THEORY AND METHOD IN SOCIO-LE

Oñati International Series in Law and Society

A SERIES PUBLISHED FOR THE OÑATI INSTITUTE FOR THE
SOCIOLOGY OF LAW

General Editors

William L F Felstiner   Johannes Feest

Board of General Editors

Rosemary Hunter, Griffiths University, Australia
Carlos Lugo, Hostos Law School, Puerto Rico
David Nelken, Macerata University, Italy
Jacek Kurczewski, Warsaw University, Poland
Marie Claire Foblets, Leuven University, Belgium
Roderick Macdonald, McGill University, Canada

Titles in this Series

Theory and Method in Socio-Legal Research

Edited by

Reza Banakar and Max Travers

Oñati International Series in Law and Society

A SERIES PUBLISHED FOR THE OÑATI INSTITUTE
FOR THE SOCIOLOGY OF LAW

·HART·
PUBLISHING

HART PUBLISHING
OXFORD AND PORTLAND OREGON
2005

Published in North America (US and Canada)
by Hart Publishing
c/o International Specialized Book Services
920 NE 58th Avenue, Suite 300
Portland, OR 97213-3786
USA
Tel: +1 503 287 3093 or toll-free: (1) 800 944 6190
Fax: +1 503 280 8832
E-mail: orders@isbs.com
Web Site: www.isbs.com

Hart Publishing is a specialist legal publisher based in Oxford, England. To order further
copies of this book or to request a list of other publications please write to:

Hart Publishing, Salter's Boatyard, Folly Bridge, Abingdon Road,
Oxford, OX1 4LB
email: mail@hartpub.co.uk
Telephone: +44 (0)1865 245533 Fax: +44 (0)1865 794882

WEB SITE http//:www.hartpub.co.uk

British Library Cataloguing in Publication Data
Data Available

ISBN 13: 978-1-84113-625-7 (cloth)
ISBN 10: 1-84113-625-5 (cloth)

ISBN 13: 978-1-84113-626-4 (paper)
ISBN 10: 1-84113-626-3 (paper)

Typeset by Compuscript, Shannon, Ireland
Printed and bound in Great Britain by
Biddles Ltd, King's Lynn, Norfolk

Contents

List of Contributors

Michael Adler, Professor of Socio-Legal Studies, University of Edinburgh, UK.

Reza Banakar, Reader in Law, University of Westminster, London, UK.

Samia Bano, Lecturer in Law, University of Reading, UK.

Andrew Boon, Professor of Law, University of Westminster, London, UK.

John Flood, Professor of Law and Sociology, University of Westminster, London, UK.

Anne Griffiths, Professor of Law, University of Edinburgh, UK.

Ole Hammerslev, Assistant Professor at the University of Southern Denmark.

Marina Kurkchiyan, Paul Dodyk Research Fellow, Centre for Socio-Legal Studies, University of Oxford.

Bettina Lange, Lecturer in Law, University of Keele, UK.

David Nelken, Professor of Sociology at the University of Macerata in Italy and Distinguished Research Professor of Law at Cardiff University, UK.

John Paterson, Reader in Law, University of Aberdeen, UK.

Thomas Scheffer, Senior Researcher, Freie Universität Berlin, Germany.

Mary Seneviratne, Professor of Law, Nottingham Trent University, UK.

Gunther Teubner, Professor of Private Law and Legal Sociology, University of Frankfurt, Germany.

Max Travers, Lecturer in Sociology, University of Tasmania, Australia.

Klaus A Ziegert, Professor of Jurisprudence, University of Sydney, Australia.

Introduction

REZA BANAKAR AND MAX TRAVERS

MOST OF THE papers in this collection were presented at a workshop that took place on research methods at the International Institute for Sociology of Law, Oñati, Spain in April 2003.[1] They illustrate how a range of topics, including EU law, ombudsmen, judges, lawyers, Shariah Councils and the quality assurance industry can be researched from a socio-legal perspective. The objective of the collection is not, however, simply to present an interesting set of papers, but to use them to explore how different methods can be used in researching law and legal phenomena, and how methodological issues and debates in sociology are relevant to the study of law.

Numerous methods texts and handbooks exist for researchers working in the fields of educational research, media studies, nursing, management, social work, criminology and even leisure and tourism. There is, however, no text that covers how one can do research about law and legal processes from a variety of social scientific standpoints.[2] Many socio-legal researchers would argue that their undertaking requires no special methods besides those already used in the social sciences. Law is, after all, only a social institution, in the same way as religion, medicine or education, and can be studied using the same methods and techniques. Having said that, criminology also requires no special research methods besides those already developed and used by mainstream sociology. Criminologists are, nonetheless, keen to produce methods textbooks on how to research crime and criminal justice and debate methodological issues arising out of their research.[3]

As we shall argue in chapter 1, too great a concern with following a prescribed method can limit creativity in research by imposing a standard way

---

[1] It also developed out of a workshop that took place in Oxford in September 2000, and two sessions on methodology organised for the first time at the Socio-Legal Studies Association annual conference in Nottingham in April 2003.

[2] Some of the earlier edited collections included a section on doing research—for example see RJ Simon, (ed), *The Sociology of Law* (San Francisco, CA, Chandler, 1968)—but more recent collections make no similar attempts to focus on the methodological issues of socio-legal research.

[3] For examples see V Jupp, *Methods of Criminological Research* (London, Routledge, 1999) and FE Hagan, *Research Methods in Criminal Justice and Criminology* (New York, NY, Allyn & Bacon, 2001). See also (2000) 41 *British Journal of Criminology*.

of investigating law and legal institutions. From this standpoint, the absence of a methods text might be seen as a good thing: it helps to maintain socio-legal research as a truly interdisciplinary field which is open to theoretical diversity and innovation. Alternatively, it could indicate a lack of interest among socio-legal researchers to engage in social scientific debates on methodology. This indifference towards methodology might be explained in terms of the relative isolation of law schools, which still provide a home for much of socio-legal research, or because many of those who do socio-legal research are not trained in social sciences. Using a similar explanation we could say that criminologists are interested in writing about methods and debating methodology partly because they are, unlike most socio-legal researchers, based at social science faculties where problems of research method and issues of methodology loom large.[4]

Whatever the reason for this 'anomaly', it has at least one important implication for socio-legal research. The absence of methods texts means that the experiences of researching law which were gained by one generation are not readily available in a systematic fashion to the next generation. This makes teaching socio-legal research difficult, and can disrupt attempts to develop robust or cumulative scholarly traditions.[5] In this connection, we should not underestimate the achievements of socio-legal researchers in using various empirical methods to study what is *legal* about legal processes, legal institutions and legal behaviour. These legal properties are not the primary concern of social scientists whose specialisations and interests do not include law and are, therefore, not addressed in their methodological writings and debates. Non-socio-legal methods textbooks tell us about the various techniques of data collection and analysis through surveys, interviews, participant observation or discourse analysis and introduce us to the broader methodological debates which engage many social scientists. Yet, they do not tell us the first thing about what it means to interview judges or lawyers in different jurisdictions, observe mediation, dispute resolution or other forms of negotiation in the context of different legal cultures or analyse legal documents in a sociological way.

The collection of papers presented in this volume does not aim to fill the methodology vacuum within socio-legal studies. Instead, it makes a modest

---

[4] Compared to socio-legal studies and sociology of law, criminology is a well-established discipline which is taught at all social science faculties. It is reasonable to expect that criminology's disciplinary standing helps to motivate many criminologists to produce methods textbooks and debate methodology. We could, however, turn this argument around and ask if the absence of similar concern with methodological issues in socio-legal studies is not one of the factors hindering its transformation into an academically stronger field of research and teaching?

[5] Not surprisingly, there have been similar discontinuities in socio-legal theorising. For a discussion see R Banakar, *Merging Law and Sociology* (Berlin, Galda & Wilch, 2003).

attempt to draw attention to the need to reflect on the methodological issues of socio-legal research and to show that socio-legal research can gain from engaging with the general debates on methodology.

A. SOCIO-LEGAL RESEARCH, LAW AND SOCIAL SCIENCE

Socio-legal studies in the UK, which provides the context of the discussions here, in chapter 1 and in the final section of the book, has grown mainly out of law schools' interest in promoting interdisciplinary studies of law. Whether socio-legal studies is regarded as an emerging discipline, sub-discipline or a methodological approach, it is often viewed in the light of its relationship to, and oppositional role within, law.[6] In that sense it should not be confused with the legal sociology of many West European countries or Law and Society scholarship in the US, which foster much stronger disciplinary ties with social sciences. The Annual Conference of the Socio-Legal Studies Association in 2003 was attended by 370 UK academics, 87% of whom were based in law departments.[7] This shows that lawyers, and not social scientists, are the main actors in the field of socio-legal research in the UK.

To further clarify the status and approach of socio-legal studies, we could, as Wiles and Campbell did some thirty years ago, contrast it with the sociology of law. The sociology of law receives its intellectual impetus mainly from mainstream sociology and aims to transcend the lawyer's focus on legal rules and legal doctrine by remaining 'exogenous to the existing legal system', in order to 'construct a theoretical understanding of that legal system in terms of the wider social structures'.[8] That is why 'the law, legal prescriptions and legal definitions are not assumed or accepted, but their emergence, articulations and purpose are themselves treated as problematic and worthy of study'.[9] Socio-legal studies, on the other hand, often employs sociology (and other social sciences) not so much for substantive analysis, but as a tool for data collection.

Admittedly, socio-legal studies has developed and become theoretically and methodologically diverse since Wiles and Campbell introduced their ideal typical distinction between the two approaches mentioned above. Socio-legal research has, for example, become on the whole less empirical— to the extent that some senior researchers in the field have declared a state

---

[6] See PA Thomas, 'Introduction' in PA Thomas, (ed), *Legal Frontiers* (Aldershot, Dartmouth, 1996) 3.

[7] Also see *The Nuffield Inquiry on Empirical Research in Law* at http://www.ucl.ac.uk/laws/genn/empirical/docs/background.doc.

[8] See CM Campbell and P Wiles, 'The Study of Law in Society in Britain' (1976) 10 *Law and Society Review* 553.

[9] *Ibid.*

of emergency to save empirical studies of law.[10] At the same time, forms of discourse analysis, cultural studies, feminism and postmodern schools of thought have gained ground within socio-legal research. This development is captured in more recent attempts to define the aims and disciplinary boundaries of socio-legal research not so much in relation to empirical research, but in terms of academic competition within law. Wheeler and Thomas, for example, perceive socio-legal studies as an interdisciplinary alternative and a challenge to doctrinal studies of law. For them the 'socio' in socio-legal studies does not refer to sociology or social sciences, but represents 'an interface with a context within which law exists'.[11] That is why, when socio-legal researchers use social theory for the purpose of analysis, they often tend not to address the concerns of sociology or other social sciences, but those of law and legal studies.

We are, however, arguing that the separation between the sociology of law and socio-legal study is an obstacle which hinders the development of the social scientific study of law.[12] We hope that the chapters in this volume demonstrate that social scientific studies of law can break new grounds and become a serious contender to traditional forms of legal research first, and only if, they develop a genuine awareness of the consequences of social scientific debates for their research practices. All the contributors to this collection, whether based at law schools or social science departments, are grappling with these issues, but also recognising the need to transcend beyond the boundaries of established disciplines such as law, sociology, political science or social anthropology. Socio-legal researchers show a far more sophisticated awareness, than in previous years, of different approaches in sociology, and recognise that there is always more to learn by participating in methodological debate. Sociologists and social anthropologists are, increasingly, recognising the need to address and understand the content of law. Anne Griffiths, to give one example, argues convincingly in her conclusion to chapter 6 that ethnography provides the most effective method for achieving this insight. There are many good examples of successful analysis of the substantive contents of law through sociological methods and theories from Max Weber's analysis of legal ideas and institutions to Doreen McBarnet's classical study of conviction and Yves Dezalay and Bryant Garth's study of international commercial arbitration.[13] These

[10] See *The Nuffield Enquiry on Empirical Research in Law*, above, n 7.

[11] S Wheeler and PA Thomas, 'Socio-Legal Studies' in DJ Hayton, (ed), *Law's Future(s)* (Oxford, Hart Publishing, 2002) 271. Also see PA Thomas, 'Socio-Legal Studies: The Case of Disappearing Fleas and Bustards' in PA Thomas, (ed), *Socio-Legal Studies* (Aldershot, Dartmouth, 1997).

[12] For a more detailed discussion see Banakar, above, n 4.

[13] M Weber, *Max Weber on Law in Economy and Society* (Cambridge, MA, Harvard University Press, 1954); DJ McBarnet, *Conviction: Law, the State and the Construction of Justice* (London, Macmillan, 1981); Y Dezalay and B G Garth, *Dealing in Virtue* (Chicago, IL, University of Chicago, 1996).

studies show that social sciences do not need to limit the scope of their studies to the external behavioural and institutional aspects of law and can, in fact, grasp and analyse the internal constitution of the law.

B. THE STRUCTURE OF THIS COLLECTION

This collection consists of sixteen chapters. The first chapter considers the nature of socio-legal research by examining the different perspectives of lawyers and sociologists and the challenges that arise in doing interdisciplinary work. Our main argument is that these perspectives are necessarily very different. Sociologists need to appreciate how academic and practicing lawyers approach, describe and use law. Similarly, socio-legal researchers, whose academic background is in law, but wish to do more than simply write generally about 'the law in context', must somehow find their way around the theoretical and philosophical debates that constitute sociology as an academic discipline.

We will present the remaining fifteen chapters in six sections. The first section on 'Method Versus Methodology' contrasts two papers, by John Flood and Klaus A Ziegert, which discuss how qualitative methods can be used to address law from opposing theoretical perspectives. Flood is an interpretivist, influenced by symbolic interactionism, an approach which is committed to addressing the perspective of the social actor. Ziegert is a systems theorist working in the tradition of Niklas Luhmann, and so argues that ethnographic research of this kind is limited, and not sufficiently concerned with 'universals'. By contrasting these two approaches, which are articulated by Flood and Ziegert, we hope to demonstrate how these foundational debates inform the study of law and society.

The next section on 'Ethnography and Law' contains three chapters by Thomas Scheffer, Samia Bano and Anne Griffiths. Scheffer's research uses actor-network theory to describe the work of judges and lawyers. Bano and Griffith's chapters adopt a feminist qualitative approach to law. These papers are grouped together here because each, in its own way, uses fieldwork and presents an ethnographic approach to the study of legal phenomena. Scheffer uses ethnography to study the everyday practices of legal work, Bano uses ethnographic observation to research the use of unofficial legal bodies, such as the Shariah Councils, by South Asian Muslim women living in Britain and Griffiths uses the fieldwork she carried out in southern Africa, among the Bakwena, to document how people experience law in their daily life and to challenge the western notions of law.

The papers in section three by Reza Banakar, Mary Seneviratne and Bettina Lange present different forms textual analysis. Banakar and Seneviratne focus on how to use textual and discourse analysis to study the works of ombudsmen. In addition, Banakar draws attention to the empirical properties of legal cases and how they can be used to carry out sociological studies of legal regulation and institutions. Lange's chapter, on the other hand, uses discourse analysis to examine the socio-legal mechanisms of the European Union in an attempt to generate new insights in the EU law.

Section four on 'Structural Approaches' consists of two chapters. The first chapter by Ole Hammerlsev shows how a sociological method inspired by Pierre Bourdieu can be employed in the study of law. The second chapter by John Paterson and Gunther Teubner contains an empirical study informed by autopoiesis theory. Hammerslev shows how Bourdieu's theory may be employed empirically to understand legal institutions and to examine the social construction of the legal profession. Paterson and Teubner provide a clear and thoughtful understanding of how autopoiesis can be used to conduct socio-legal research by examining the conflicts between regulators, offshore oil industry and engineers. Despite the apparent differences between the theoretical frameworks used by Hammerslev and Paterson, both these approaches represent examples of how structural functionalism can be used to study law.

In section five we turn our attention to how the concept of 'legal culture' can be used to conduct socio-legal research. The first chapter in this section is by David Nelken, who provides an overview of comparative socio-legal research into criminal justice systems from a cultural standpoint. Nelken also describes some of the conceptual and methodological issues arising out of doing research in, and about, different (legal) cultures. The second chapter is by Marina Kurkchiyan who also engages with problems of studying legal cultures, but this time in the context of the recent transformation of the Russian legal system and with the intention to explain how law is conceived in post-soviet Russia. Kurkchiyan's chapter provides an insightful account of the process involved in the study of a legal culture in transition.

Scholars based in different countries and representing different traditions of research wrote the first five sections of this book. These studies were organised in accordance with their methodological orientations, rather than the national origins of their authors. Presenting these studies without taking into account the tradition of research in various countries gave an overview of how socio-legal research is developing. Needless to say, the studies presented here do not provide us with a sufficiently broad international base for generalising about the direction of socio-legal research worldwide. Yet, they do give us a general idea about the methods, theories and research topics, which interest socio-legal researchers.

In the final part of this book, in section six, we turn our attention to how socio-legal research has developed in the UK. Michael Adler provides an example of the applied research conducted for government agencies. He describes what was involved in designing questions for a national survey to investigate people's experiences of administrative bureaucracies and how they pursue complaints about government departments and public bodies. The two concluding papers, by Andrew Boon and Max Travers, look at changes in the research environment that may have important consequences for socio-legal research: the rise of the ethics committee, and pressures to conduct evaluation research. The last section has a slightly different focus in that we are also looking at the debate between applied and pure research, which is particularly relevant at the moment when there is great pressure to gear our activities as researchers and the university curriculum to the needs of government agencies.

This is, to some extent, an arbitrary division of the papers, although it allows us to show how the general debates in sociology, and methodological issues that we review in the next introductory chapter, are relevant to socio-legal research. We will also use the section introductions to explain bodies of theory or methodological issues raised in the papers, so we hope that reading the papers in conjunction with the introductions should provide some useful insights, and suggest further reading in the same way as our text on law and social theory.[14]

We should make it clear at the outset that only a limited range of theoretical traditions were represented at the workshop, and we are not trying to produce a general handbook that demonstrates systematically how social scientists can study socio-legal topics. There was a lively debate between ethnographers in the symbolic interactionist and ethnomethodological traditions and researchers influenced by systems theory, but many methodological positions were not represented, so we did not have, for example, a debate between poststructuralists and critical theorists, nor did we explore the distinction between particular approaches within one methodological camp. There is, however, no need for this book to be comprehensive. We will simply be trying to convey the critical discussions about the nature of law as a topic and the difficulty of studying it that took place during the workshop.

We are pleased that the collection contains contributions from socio-legal researchers working or researching in a number of countries, including Australia, Denmark, Germany, Italy, Russia, Sweden and United Kingdom. We hope that the examples we use will demonstrate why methodological debate and discussion is valuable for socio-legal research, and indeed the only way forward to develop the field. We would also ideally like the book to raise questions and problems, rather than giving the impression that everyone agrees over how to study the social world.

---

[14] See R Banakar and M Travers, *Introduction to Law and Social Theory* (Oxford, Hart Publishing, 2002).

ACKNOWLEDGEMENTS

We are grateful to the International Institute for the Sociology of Law for supporting our workshop in March 2003 and facilitating the publication of this volume. We would also like to thank the contributors for their commitment and patience—there was a long editing and reviewing process, but we are pleased that the collection has finally been published. The ideas and arguments are certainly still current!

We acknowledge permission from *Social and Legal Studies* to publish material from Volume (1999) 7(4) entitled 'Changing Maps: Empirical Legal Autopoiesis' in chapter 11.

1

Law, Sociology and Method

REZA BANAKAR AND MAX TRAVERS

SOCIO-LEGAL RESEARCH IS, in some respects, founded on a paradox in that, while it claims or aspires to be an interdisciplinary subject with particular ties with sociology, the majority of its practitioners are based in law schools, and have not received any systematic training in either sociological theory or research methods.[1] There are, of course, many academics from other disciplines who have contributed to the field over the years, and whose studies appear on undergraduate reading lists. There has also been genuine collaboration between academic lawyers and social scientists that has resulted in many interesting and insightful studies about law. Nevertheless, we would argue that this inter-change has been limited to a few institutions, and that a sustained and open dialogue with sociology, or for that matter with other academic disciplines, has not so far taken place.

In this chapter we will consider the nature of socio-legal research, especially as it has developed in the UK, and the challenges of working in an interdisciplinary field. We will then introduce some general debates in sociology about method and show how these are relevant to studying socio-legal topics. We will conclude this chapter by referring to the *Nuffield Foundation Inquiry on Empirical Research in Law* which expresses concern for the 'dwindling of capacity to undertake rigorous empirical research in law'.[2] We will argue that to create a sound foundation for empirical research into law we need to introduce research methods and project work into the undergraduate law school curriculum, despite the current pressures in the direction of a narrow degree based almost entirely on studying legal rules.

[1] We are grateful to Julian Webb and Simon Halliday for commenting on the first draft of this chapter.
[2] See *The Nuffield Foundation Inquiry on Empirical Research in Law* posted at http://www.ucl.ac.uk/laws/genn/empirical/docs/background.doc. Also see 'Nuffield Inquiry Into Empirical Research: Progress Report' (2004) 44 *Socio-Legal Newsletter* 1.

A. THE NATURE OF SOCIO-LEGAL RESEARCH

The fact that the overwhelming majority of socio-legal researchers are based at law schools does not by itself mean that they do not, or cannot, produce sociologically-informed research about law.[3] It rather means that their academic point of reference is influenced in the first place by the aims and aspirations of law, legal education and legal studies.[4] They are, for example, more often exposed to debates within legal theory than in sociology or anthropology. This has an adverse effect on the degree to which they participate in the internal debates of other disciplines. In addition, one should not forget that legal studies does possess its own disciplinary debates and concerns too. Socio-legal scholars who make their careers in legal education and legal research have to remain informed about legal debates if they are to continue as legal scholars. They are not, however, expected to engage in debates within sociology. In fact, those very few scholars who attempt to engage in debates in both law and sociology soon discover that they are spreading their intellectual resources too thin.

Similarly, mainstream sociology pays very little attention to law and no attention to academic debates within legal studies. This is perhaps only to be expected because after all sociologists are not using legal theory and methods to conduct research. Yet, sociology's relationship to law becomes slightly more complicated when we realize that the study of law played a significant role in the formation of classical sociology and social anthropology. However, the interest originally shown by the forerunners of sociology and anthropology, such as Weber, Durkheim and Malinowski to name a few, in studying law, legal behaviour and legal institutions was not sustained by modern sociology. Besides social philosophers such as Jürgen Habermas and the systems theorist Niklas Luhmann (who happened to be a lawyer by training), we find few contemporary scholars who seriously engage with the study of law in order to develop a sociological theory. Those few who do so are not based at sociology departments, but often attached to a handful of research institutes devoted to promoting socio-legal research. Looking at the work that most of these scholars produce, we

---

[3] As pointed out in the introduction, only 13% of the participants in the Annual Conference of the Socio-Legal Studies Association (SLSA) in 2003 were based in departments other than law. This disparity is also confirmed by the general membership of the SLSA.

[4] This discussion refers primarily to the state of socio-legal studies in the UK, which has its own specific characteristics distinguishing it from the traditions of legal sociology or law and society research in other countries (for a brief discussion on the differences see the introduction to s 7). We should also mention that the notion of sociology is used here broadly to include much of what is generally regarded as legal anthropology. This is neither to overlook the theoretical differences between sociology and social anthropology, nor to play down the important contributions of legal anthropology. Instead we adopt this approach, because for our limited purposes, sociology and social anthropology have similar assumptions in studying law when compared to traditional legal scholarship.

often find attempts to use ideas and approaches of modern social theorists to study of law.[5] The diminishing interest of mainstream sociology in law is also reflected in sociology curricula and courses offered by sociology departments in most countries. While courses in sociology of crime, race, science, education, health (or medicine) and sport are offered by most sociology departments, courses in sociology of law are conspicuous only by their absence.

Roger Cotterrell, in what is still the most widely-read introductory text on sociology of law, argues that the interdisciplinary approach to the study of law should transcend the narrow disciplinary perspective of 'academic sociology'. Drawing on Bauman, he aligns himself with 'postmodernism's harsh judgment on science as a network of specialisms': 'Science has lost its capacity to enlighten ordinary citizens as it has become so intricate and esoteric that only the masters of sub-specialisms of specialisms within scientific disciplines can follow selected pathway's through science's knowledge-mazes'.[6]

This criticism of sociology is, to some extent, misplaced since one way of understanding the history of the discipline is as a series of debates over whether it should become like natural science. Avowedly anti-scientific intellectual movements like postmodernism and poststructuralism can also be criticised for becoming specialisms with their own technical language, and methods.[7] One can see, however, that even without this theoretical justification, the view that socio-legal scholarship does not need to engage with sociological theory or method too deeply might appeal to researchers who would otherwise have to undertake much work understanding specialist debates in sociology and acquiring a competence in technical, demanding methodologies such as log linear or conversation analysis. We have also come across academics from other disciplines who are full of praise for the interdisciplinary character of socio-legal studies after attending conferences. They like the fact that it is a friendly, tolerant field, and they do not have to face the critical responses about theory and methodology they would expect from colleagues in their own discipline.

---

[5] For such examples see Ole Hammerslev's application of Bourdieu's theory in ch 10. Other interesting attempts can be found in the application of ideas borrowed from Michel Foucault to the study of governance and gender studies. See A Hunt and G Wickham, *Foucault and Law: Towards a Sociology of Governance* (London, Pluto Press, 1994); and C Smart, *Feminism and the Power of Law* (London, Routledge, 1995).

[6] Z Bauman, *Intimations of Postmodernity* (London, Routledge, 1992) 37; cited in R Cotterrell, *The Sociology of Law: An Introduction* (London, Butterworths, 1992) 311.

[7] Postmodernism is used by writers like Cotterrell and Bauman inter-changeably with poststructuralism to refer to the critique of scientism advanced in recent times by poststructuralist thinkers, such as Lyotard, Foucault and Derrida. For evidence of how poststructuralism can become a sociological method, see G Kendall and G Wickham, *Using Foucault's Methods* (London, Sage, 1999).

Our own position is that socio-legal research would benefit from more engagement with sociology, and in particular with the debates about method that take place between and within different theoretical traditions. This aspiration characterised the first thirty years of the American law and society movement, and the initial period of socio-legal research in Britain. It has, however, only had limited success in attracting academics from outside law schools into the movement, or breaking down the intellectual boundaries between the two fields. In more recent time, the field has become divided between policy researchers who have a positivist understanding of method, and critical scholars who have little interest in doing empirical research.[8] The sociological research on law that has been conducted is fragmented, and theoretically undeveloped in relation to sociology.[9] There have also been relatively few empirical studies of law when compared to the large literatures in the sociologies of medicine, education or science. It is important to understand this intellectual and institutional context, before considering how sociologists understand the question of method.

B. THE CHALLENGES OF INTERDISCIPLINARITY

Concerns with methodological issues emerge as part of attempts of various fields of research to present their labours as systematic, reliable and rigorous sources of knowledge. Once these fields are transformed into established disciplines, they use methodology to monitor and sustain the quality of the research conducted within their realms, but also to 'discipline' the newcomers. In other words, methodology has two closely interrelated functions: It, firstly, guarantees a degree of quality control and, secondly, it ensures the internalisation of standards and values underlying any particular discipline by the newcomers to that discipline.

That is why originality and innovation do not go comfortably hand in hand with methodological restrictions and standards. Those who would like to develop new ideas and approaches soon find themselves confronted with, and forced to defy, the methodological restrictions of established disciplines. Having said that, it is important to add that original pieces of

---

[8] It is still possible to conduct policy research without being a positivist, so for example, one can obtain funding to conduct ethnographic research in institutional settings that complements quantitative studies. There are, however, pressures to produce cut-and-dry findings, and analyse data in less depth, and one cannot employ interpretive or poststructuralist ideas in a fully-fledged way for government agencies.

[9] A Hunt, *The Sociological Movement in Law* (London, Macmillan, 1978); M Travers, 'Putting sociology Back into Sociology of Law' (1993) 20 *Journal of Law and Society* 443; and R Banakar, *Merging Law and Sociology: Beyond the Dichotomies of the Socio-Legal Research* (Berlin, Glada and Wilch Verlag, 2003).

research often defy methodological rules *consciously* and intentionally. The 'perpetrators' who produce original work are knowledgeable or experts in what they are defying and the methodological rules that they are violating. Thus, the ignorance of methodological issues can seldom become a source of originality or innovation.[10] Expressed differently, our ignorance of sociological methods cannot be justified as a 'method' to escape the disciplinary restrictions of sociology, or presented as part of the attempt to create original socio-legal work.

Interestingly enough, there is an important connection between the rise of interdisciplinary research and the problem of methodology. Interdisciplinary research indicates an ambition to understand and integrate aspects of two or several disciplinary perspectives into one single approach. Sociology and psychology are, for example, brought together to create the new field of social psychology, biology and chemistry to create bio-chemistry or, as in our case, law and social sciences to create socio-legal studies.[11] The objective of this exercise is ultimately to combine knowledge, skills and forms of research experience from two (or several) disciplines in an attempt to transcend some of the theoretical and methodological limitations of the disciplines in question and create a basis for developing a new form of analysis. At the same time interdisciplinarity provides a 'space of encounter' at the cross-section of disciplines which offers temporary relief from methodological and theoretical restrictions of established disciplines (perceived as an hindrance to innovation).[12]

This disciplinary reprieve comes with a price tag. In order to create an interdisciplinary space, the researchers have to establish communicative links between disciplines. These links assist them to visualize the world from the standpoint of the other relevant disciplines and appreciate the value of the knowledge and skills developed by them. This often requires them to develop double competence and to master two or several academic discourses, which is easier said than done. In addition, mono-disciplinary researchers might, and often do, regard the interdisciplinary form of

---

[10] Breakthroughs and discoveries have been made accidentally within natural and experimental sciences when researchers failed to follow the established methods of research. However, this type of accidental discoveries is not relevant to social sciences, within which research is a discursive process rather than a laboratory based activity, conducted in isolation from various social forces and interests.

[11] Interdisciplinarity should be distinguished from 'multidisciplinarity', which juxtaposes several disciplines without any attempt to integrate or synthesis aspects of their knowledge and perspectives. It should also be distinguished from 'transdisciplinarity', which indicates interactions that transgress the boundaries of the science system. For our purposes here interdisciplinary research combines different approaches into one new approach, while the multidisciplinary research employs multiple approaches at the same time.

[12] See L Kalman, *The Strange Career of Legal Liberalism* (New Haven, CT, Yale University Press, 1996) 139–40; and DW Vick, 'Interdisciplinarity and the Discipline of Law' (2004) 31 *Journal of Law and Society* 163–93.

knowledge/power as a threat to their academic prestige and other vested interests and hence dismiss it as a form of dilettantism. Their tendency to dismiss the fruits of interdisciplinary research increases if the interdisciplinary undertaking contains, or when it brings about, an explicit critique of the shortcomings of the traditional disciplines in addressing certain fundamental questions. Thus, interdisciplinarity can be perceived (often correctly) as 'a threat to the existing identity of a discrete discipline'[13] and an attempt to undermine the authority of traditional disciplines. Also, as pointed out by Moran, 'interdisciplinarity is always transformative in some way, producing new forms of knowledge in its engagements with direct disciplines'.[14] The transformative character of interdisciplinary research is not welcomed in academic settings with a vested interest in preserving the traditional methods of research and education.[15]

It is, however, important to note that there is no single definition of interdisciplinarity for the simple reason that it means different things to different researchers. Not only do different researchers turn to interdisciplinary research for very different reasons, but they also borrow in different degrees from different disciplines. If we agree that interdisciplinarity involves integrating and organising traditional forms of knowledge, skill and experience in a new and original fashion, then we should resist attempts to formulate an all-encompassing definition of interdisciplinarity. A single definition would indicate the emergence of a new discipline, with its own theoretical and methodological restrictions, from which interdisciplinary researchers would wish to escape.

Let us now take a brief look at law and sociology, from an interdisciplinary point of view, to see how the issues debated here are relevant to the development of sociology of law and socio-legal studies.

C. LAW AND SOCIOLOGY

The fact that law is a formal instrument of regulation (ie, a tool in the hands of policymakers), a body of rules and decisions (ie, a system of norms), an occupational setting (ie, a profession), an academic discipline (as reflected by *scientia iuris*, legal studies and jurisprudence), a form of learning, teaching and training (ie, an education) at the same time, and can also be seen and experienced as a source of justice by some people, and a form of oppression by others, makes it impossible to generalise about its nature. We

---

[13] Vick, *ibid*, p 173.
[14] J Moran, *Interdisciplinarity* (London, Routledge, 2002) 16.
[15] A heated debate is currently going on between social scientists and humanists on the need to rethink interdisciplinarity. An academic website devoted to these discussions can be found at http://www.interdisciplines.org/interdisciplinarity.

always have to consider which aspect or manifestation of the law we are discussing, and from whose perspective we are presenting that aspect. This idea is far from alien to jurisprudence, within which we find many orientations and schools of thought that implicitly or explicitly recognise the sociological diversity of law. But interestingly enough, the image of law as a highly rationalised rule-based activity, ie, as a system of rules, norms and principles designed to guide legal analysis and justify decisions, occupies a central position in both common law and civil law discourses. This does not mean that legal reasoning, as articulated by doctrinal studies of law or legal theory, follows rules, norms and principles blindly, mechanically or at all times, but that it either searches for, examines or employs rules and principles as part of its general approach. Doctrinal studies of law, for example, use interpretive methods to examine cases, statutes and other sources of law in an attempt to seek out, discover, construct or reconstruct rules and principles. It then systematises and employs them to conduct descriptive analysis and normative evaluation of the process of decision-making.[16] This reliance on legal rules and principles turns much of law, legal reasoning and legal studies into a *formal* activity.

Many theories of law, in particular those rooted in legal positivism, are also influenced by this rule-based approach. These theories often hold that 'legal rules are constitutive of law and that the force of rules ... derives in general from their having been enacted by institutions authorised to make rules'.[17] HLA Hart's idea of 'primary' and 'secondary' rules and Hans Kelsen's 'pure theory of law', each in its own way, draw on, and contribute to the development of, the rule-based approach to law. Hart, with his roots in the common law tradition, and Kelsen, in the civil law, disagreed on many fundamental issues, but not on the definition of law as a system of rules and norms.[18] Even Dworkin's approach, which questions Hart's rule-based model by arguing that lawyers 'make use of standards that do not function as rules, but operate differently as principles, policies and other sorts of standards' would still agree that the overwhelming majority legal analysis and decisions are made in reference to legal rules.[19] Taking Dworkin's theory at face value, his 'standards' are evoked in hard cases when the problems with legal rights and obligations become acute.

[16] According to Aleksander Peczenik, legal doctrine aims to increase the coherence of law, to present it as a systematic whole, to present legal rules under the umbrella of principles, to present law as a stable entity (which 'may change but not all at once') and to ensure the unity of legal validity. See A Peczenik, 'Can Philosophy Help Legal Doctrine?' (2004) 17 *Ratio Juris* 107.

[17] J Elkins, 'Frederick Schauer on the Force of Rules' in L Meyer, (ed), *Rules and Reasoning* (Oxford, Hart Publishing, 1999).

[18] HLA Hart, *The Concept of Law* (Oxford, OUP, 1988); and H Kelsen, *Introduction to the Problems of Legal Theory* (Oxford, Clarendon Press, 2001).

[19] RW Dworkin, 'Is Law a System of Rules?' in RW Dworkin, (ed), *Legal Philosophy* (Oxford, OUP, 1977) 43.

To make matters more complicated, most lawyers recognise that law as a form of practice encompasses many forms of skill, some of which cannot be reduced to the application of rules. Yet, we find that they still confer an important role to lawyers' ability to handle rules. For example, in *How to Do Things With Rules*, William Twining and David Miers point out that legal practice contains diverse activities ranging from advising on the procedure of a particular course of action to advocacy, drafting statutes, communicating information about legal rules and so on. They also emphasise that 'rule-handling is only one aspect of the crafts of law' and that 'interpretation is only one aspect of rule-handling'. Yet, they go on to argue that interpretation plays a basic role in the exercise of law as a practical art: 'first, because most rule-handling activities involve or presuppose it and secondly, because a clear understanding of what is involved in interpretation inevitably throws light on a number of other matters as well'.[20] By conferring a central role to interpretation—as one aspect of rule-handling—they confirm, indirectly as it might be, the central role played by rules in legal reasoning and practice.

The rule-based paradigm sets the parameters—defined in terms of a particular set of questions or concerns—for examining any factual situation or legal problem. It might, for example, be used to determine the rights and duties of the persons or entities involved in a particular situation. In addition, it provides a context for using various methods to identify the applicable sources of law, to critically examine their underlying policies and to analyse them in order to determine the valid rules of law. It also helps to synthesise the valid rules into a coherent system in which the more specific rules are grouped under the more general ones, to research the relevant facts and, finally, to apply the structure of rules to the facts of the case to ascertain the rights or duties created by these facts.

The rule-based paradigm also sets the context in which the law students are taught to read and criticise legal, moral and policy arguments. This can directly or indirectly convey to students the image of law as a normatively closed system, which can be studied by the exegesis of authoritative texts. Tony Bradney points out that legal doctrine teaches students to 'particularise and narrow down argument', to carry out 'close reasoning' and to pay 'the utmost attention to textual contexts',[21] but

> it forbids the making of the connections with the wider questions which lie at the roots of human inquiry. Reasoning in doctrinal study must be about a particular range of questions. *The question which cannot be legitimately answered by reference to a statute or judgment lies outside the doctrinal gaze* (our italics).[22]

---

[20] W Twining and D Miers, *How to Do Things With Rules* (London, Butterworths, 1996) xviii.
[21] A Bradney, 'Law as a Parasitic Discipline' (1998) 25 *Journal of Law and Society* 71, 76.
[22] *Ibid.*

The doctrinal gaze does not, however, provide a satisfactory explanation of how a practising lawyer operates or employs his or her various skills. The practising lawyer has a more pragmatic understanding of law than what is mediated by the rule-based paradigm. He or she might indeed be quite unruffled by jurisprudential concerns or the need to preserve the integrity of law as a coherent system of rules. From the standpoint of the practicing lawyer all matters of law are open to debate and bargaining. Where the boundary of the law is to be drawn and how the content of legal rules are to be determined in order to decide a case is a matter of negotiation in legal practice. Hence, the legal reasoning of doctrinal scholars becomes only one among a number of devices (or 'resources') to be employed if, and in so far as, it serves to negotiate the boundaries of the law in one's favour. It is abandoned in favour of other tactics when it no longer serves to bring about the desired effect.

It should not come as a surprise if doctrinal studies remain the aspect of law least interested in interdisciplinary research. Parasitic as this form of scholarship might be on the work done by others,[23] it nonetheless constitutes an activity, which sees no use for social scientific insights or methods of analysis.[24] Having said that, it is important to remember that doctrinal studies of law constitute only one aspect of law. Other manifestations of law, such as non-doctrinal legal research and legal education, but also certain areas of legislation, which are closely linked to the implementation of social policies and regulation, such as welfare and administrative laws, have been greatly influenced by socio-legal research. That is why the move towards interdisciplinary research has become more acceptable within the British law schools. To quote Bradney again:

> Law schools have seen the rise of a host of movements such as socio-legal studies, sociology of law, economics and law, feminism, Critical Legal Studies, queer theory and law and literature.... In the contemporary era whole departments are given over to modes of scholarship that would have been unthinkable in a law school in 1960.[25]

Similarly, in a recent empirical study of academic lawyers in the UK, Fiona Cownie describes the relationship between doctrinal studies and socio-legal studies in the following way:

> [L]aw is a discipline in transition, moving away from traditional doctrinal analysis towards a more contextual, interdisciplinary approach ... [T]he legal

---

[23] *Ibid.*
[24] For a debate related to this issue see R Cotterrell, 'Why Must Legal Ideas be Interpreted Sociologically?' (1998) 25 *Journal of Law and Society* 171–92; and D Nelken, 'Blinding Insights? The Limits of a Reflexive Sociology of Law' (1998) 25 *Journal of Law and Society* 407–26.
[25] A Bradney, *Conversations, Choices and Changes: The liberal Law School in the Twenty-First Century* (Oxford, Hart Publishing, 2003) 9–10.

academics I interviewed were evenly divided between those describing themselves as 'black-letter' ... and those describing themselves as 'socio-legal/critical
legal'. However, given the propensity of those adopting a socio-legal approach
to stress the necessity for an understanding of cases and statutes before more
theoretical analysis can be undertaken, and the equally strong comments made
by the great majority of 'black-letter' lawyers about the importance of introducing contextual issues into their analysis, one could accurately characterise the
dominant mode of academic law as 'concerned with doctrine and with placing
those doctrinal materials in their social context'.... There is clear evidence from
my study that the discipline of law as a whole has left behind the pure doctrinal analysis with which it started when it was first taught in English universities
at the end of the 19th century.[26]

Now let us turn to sociology. In contrast to positive law and doctrinal legal
studies, sociology is, to use Philip Selznick's phrase, 'anti-formalist in spirit' and capable of looking 'beyond what is given and immediate to what is
latent and inchoate'.[27] Sociology allows and encourages borrowing of ideas
and concepts from other disciplines and attempts to develop new paradigms. This freedom is only restricted by a general concern with the social,
an engagement with epistemological questions on how one can obtain
knowledge about the world, and a commitment to empirical enquiry (which
distinguishes it from speculation or metaphysics). Sociology is, in this sense,
a multiple-paradigm subject, embracing 'hard' scientific programmes influenced by Durkheim, but also interpretive traditions represented by Weber,
and most recently by poststructuralist thinkers who challenge the idea that
we can ever fully know social reality.[28] Different sociological traditions have
attempted to produce a more accurate description of society and social life
over the last 250 years, although there is no agreement about even basic
concepts such as 'power' or 'social class'. While sociology is engaged in continual debates that produce insights into the diversity and complexity of
social life, the legal system struggles to limit its single vantage point and
thereby, to use Niklas Luhmann's sociological description of the law as a
system, reduce its 'complexity' in relation to its social environment.[29]

There are also significant differences at the level of the individual
practitioners who are involved in the reproduction of the field of law and

---

[26] F Cownie, *Legal Academics: Culture and Identities* (Oxford, Hart Publishing, 2004)
197–8.
[27] P Selznick, 'Sociology and Natural Law' in D Black and M Mileski, (eds), *The
Organisation of Law* (New York, NY, Seminar Press, 1973).
[28] For a discussion of similarities between Weber and poststructuralist thinkers, see N Gane,
Max Weber and Postmodern Theory: Rationalisation versus Re-enchantment (London,
Routledge, 2002).
[29] N Luhmann, 'The Self-Reproduction of Law and its Limits' in G Teubner, (ed), *The
Dilemma of Law in the Welfare States* (Berlin, Walter de Gruyter, 1986).

sociology. Here we find that lawyers tend to think in terms of individual (abnormal or exceptional) cases, while sociologists try to generalise, taking into account routine and typical conditions.[30] The practicing lawyer's pragmatically formed approach to law is firmly rooted in legal practice and is related to the functional character of the law. This approach is, however, sustained and reproduced through a legal education that fosters the reductionistic tendencies of the legal system.[31] In brief, law as a field of practice, and sociology as an academic discipline, relate themselves to society in fundamentally different ways and seek different ends. Laws are introduced by the legislature to change society by enabling (or conferring power on) or restraining certain types of action, regulating social institutions and coordinating groups and individual behaviour in an effective and rational manner. Lawyers are socialized to think in a pragmatic and eclectic manner, focusing on individual cases.[32] The legal system is, in turn, expected to contribute to shaping social behaviour and bringing about the changes desired by legislatures. Whether or not law does in actual fact regulate behaviour or change society is, of course, another matter all together which falls outside our immediate concern here.

Sociology, on the other hand, is ultimately driven by sociologists' curiosity about social life as reflected in their attempts to explain and understand social reality. The most valuable asset of a sociologist is, to use Erving Goffman's words, 'the bent to sustain in regard to all elements of social life a spirit of unfettered, unsponsored inquiry and the wisdom not to look elsewhere but to ourselves and our discipline for this mandate'.[33] It does not mean that sociologists do not have civic commitments or sociology is free from all forms of pragmatism and instrumentalism. Neither is it implied that all sociological studies are as a rule driven by the ambition to enlighten. In fact, one can argue that sociology has become increasingly pragmatic in recent years and that many sociologists tend to see their role as the provider of scientific knowledge to the decision-makers.[34] But the essence of sociology, which bestows it with a unique understanding of social phenomena and transforms it into 'a form of life', will remain the curiosity about social life and the urge to reveal the hidden social structures.[35]

---

[30] A Podgórecki and CJ Whelan, (eds), *Sociological Approach to Law* (London, Groom Helm, 1981) 11.
[31] KA Ziegert, 'Legal Education at Work: The Impossible Task of Teaching Law' (1988) 5 *Tidskrift för rättssociologi* 184.
[32] *Ibid.*
[33] E Goffman, 'The Interaction Order' (1983) 48 *American Sociological Review* 1–17.
[34] TC Halliday and M Janowitz, *Sociology and its Public: The Forms and Fates of Disciplinary Organisation* (Chicago, IL, University of Chicago Press, 1992).
[35] The type of sociologist who is above all driven and motivated by an unlimited curiosity about social life is undoubtedly a threatened species within socio-legal studies.

Broadly speaking, mainstream sociology has two major commitments: firstly, to develop an intellectual tradition within the scientific community; and secondly, a civic obligation to the wider public.[36] In contrast to the lawyer, the sociologist is interested in the general characteristics of social phenomena and his/her scientific activities are directed towards producing a general knowledge of society, ie, social theories. Individual cases *in themselves* and *for themselves* are of no significance to the sociologist (although different traditions disagree on how one can generalize from cases).[37] Thus, sociology and law are founded on two different, and in some ways irreconcilable, approaches to social life. These approaches or strategies are broadly speaking based on two epistemological premises: law's knowledge of society is obtained above all by communicating about and processing individual cases, while sociology's knowledge is obtained from examining generalisable social conditions. This does not mean that sociology, or legal studies for that matter, are epistemologically monolithic. In actual fact sociology contains many epistemological approaches and is ridden with internal debates and disagreements on the nature and scope of knowledge and how to identify and access 'reliable knowledge'. Poststructuralists would also challenge the idea that certain knowledge is possible, although few sociologists, influenced by this epistemological position, have thought through the implications for how one conducts and writes up empirical research.[38] The point made here is that law's understanding of society and social relations, being a form of knowledge, is at a general level derived differently from that of sociology's.

What does all this mean for sociological studies of law? It means that the field of the sociology of law is given the difficult (if not impossible) task of uniting two fundamentally different images of society: a legal image derived through processing individual cases and shaped by formal practice and a sociological image aspiring towards generalisable knowledge of society and formed through intellectual scientific curiosity. The result is the creation of a socio-legal field of research characterised by a constant tension caused by these two different images of society. This interdisciplinary tension can be, and has been, turned into a fruitful and useful source of socio-legal research, enabling sociologists of law to highlight issues that neither law

---

[36] T Parsons defines the primary role of sociology as 'the advancement and transmission of empirical knowledge "knowledge"' pertaining to social life. See T Parsons, 'Some Problems Confronting Sociology as a Discipline' (1959) 24 *American Sociological Review* 527.

[37] An ethnomethodologist in looking at a legal case might be interested in showing how general cultural knowledge and interpretive methods are employed by legal professionals. A structural-functionalist might be interested in showing how general structures in social life shape the outcome. These different sociological interests can be contrasted with that of the legal scholar who seeks to explain how the law develops on a case-by-case basis.

[38] For an example of a text that takes poststructuralism seriously, see M Ashmore, *The Reflexive Thesis: Righting the Sociology of Scientific Knowledge* (Chicago, IL, University of Chicago Press, 1989).

nor sociology alone can study and grasp adequately. In that sense, the tension between these two forms of knowledge constitutes the disciplinary core of the socio-legal field. However, the same tension has also brought doubts and uncertainty regarding the aims, aspirations, foundations and methods of socio-legal research.[39] Although such doubts are part and parcel of any interdisciplinary undertaking, they need to be taken seriously and debated critically if the vitality of socio-legal research is to be sustained over time.

D. A CYNICAL VIEW?

We can hardly overstate the power of law, as an academic discipline, a field of practice and a profession, in preserving its values and aspirations and forcing its own image of society on outsiders who break into the realm of law. Llewellyn and Hoebel express this in the following way:

> [Modern law] becomes a world of its own. It is a world like Alice's Looking-Glass—both difficult to break into and difficult, once one has become acclimated to it to break out of. [...] Even the specialists of the social disciplines find the self-contained world of authoritative legal doctrine a sort of uncharitable fourth dimensional space. Effort after effort at synthesis of the social disciplines over the past ten years has made worthwhile headway in all respect, except that of integrating law-stuff with the rest. [...] The obstacle is the acceptance of the realm of Law as being a different order, that sets its own premises and becomes impenetrable on any premises except its own.[40]

The picture of the spread of interdisciplinary research into the law schools, as painted above by Bradney and Cownie, might be a source of encouragement to some researchers who are interested in socio-legal studies. But as sociologists of law we need to view this development with caution, for it might disguise law's attempts to 'neutralise' rather than 'internalise' the skills, theoretical knowledge and experiences which are developed within other disciplines, such as social anthropology, sociology, political science or psychology. Expressed differently, we need to ask whether law as an academic discipline is opening up to social science disciplines and humanities to integrate its brand of knowledge with their forms of knowledge in order to broaden its intellectual and academic horizons, raise new questions and devise new methods to approach these questions, or if it imports their knowledge selectively and strictly on its own disciplinary terms to address the same disciplinary concerns as before. There cannot be a clear-cut answer to this question and law might very well be trying to achieve many

---

[39] For a critical discussion on the state of socio-legal research see BZ Tamanaha, *Realistic Socio-Legal Theory: Pragmatism and a Social Theory of Law* (Oxford, Clarendon Press, 1997); and Banakar 2003, above, n 2.

[40] KN Llewellyn and EA Hoebel, *The Cheyenne Way* (Norman, OK, University of Oklahoma Press, 1940).

different goals at the same time, some of which might not even be compatible with each other, by importing other disciplinary approaches into its realm. Yet, much evidence arguably supports the latter form of knowledge organisation by law, ie, law allows the import of extra-legal methods and forms of knowledge in so far as they do not question law's gaze or disciplinary identity. If so, then the question becomes whether the 'import' of theories and methods on law's terms suffices to bring about the type of critical reflexive approaches we find within social sciences, aimed at questioning the taken-for-granted values of legal profession and legal academics? It is precisely in connection with this question that we are once again confronted with the issue of methodology. On the one hand, we must examine if a selective import and application of social science methods by the law provide the methodological distance required to escape disciplinary blindness to its taken-for-granted values and practices and, on the other hand, if sociology (assuming that it is integrated with legal studies) can climb out of its skin and step into law to see and experience it from within?

E. RESEARCH METHODOLOGY IN SOCIOLOGY

Although sociology has generated what looks at first sight as a bewildering range of methodologies, each of which has its own technical language, it should be remembered that there are really only a few general methods that can be used in researching any topic or social setting. Quantitative methods involve using a range of techniques to collect data, including administering questionnaires or surveys, and analysing this using statistical techniques. Qualitative methods involve conducting semi-structured or unstructured interviews, doing ethnographic fieldwork, or analysing tape-recordings or textual materials.[41] There is a lot one can say about the technical issues involved in using these methods. However, we feel that it is more important in this introductory chapter to focus on the epistemological positions and debates that inform how they are used in the discipline. We will start by reviewing the debate between positivism and its critics which is still of central importance in sociology. We will then look at some recent criticisms made by ethnomethodology, feminism and postmodernism and their implications for how one conducts empirical research.

F. POSITIVISM AND ITS CRITICS

The term positivism was first used by Auguste Comte who believed that sociology should model itself on the natural sciences, and seek to produce

---

[41] There is a huge range of specialist guides to different methods. For examples of general introductory texts, see N Fielding, (ed), *Researching Social Life* (London, Sage, 1993); and E Babbie, *The Basics of Social Research* (Kentucky, Wadsworth, 2002).

objective findings about the structure of society.[42] Shortly afterwards Adolphe Quetelet developed what became the science of social statistics: a means of investigating regularities in society, such as crime rates, and identifying possible causes through their relationship to different variables. They developed these ideas in the aftermath of the French Revolution so the discipline can be seen, at least initially, as a conservative attempt to manage social change after the failure of the utopian hopes of Enlightenment thinkers such as Voltaire or Rousseau.

It is important to recognise that the development of statistical analysis as a method cannot be separated from how positivism has been promoted as a philosophical position in social science. The sophisticated techniques used to analyse large data-sets today were first developed in the 1940s by American sociologists such as Paul Lazarfeld. The most influential advocate of positivism was, however, Emile Durkheim who argued at the end of the 19th century that sociology should be concerned with identifying the causal relationship between 'social facts', and that there was consequently no need to address the subjective understandings of individuals.[43]

The view that sociology should become like natural science was contested by many German thinkers during the 19th century, partly as a conservative reaction against the view that progressive change can be achieved by social engineering. At its root, however, was a philosophical objection to the idea that one can explain human action in the same way as phenomena that could be measured and observed in the natural world. This interpretive objection was expressed in different ways, but led proponents, like Max Weber, to advocate methods that address the meaningful character of human activities. Qualitative methods were developed as a set of techniques by the Chicago School, and American urban anthropologists in the first half of the 20th century. Interpretivism has also been advanced as a philosophical position by Alfred Schutz and Peter Winch.[44]

Interpretivism is not, however, the only tradition in sociology that has been critical towards positivism. Another epistemological position that is equally influential is the critical realism advanced by Karl Marx, and later by the Frankfurt School. In some respects, this has something in common with positivism, in that the analyst produces a scientific explanation of society which is intended to correct the falsehoods promoted by economically dominant groups. On the other hand, the main target is the positivist belief that research can produce neutral and objective findings.

All this can become quite complicated, but it is worth making these distinctions because they are relevant to how one understands questions of

---

[42] A Comte, *System of Positive Polity*, vol 1–4 (New York, NY, Burt Franklin, 1968).

[43] E Durkheim, *The Rules of Sociological Method* (New York, NY, Free Press, 1966).

[44] For a review of these debates, see J Hughes and W Sharrock, *The Philosophy of Social Research* (London, Longman, 1997).

method which are not always given adequate treatment in texts or review articles about sociology of law. It is, for example, easy to combine theoretical approaches informed by critical realism and interpretivism, since they are each opposed to positivism. If one looks more deeply, it becomes apparent that they have opposing epistemological assumptions that lead to different understandings of research method. Critical realists are, for example, open towards combining qualitative and quantitative methods, since any form of data can be used to advance a progressive viewpoint. By contrast, interpretive sociologists, such as symbolic interactionists influenced by Herbert Blumer, have a commitment to fieldwork as the only way of addressing meaning.[45]

It is also worth making the point that one does not necessarily need to have an interest in the philosophy of social science or be committed to the use of sophisticated statistical methods to be a positivist. The most common research conducted for governments today uses a combination of qualitative and quantitative methods in evaluating the effectiveness of policies or programmes. This is often described as empiricist, but it shares a set of philosophical assumptions with positivism, including a commitment to using scientific methods, and a belief that it is possible to describe the world objectively. From an interpretive perspective, the short interview extracts that appear in evaluation reports do not adequately address the full range of viewpoints one can find in an organisational setting such as a law court. From a critical realist perspective, they do not ask critical questions about government policy or the nature of society.

1. Some Recent Criticisms

Although methods can be understood as a set of techniques, that can be combined with epistemological and theoretical positions, it is very difficult to separate them in practice. This will be apparent in the kind of research undertaken by three recent intellectual movements which are critical of positivism.

Ethnomethodology, which was founded in the 1960s by the American sociologist Harold Garfinkel, is a diverse movement which has various subfields including ethnomethodological ethnography and conversation analysis.[46] It is deeply anti-positivist, in the sense that it goes further than Weber or the symbolic interactionists in investigating the nature of meaning. This has resulted in a radical re-conceptualisation of qualitative research, so that

---

[45] For a review of debates within symbolic interactionism about method, see M Travers, *Qualitative Research Through Case Studies* (London, Sage, 2001).

[46] For an introduction, see J Heritage, *Garfinkel and Ethnomethodology* (Cambridge, Polity Press, 1984).

instead of trying to produce a determinate account of meaningful activities in a setting, it instead looks at the interpretive procedures by, and through which, meaning is produced. An example would be Lawrence Wieder's study of a half-way house for drugs offenders, in which he describes the methods he employed to make sense of what was happening in the house.[47] Similarly, conversation analysts are interested in studying the methods used in conversation in everyday and institutional settings. Without going into this field in any depth,[48] one can see that pursuing a philosophically-driven argument against positivism results in a different way of conducting and conceptualising qualitative research.

Feminism is another movement that has been critical towards positivism, although this is complicated by the fact that some feminists favour the use of quantitative research methods. The literature on feminist methodology is now extensive, although only a few of these debates have been taken up by socio-legal researchers. Many feminists see quantitative methods as serving male interests in a society where women are excluded from positions of power and influence. They have, therefore, promoted a reflexive version of qualitative research that is sensitive towards power relations and the ethical position of the researcher.

Finally, the intellectual movement that has mounted the most sustained challenge to positivism in the last two decades is poststructuralism. This draws on the idea, implicit in interpretivism, that there might be multiple viewpoints in any social setting, but it combines this with a sceptical philosophical argument against the Enlightenment belief in reason and progress. Theorists who use poststructuralist ideas often fall back on critical realist arguments (a version of what Woolgar and Pawluch term 'ontological gerrymandering'),[49] and one can find many examples of this in fields like critical legal studies. There have also, however, been attempts to develop new forms of ethnographic writing that celebrate multiple meanings, or the fact that every theory can be challenged.

G. SOCIOLOGY, RESEARCH METHODS AND LAW

A wide range of methods are used in socio-legal research ranging from the statistical analysis of survey research to the analysis of transcripts from tape-recordings of judicial hearings. There are socio-legal researchers who have employed quantitative methods, qualitative methods or a combination

---

[47] DL Wieder, *Language and Social Reality: The Case of Telling the Convict Code* (The Hague, Mouton, 1974).
[48] See M Travers and JF Manzo, (eds), *Law in Action: Ethnomethodological and Conversation Analytic Approaches to Law* (Aldershot, Ashgate, 1997).
[49] S Woolgar and D Pawluch, 'Ontological Gerrymandering' (1985) 32 *Social Problems* 214–17.

of both in addressing socio-legal questions. There are also researchers who have employed discourse analytic methods in studying legal texts, or conducted in-depth interviews with judges, or spent time as fieldworkers looking at law in non-western societies. Much of this work has been of high quality, and is comparable with the best research in other sociological subfields.

The problem from our perspective is that many of these studies have been conducted by researchers outside the law school. Here we need to address the difficult issue that many interesting studies about law and legal institutions are published each year in a variety of journals that are never cited in the main socio-legal journals or book series. There are a number of possible reasons. To begin with, the editors and editorial boards are inevitably only interested in, or knowledgeable about, only a sub-set of the sociological approaches that have been used to study law, and may reject papers that do not fit their preconceptions. There is also the problem that researchers find more satisfaction in being reviewed by scholars who have similar interests, and so do not apply to inter-disciplinary journals. A related issue is that disciplinary specialists do not always want to address wider audiences, or supply suitable literature reviews for a general readership.

Perhaps one has to accept that law is not necessarily the property of scholars based in law schools. Since law, as we are often told, is everywhere, and relevant to most social topics, it is inevitable that it can be studied from many disciplinary perspectives. One might, therefore, want to argue that socio-legal studies should be understood as a clearing house or point of exchange for different discipline-based studies about law, rather than an academic discipline or sub-discipline in its own right. In this case, one would want to see more review articles in law and society journals explaining research about law conducted by other disciplines.

Socio-legal studies has also, however, had the aspiration of developing sociology of law and empirical policy research inside law schools. Here we would argue that there has only been a limited amount of success, although many law-school academics have sought out contact with sociologists, and in some cases like Roger Cotterrell registered for higher degrees in sociology.[50] It is generally recognised that most socio-legal researchers use only a limited range of research methods and do not fully engage with the methodological debates that take place in sociology. Moreover, there is no sense of a field having developed, comparable to the sociologies of medicine, education or social work, in which academic lawyers take ownership of sociology as an empirical discipline and apply it to law.

---

[50] Fourteen of the contributors to this collection are based in law schools, and five in departments of social science. John Flood and Max Travers trained as lawyers, before doing doctorates in departments of sociology.

We would argue that the root of this problem is not so much the technical skills and training available to law-school academics, but how they understand the nature of sociology, and in particular the relationship between theory and method. We would, therefore, like to use the rest of this introduction to make some general points about the relationship between theory and method in studying law, the craft of doing empirical research, and the difficulties involved in studying the content of legal practice. These conceptual issues have still not been adequately addressed by the few introductions and review articles on sociology of law, but are arguably central to developing sociology of law in law schools.

H. THE RELATIONSHIP BETWEEN THEORY AND METHOD

It should already be apparent that one cannot talk about methods in socio-legal studies without also talking about how these are understood in different theoretical traditions. We will be trying to show throughout this collection that theory and method are inextricably inter-linked. Methods are not simply techniques that can be used in obtaining facts about the social world, but are always used as part of a commitment to a theoretical perspective, even if this is not discussed explicitly in a research project.

Here it is worth briefly considering two exemplary studies, in the sense that they are well-theorised, and represent different ways of studying a court setting. Perhaps inevitably, the researchers were trained and based in disciplines outside the law school, although they each collaborated with legal scholars, and court personnel during the research.

The first study is Sally Merry's ethnography of disputes in the lower courts in a New England town.[51] Merry is an anthropologist, but belonged to an inter-disciplinary group of legal theorists, socio-linguists, political scientists and sociologists who met together during the 1980s to develop a common perspective on law. In this study, Merry addressed the local understandings of the participants to build up a detailed picture of the social relationships in this community and how they are regulated by law. However, she continually relates this to a theoretical understanding of the nature of American society that draws on what might loosely be called the conflict tradition in sociology: the view that law benefits economically dominant groups and is also a vehicle for promoting ideas that benefit those groups. It is a crucial part of her analysis that the people she studied were unaware of how their actions were shaped by, but also reproduced, this wider structural context.

---

[51] S Merry, *Getting Justice and Getting Even: Legal Consciousness Among Working Class Americans* (Chicago, IL, University of Chicago Press, 1990).

Although Merry does not discuss this explicitly, her study is informed by the epistemological assumptions of critical realism.[52] By contrast, there are other theoretical traditions in sociology, influenced by interpretivism, that would only be interested in how the lawyers and litigants in this court understood their own activities. The claim by an analyst to know more about the history or political structure of society would be seen as an illegitimate move inside this tradition. Robert Emerson's ethnographic study of a juvenile court can be used to illustrate this difference in theoretical perspective. In looking at the court as symbolic interactionist, he focuses on the different perspectives of judges, lawyers and litigants, and attempts to address how they understood what was happening.[53] He was interested, for example, in how lawyers were able to mitigate certain offences by using the idea of a criminal career. Emerson's study, consequently, gives more detail about the practical concerns of the lawyers and judge, and has much less focus on the structure or history of American society.

Finally, it is worth noting that this is a good example, for our purposes, because the methods employed by Merry and Emerson were similar. They each conducted ethnographic fieldwork over a long period, and as a result obtained some rich data about, respectively, neighbourhood disputes and juvenile crime. It was, however, the theoretical framework that determined how they used and interpreted the data. Although the research studies we will be presenting in the different sections of this collection are not of the same quality as these studies (for one thing, they have not benefited from the same level of funding), they also illustrate how one cannot separate a discussion of methods from theory.

I. THE CRAFT OF DOING EMPIRICAL RESEARCH

One difficulty facing socio-legal researchers who wish to learn more about methods is that sociologists do not acquire a competence as empirical researchers through reading research manuals or attending courses. Each method can be understood as a set of craft skills one learns from experienced researchers or from encountering problems while doing research. Each also requires learning how to think and talk about a specific set of methodological issues. To give two examples, researchers using ethnographic methods often have to consider ethical issues when researching closed or sensitive settings, whereas quantitative researchers will need to think about the respective merits of different statistical tests.

---

[52] Merry belongs to a tradition in anthropology known as 'interpretive anthropology'. This is where interdisciplinary fields can become confusing since she has arguably more in common with the critical realist tradition than with interpretive approaches, such as symbolic interactionism in sociology.

[53] R Emerson, *Judging Delinquents: Context and Process in Juvenile Court* (Chicago, IL, Aldine, 1969).

There are usually no clear answers to such methodological problems. One should note, for example, that it would be quite legitimate for a sociologist to defend what others might view as unethical behaviour, for example by pursuing covert observation when it is not possible to obtain information through other means.[54] Similarly, there are many ways of analysing and interpreting quantitative data. Competence in a research method means being able to situate your own work in relation to debates in a particular literature, and to demonstrate an understanding of the technical issues that arise within that community.

More generally, it involves being able to justify your choice of method over alternatives, which can involve admitting that practical considerations made it impossible to pursue what was originally planned. Many ethnographers have, for example, set out with the goal of comparing two institutions, only to realise that this is impractical in terms of time. Here, the matter is complicated by the fact that one could also justify the decision to study one setting on methodological grounds. From an interpretive perspective, it is usually preferable to conduct one in-depth case study, based on a long period of fieldwork, as opposed to spending shorter periods of time in two or more settings. Again, one can see there is no clear answer to this methodological issue: what counts is being able to justify a particular decision in relation to your research question, while demonstrating an understanding of how other researchers have encountered similar problems.

The different chapters in this collection show socio-legal researchers doing exactly this. They are not simply applying sociological theories and methods to legal topics, but working creatively within the constraints of different traditions.

J. ADDRESSING THE CONTENT OF LAW

A central issue that was raised in the first half of this chapter was the extent to which sociologists, as outsiders, can address the content of legal practice. A common complaint is that sociological research has so far failed to address the content of law as a lawyer would understand this. One can also again see how this is not simply a question of theory (the sociological questions one can ask about law) but also has methodological implications for how one might address this omission.

To secure and enhance its professional standing, law often presents itself as a formal and coherent body of rules, doctrines and principles. According to this view, the centre of gravity of the legal system rests on an esoteric

---

[54] For an example of a study based on covert observation (or at least where the real objectives of the study were concealed), see J Pierce, *Gender Trials: Emotional Lives in Contemporary Law Firms* (Berkeley, CA, University of California Press, 1995).

body of knowledge, which requires considerable exegetical skills of interpretation. Law becomes essentially concerned with interpretation of acts
and case readings, expounding legal doctrines, and constitutes itself through
textual manifestations of legal decisions, judgements, and opinions.

As has been suggested in previous sections, the reality of law understood
strictly in terms of explicating the correct meaning of legal rules does not
require, and cannot be reduced to, sociological concepts, insights, or ideas.
However, besides reading legal matter and doing legal research, the practicing lawyer is involved in a range of other activities—such as conferring with
clients, doing office paper work, doing court work, negotiating, conferring
with other lawyers[55]—where sociological insights and knowledge can be
decisive. The dependence of legal practices and processes, which create the
contexts of legal decision-making, on institutional facts reveal the interdependence of legal discourses (ie, reflecting factors internally constructed by
law) and social discourses (institutional factors external to law). Thus,
focusing the reflexive lenses of sociological analysis on the practice-based
features of the law, can potentially enable us to uncover the institutional
limits of the legal practice, in a way that traditional forms of legal studies
cannot do.

Sociologists have already done this using a variety of methods, and from
a variety of theoretical perspectives.[56] Marxist studies have, for example,
looked at the development of protection for workers in 19th century
England through the Factory Acts.[57] The two ethnographic studies we have
already discussed by Merry and Emerson, are also concerned with how
lawyers and clients understand the practice of law. Nevertheless, one can
see that these and other sociological studies are rarely interested in the
development of legal doctrine in the same way as black-letter lawyers. This
makes it possible to complain that sociology only addresses the effects of
law on society rather than the essence of law.

It would be nice to have some empirical studies that examine how judges
make decisions through using legal rules. Alan Paterson has shown what
can be achieved through interviewing judges in the higher courts about their
work, even though he did not look at the nature of decision-making in
much detail.[58] We know of two research projects currently underway in

---

[55] See EO Smigel, 'Work of the Wall Street Lawyer' in R James Simon, (ed), *The Sociology of Law* (San Francisco, CA, Chandler, 1968).

[56] See DJ McBarnet, *Conviction: Law, the State and the Construction of Justice* (London, Macmillan, 1981); A Paterson, *The Law Lords* (London, Macmillan, 1982); and M Travers, *The Reality of Law: Work and Talk in a Firm of Criminal Lawyers* (Aldershot, Dartmouth, 1997).

[57] WG Carson, 'Symbolic and Instrumental Dimensions of Early Factory Legislation: A Case Study in the Social Origins of English Law' in R Hood, (ed), *Crime, Criminology and Public Policy* (London, Heineman, 1980) 107–38.

[58] See Paterson, 1982, above n 56.

England and Australia that have obtained permission to interview judges about their work.[59] It might be that these will focus on the occupational socialisation of judges, or their social backgrounds, as opposed to how legal reasoning takes place. This will, however, depend on the theoretical questions addressed, and the methods employed to pursue these.

Socio-legal researchers based in law schools are well-placed to conduct studies that address the content of legal rules, as well as the wider social context. It is also worth noting that the outsider/insider distinction can be exaggerated: it is possible for a non-lawyer to understand legal principles and reasoning; and, as many studies have shown, decision-making in many legal settings involves very little law in the sense of the skills taught in law degrees. Much of the problem may not be conceptual or philosophical at all, but simply the practical issue of the extent to which one can interview or observe practitioners, as an outsider so that one develops an understanding of what actually happens in legal work.

K. RESEARCH METHODS TRAINING IN THE LAW SCHOOL

Much of what we have said in this chapter may be summarised by discussing the recent debate on empirical legal research in the UK. As previously mentioned in the introduction, a number of senior academics with many years of experience in socio-legal research have recently joined voice in drawing attention to what they describe as the 'dwindling of capacity to undertake rigorous empirical research in law'.[60] Their concern 'goes well beyond the need and interests of academic practitioners and users' and embraces many areas of legal policy, such as the public funding of legal services. These legal policy areas need to be underpinned by 'rigorous empirical research of law and the institutions of law *as they operate*'.[61] This crisis in legal empirical research is in parts placed in the context of the ESRC commissioned Review of Socio-Legal Studies in 1994 which noted that there was 'a shortage of staff within law departments to provide training in socio-legal research'. This review also pointed out that social science departments did not have legally trained academics who could teach or promote research about law. The task of training socio-legal researchers was, thus, left to the law schools.

It should be noted that nowhere in the Nuffield Enquiry we are told what 'rigorous empirical research' is. Also, the quest for finding ways of revitalising empirical legal research comes at a time when, according Wheeler and

---

[59] These are being conducted by Penny Derbyshire of Kingston University in the United Kingdom and Sharyn Roach Anleu of Flinders University, Australia.

[60] See above, n 2.

[61] See above, n 2.

Thomas, socio-legal research is at the height of its academic popularity and success.[62] This implies that 'rigorous' research is other than the type of research (mainly of the qualitative interpretive kind) currently undertaken by most socio-legal researchers in the UK. The other interesting aspect of this document is that it places emphasis on the 'policy-relevant empirical examinations' and the need to train staff to conduct empirical research. However, it does not refer to the role of 'methodology' or 'theory' in training such researchers. Our argument is that to collect hard data on the operations of legal institutions requires an awareness of the theoretical issues of law and social sciences if this data is to enhance our understanding of how law and legal institutions operate in relation to various social factors. There is no need or urgency to train research staff who can conduct 'rigorous' empirical studies, if these are to be done without taking into consideration the debates on the relationship between social scientific methodology and theory. Statisticians, many of whom are even trained in the social sciences, are well capable of studying the flow of cases through courts and the rate of litigation in a 'rigorous' fashion.

Looking back at the discussions presented in this chapter we cannot see how empirical research, which helps us to understand legal institutions and legal behaviour in relation to broader social interests and factor, can be conducted without full theoretical engagement and commitment to advancing social scientifically aware socio-legal research. We thus conclude this chapter with a plea for placing more emphasis on teaching research methods, and allowing students to conduct empirical projects in law schools.

One reason for holding our workshop on research methods in Oñati was to provide an opportunity for law school researchers who were interested in different types of methods to discuss shared intellectual interests. We all believe that holding the occasional workshop is beneficial for the participants, but increasing the quantity and quality of socio-legal studies really requires changing the law school curriculum. This might be seen as pursuing something of a hopeless cause at present, given the pressures on law schools, at least in Britain, to become more vocational, and even incorporate 'nuts and bolts' courses that are presently taught on the Law Society Final's Course.[63] The postgraduate law degree offered in America continues to be narrowly vocational, although at least students are required to obtain experience of a wider range of subjects in their first degree.

As we noted in our previous text on law and social theory, we are happy to stand alongside reformers like Karl Llewellyn who have argued that law students should do more than learn legal rules. We would argue, with

---

[62] S Wheeler and P Thomas, 'Socio-Legal Studies' in DJ Hayton, (ed), *Law's Future(s)* (Oxford, Hart Publishing, 2002) 274.

[63] See C Sanders, 'Law Courses Set for Radical Shake-up', The Times Higher Education Supplement, 21 November 2003.

Anthony Bradney and Fiona Cownie, that lawyers need to have a general education if they are to contribute most effectively to legal practice at a time of rapid social change. Students taking nursing, or management, or social work are usually required to do an empirical project as part of their degrees, and find that this encourages them to reflect critically about professional practice. There are already law degrees where students are offered an opportunity to do work experience, or participate in a legal clinic, and we feel that learning something about research methods in the degree would add something to this experience. We hope that this collection will demonstrate the variety of topics that can be addressed, and suggest ways in which one could develop an appropriate methods course for law schools.

Section One

Method Versus Methodology

REZA BANAKAR AND MAX TRAVERS

A CENTRAL THEME running through this collection is that it is impossible to understand the issue of method, without also considering how methods are used by different theoretical traditions: this is the distinction between 'method' and 'methodology'. This quickly became apparent in the workshop we held at Oñati, in that from the outset there was a lively debate between socio-legal researchers committed to what we described in chapter 1 as the epistemological positions of positivism and interpretivism. This is also often described in textbooks as the action-structure debate, and developed out of methodological debates that took place in the 19th century over how sociology should develop as a science.

It is worth noting before reading the two papers in this section that there are many positions one can take in this debate, and one argument favoured by many contemporary social theorists is that one can move beyond the divisive paradigm wars of the past, and build a social science that can address both structure and action. Whatever one feels about this recent attempt to provide sociology with an agreed framework in which it can advance and prosper as a science, most of the socio-legal researchers who attended this workshop did not share this vision. The structural tradition was represented by a group of researchers whose work is influenced by the systems theory of Niklas Luhmann. The action tradition was represented by a group of researchers influenced by symbolic interactionism and ethnomethodology. It was clear that each understood the practice of research very differently, and in particular how one should collect and analyse qualitative data.

The two papers in this section by John Flood and Klaus A Ziegert give a flavour of the arguments used by each side, but they should also be seen as representing different styles of sociological work which are characteristic of the two paradigms. Klaus A Ziegert writes in the formalistic, theoretical style favoured by theorists like Luhmann and Talcott Parsons who are seeking to develop a thorough and 'objective' understanding of society. It is also written using a theoretical terminology (terms such as 'autopoiesis', 'binary codes', 'self-reference' and 'node') that one can only properly understand by already knowing something about this theoretical tradition. Although no brief account of Luhmann's systems theory could do it justice, it might nonetheless be helpful to introduce some of its features, which are methodologically relevant and of interest to the discussion here, very briefly.

Luhmann places the idea of self-reference at the heart of autopoiesis, or his theory of operatively closed systems.[1] It is important to note that autopoiesis is not a theory of specific objects, processes or relationships, but a theory that observes reality or systems using the specific distinction of system/environment. Hamberto Maturana and Francisco Varela orig-inally coined the concept of autopoiesis within theoretical biology to describe the self-reproduction of living cells through self-reference.[2] Maturana and Varela postulated that living systems maintain their autonomy and unity through their very own operations, which are based on controlling the selection of external causes (required for their survival and reproduction) through internal operations. Thus, autopoiesis indi-cates the process characteristic of life by which systems organise them-selves out of disorder, forming a responsive, self-reflecting, self-maintain-ing network.

Luhmann's systems theory transcends the classical understanding of object/subject by regarding communication (and not 'action') as the basic element of any social system. He breaks with traditional systems theory of Parsons and descriptions based on cybernetic feedback loops and structural understandings of self-organisation of the 1960s. This allows him to work towards devising a solution to the problem of the humanised 'subject'.

Perhaps the most challenging idea incorporated in the theory of auto-poiesis is that social systems should not be defined in terms of human agency or norms, but of communications. Communication is in turn the unity of utterance, information and understanding and constitutes social systems by recursively reproducing communication. This sociologically radical thesis, which raises the fear of a dehumanised theory of law and society, attempts to highlight the fact that social systems are constituted by communicative *events*, and reproduced by recursively using events to produce events.[3] It

---

[1] According to KA Ziegert, N Luhmann's systems theory was branded as 'autopoietic theo-ry' by others. Autopoietic means self-creation in Greek, but also implies self-reference See KA Ziegert, 'The Thick Description of Law: An Introduction to Niklas Luhmann's Theory of Operatively Closed Systems' in R Banakar and M Travers, (eds), *An Introduction to Law and Social Theory* (Oxford, Hart Publishing, 2002).

[2] HR Maturana and FJ Varela, *Autopoiesis and Cognition* (Boston, MA, Reidel, 1980).

[3] G Teubner, 'Juridification: Concepts, Aspects, Limits, Solutions' in G Teubner, (ed), *Juridification of Social Spheres: A Comparative Analysis in the Areas of Labour, Corporate, Antitrust and Social Welfare Law* (Berlin, Walter de Gruyter, 1987) 3.

means that what turns law into an integrated whole is neither legal norms nor social actors and institutions, but the unity of legal communications. From an empirical point of view, the communicative events 'occur whenever people express themselves in terms of lawful/unlawful, legal/illegal, and whenever their communicative acts are directed towards claim-making and claim-defending'.[4] It appears as if systems theory defines and positions empirical data by the application of what is ultimately a set of *a priori* theoretical assumptions and propositions. This point is, however, refuted by Ziegert, who on the contrary argues that systems theory is better equipped for conducting genuine empirical research than, for example, the grounded theory approach. We can perhaps better assess the implications of doing research as suggested by Ziegert when we compare it with the approaches of the interpretive traditions, which are described by John Flood in this section.

Flood writes in the essay style favoured by American interactionists like Everett Hughes, Herbert Blumer or Howard Becker.[5] One finds in this tradition a distrust of scientism and abstract terminology, and this is reflected in how researchers present findings and write about methodology.

Flood's piece can be seen as a characteristic attempt of interactionists, particularly those associated with the 1940s Chicago School, to side-step the epistemological and theoretical debates that trouble or excite other social scientists, and to present research as simply what one learns by observing different groups and institutions at close quarters. However, the argument is slightly more pointed than this. Like other interactionists in this tradition, Flood believes that too much theorising is bad for sociological research. He notes that 'the blinders imposed by the systems approach are desensitising, and the core of ethnography is to be sensitive to everything around you, not just segments of theoretical reality'. The central interpretive message is that the objective of research should be to address how members in the group being studied understand their own activities, whether these are barristers' clerks or managers in the Financial Ombudsman Service. This is not possible for researchers who are interested in building elaborate theories which are presented as superior to our ordinary, common-sense knowledge about the social world.

Ziegert's piece takes the opposite view, in that he argues that theory is necessary to understand qualitative data, and that the descriptive work favoured by Flood fails to address the underlying structures that shape and

---

[4] M King, 'The "Truth" About Autopoiesis' (1993) 20 *Journal of Law and Society* 218, 224–25. Also see G Teubner, *Law as an Autopoietic System* (Oxford, Blackwell, 1993) 225.

[5] See E Hughes, *The Sociological Eye* (Chicago, IL, Aldine, 1971); Becker, *Howard Sociological Work* (Chicago, IL, Aldine, 1971); and H Blumer, *Symbolic Interactionism: Perspective and Method* (Englewood Cliffs, NJ, Prentice-Hall, 1969).

determine the nature of law.[6] What is perhaps most striking about the chapter, and characteristic of all structural theoretical approaches, is that he presents autopoiesis as a map that allows one to see society as a whole, with all the individuals and institutions on a grid or matrix which enables the analyst to zoom in or zoom out, and to study how institutions have developed through history. The assumption that the theorist has an objective vantage point and can investigate society in this way is shared by thinkers like Durkheim and Marx, but is opposed to the interpretive tradition in which one can only address how different groups and individuals understand the world around them, or to continue with the metaphor, how they make their own maps.

The implications for method are most clear in the diagram Ziegert presents for a comparative project that looks at how law is changing as an autopietic system in different societies. At the workshop, he presented a larger and more elaborate diagram in which tiny figures of individuals were presented as part of larger systems. He proposed that one could investigate these relationships scientifically by zooming in and interviewing two representatives from different groups, and use this data as part of a theoretically-driven analysis. One can, however, see how from an interpretive perspective, this does not adequately address how lawyers, judges or other social actors understand their own social worlds. The objection is partly on theoretical grounds since autopoiesis, as a structural approach, presents individuals as objects that are shaped and moulded by social systems and structures, whereas interpretivists see society as only consisting of individuals.

However, it also concerns how one chooses to study the world. It is significant that structural traditions usually favour methods like statistical analysis (see Ziegert's favourable comments on the Norwegian sociologist Stein Rokman) or structured interviews to investigate social life. They are not interested in the extended ethnographic fieldwork advocated by symbolic interactionists like Becker and Hughes which, according to ethnographers, allow one to obtain a much richer and more complex understanding of different social worlds.

---

[6] Ziegert's main target is the related tradition of grounded theory, which was developed by Barney Glaser and Hughes' student Anselm Strauss. See BG Glaser and A Strauss, *The Discovery of Grounded Theory, Strategies for Qualitative Research* (New York, NY, Aldine de Gruyter, 1967) and for a practical guide A Strauss and J Corbin, *Basics of Qualitative Research* (London, Sage, 1990). This was intended to be a more scientific version of interpretive research that involved systematic procedures for organising qualitative data into themes or codes. They defended inductivism on scientific grounds against the deductive procedure favoured by quantitative analysts who typically set out to test hypotheses through establishing causal relationships between variables. Ziegert is particularly concerned to criticise grounded theory in this chapter, since it has become popular in Germany. Interestingly, his main complaint is that grounded theory does not produce scientific, structural theory of the kind supplied by the autopoiesis tradition; whereas a grounded theory researcher might respond that this is exactly the kind of *a priori* deductive theorising they want to challenge.

These two papers, therefore, raise general issues that are immensely difficult and complex, and have generated protracted debates about method in the philosophy of social science for over two hundred years. One can, in fact, argue that most discussions today about how one conducts social science research, and whether objectivity is possible or even desirable, started with these 19th century debates on whether sociology should be a science in the same way as natural science. Durkheim and Weber are the best examples of scholars who developed well-thought out methodological statements on these issues, and most 20th century theorists have also engaged with, or attempted to transcend the action-structure debate.[7] In sociology, this is to some extent old-hat, and one can argue about whether people who suggest this are really trying to declare victory for their own position, rather than acknowledging that there is always another side in this kind of foundational debate. Although there are many positions on the issue, no one would dispute that it has not only generated a great deal of productive and interesting theorising, but also a great deal of empirical research. In our view, there is not nearly enough discussion or debate about this issue in sociolegal studies, so we are pleased to publish these two methodological statements that are relevant to any research project.

---

[7] For discussion on how Weber's methodological writings are relevant to postmodernism, see N Gane, *Max Weber and Postmodern Theory* (Basingstoke, Palgrave, 2004).

2

Socio-Legal Ethnography

JOHN FLOOD

We cannot think of any object apart from the possibility of its connection with other things' (**Wittgenstein**)

A. PREMISES

ETHNOGRAPHY TAKES US back to our roots where social interaction is at the base of our research. Hobbes talked of the problem of order as the most basic and this, in essence, is what we study. Many research methods have been devised to cope with the problems of social research—social surveys, observation, interviewing, social experiments—but only one gives us insight into the richness of social life. Ethnography makes us simultaneously stand inside and outside the *mise en scène* as we research. It is both a literary and scientific endeavour without privileging one over the other.

I make no apology for starting this essay in such a bald vein. But part of the reason for my so doing is that contemporary methodology has suffered a diminution of scale. For much of the time the empirical is ignored for the benefit of the abstract. The abstract becomes a palimpsest on which anything can be inscribed and argued about without recourse to social interaction. Too often the research process is truncated so the 'essential' work of theorising can be undertaken. Methodology needs to be brought back into the mainstream as an activity that is seen as central to the research enterprise.[1] My argument is not against theory itself, but rather one where theory is to be viewed as part of the research process, not its goal nor necessarily its starting point. Even the hyper-theorists such as Levi-Strauss and Bourdieu did fieldwork in Brazil and Algeria, respectively, before retreating to the Collège de France.

[1] The effects of this can be seen in the efforts of research funders to attempt to increase the future numbers of trained researchers. In their eyes there will soon be a research deficit.

Ethnography has about it an anarchic atmosphere that sidesteps system building. It is contextual, dynamic, reflexive, that is, it is open to all sorts of stimuli. This is not to say that ethnography cannot produce systematic results, but it is not overly concerned with questions of validity and reliability in the conventional way, say, that quantitative approaches are. The research process for ethnography is different from others: it is tentative, multi-textured, open-ended and discursive. It starts from a point of learning and enquiry that recognises we know little rather than supposing a state of knowledge which is subject to *ex post facto* ratification.

Systems theorists who see the world as a series of texts will find ethnography an uncomfortable method. The blinders imposed by the systems approach are desensitising whereas the core of ethnography is to be alert and attentive to everything around you not just particular segments of theoretical reality.

Law, as a topic for research, raises exciting questions in this context. It is situated at the intersection of life and theory. The problem is that most lawyers do not realise it. For them life is constructed out of the narratives told by judges, some of whom occasionally have a literary approach, as did Denning. These narratives are proxies for the real world. It took me some time before I realised that the worlds constructed by judges were often illusory. For example, as students we religiously learn about the snail in the ginger beer bottle and learn to control our gagging reflexes, but in fact we do not know if that snail existed or not.[2] As heuristic devices, law reports have utility; as devices for engineering social action, they are disturbing. The key for system theorists is that law appears to be a system as a result of the ways it is constructed by its practitioners. Judges and lawyers endow law with an authority that it cannot sustain under examination, especially from the ethnographer.

In my guise as a first-year law student I encountered this difference with drama. One of my teachers, Michael Zander, was fond of engaging his students in his research projects. We did not always know what we were doing or what the repercussions of what we were doing would be, but we enjoyed the immediacy and the action. For example, he decided to find out if police stations had all the necessary information on hand for those brought into custody. This was in the 1970s. The English Legal System class was organised to fan out through London and enter as many police stations as possible at roughly the same time and ask to see this information. Since no one had warned the police stations we were coming, the desk sergeants were shocked and not very pleased when many young persons arrived and

---

[2] For interesting insights into one of the most enduring legal cases see *Donoghue v Stevenson* [1932] AC 562; and the Scottish Council of Law Reporting *Donoghue v Stevenson* digital resources page at <http://www.scottishlawreports.org.uk/resources/keycases/dvs/donoghue-*v*-stevenson.html>.

demanded to see their booklets. Some of us were allowed to see them and many of us were evicted, in part because the stations did not have any, and the telephone lines buzzed between Scotland Yard and the LSE. It was fun if uncertain as to how it would turn out.[3] Having seen how exciting field-work could be, the students reacted extremely differently. There were those, like myself, who became captivated and there were those who were horri-fied by the experience and quickly reopened their law reports never to leave the library.

I now teach a course in research methods to, largely, law graduate stu-dents. Very few have any familiarity with formal presentations of theory and methodology; the scientific method is an unread catechism to them. Perhaps the most difficult notion for them to grasp is that of the research question. I try to tell them that research questions are a guide to influence their thinking about their research topics, something that will set up inter-nal arguments that they can carry on in their research. Even though I con-tinue to teach them about the role of theory and the various methods they can use to do their research, my main concern is that they generate an inter-est in their topics and ask questions because these will stimulate them fur-ther. What I try to avoid is overbearing them with discussions about the necessity for constructing theoretical frameworks as a starting point for their research. If they do start at this point the usual result is that they become stuck in a theoretical quagmire from which it is difficult to escape. For example, Donald Black's attempt to impose a false natural science cloak on social science fits in with this style of thinking.[4] One of the joys of ethnography is that it is not enslaved by a theoretical straitjacket. Therefore it does not encounter the definitional problems of 'structural coupling' or 'habitus'. It opens the field to many interpretations. The essence then of ethnography is its liberating power. In the field of law, liberation is essen-tial.

What follows is part biography and part analysis. My own journey into ethnography and my feelings about it are a product of my first encounters and disillusionment with academic law.

Originally I was drawn to law by a feeling that law possessed the power to effect change, to help the dispossessed and heal society's ills. Many stu-dents start with these ideals in mind. Scott Turow's *One L* chronicles the first year law student's journey from search for justice to the Socratic pleasures of legal reasoning. Appeals to justice are met with scorn from the professors.[5] As the students engage with the minutiae of the law reports,

---

[3] As a research exercise, there are innumerable problems with the way this experiment was carried out. But to unravel this is not my purpose here.

[4] D Black, *The Behavior of Law* (New York, NY, Academic Press, 1980).

[5] S Turow, *One L: The Turbulent True Story of a First Year At Harvard Law School* (New York, NY, Farrar Straus & Giroux; Reissue, 1977).

they revel in their command of the nuanced distinction, they are won over, they become adepts. In my case the law reports lacked life and they were soulless. The potential for transformative engagement slithered away and I was left feeling deprived. Law was failing me and I was failing it. The way I have described this so far already carries the portent of some epiphanic moment. It came when I found myself rejecting all the courses necessary to become a lawyer, that is, those that gained one exemptions from professional examinations, and taking instead a range of divergent or, in the eyes of some, 'marginal' courses. Chief among them was the anthropology of law.[6] Here law ceased to be an idealised form and became instead a variety of forms and action by and through which people made sense of everyday life, which of course is saturated with normative activity.[7]

The anthropology of law revealed two things to me: that law was not something imposed from above mainly by a state; and that anthropologists carried out their research in markedly different ways to conventional lawyers. Anthropologists felt it necessary to engage with everyday life and the people who lived it. They were the *Empiriki*.[8] That law was constituted by everyday concerns opened an array of possibilities for its analysis. During the course I focussed on a little-known group of people known as the Lepchas in Sikkim who apparently practised four religions simultaneously and lived by their agricultural cycle.[9] Linearity was alien to them as life constantly repeated itself in cyclic fashion. Their acephalous society, through bonds of reciprocity, maintained an equilibrium that made courts, officials and police redundant. Nevertheless order was maintained and punishment could be meted out if necessary. Gorer lived among the Lepchas recording their daily activities, listening to their stories and myths. I felt I understood more profoundly the processes of Lepcha social order and disputing than I understood of my own society. By comparison with the anthropology of law, law itself represented itself as an instrumental set of disembodied and narrow techniques. The anthropology of law opened up to me the virtual impossibility of attempting to confine law to state-backed action. We lived in a normatively pluralistic world.[10]

---

[6] The course was eventually published as S Roberts, *Order and Dispute: An Introduction to Legal Anthropology* (Oxford, Martin Robertson, 1979).

[7] William Twining used to make his Warwick first year law students read a broadsheet newspaper for articles about law. The result was that they often picked articles with court cases but missed the items on pensions reform or the difficulties of transferring footballers from one club to another.

[8] R William, *Keywords: A Vocabulary of Culture and Society* (London, Fontana, 1976) 99.

[9] G Gorer, *Himalayan Village: An Account of the Lepchas of Sikkim* (London, Michael Joseph, 1938).

[10] There are many debates surrounding this issue. Bradney and Cownie review many of them in ch 1 of their study of dispute resolution among Quakers. See A Bradney and F Cownie, *Living Without Law: An Ethnography of Quaker Decision-Making, Dispute Avoidance and Dispute Resolution* (Aldershot, Ashgate, 2000).

In order to experience that world and portray it, fieldwork was key. It is through fieldwork that one begins to enter the mentality of the other. The primary means for doing so is language; knowing and understanding the language of the group. Understanding language means learning language, appreciating how it is used both prosaically and poetically. Both are necessary just as the right and left hemispheres of the brain are essential for complete human beings. In other words, we need to be scientific and artistic. The artistic or poetic aspect emerges when we attempt to play with the nuances of language, and so often get it wrong. Santos was run out of a *favela* at gunpoint when he told an inhabitant of one that he was doing research on *favelas*.[11] Unfortunately, the appropriate word for researcher in Portugal translated into police investigation in Brazil. Becker also showed how tyro marijuana smokers had to learn to get 'high'—the term was not self-explanatory or self-executing—since impostors could be identified by experienced smokers.[12] Group norms are demonstrated in interaction—ours and theirs. Without interaction scientific description of our world will be lifeless and most probably incorrect.[13]

B. BECOMING AN ETHNOGRAPHER

Although the anthropology of law was a well-stocked field with studies of groups around the world, the sociology of law was relatively empty.[14] It seemed once the state claimed the major role in law production, regulation and administration, law reverted to its formal characteristics in the Weberian sense rather than containing any impression of being socially constructed.[15] It was difficult to encounter texts that would explain how the 'law jobs' were being done in modern western society. One could see occasional

---

[11] B de Sousa Santos, 'Science and Politics: Doing Research in Rio's Squatter Settlements' in R Luckham, (ed), *Law and Social Enquiry: Case Studies of Research* (Uppsala, Scandinavian Institute of African Studies; and New York, NY, International Center for Law in Development, 1981).

[12] HS Becker, 'Becoming a Marijuana User' (1953) 59 *American Journal of Sociology* 235–42.

[13] An interesting contrast to this claim is found in the work of Goffman who although engaged gives an impression of complete disengagement. See, for example, E Goffman, 'On Cooling the Mark Out: Some Aspects of Adaptation To Failure' (1952) 15 *Psychiatry: Journal for the Study of Interpersonal Processes* 451–63; and HS Becker, 'The Politics of Presentation: Goffman and Total Institutions' (2003) 26 *Symbolic Interaction* 659–69.

[14] I am making an artificial contrast between the anthropologist as student of preliterate societies and the sociologist as the student of the modern.

[15] 'An order will be called *law* if it is externally guaranteed by the probability that physical or psychological coercion will be applied by a *staff* of people in order to bring about compliance or avenge violation'. M Weber, G Roth and C Wittich, (eds), *Economy and Society: An Outline of Interpretive Sociology* (Berkeley, CA, University of California Press, 1968) 34. See also AT Kronman, *Max Weber* (Stanford, CA, Stanford University Press, 1983) 31.

glimpses but not much else. For example, I became interested in the role of the barristers' clerk, an agent who supplies work to barristers and collects their fees.[16] To my naïve view of the world, it seemed ridiculous that the legal profession could base itself on Dickensian class divisions and that barristers' clerks were truly a relic of the 19th century. Yet, as the study evolved, I came to see that clerks were an important part of the English legal system, providing a network through which different parts could coordinate. The entire court listing system was balanced around the clerks' diary manipulation: this way they could keep the courts' case docket moving and maintain a steady schedule of work for their barristers.

Let me provide a brief account of the barristers' clerk's world so that this chapter remains intelligible. Essentially the clerk is the middleman, or mediator, between the diverse interests of the legal system, namely those of barristers, solicitors, judges, list officers, and occasionally the client upon whom the system depends. Although these groups are discrete, they are interdependent. But their interdependence does not prevent them from pressing divergent demands that must somehow be resolved into a common aim if the legal process is to function reasonably smoothly. How is this resolution effected? By the clerk—and in so doing he assumes different roles to satisfy the demands, but keeping in mind his own interests. Broadly, there are three such roles: counsellor, negotiator, and 'fixer'. Perhaps the most important is that of fixer, since the others are variants of it. While performing these roles the clerk carries out a number of tasks. The main ones are negotiating his barristers' fees and collecting them, obtaining work for his barristers, supervising their and the chambers' accounts, helping to schedule cases and checking the daily court lists for his barristers and the solicitors.[17] The barrister's clerk has a wide range of duties delegated to him.[18] The ostensible rationale of his existence is to relieve the barrister of the day-to-day routines of office administration so that the latter can concentrate entirely on legal work. But the clerk does much of the 'dirty work' of the Bar. He fulfils a role that would be difficult, both theoretically and practically, for the Bar to do without. For example, he generates work for barristers, permitting them the claim that they conform to their rule against advertising: he can refuse to accept work on a barrister's behalf by, say, charging an exorbitant fee, allowing barristers to say that they conform to the supposedly inviolate cab-rank rule. Clerks have a lively history appearing in novels by Surtees and Trollope, and Charles Lamb wrote about his father who was a clerk.

---

[16] J Flood, *Barristers' Clerks: The Law's Middlemen* (Manchester, MUP, 1983). <http://www.johnflood.com/Barristers_Clerks_book.pdf>.

[17] *Ibid*, p 3.

[18] At the time of the research approximately 4% of clerks in London were female, hence the use of gender specific language.

The single most contentious point raised about barristers' clerks by their critics is the form of their remuneration. Clerks generally receive a clerk's fee which is paid by way of a percentage commission. They take great pride in their commissions, though it may, to some, appear a dubious form of payment within the Bar, which considers its own fees *honoraria* and is unable to sue for them. Critics condemn the clerk's fee for the reason that clerks have a personal stake in extracting the largest possible sum from the client. Superficially the criticism sounds plausible, but it ignores the manner in which clerks conduct their business. Overcharging would simply prevent solicitors from returning to a particular set of chambers. The clerk's goal is to generate a constant supply of work. The fixing of fees thus requires careful deliberation. At one time receiving 10% of the brief fees was a sign of great esteem, 'a ten per cent man'.

I end this account with three vignettes that illuminate the role and status of clerks.

— In 1976 a senior clerk described his tasks thus: 'a barrister's clerk does everything for his governor, even sewing on his fly-buttons, because the typist couldn't do it, as there was no time to take his trousers off'.

— A common law clerk explained why the bar needed clerks, 'I tell you, barristers need clerks, because they've got no common sense, and that's what a clerk's got. These barristers go to university and they get pumped full of law through one ear and their common sense comes dripping out the other side' (said replete with gestures: fingers in at one ear and the others waving away from the other).

— A junior clerk describing his initiation into the Temple remembered the rules laid down by his first senior regarding status and hierarchy: 'When I call someone by their first name, you call them Mr So-and-so; when I call someone Mr So-and-so, you call them Sir; when I call someone Sir, you don't speak to them'.

I had to make sense of a way of being that was largely alien to me. Barristers' clerks were working class men with little or no education. I, as a middle class, educated student was remote from them. In many ways doing ethnography is a way of developing empathy, which also means finding out more about oneself in the process. I am trying to present myself as someone who will make sense of their world to me and to them. Being a researcher is a strange occupation to others. Others have a good idea of what they do because they do it. That does not mean they can articulate what they do since in most likelihood they have not had time to reflect on their actions. The researcher plays the role of the external reflector. But for the researcher to take on that role there must be trust, which needs empathy. Without it there will be no worthwhile results.

Occasionally the criticism will arise that ethnography can observe only the surface of interaction. It is unable to determine the deep structure that produces 'universal' ideas of what makes the world. Certainly we cannot read minds and so we cannot know or verify internal states, but that is not what interests us. If we are unable to produce an objective account of reality as something 'out there', then the alternative is to explore subjective accounts and determine how they constitute sociological understanding through the process of social interaction.[19] Ethnography is provisional, never absolute. The very way that ethnographers go about their tasks suggests they are constantly learning and uncovering new interpretations and meanings. Ethnographers' findings are of a different character to those of social surveys. We are not concerned about our degrees of freedom, but whether we have understood sociality better than we did before we undertook our fieldwork.

I felt vindicated about my method of researching barristers' clerks after I listened to a group of them talk about their careers at a Bar Conference in the 1990s. They were contrasting the way barristers' clerks ran a set of chambers with the more bureaucratic modes of administration adopted by practice managers. The latter could be good at instituting systems for record keeping, billing and so forth, but they lacked the interpersonal skills to deal with advising barristers when to move from one type of work to another, for example, criminal to personal injury, or when to apply to become a Queen's Counsel (QC) with its consequential effect on the types of work a QC would be hired to do. The clerks' accounts of their work and roles were rich and contextual. At the conclusion of the panel I went to speak to them. As I introduced myself, they told me, 'I used your book to prepare my speech'. My journey through the clerks' world and its results corresponded with their own understanding. I had been able to make the barrister's clerk's world intelligible internally as well as to the outside world.

Ethnography presents a unique set of problems for the researcher, in part because it is a messy process. There are problems of entry, developing trust and empathy, recording interaction, and making sense of ethnographic data. The first three of these are largely absent from many other types of research.

Gaining access to groups exemplifies this point. In the three ethnographic studies I have engaged in, gaining access presented different problems each time. With the barristers' clerks my main difficulty was that I didn't know any nor did I know how to make contact with them. As a first-time researcher, it hadn't occurred to me that I should consider this aspect of the

---

[19] This in part relies on Weber's approach to sociological method. M Weber, 1968, above, n 15 at 4.

research when selecting my topic. Official sources were of little help including the Barristers' Clerks Association, which genteelly ignored my requests for help. I was concerned that no access was going to mean no research. At this stage I was expecting to carry out interviews as my main research method. A stroke of good fortune changed my situation when a friend of mine, who worked in a neighbourhood law centre, told me he knew a junior clerk and would arrange an introduction. Although the subsequent meeting was successful and the clerk wanted me to sit in the clerks' room to experience the frenetic pace of the job, circumstances almost conspired to block me. I had telephoned the senior clerk to submit a firm date for my visit. He enquired whether I had read the *New Statesman* that day. I told him I had not. He then launched into a lengthy rant against an article entitled 'NCOs of the law'.[20] There was one paragraph, in particular, that had greatly upset him.

> One person who felt the clerks' prejudice is a clerk herself: Mary Hickson, the clerk of the most unusual chambers in Britain, those of Lord Gifford in Lambeth. She works in an office that has a notice 'Sue the Bastards!' by the door and an anti-anti-abortion poster in the window. As part of her training for clerking, she spent two months in 'The Cloisters' ... 'I learned how much I disliked the Temple and how much they don't want a woman to be a clerk. The senior clerk there just told me to go away and get married'. This prejudice is exercised against women as barristers, though, says Hickson, 'they think they're okay for some things like matrimonial work'.[21]

In addition the article referred to the criticism that the barrister's clerk's commission tended to inflate the fees charged to clients. The senior clerk vehemently denied that clerks were biased against women; he even said that when a new set of chambers was being established he had recommended a woman as clerk. The description of the clerks' room, including its posters, represented to him a gross violation of good taste and proper conduct. 'I certainly wouldn't have posters and a sign saying "Sue the bastards!" in my clerks' room'. He also felt that clerks were being unjustifiably attacked over the question of counsel's fees and put forward the defence that certain occasions and circumstances demanded he reduce or even waive some fees. Sometimes, he said, the fault lay with solicitors, who offered unnecessarily high fees to counsel: for example, one solicitor suggested a £50 fee for a matrimonial matter that, at best was worth only £25.

The upshot was, according to him, that no barrister's clerk would allow me, or any other researcher, to enter their chambers—a total, eternal ban. I

---

[20] The article was written at the time that the Benson Commission was investigating legal services. *Final Report of the Royal Commission on Legal Services*. Cmnd 7648 (London, HMSO, 1979).

[21] J Bugler, 'NCOs of the Law', *New Statesman*, 5 March 1976, p 287–87.

felt faint with shock, but for the following twenty minutes I virtually plead-
ed with him to change his mind. I pointed out the advantages, in that I
would be able to present a fair and objective picture of clerking, which
would naturally suffer through my not having experienced the urgency and
frenzy of the clerks' room. And, as a final argument. I offered him the
opportunity to read and comment on my writing, but without assigning any
editorial control to him. To my relief the arguments had some effect. He
began to retreat from his position and question me about the length of my
stay. I answered that two or three days would be sufficient. Again he raised
objections but, greatly to my surprise, now considered it short and instead
suggested I extend the visit to a week, when he could take me to the Old
Bailey and the Law Courts. Paradoxically my situation had actually
improved as a result of this apparent catastrophe. It was as though he wanted me to prove the article false.[22] Eventually, I remained in various clerks'
rooms for several months having become an accidental ethnographer.

In my second study the process of gaining entry was supposed to be
much smoother. My purpose was to do an ethnography of a large law firm
in Chicago.[23] On this occasion I was fortunate to have as one of my dissertation committee members Jack Heinz, a law professor at Northwestern
University and then executive director of the American Bar Foundation.
Many of the city's lawyers had been taught by him, so he was knowledge-
ably placed to advance my chances of gaining entry to a law firm. One of
the key obstacles was the problem of my presence violating attorney-client
privilege. The first law firm I approached was supportive of my aims until
one of their clients was found shot dead, allegedly by the Mafia, in a
Chicago parking lot. As this would result in an awkward investigation by
the authorities, the firm decided they should decline my offer to observe
them. The next firm that was approached agreed to take me as observer,
again the way smoothed by my supervisor, provided they could hire me on
a temporary basis to overcome the difficulty with attorney-client privilege.

My third study of the Financial Ombudsman Service (FOS) was another accidental ethnography. While at a reception for someone leaving the
Law Society, I met her predecessor. In the usual small talk of receptions I
asked him what he was now doing. He replied he was chief ombudsman
at the new FOS. 'What's that?', I asked. He told me about the different
ombudsmen organisations—eg, banking, investment, insurance—that
were being integrated to form a unified financial ombudsman service.[24]
After we parted, rather in the style of *esprit d'escalier*, it occurred to me

---

[22] J Flood, 'The Middlemen of the Law: An Ethnographic Inquiry into the English Legal
Profession' (1981) *American Bar Foundation Research Journal* 377–405.

[23] J Flood, 'Anatomy of Law: An Ethnography of a Corporate Law Firm', (PhD dissertation,
Department of Sociology, Northwestern University, 1987).

[24] See <http://www.financial-ombudsman.org.uk>.

that there existed a research possibility in this new organization. My subsequent conversations with the chief ombudsman indicated he was of a
mind to encourage research on his fledgling service. He patiently spent two
hours telling me about the organisation, but revealed that he was reluctant
to have his employees give up large amounts of time to be interviewed by
me. Could I do the research in a less invasive way? I suggested he let me
hang around him and his colleagues and observe them. He warmed to this
approach and I began my ethnographic study of the FOS.

In ethnography one has to deal with life in real time, with interaction as
it occurs. It is not possible to wait and go back and ask, 'How was it for
you?' The point of ethnography is not to recover memory, as in oral history, except as something auxiliary to action observed. Although I refer to
observation as though it were some passive activity like watching a film, it
never is so remote from what is happening. Ethnography is often referred
to as 'participant-observation', which I would argue is more common than
mere 'observation'. It is difficult to be disengaged from interaction and the
researcher is frequently drawn in by stealth.[25] For some researchers this
kind of involvement is disturbing because it may diminish their neutrality
and impartiality. They can be seen as taking sides by being implicated in
that which they are observing. But this is not always the case. During my
time with the barristers' clerks I would happily answer the phone and check
diaries, especially if the clerks' room was shorthanded. This mundane activity helped me understand how the clerks' room actually functioned day to
day. For the clerks the busiest time of day was around five to six o'clock in
the evening when the solicitors called in to get barristers for the next day. It
was like rush hour—phones ringing continuously, clerks calling across the
room to each other for information. No one could stop until the phones
stopped ringing.

Being active in the field as participant can mean that others identify one
as belonging to a particular group. Most barristers who encountered me in
the clerks' room saw me as another clerk, which put me below their sights.
My being so categorised meant that my situation was perceived as harm-
less and enabled me to observe things that I might not have been able to
see if my position had been different. For example, part of my research
interest was how clerks and barristers interacted with each other given that
they came from different backgrounds, classes, differed extremely in educational level, yet endured a considerable degree of interdependence.
Quintin Hogg, a former lord chancellor, had once said: 'A solicitor is a

---

[25] Conversely in their study of divorce lawyers and clients, Sarat and Felstiner observed
through the medium of the tape recorder in the lawyers' offices while they were absent which
kept them firmly distanced from the action. See A Sarat and WLF Felstiner, *Divorce Lawyers
and Their Clients: Power and Meaning in the Legal Process* (New York, NY, OUP, 1995) 8–10.

man of business, a barrister an artist and a scholar'.[26] The bar had surrounded itself with traditions, often newly-minted, that seemed to insulate it from the pressing concerns of commercial life.[27] Since not every barrister was accompanied by a private income, the need to generate money was ever present. The difficulty for the bar was how to overcome the impurity of being directly concerned with negotiating fees and collecting them.[28] The solution to the dilemma was the clerk: he would bring in the money and the work. The world of work surrounds itself with ideas of cleanliness and dirt and different occupations are esteemed according to their degree of moral purity. Everett Hughes coined the term, 'good people and dirty work', which is where the clerks are situated.[29]

Even if there is no actual identification with a group, there may be ascribed identification in that others are convinced you are a part. In the Chicago law firm most clients saw me as another attorney with his yellow legal pad. This is often a useful attribution. What others think has an impact on the group and they begin to think the researcher is one of them. Admittedly these multiple attributions and ascriptions can become confusing, but the task of the ethnographer is to accept the challenge of multiple roles and identities. There were times when I would find the confusion overwhelming. The main one was when the clerks went to the pub. Clerks spent a lot of time in pubs because that was the best meeting place to exchange news and gossip. Gossip is an essential means of communication since it enables people to trade information especially in situations where little is written down. In addition to talking, the clerks drank. I was not used to drinking heavily but I had to participate otherwise any pretence of being in with the clerks would collapse, despite the consequences of my own physical collapse. In a way, I was no different to Becker's marijuana smoker learning about being high.[30] I had to learn to drink and behave in ways that were unfamiliar to me.

---

[26] S Aylett, *Under the Wigs: The Memoirs of a Legal King-Maker* (London, Eyre Methuen, 1978) 160.

[27] This is clearly a tradition of mythic proportion. Abel has conclusively demonstrated that for many years a large proportion of the bar has relied on the state via legal aid to support it. See RL Abel, *The Legal Profession in England and Wales* (Oxford, Blackwell, 1988); and RL Abel, *English Lawyers between Market and State: The Politics of Professionalism* (Oxford, OUP, 2003). Hobsbawm astutely noted that, 'Inventing traditions ... is essentially a process of formalization and ritualization, characterized by reference to the past, if only by imposing repetition'. E Hobsbawm and T Ranger, (eds), *The Invention of Tradition* (Cambridge, CUP, 1992).

[28] M Douglas, *Purity and Danger: An Analysis of the Concepts of Pollution and Taboo* (Harmondsworth, Penguin, 1970).

[29] EC Hughes, *The Sociological Eye: Selected Papers on Work, Self, and the Study of Society* (Chicago, Aldine Atherton, 1971) 87–97, 338–47.

[30] Becker, 1953, see above, n 12.

Any research setting is potentially daunting for the researcher. How is one going to be received? Are the people friendly? Will I make a fool of myself? When I first met the lawyers in the Chicago law firm I was about to study, someone shouted, 'Here's the company spy!' But all of this goes to the task of developing trust. The scale of the setting has a big effect. With clerks I dealt only with a few at a time and it was easy to be vouched for as I moved around different clerks' rooms. My last two stints of fieldwork were within large organisations where there were a variety of coalitions, alliances, groups, and networks to contend with. Here it is easier for one to be identified with particular groups and their interests. I was most aware of being categorised in this way when I researched the Financial Ombudsman Service. At the FOS I started my fieldwork with the management who were reconstructing eight different ombudsman services into an integrated whole. Some of these eight had been privately run, others were state institutions. The cultural divergences were enormous at times even though everyone I encountered seemed eager to bring about this integration. I felt I had to stay within the group that I was observing as they were doing the core work of designing the integration. For the remainder of the organisation there were thousands of financial services cases to be dealt with, some under the separate ombudsman rules and the newer ones under the integrated service rules. With a caseload of 45,000 disputes spread among approximately 400 employees, little time was left for the organisation itself. Nonetheless, for the management determining how the FOS would evolve was crucial. The governing legislation had produced a hybrid form of control where the FOS was fundamentally autonomous but its budget had to be approved by the Financial Services Authority (FSA).[31] Approving the budget became the entry point for the FSA to attempt to micro-manage the FOS. For me, the ethnographer, the meetings between the FOS and the FSA were highly charged dramatic scenes where the two sides struggled and bitterly contested control. In this context I became very much identified as a member of the FOS management by both sides, which, at times like these, was inescapable for me. One cannot say, 'this is nothing to do with me,' for one is explicitly implicated.

C. MAKING SENSE OF ETHNOGRAPHY

The data collected in fieldwork are multifaceted. They cover conversations, observations, impressions, and so forth. It is at this point that ethnography gets epistemological qualms. Is it looking for similarities or differences, convergence or divergence? The Chicago School would

---

[31] See Financial Markets and Services Act 2000, ss 225–34 <http://www.hmso.gov.uk/acts/acts2000/20000008.htm>.

emphasise the former,[32] while Burawoy expresses the latter.[33] Perhaps it is at this stage that theory fulfils a role for ethnography. Once one engages in analysis, one cannot help but theorise. But what is indicative of the ethnographic approach is the link to inductivism and grounded theory. By this I mean that it is not always possible to set up prior theoretical frameworks in ethnography no matter how precise one tries to be, because the researcher does not always know what the outcomes will be. Ethnography is constant surprise. It gives rise to fresh theoretical insights as it evolves.[34] This rolling style of theorising facilitates the creation of an 'organisational epistemology' that assists ideas to build on each other as the research progresses.[35]

Social scientists make unfair generalisations about ethnography, frequently that because it focuses on small-scale activities, it must ignore the world-at-large. There is no reason, for example, why such grand themes as globalisation cannot be brought into the realm of ethnography. The Financial Ombudsman Service is now an integral part of the apparatus that governs the delivery of financial services. Its success has led to governments in Asia and Latin America considering adopting the model for their societies. The ombudsman has generally become a powerful means of resolving disputes in many areas of life from financial services to funerals. Ethnography can help interpret these movements by understanding the processes and steps that societies and organisations must go through in order to produce workable and reasonable solutions to problems encountered by the citizenry.

Making sense of ethnography should be simple. The books of Studs Terkel telling of life in Chicago through the words the people he talked with are powerful and redolent of the struggles and indignities that life throws at working class people.[36] The stories speak to us and they are also the kind

---

[32] MJ Deegan, 'The Chicago School of Ethnography' in P Atkinson, *et al*, (eds), *Handbook of Ethnography* (London, Sage, 2001).

[33] M Burawoy, 'Revisits: An Outline of a Theory of Reflexive Ethnography' (2003) 68 *American Sociological Review* 645–79.

[34] Compare, however, Wacquant's claim that, 'To fail to exercise theoretical control at every step in the design and implementation of an ethnographic study-as with every other method of social observation and analysis-is to open the door to *theoretical simple-mindedness* whereby ordinary notions issued out of common sense fill in the gap and steer crucial decisions on how to characterize, parse, and depict the object at hand ...'. L Wacquant, 'Review Symposium: Scrutinizing the Street: Poverty, Morality, and the Pitfalls of Urban Ethnography' (2002) 107 *American Journal of Sociology* 1468, 1524.

[35] HS Becker, 'Theory: The Necessary Evil' in DJ Flinders and GE Mills, (eds), *Theory and Concepts in Qualitative Research: Perspectives from the Field* (New York, NY, Teachers College Press, 1993).

[36] S Terkel, *Working: People Talk about What They Do All Day and How They Feel About What They Do* (New York, NY, Pantheon Books, 1984). See also <http://www.studsterkel.org>.

of stories that people listen to and act on. According to some oral historians and social scientists these stories are not generalisable, they are *ad hoc*,
personal, occasional. They do not constitute a basis on which to theorise or
make policy. Just as I am a legal pluralist, I am a methodological pluralist.
I believe the battle lines between qualitative and quantitative approaches
are illusory and unnecessary yet they persist. If social science had the confidence not to attempt to replicate the natural sciences, its impact on the
world would potentially be greater. However, the lines are drawn and the
main critique from the 'quantoids' is that qualitative research concentrates
too much on the particular at the expense of the general—only large Ns can
tell the truth.

Part of the problem is a misunderstanding that some have about ethnography. Ethnography is about interpretation not causal analysis. And
ethnography also includes history; time is an essential element. If we want
to understand the complexity of lawyer-client or doctor-patient relationships, we need to know what happens in those interactions, we need to
observe them as they unfold and play out. A survey that recollects dim
memories will not tell us much. If we want to know how organisations
attempt to create a culture and establish their niche, we need narrative
because these things are contested, ambiguous and inchoate.[37] The case of
the FOS is interesting. Here is an organisation that came together from
many and over time came to play a central role in the financial services
industry. It had to coordinate its strategies to accommodate the needs of the
industry, the regulators and government, and yet establish its own identity
and role. This was not something that could be created on a template since
it required careful negotiation in order to establish its bona fides with these
groups. The backgrounds of the managers—they came from a mix of legal
and regulatory careers—assisted in these processes since they embodied
some of the values recognisable by others in the network. By understanding
the processes that form organisational culture and identity, we can do
things like formulate good practice elsewhere, but we need to be able to
identify the constituent parts not merely the end result. As Van Maanen
nicely encapsulates it: 'Narrative is not an ornamental or decorative feature
designed to make ethnography more palatable or audience-friendly, but a
cognitive instrument in its own right'.[38]

Perhaps one of the most telling points about ethnography is its adoption
by corporate enterprises as a means of understanding their businesses and
consumers' responses to them. The technology industry has led the way

---

[37] J Van Maanen, 'Afterword: Natives "R" Us: Some Notes on the Ethnography of
Organisations' in DN Gellner and E Hirsch, (eds), *Inside Organisations: Anthropologists at
Work* (Oxford, Berg, 2001).
[38] Van Maanen, *ibid*, p 256.

through its realisation that the views of software engineers and consumers do not necessarily coincide and that the social implications of computing are increasingly important.[39] Moreover, 'anthropologists are now regarded as a necessity at such firms'.[40]

To bring this essay to a close, I would reiterate a telling point made by Everett Hughes many years ago. It is in connection with the stated problem that others sometimes have with ethnography, that we cannot learn anything beyond the details of the story told. Hughes wrote:

> I am suspicious of any method said to be the one and only. But among the methods I would recommend is the intensive, penetrating look with an imagination as lively and as sociological as it can be made. One of my basic assumptions is that if one quite clearly sees something happen once, it is almost certain to have happened again and again. The burden of proof is on those who claim a thing once seen is an exception; if they look hard, they may find it everywhere, although with some interesting differences in each case.[41]

---

[39] For example, see L Suchman, *Plans and Situated Actions: The Problem Of Human-Machine Communication* (Cambridge, CUP, 1987).

[40] 'Off With the Pith Helmets', *Economist Technology Quarterly*, 13 March 2004, p 6.

[41] Hughes, 1971, above, n 29 at ix.

3

Systems Theory and Qualitative Socio-Legal Research

KLAUS A ZIEGERT

IT IS WIDELY taken for granted that systems theory, especially in the form of the extensively elaborate work of Niklas Luhmann, is just another example of sociological grand theory. The underlying assumption is that the approach is useless for social research. This understanding may be based on a myth. In this case, it was a way for sociology, mainly in the USA, to deal with the trauma afflicted on it nearly seventy years ago by Talcott Parsons. His attempt at tying Weberian grand theory to pragmatist social science research culminated in what was then called systems theory.[1] It split sociologists deeply over the way in which to study and understand society and in relation to the question as to the best methodology to fit a socially constructed and deeply troubling world. Since then sociology has become more methods-pluralist or, in the version of 'postmodernist' deliberations, even methods-indifferent. Yet, the sociological trauma of Talcott Parson's theory construction has persisted as a label for systems theory in the mythopoetical way that labels always do.

The theory of Niklas Luhmann has deliberately, and maybe provocatively, embraced not only the label but also the programme of systems theory.[2]

---

[1] T Parsons, *The Social System* (Glencoe, IL, Free Press, 1937).

[2] As a matter of fact, Luhmann turned sociologist (from administrative lawyer) by joining Talcott Parsons at Harvard for studying formal organisation for over a year and returning home as the only major protagonist of systems theory in Germany at the time (1968) but a systems theory entirely on his own terms. See for more biographical detail of Luhmann's work, especially in relation to socio-legal research, KA Ziegert, 'Rechtstheorie, Reflexionstheorien des Rechtssystems und die Eigenwertproduktion des Rechts' (Legal theory, reflexive theories of the legal system and the production of the intrinsical value of law) in H de Berg and J Schmidt, (eds), *Rezeption und Reflektion. Zur Resonanz der Systemtheorie Niklas Luhmanns außerhalb der Soziologie* (Frankfurt, Suhrkamp, 2000) 93–133; and KA Ziegert, 'The Thick Description of Law: An Introduction to Niklas Luhmann's Theory of Operatively Closed Systems' in R Banakar and M Travers, (eds), *An Introduction to Law and Social Theory* (Oxford, Hart Publishing, 2002) 55–75.

However, Luhmann has explicitly rejected the theoretical tenets of Parsons' approach[3] and, above all, fundamentally reworked Parsons' methodology. In doing so, he has, on the one hand, distinctly diverged from the substance of arguments which systems theory today does no longer support. On the other hand, he has based radically new arguments on an uncompromising empirical conceptualisation of society. Therefore, it will be the central argument of the following observations that a thorough evaluation of the process of Luhmann's theory building over thirty years can show that it was above all the *methodological turn*—and not a theoretical turn—which put Luhmann's systems theory on the tracks of a radically new approach to sociological theory. Arguably, then, it is also this methodological aspect that makes systems theory eminently relevant for socio-legal research.

I have argued elsewhere that Luhmann's project of a 'functional analysis of society' was driven from the outset by the idea of sociological enlightenment.[4] For Luhmann that meant that only sociology could offer a *scientific methodology* for working out a general theory of social organisation including law. This is reminiscent of particularly Eugen Ehrlich, Max Weber, and Theodor Geiger among many more in the past, and in the present, who were or are lawyers in search of a scientific foundation for unreduced knowledge about human practice, and in particular law. They all made valuable methodological contributions and it should be remembered that particularly the three mentioned above conducted pioneering empirical studies of law and society in spite of being sociological 'loners' without much connection to sociological schools or specific research traditions.

It can be argued that the similarly undeterred and lonely methodological drive of Luhmann's sociological enlightenment builds on the conceptual work of these predecessors and finally succeeds in stringing together radically abstracted concepts which can be empirically tested to form a cohesive theoretical matrix for functional analysis. The result is clearly not empirical social science research in the conventional meaning of variables research— which Luhmann rejected as meaningless.[5] Rather it puts his approach closer to 'thick' (qualitative) empirical conceptualisations of society, such as

---

[3] This is not the place for a more thorough exposition of the evident, deeply cultural difference in the histories of ideas on which Parsons and Luhmann draw respectively. Parsons' history of ideas is the specific adaptation of the sociological categories of Max Weber to the US tradition of pragmatism. Luhmann draws on a much longer history of idealist philosophy (Hegel), philosophical anthropology (Gehlen, Plessner) and phenomenology (especially Husserl) which all have been bypassed by US American sociology more or less completely. This observation is also important for the comparison with grounded theory in this chapter.

[4] Ziegert, 2002, see above, n 2.

[5] See only N Luhmann, 1993, *Das Recht der Gesellschaft* (Frankfurt, Suhrkamp, 1993); N Luhmann, KA Ziegert, (tr), *Society's Law*, (Sydney, Faculty of Law Notes, 2000); N Luhmann, F Kastner, *et al*, (eds), KA Ziegert, (tr), *Law as a Social System* (Oxford, OUP, 2004) pp 18, 31, 41, 45 (n 15), 46 (n 17), 77 (n 146), 124, 127, 149 and in the context below.

grounded theory. And it is definitely not abstract theory for theory's sake, such as sociological grand theory or whatever this label designates.

This paper explores the hypothesised methodological affinity between qualitative social science research and the way in which Luhmann discovers[6] society with systems theory. I will argue in the following section that Luhmann's concepts are, contrary to widely held opinion, an excellent mapping device in the methodological framework of qualitative empirical research. This will lead to a juxtaposition of systems theory and grounded theory as in many ways comparable approaches when qualitative social science research is concerned. The evaluation of the two approaches will, then, provide criteria that allow us to argue that systems theory is the better bet as far as research technology is concerned and that Luhmann's thick description of law makes systems theory particularly fit socio-legal research requirements. The functional analysis of the operation of the rule of law in different social settings can, finally, provide a schematic example for the potential of systems theory when it is discovery that researchers require and not just confirmation of what they already know.

A. MAPPING SOCIETY

Luhmann, though an administrative lawyer by professional socialisation, was not primarily interested in law and, in fact, quite reluctant to get involved in sociology of law. What he was interested in, probably as a result of studying law under the harsh conditions in Germany immediately after the end of WWII, was to discover how social order was possible if the contrary, chaos, was so much more plausible.[7] But what he came up with seems to be, at least at first sight, sociology with the conceptual tools of jurisprudence. By that I mean an extreme, even obsessive, care for the differentiation of terms, definitions and concepts, their comprehensive registration and indexation and their conceptually tight fit with well-defined, specific social domains. This then is the method of this 'jurisprudential approach': the careful observation of what can be found in the mapped area and the

---

[6] Discovery, rather than the mere confirmatory testing of hypotheses, is of course one of the overriding concerns of qualitative and interpretive social science research; see, for example, Kirk and Miller, especially when they state 'Most of the technology of confirmatory, non-qualitative research in both the social and natural sciences is aimed at preventing discovery'. See J Kirk and ML Miller, *Reliability and Validity in Qualitative Research* (Beverly Hills, CA, Sage, 1985) 15.

[7] See interview with Pierre Guibentif in P Guibentif, *Pierre Guibentif in Bielefeld 1991*, Interview first published (in French) in AJ Arnaud and P Guibentif, (eds), *Niklas Luhman: Observateur du Droit* (Paris, Librairie générale de droit et jurisprudence, 5 Droit et société, 1993, at 187–229) in the German original transcript version P Guibentif, 'Niklas Luhmann und die Rechtssoziologie: Gespräch mit Niklas Luhmann, Bielefeld, 7 January 1991' in (2000) 21 *Zeitschrift für Rechtssoziologie* 217, 220ff.

construction of universally applicable concepts which are consistent with each other throughout and which, more importantly, follow from each other in whatever direction one is guided by them. Thus systems theory is the endless 'grid' of everything that constitutes society. Luhmann was aware of the enormity of the task of finding a formulaic expression for that grid. However, he did not shy away from making *complexity* his business and systems theory reflect that complexity. The result is a conceptual grid that can be read semantically in any direction—and in the logical form of a text from the beginning to the end or from the last chapter to the first. In this sense, metaphors for this enterprise, such as 'map', must mislead, as they do not really reflect the 'spherical' construction of the conceptual 'grid' which in fact connects all its nodes with each other and yet returns every departure eventually to the point from where it started.

The objective of the enterprise is thus not so much 'theory building' as producing 'good science'. Luhmann's overriding concern is clearly focussed on the good fit between observed phenomena and the concepts that capture them but he never overlooks that *only theory*, not the concepts themselves, provides the basis for a reality check.[8] We can, therefore, conclude that Luhmann's methodology for a scientific universal explanation of society was effectively driven by the jurisprudential experience of the *practical importance* of tightly fitting concepts that can be tested only in the theoretical framework in which they are developed and thus 'ground' systems theory. As a result, the theory of operatively closed systems is, in the methodological sense, a thick (concept-rich) universal description of society.

Seen in this methodological perspective, one can understand why Luhmann had the courage—Luhmann used to say more directly: 'pig-headedness' (Bockigkeit)—to build his theoretical concepts from the ground up independently of any scholastic conventions[9] and to pursue this methodological strategy with an astonishing sense of direction.[10] The most important

---

[8] Luhmann 1993, p 45, see above, n 5.

[9] See the collection of early sociological essays (1962–1968) in N Luhmann, *Soziologische Aufklärung* (Opladen, Westdeutscher Verlag, 1970).

[10] See the series of books on functional systems starting with the conceptual map in N Luhmann, *Soziale Systeme. Grundriss einer allgemeinen Theorie* (Frankfurt, Suhrkamp, 1984), and in the English edition: N Luhmann, *Social Systems* (Stanford, CA, Stanford University Press, 1995); N Luhmann, *Die Wirtschaft der Gesellschaft* (Society's economy) (Frankfurt, Suhrkamp, 1988); N Luhmann, *Die Wissenschaft der Gesellschaft* (Society's science) (Frankfurt aM, Suhrkamp, 1990); N Luhmann, *Das Recht der Gesellschaft* (Frankfurt aM, Suhrkamp, 1993) (see n 9); Luhmann, *Die Kunst der Gesellschaft* (Society's fine art) (Frankfurt aM, Suhrkamp, 1995); N Luhmann, *Die Religion der Gesellschaft* (posthumously, Society's religion) (Frankfurt, Suhrkamp, 2000); N Luhmann, *Die Politik der Gesellschaft* (posthumously, Society's politics) (Frankfurt, Suhrkamp, 2000); and ending with the grandiose account of society in the setting of global society in N Luhmann, *Die Gesellschaft der Gesellschaft* (Frankfurt, Suhrkamp, 1997).

elements of this strategy for obtaining and grounding scientific knowledge are the following[11]:

1. an observation of a *material continuum* which happens but remains unfathomable as to its full complexity; it can be called 'states of affairs' (Sachverhalte) or 'world';
2. the observation that states of affairs (world) are neither obvious nor self-explanatory ('natural');
3. the observation of observers: a state of affairs can be scientifically observed and explained; this may result in different points of views of different observers;
4. the observation of the *construction* of the observed: phenomena are not 'made up' by the observers, however different their views are. Observers reach intersubjectively a shared understanding of what things 'mean'—not what they are—and are intersubjectively held to that accepted meaning;
5. the observation that the construction of scientific meaning (knowledge) has to proceed empirically and by solidly grounding theoretical concepts on accurate observations in order to make them intersubjectively acceptable. Theory which is *a priori* and predictive (prognostic) is useless (impractical) for explanation;
6. the observation that a *comparative approach* provides the most accurate observations and the most solid empirical grounding for concepts;
7. *the comparative observation* that the *most distinctive* features of phenomena (states of affairs)—when compared—are their *functions* and not their forms.
8. the comparative observation that the crucial aspect of functions is not the fact that they exist or whether or not they are fulfilled, but that functions become *possible* by evolution;
9. the comparative observation that possibilities are contingent. This means that if something (that exists/happens) is possible, it is also possible differently, ie, there are functional equivalents within different forms increasing complexity. Contingency and complexity defeat causal explanations (for instance as in quantitative research based on variable analysis);
10. the observation that functional equivalents and how they happen are useful reference points for structuring comparisons and for condensing observations into concepts and concepts into theory.

---

[11] See in more detail Ziegert, 2002, see above, n 2, p 57–58.

11. the good science test: the observation that good theory must be able to answer the question as to how things (state of affairs/ world) can become possible; this means, that good theory must be able to answer the question as to how something can create its (own) boundaries in relation to the environment in which it happens[12];

12. the observation that *systems* are phenomena which can be observed and conceptualised as ones which become possible by creating their boundaries by their own operations. In this way, social systems are the 'research fields' or 'sites' of empirical research which is guided by systems theory.

13. *the strategic decision* that the theory of social systems is good science which passes the good science test.[13] In fact it is, as far as can be seen, the only sociological theory that does that.

B. SYSTEMS THEORY AND GROUNDED THEORY

The methodological points which we have selected above from the profuse work of Niklas Luhmann are often hidden under the overwhelming intricacies of conceptual detail. However, this is the very essence of a thick description and it is nevertheless clear and unambiguous. The objectives of such a detailed but consistent description are discovery and good science and at the same time the exposure of the traps of *a priori* (predictive) diagnostics and of the fallacies of poorly empirically grounded concepts such as insufficiently explained variables in quantitative research, or arguments which are not empirically based at all such as doctrinal arguments, normative (value) judgments and ideological positions. These are objectives which remind us of the path-breaking work of Theodor Geiger in Denmark during and immediately after WWII.[14] These objectives are also very similar to the ones established by the specific approach under the name of *grounded theory* thirty years later. This is not the place to follow up on the intellectual history of a strongly anti-metaphysical and anti-ideological sociology and it must suffice to sketch here only its methodological consequences in the form of *grounded theory*.

---

[12] Luhmann 1993, p 15, see above, n 5.

[13] See point 11 above and next section below.

[14] See T Geiger, *Vorstudien zu Einer Soziologie des Rechts* (Preliminary studies for a sociology of law), (Acta Jutlandica XIX, Aarhus, 1947). Unfortunately, Geiger died before he could take his studies to full fruition for socio-legal research but he left a strong legacy for Nordic, above all Danish (T Agersnap, BM Blegvad, A Weis Bentzon) and Norwegian (J Galtung, R Rommetveit, S Rokkan), sociological research. He wrote mainly in Danish and German and there are to my knowledge no translations of his major works into English.

Given substantial differences in the philosophy of science between US American and European sociology, it may not be so surprising that there is no, or very little, direct interaction between Luhmann's approach and the approach of grounded theory. It is more striking that both approaches arrive at the same objectives from apparently almost diametrically opposed starting points. Where Luhmann pursues radically accurate theoretical concepts, grounded theory pursues radically 'pure' empirical research activities.[15] The latter may have created a wrong perception of an uncompromising inductive methodology among researchers, especially when inductive research is defined as synonymous with qualitative research in many methodology textbooks and research manuals.

However, as far as grounded theory is concerned, the seemingly 'oxymoron' label is ultimately rather precise in defining the nature of the approach: 'Grounded theory is a nonreductionist systematic approach to the simultaneous collection and processing of data to the formulation of theories that are said to be "grounded" in the real world of the participant.'[16]

Or in the words of Anselm Strauss, together with Barry Glaser (1967), the founder of the approach:

> Grounded theory is one that is inductively derived from the study of the phenomenon it represents. That is, it is discovered, developed, and provisionally verified through systematic data collection and analysis of data pertaining to that phenomenon. A well-constructed grounded theory will meet four central criteria for judging the applicability of theory to a phenomenon: fit, understanding, generality, and control.[17]

Also grounded theory is directed at the fallacies of 'empirical social science research':

> In contrast [to quantitative studies], with GT research, rather than testing the relationships between variables, we want to discover relevant categories between them; to put together categories in new, rather than standard ways.[18]

Or, more specifically methodological:

> The analytic procedures of grounded theory are designed to 1) build rather than only test theory; 2) give the research process the rigor necessary to make the theory 'good science'; 3) help the analyst to break through the biases and assumptions brought to, and that can develop during, the research process; 4) provide

---

[15] That is not to admit theoretical concepts that have not been empirically grounded at first.

[16] WC Chenitz and JM Swanson, 'Qualitative Research using Grounded Theory' in WC Chenitz and JM Swanson, (eds), *From Practice to Grounded Theory: Qualitative Research in Nursing* (New York, NY, Addison-Wesley, 1986) 471.

[17] A Strauss and J Corbin, *Basics of Qualitative Research: Grounded Theory Procedures and Techniques* (Newbury Park, Sage, 1990) 23.

[18] *Ibid*, p 49.

the grounding, build the density, and develop the sensitivity, tightly woven, explanatory theory that closely approximates the reality it represents.[19]

Evidently, also this approach leads to the empirical sensitivity for structure as a pattern for possibilities or conditions, rather than the observation of unrelated incidents or events. In grounded theory this 'condensation' of concepts is achieved in the form of a *conditional matrix*:

> [A conditional matrix is] an analytical aid, a diagram, [which is] useful for considering a wide range of conditions and consequences related to the phenomenon under study. The matrix enables the analyst to both distinguish and link levels of conditions and consequences related to the phenomenon under study.[20]

The consistent grounded conceptualisation allows for multi-directional and multi-sites comparisons of phenomena in the form of a *conditional path*:

> [A conditional path enables] ... the tracking of an event, incident or happening from action/interaction through the various conditional and consequential levels, and vice versa, to link them directly to a phenomenon.[21]

The construct of a conditional matrix thus helps to

> 1) be theoretically sensitive to the range of conditions that might bear upon the phenomenon under study, 2) be theoretically sensitive to the range of potential consequences that results from action/interaction, 3) systematically relate conditions, actions/ interaction, and consequences to a phenomenon.[22]

Hopefully, this conceptual work 'from the ground up' facilitates the construction of multi-level conditional matrices ('international, national, community..' or 'communication society, culture, sub-system')[23] and so addresses the major failings of quantitative research based on variable analysis[24]:

> [...] Most writings on [research on negotiations and legal procedure] fail to detail the structural conditions under which [negotiations] occur; or if these conditions are discussed, they are brought into the picture only as a descriptive background. Thus, what is missing in these writings is specific linkage of broad conditions to action/ interaction.[25]

---

[19] *Ibid*, p 57.
[20] *Ibid*, p 158.
[21] *Ibid*, p 158.
[22] *Ibid*, n 17, p 161.
[23] *Ibid*, pp 162, 163, 165.
[24] See also M Ekström, 'Sociologiska förklaringar och Variabelanalysens Gränser: En Kritisk Analys med Exempel Från Medicinsk Sociologi' (Swedish Sociological Explanations and the Limits of Variable Analysis: A Critical Analysis with Examples from Medical Sociology) (1993) 30(2) *Sociologisk Forskning* 26; and KA Ziegert, 'Aufgaben der Rechtssoziologie als Soziologie für Juristen in der Rechtsforschung und Juraausbildung' (Objectives of the sociology of law as a sociology for lawyers in legal research and legal education) (1994) 15(1) *Zeitschrift für Rechtssoziologie* 13–23.
[25] Strauss & Corbin 1990, see above, n 17, p 165.

These few references may suffice here to remind the reader of the major tenets of grounded theory. In sum, and in spite of the remarkably vague and formulaic advice, grounded theory promises to go a long way towards its stated objective of 'good theory'—but can it attain it?

Before answering this question, we should make brief reference to a comparative third position of 'good theory' by mentioning another eminent social scientist and his quest for theory.[26] This is the approach of Stein Rokkan, a Norwegian researcher and member of the 'Nordic Club' of recipients of large research grants mainly from US American foundations after WWII to study the 'democratisation' of Europe.[27] He cannot—in view of his work in collections and evaluations an huge amount of *quantitative data*—be easily dismissed as having suffered from aspirations to 'grand theory'. And yet, there is a remarkable u-turn in Rokkan's work over the period of his life.[28] His approach is best characterised as comparative historical sociology. It led him from research on European political systems, operationalised under the influence of US American political sociology on the variables that influence voting behaviour, to a more comprehensive appreciation of the structures of the historical and political environments. In encountering the gap between theory and the models of quantitative research, Rokkan shifted to structural explanations in trying to 'discover theory from data'.[29] This is reminiscent of Strauss and Glaser, and indeed Rokkan followed a similar path by observing structural dimensions and designing area-specific maps for theoretical concepts based on the strength of their evidence from the *structural relational patterns* reflected in the quantitative data. In his way, then, also Rokkan arrived at the conclusion of the relevance of 'well-grounded' theory,[30] which is not predictive, which as a 'process [is] rich, complex and dense'[31] and which 'aids in understanding the specificity of cases in an analytical way by comparing them along several general dimension'.[32] Most importantly for our observations here, Rokkan realised that 'good theory' is one that allows for generalisation 'not ... across cases ... but within them'.[33] At the same time Stein Rokkan's approach highlights the fact that it is not quantitative data *per se* which

---

[26] See L Mjöset, 'Stein Rokkan's Thick Description' (2000) 43 *Acta Sociologica* 381, 394 with reference to C Geertz, 'Thick Description: Toward an Interpretive Theory of Culture' in C Geertz, (ed), *The Interpretation of Culture* (New York, NY, Basic Books, 1973) 3, 25, another prominent pioneer of qualitative research methodology.

[27] L Mjöset, 2000, see above, n 26. See also the reference to T Geiger, above, n 14.

[28] It is a fascinating biography in relation to social science research methodology and well documented by Mjöset, 2000, see above, n 26.

[29] Mjöset, 2000, see above, n 26, p 393.

[30] *Ibid.*

[31] *Ibid*, p 391.

[32] *Ibid*, p 394.

[33] *Ibid.*

makes the grounding of theory difficult if not impossible. On the contrary, quantification supports theory building by a considerable increase of the potential for the condensation of concepts based on data.[34] The issue is with the theory-empty use of concepts for the testing of hypotheses in variables research which established itself as the dominant paradigm of so-called empirical social science research.[35]

The detour via the intellectual biography of Stein Rokkan brings us back to the issue of the strategic position of theory in social science research that Luhmann raised so indefatigably. Both Luhmann and Rokkan stress, the one from the beginning, the other at the end of his journey, that only well-constructed theory relates to the 'real world of the participant' and not the more or less well fitting individual concepts that researchers may pursue. The advocated pragmatic activism of grounded theory makes the researcher easily overlook the fact that in spite of all 'condensing', 'open, axial, and selective coding', sampling and resampling, a theory cannot be discovered or found. Theory must be built. And it must be built with concepts that tightly fit the studied phenomena. But the fit must relate likewise to the theory that directs the systematic and consistent development of concepts.

It can be argued, then, that grounded theory may send off doctoral students and hapless researchers on a wild-goose chase with the mirage of good theory and a 'saturation point' of the sampling and evaluation of their qualitative data never to arrive. It can be further argued that while grounded theory only promises a 'grounded' theory, the systems theory approach already delivers.

Undeniably and perhaps ironically Luhmann exudes *theoretical sensitivity* which is one of the required personal qualities of a researcher as seen by grounded theory, the other personal qualities being a 'maintained attitude of scepticism' and consistency in the research procedure.[36] More seriously, grounded theory seems not to be able to follow what it preaches in terms of theoretical sensitivity and scepticism. How else can it be explained that, as the attentive reader has no doubt noticed, concepts like 'structure' and 'action/interaction' are introduced as self-evident formulas and no further effort is made to ground them theoretically? They explain nothing, do not lead anywhere, and send the researcher off on a false start. A 'theoretically sensitive' and sceptical researcher cannot accept concepts such as 'structure' and/or 'action' as self-explanatory, and Luhmann does not. By 'drilling down', like Rokkan, to the specificity of cases, systems theory arrives with

---

[34] This is also where computer assisted research has its place, for instance by computer assisted simulation of complexity models or the handling and systematisation of large amounts of data to determine structural patterns; see, for instance, U Kelle, (ed), *Computer-aided Qualitative Data Analysis. Theory, Methods and Practice* (London, Sage, 1995).

[35] Ekström, 1993, see above n 24.

[36] Strauss & Corbin, 1990, see above, n 17, p 41.

the concepts of system and system operations at a seamlessly generalisable but never finished grounded theory.

It can, then, finally be argued that systems theory is not only grounded *both* in the 'real world of the participant' *and* in 'theory as process'. It delivers 'good science' by *the tight fit of the three elements of research*: theory, methodology, and the phenomenon under study, so that they feed on each other. This means that sociological research only 'fires' if there is sufficiently rich, complex and dense theory. But this requires the procedural energy of research methodology and a thorough reflection of the rich, complex self-description of social structure which only society itself can provide.

C. MAPPING SOCIETY'S LAW

The systems theory approach does not require that researchers start their projects at 'ground zero' for discovery. But it is also a misunderstanding of the objectives of grounded theory, however empty its theory concepts are, that it can only succeed with uncompromising inductive research 'from the bottom up'. The fundamental difference between the systems theory approach and grounded theory approaches *is the much more serious reflection of the 'human condition'*[37] in the theoretical (conceptual) groundwork of the systems theory approach. This provides a clear sense of theoretical direction and gives researchers a head start through the case-specific and area specific dense conceptual groundwork already done and stimulated by systems theory.

At a first glance, this triangulation of thorough theoretical conceptualisation, systematic methodological consistency and the *self-description* of society found in the autopoietic patterns of the operations of the social system seems to be particularly apposite in the case of the legal system because of its universality and an exceptional high degree of formalised self-description. However, on a more thorough reflection, society's law is no different from any other social phenomenon *on that level* of a functional system, such as society's economy, society's political system or society's families.

This observation answers the question as to whether socio-legal research needs any specific or distinctive research methodology in the negative. However, it confirms *that socio-legal research is an area-specific and case-specific research* with all the advantages of a condensation of theoretical concepts. Undeniably, systems theory has made a valuable contribution to this condensation of theoretical concepts for socio-legal research. But systems theory is useful for socio-legal research precisely because it is not a 'dedicated' socio-legal research methodology but a sociological thick description that maps society as a whole. In order to demonstrate how this

---

[37] In the sense of evolutionary conditions for the possibility of social systems.

seamless mapping of society relates to area-specific socio-legal research, it is sufficient to briefly single out particular *conceptual nodes* of this area.[38] These provide conceptual links to be made 'inwards' (zoom in) to more micro-sociological concerns of socio-legal research, like courtroom-communication, or 'outwards' (zoom out) to more macro-sociological concerns, like global law, or sideways to other social systems on comparable levels, like the political system or the economic system. In turn, linking these conceptual nodes can enrich our theoretical sensitivity for observing and describing a phenomenon, like the 'rule of law', in even better detail, that is, by 'zooming in' in terms of our mapping device.

The largest scale for our grid, namely the *evolutionary process*, must be assumed in revisiting the initial rather abstract observation of the requisite variety of possibilities for *the self-creation of systems through their operations*. Zooming in on our specific area, and what makes it specific, focuses on this *process of differentiation*. We can also zoom in further, in order to obtain a sharper focus on lawyers, the legal profession, decision-makers, judges, and zoom out to examine an arrangement of the *communication of second order law observers,* that is legal communication. This communication establishes *itself* as society's law by its own operations (the communication *between* legal decision-makers as to what they deem is legal) and invisibilises its paradoxical stand—that it is society and at the same time something other than society—by *operative closure*. We can call this special communication *closed* because the references made here refer exclusively to operations which are the system's own operations (for instance, previous legal decisions [precedents] or previous legislation/statutes, doctrinal texts etc.). We can call this communication *operatively closed* and can compare this kind of closure with the function of (biological) membranes, eg, the ear 'drums', which protect the self-containment of the system operations while at the same time optimising stimulation or irritation of the system from the environment. We can see—zooming out to *historical comparisons*—such an operative closure of legal communication in order to distinguish what is legal by self-reference to the operations of lawyers as early as in Roman law or in pre-medieval English case law and the early beginnings of the formation of a legal profession.

Generally, when looking from outside in, this puts the focus on *system boundaries* and specifically the boundaries of the legal system. When looking from inside out this is the question as to what constitutes *the unity of legal operations*. Legal operations can refer to ('interpret') the operations in other social systems. But they do not have a key to operate the operations of other functional systems. Therefore, references are typically the operations

---

[38] For a full account see Luhmann, 1993, above, n 5; for a 'short-cut' interpretation see Ziegert, 2002, n 2.

of the referring system, here the legal system, and not of the referenced system[39]—such as reading reports, interpreting decisions, establishing facts. The communication that drives *all* legal operations, and thus forms the boundary of their unity is the 'quaestio iuris'—what is law and legal and what is not? This is *the binary distinction* between law and non-law and its encryption as the code for all legal operations. In this way, all communication operations that relate to legal communication carry the 'law DNA' and can be distinguished from all other, non-law operations. It is, then, the function of the binary code to guide the selection and confirmation of those norms in society, which are deemed to be legal norms and which can be expected to prevail over non-legal norms. This better strategic chance of legal norms to prevail and to be expected to prevail constitutes the *function of law, namely the stabilisation of some normative expectations* in society at the expense of others. This is the only function of law which can be empirically assessed and found with any certainty.[40] In other words, legal decisions are, as legal operations, not designed to achieve certain intended outcomes (for instance, to stop crime/ illegal consumption, or regulate economic decision-making) even where such itentions are expressed,[41] for instance, in legislation, in the concluding address of a judge to a convicted defendant or in the preamble of a constitution. Legal decisions are designed to state what the law is and to resist non-legal change. This higher 'durability' of legal norms compared with other norms is a remarkable speciality of the function of law and directs the focus of our research efforts on the *time dimension of meaning.*[42] It is an important aspect of the function of law that law provides a degree of certainty in the face of an always open future that no other communication system can. While also law like the rest of society world wide cannot know the future, it can 'bind time' through its normative operations, for instance, in a judicial order, in a will or a contract, and so makes an open future at least manageable.

---

[39] The observation of communication research that the receiver and not the sender determines the meaning of a message supports this statement.

[40] Luhmann, 1993 pp 60 and 125, see above, n 5.

[41] This vexing circumstance that communication cannot control what will actually happen is always the case but rarely reflected in the communication itself. The more accurate observation that communication is *acratic* (from Greek 'out of control') makes an important distinction between the different levels on which communication operates. On a surface level, communication has to satisfy demands (expectations) of 'making sense' in the 'things we say'. On the deeper structural (invisible) level of complex communication patterns, communication can only recur to the respective system operations and its self-reproduction. Everything else is 'ultra vires' for the communication operations in question. See for more detail KA Ziegert, 'Courts and the Self-Concept of Law. The Mapping of the Environment by Courts of First Instance' (1992) 14 *Sydney Law Review* 196.

[42] The other dimensions are social (constructing generalised meaning in relation to what people do) and a factual dimensions (constructing generalised meaning in relation to what things are). See N Luhmann, *Social Systems* (Stanford, CA, Stanford University Press, 1995) pp 59–102.

The careful observation of the function of law—and limits of that function—leads back to an unequivocal positioning of the legal system in society as one of its differentiated *functional systems*. Law is defined by its own operations and not by normative (political) boundaries, for instance, the feudal class in a stratified society, or a territorial 'nation' state of a modern society. The conventionally so-called legal systems (eg, the Japanese legal system, the English legal system, etc.) are on closer socio-legal inspection a *network of legal communication* in a historically and locally highly varied array of communication relations between different legal regimes in the contexts of more or less different social systems. These regimes have their unity in the network array of legal communication and not in any individual, mostly politically defined, domestic regime. Moreover, there is no hierarchical order between the 'sites' to which legal operations refer internally. Rather, they are *functionally* related to each other. The unity of all legal operations as they have evolved locally over time is global law as the universal legal system of a universal society which moves and always has moved across boundaries.

Mapping the differentiation of society *historically* on the way to modern law reveals the many ways in which the legal system is increasing its complexity through *structurally coupling* with other functional systems.[43] This in turn increases the differentiation of these other systems and 'lifts' them irreversibly to new levels of functioning. The structural coupling of the legal system with the political system through the constitutional arrangement of *the rule of law* is only one, even if historically highly significant example. The co-evolution and co-operation of law with *the family system*, *the economic system* and *the emerging (global) civil society* respectively are other examples.

We want to conclude this rather cursory review of the many directions that the differentiation of the legal system can take by mapping the structural patterns of local and locally developing regimes. These local legal operations can be observed as being firmly centred in the legal decision-making, that is, *communication in the courts*. Accordingly an empirically founded map for the legal communication of any domestic regime will invariably show *local legal communication* as *an array of concentric (centripetal) communication flows* with the *courts and legal profession in the*

---

[43] Structural coupling is the 'flip-side' of the autopoiesis of systems. Due to the self-referential communication that constitutes social systems, differentiated functional systems *cannot* communicate *with each other*. Structural coupling is a structural two-sided form (not a mechanism!) that has the operations of different systems on either side. They can only succeed with their respective autopoiesis if the conditions for self-reference are met by the operations of the respectively other system. The rule of law is such a form that requires that the political system and the legal system co-operate, usually in the form of a constitution and constitutional law. See for more detail Luhmann, 1993 p 45, see above, n 5, and especially 440ff.

centre of that communication network and all other forms of legal communication—from legal doctrine to legal education and legislation—in a more or less complex periphery. In this form the decision-making in the courts can be observed as exercising a structuring selective pull on all legal operations in the periphery; the courts are empirically the real shadow that law casts over all legal communication. This central structural importance of courts for legal communication also justifies directing observations to the more basic, micro-sociological level of socio-legal research, namely the mapping of *courtroom communication*[44] and the quite specific structural conditions of *the episodic nature of hearings and judicial decision-making*.[45] The periphery on the other hand can be analysed in its buffering or filtering of the 'noise' in society at large and how it establishes from that the 'seriously' legal communication in the centre. Many legal operations in the periphery, like advice in the lawyers' offices, concluding contracts, mediation and arbitration but also legislation, legal doctrine and most legal theory, including critical legal studies and feminist jurisprudence remain peripheral and thus optional for the most part of legal operations. However, establishing and maintaining the validity of law is vital and not optional for the legal system and can only be reproduced by the legal operations in the centre. The form of the centre-periphery structure of legal communication is also consistent with the observation of early regimes of legal communication, such as tribal law and religious law, and develops from here, among others, to the more differentiated forms of Roman law, early common law and the medieval *lex mercatoria*. Here legal communication is already fully functional in a rather lean form of providing largely only the decision-making operations in the centre without much other legal communication apparatus necessary in the periphery. Accordingly, due to the historically and geographic-locally specific evolutionary conditions, *the proportions of legal communication in the centre and in the periphery of domestic legal regimes* can vary considerably when compared with each other. For instance, local legal regimes linked to the common law tradition have a comparatively lean (little differentiated) periphery and high status and dominance of the centre, local legal regimes linked to the European continental tradition have a comparatively huge (highly differentiated) periphery with a relatively high status and dominance over the centre. Local legal regimes linked to the Nordic law tradition take a pragmatic middle ground of a tight integration of administrative decisions and court decisions with both a lean centre and

---

[44] KA Ziegert, 'The Complex Courtroom Communication Scheme: Towards a Transnational and Transcultural Inventory for Measuring Legal Impact: Observations from a Study of Australian, Danish, German and Swedish Courts', paper presented at the *Law & Society Association Annual Meeting*, Phoenix, AZ, 16–19 June 1994.

[45] Luhmann, 1993, see above, n 5, p 208.

lean periphery. Subsequently, one can observe that these different structural patterns are reflected in different legal ideologies, legal theories and doctrines, for instance the insistence on different 'sources of law' in doctrine: Divine? Precedent? The code? Notwithstanding such normatively invoked differences, insisted on by reflexive theories and legal self-descriptions by lawyers for lawyers, empirically all legal operations and courts everywhere in the world operate essentially in the same way. However, where they differ in fact, ie, empirically, is in the structural effects of legal operations due to the variations of structural coupling patterns, which have not developed evenly throughout the world. These differences involve highly complex co-operation arrangements between the various functional systems that evolve or do not evolve and which correlate strongly with social indicators, for instance poverty. Thus we can find, when conducting comparative structural analyses, great differences between, for instance, Islamic law and law in Europe, and also considerable barriers which prevent an easy development to modern law, for instance, the 'democratic centralism' in countries which still maintain the Soviet design of Socialist Law.

D. CONCLUSION: DISCOVERING THE RULE OF LAW—AN EXAMPLE

The mapping of society's law with systems theory has provided us with a multi-dimensional multi-tier, socio-legal research agenda. It contains the 'classical' fields of empirical socio-legal research but 'stitches' them together in a seamless matrix for meaningful qualitative research. We want to conclude this brief introduction into the methodological aspects of systems theory and its advantages for qualitative socio-legal research with an example by contrasting an early, in many ways pioneering, approach to empirical sociology of law in early 1970 to 1980 with the possibilities that systems theory can open up today. The earlier research flowed from the central research problem of early sociology of law, namely the issue of the authority and 'binding' power of law, or in other words the question as to what made people observe the law and respect legal rules. This research problem came to be known under the title of 'the general sense of justice'[46] and the numerous studies that followed, mainly in Europe, went by the label of KOL-studies or

---

[46] See B Kutchinsky, 'Law and Education: Some Aspects of Scandinavian Studies into the "General Sense of Justice"' (1967) 10 *Acta Sociologica* 21–41; A Podgórecki, 'The Prestige of Law (Preliminary Results)' (1967) 10 *Acta Sociologica* 81–96; CJM Schuyt and JCM Ruys, 'Die Einstellung gegenüber neuen sozio-ökonomischen Gesetzen' (Attitudes towards new socio-economic legislation) (1972) 3 *Jahrbuch für Rechtssoziologie und Rechtstheorie* 565–598.

studies of the knowledge and opinion about law.[47] At the time, these studies were almost synonymous with empirical sociology of law. For the first time, large sample surveys and questionnaires were employed by socio-legal researchers in order to find how a general population felt about law, knew about law and was more or less guided by legal, or at least normative principles. The findings of these studies were, as is typically the case with surveys and opinions research, largely inconclusive as far as the research question was concerned[48] but canvassed considerable differences between different groups in society especially when differentiated by age, education and socio-economic status. In the 1980s, studies of this kind disappeared from the research agendas without a trace.

There are at least two reasons why sociology of law could not benefit better from these studies. The first and major reason for the failure was the insensitivity of the quantitative approach to the social context, in which respondents lived and worked. The second reason was the blindness of the approach as to the complex functioning of law; actually the KOL-studies did not research the functioning of law at all. The mapping of society by systems theory can address the deficiencies of socio-legal studies like the KOL-studies while both covering very much the same ground—how do people do things with law, and if not why not, why does the law work, and if not why not?

In order to answer these questions, qualitative research provides the array of 'sensors' which can be brought to bear on society in order to make the boundaries of the operations of law visible, and the mapping of systems theory provides the meaningful grid for positioning the array of sensors at those 'fault' lines between legal operations and those of other social systems where the visibility of the boundaries of law is most likely to occur. In this way, we can replace the futile search of the KOL-studies for a 'general sense of justice' by the empirical measurement of the rule of law. We could then, for instance, compare or even benchmark the rule of law of one legal regime, say in Sweden, with the rule of law of another regime where it is problematic, say Ukraine or Vietnam.

---

[47] See B Kutchinsky, 'Knowledge and Attitudes Regarding Legal Phenomena in Denmark' in N Christie, (ed), *Scandinavian Studies in Criminology II* (Universitetsforlag, Oslo, 1967); W Kaupen, 'Das Verhältnis der Bevölkerung zur Rechtspflege' (Attitudes towards the administration of justice) (1972) 3 *Jahrbuch für Rechtssoziologie und Rechtstheorie* 555–63.

[48] For a critical overview over these early empirical studies see KA Ziegert, *Zur Effektivität der Rechtssoziologie: die Rekonstruktion der Gesellschaft durch Recht* (Towards the effectiveness of sociology of law: the reconstruction of society through law) (Stuttgart, Enke, 1975) p 191; and also D Lucke and OG Schwenk, 'Rechtsbewusstsein als empirisches Faktum und symbolische Fiktion' (Legal consciousness as an empirical fact and symbolic fiction) (1992) 13(2) *Zeitschrift für Rechtssoziologie* 185–204.

As briefly outlined above, the rule of law can be seen as a specialised structural form resulting from the co-evolution and co-operation of functional systems, in this case the legal and the political systems.[49] However, the effective structural coupling of law and politics (rule of law) is not the only condition for delivering a functioning law. Here specific forms of the co-evolution of law and the family system, law and the economic system and more recently law and civil society (the political system that is not state-centred, itself a result of the differentiation of law, in particular international law and human rights) enter the picture and together spell out the status and degree of differentiation in a given setting. In this sense the operation of the rule of law cannot be measured on the terms of the legal operations only but must be also observed in the standards and practices that are applied in everyday coping in the respective functional systems. This means that our array of sensors are the qualitative interviews that are conducted with respondents not only at critical positions for the legal system (courts, prosecution, legal profession, see appended example plan for a study in Vietnam) but also at critical positions for the political system, the economic system, the family system and civil society (see project plan).

The sensitivity of this basic grid of sensors can be further enhanced, that is approximated to the complexity of society, if sensors are additionally placed, ie, qualitative interviews conducted, at the differentiated levels of respective system operations on the centre-periphery spectrum. For instance, poor rural families can be expected to cope with everyday life with standards and practices which are quite different from rich urban families, as much as the standards and practices in local branches of banks may differ from the standards and practices of central bankers.

The resulting interviews can be recorded and 'benchmarked' as a complex *matrix of standards and practices* that form the conditions (conditional matrix) for the rule of law to work or not. It can be applied longitudinally and repetitively for purposes of monitoring and evaluating social and legal change in one society over time; or it can be benchmarked comparatively between two or more societies. In either case the concrete but largely open research question whether or not everyday coping be improved by the rule of law can be approached with a definitive research plan guided firmly by the qualitatively thick mapping of systems theory.

---

[49] Luhmann, 1993, see above n 5.

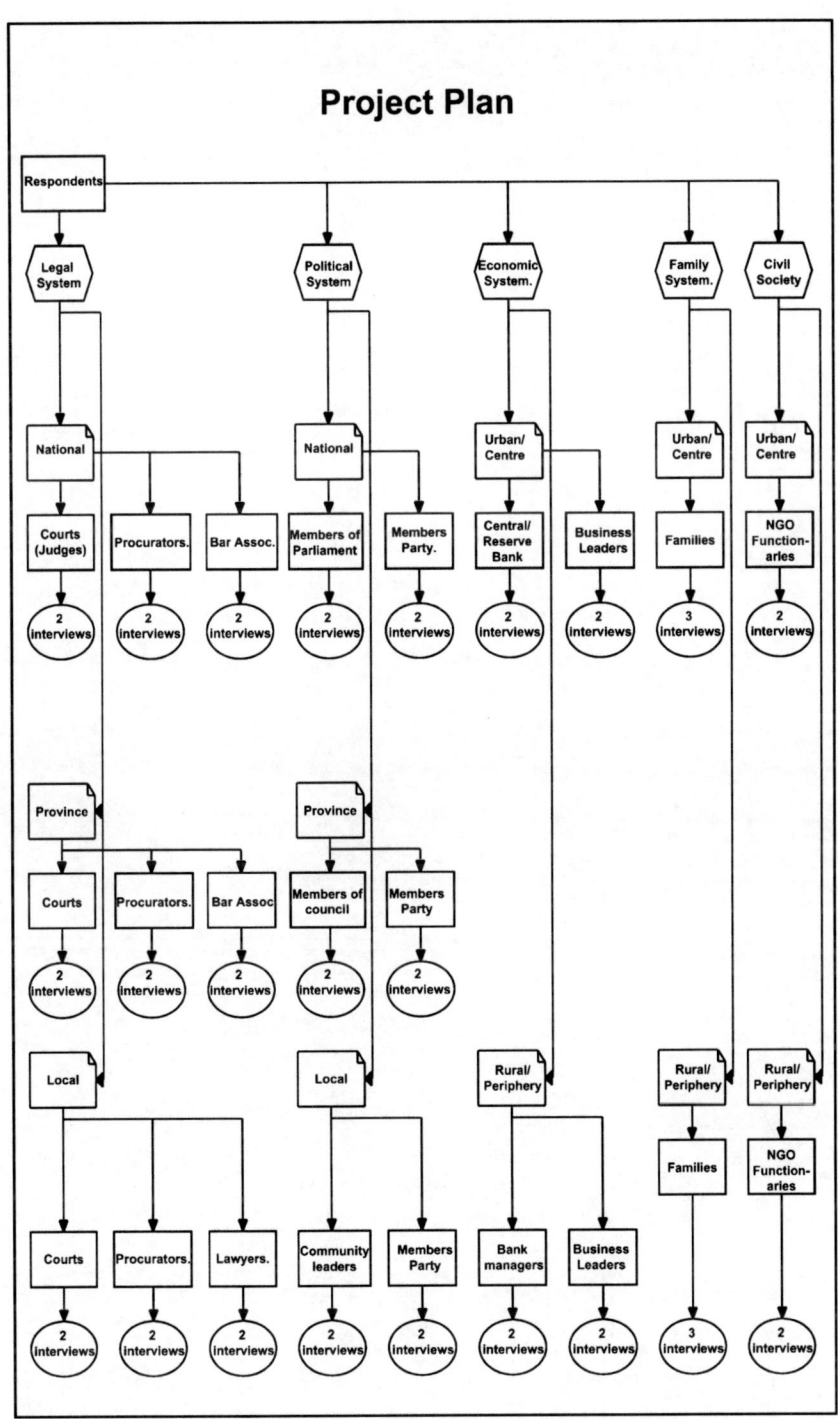

Section Two

Ethnography and Law

REZA BANAKAR AND MAX TRAVERS

T HIS IS NOT intended to be a comprehensive handbook on research methods and socio-legal research. If we were writing such a text, there would have to be chapters on a wider range of methods, and also on different ways of analysing data. To give an example, the most common method used in qualitative research is interviewing, and one can analyse interviews from a variety of theoretical perspectives.[1] The most common in social science is some variant of the grounded theory tradition in which data is analysed into themes or codes. It is particularly popular as a method in health studies and management, but is also taught on many sociology programmes internationally, and is promoted through software packages such as NUD*IST.[2] There are large literatures one can consult about grounded theory, and all kinds of debates within the field. Nevertheless, despite its popularity in sociology, we cannot think of any articles published in socio-legal journals that employ this method of analysis.

The three chapters in this section are partly based on interviewing, although they have each spent a long period of time observing or participating in a particular institution or community. Thomas Scheffer spent several months observing solicitors preparing cases for crown court hearings in England. His research is distinctive in focusing on the documents produced during a case and how they are used during the proceedings. He describes how he developed a method of 'tracing selected issues through the files on their way to court'. Samia Banio observed mediation hearings in Sharia Councils, the community bodies that decide family disputes for British Muslims, conducted a content analysis of case files, and interviewed 25 Pakistani women about their experiences of obtaining a divorce.

---

[1] See J Gubrium and J Holstein, (eds), *Handbook of Interview Research: Context and Method* (Thousand Oaks, CA, Sage, 2002).

[2] This stands for Non-numerical Unstructured Data. Indexing, Searching and Theorising.

Anne Griffiths conducted anthropological fieldwork in a village in Botswana over a period of seven years with the aim of understanding how women experience and are governed by family law. In each case, the same methods were used (interviewing, observation and documentary analysis) although for distinct theoretical, and in the case of the last two papers, political purposes.

There have been a number of studies about legal practice using ethnographic methods, not nearly as many as one finds in fields like the sociologies of medicine, education or science. The language and power tradition has arguably made most impact on the law and society movement since it is theoretically compatible with the critical perspectives in sociology that still inform many papers published in socio-legal journals. Sociolinguists have examined interaction in different institutional settings, and located this in wider structures of inequality.[3] Two other influential traditions have been ethnomethodology and conversation analysis. Ethnomethodological ethnographers have described the practical considerations involved in legal work in different settings. Conversation analysts have produced a large body of work about courtrooms, but are also starting to study interaction inside legal offices.[4]

The distinction between these two bodies of research, and the methodological debates that take place between them, relates to the general issues about the foundations of sociology we reviewed in the previous section. Ethnomethodologists and conversation analysts disagree amongst themselves over the issue of whether studying discourse is sufficient to understand work in legal settings.[5] Nevertheless, they each have a commitment to addressing how the people they study understand their own activities, as opposed to claiming to know more as analysts. These arguments become more pointed in that structural traditions often claim that ethnomethodology and conversation are morally deficient for not addressing wider social structures; whereas they argue that critical sociolinguists do not adequately address what happens in legal settings, or impose their own political views over the people they are studying.

---

[3] For a general review, see JM Conley and WM O'Barr, *Just Words: Law, Language and Power* (Chicago, IL, University of Chicago Press, 1998). For examples, see J Conley and WM O'Barr, *Rules Versus Relationships: The Ethnography of Legal Discourse* (Chicago, IL, University of Chicago Press, 1990); A Sarat and W Felstiner, *Divorce Lawyers and their Clients* (London, OUP, 1995); and S Trinch, *Latina's Narratives of Domestic Abuse* (Philadelphia, PA, John Benjamins, 2003).

[4] For an introduction, see M Travers and JF Manzo, (eds), *Law in Action: Ethnomethodological and Conversation Analytic Approaches to Law* (Aldershot, Ashgate, 1997).

[5] See M Travers, *The Reality of Law: Work and Talk in a Firm of Criminal Lawyers* (Aldershot, Ashgate, 1997); M Moerman, *Talking Culture: Ethnography and Conversation Analysis* (Philadelphia, PA, University of Pennsylvania Press, 1988); and D Maynard, *Bad News, Good News: Conventional Order in Everyday Talk and Clinical Settings* (Chicago, IL, Chicago University Press, 2003) ch 3.

This background should help in understanding Scheffer's chapter. He refers at various points to the language and power tradition, ethnomethodology and conversation analysis, as well as interactionist ethnography of the kind advocated by John Flood in chapter 1.[6] There is also a reference to Dorothy Smith's paper on textually-mediated interaction. Although no contributor in this collection has drawn on this theorist, it is worth noting that she provides yet another potential resource one can use in socio-legal research, especially since her most recent work has concerned procedures in policing domestic violence. The method of institutional ethnography she developed in the 1970s invites students to use ethnographic methods in investigating everyday life, with an ethnomethodological sensitivity to local practices and understandings, and from there find ways of addressing structures of power and inequality (what she calls the 'relations of ruling').[7]

What makes Scheffer's chapter distinctive, however, is the way it also draws on a theoretical tradition associated with Bruno Latour, and researchers in the sociology of science, known as actor network theory. One reason why this has generated attention and controversy is because of Latour's insistence that non-human agents, such as machines or microbes, should be recognised and described as actors in the same way as human beings. Although this should partly be understood as a provocative philosophical claim, it is also interesting sociologically for two reasons. It is, firstly, the latest attempt to overcome the action-structure divide. Pursuing this type of analysis also allow us to see how objects and outcomes are produced through complex human activities in institutions like scientific laboratories or, in Latour's most recent work, law courts.[8]

Scheffer is, arguably, not as consistent as Latour in the way he treats objects in a solicitor's office, like legal statements or files, as having agency. However, his analysis does make one think, in a way one does not usually find in interactionist or ethnomethodological accounts, about the way cases develop over time, from pieces of information being brought together, and of the contingent nature of what eventually becomes the case. As he observes, if we can follow 'how probes of soil enter an academic paper' (a reference to a study by Latour about soil scientists in the Amazon forest), 'why cannot we also follow a statement on its way to court?'.

One can, of course, argue that despite having invented a new theoretical language, Latour has been no more successful than previous theorists in over-coming the action-structure debate, or that, in theorising about the

---

[6] See M Travers, 'Symbolic Interactionism and Law' in R Banakar and M Travers, (eds), *An Introduction to Law and Social Theory* (Oxford, Hart Publishing, 2002) 209.

[7] See, for example, D Smith, *The Everyday World as Problematic* (Milton Keynes, Open University Press, 1987); M Campbell and A Manicom, (eds), *Knowledge, Experience and Ruling Relations* (Toronto, University of Toronto Press, 1995).

[8] See B Latour, *La Fabrique du Droit: Une Ethnographie du Conseil d'Etat* (Paris, la Decourverte, 2002).

world, he does not adequately describe lived experience. For all the claims made about the deficiency of other ethnographic approaches, the actual considerations that matter to people at any stage of a legal case, including how they understand the law, are not described. Against this, the chapter illustrates what can be done by conducting ethnographic research inside legal offices, and the potential wider implications for understanding law: it would be good to see more studies of this kind, from different theoretical perspectives, being published in socio-legal journals.[9]

The researchers in the next two chapters also used ethnographic methods, although they look at the experience of people affected by legal institutions rather than the work of professionals (and it is interesting, in this respect, that the client in Scheffer's chapter remains a shadowy figure in the background, or an object to be 'inscribed' in legal files). They are also writing from a feminist perspective, and this influences how they write about method, and also the way they present and analyse ethnographic data. There are all kinds of debates within feminism, and it should not be seen as a unified or homogeneous tradition.[10] Debates about feminist epistemology and method can become every bit as heated, in their own way, as those between interpretivists and systems theorists, and this again illustrates how arguments about theory and method are central to sociology as an academic discipline. We would, however, argue that what is distinctive about these papers is their political slant. They each present women as an oppressed group, both through the family and legal institutions controlled by men.

Samia Bano interviewed British Pakistani women about their experiences in using Sharia Councils to obtain a divorce. This is a sensitive topic, and it is worth noting that only 25 of the 45 women she approached agreed to participate. One reason given was that 'the research might contribute to the stereotype of Muslim women as victims of a patriarchal cultural/religious system'. This is a common theme in the American black feminist literature and part of the way women experience 'dual oppression'. Theorists like Bel Hooks recognise that African-American women are victims of both sexism and racism, but that negative accounts about their own community play into the hands of the racists.[11]

---

[9] See also J Morison and P Leith, *The Barrister's World and the Nature of Law* (Buckingham, Open University Press, 1992).

[10] Some feminists are, for example, strongly committed to qualitative research methods, and see quantitative research as a masculine, objectifying way of relating the world. Others have argued that one can use quantitative methods as a feminist. Compare, for example, L Stanley, (ed), *Feminist Praxis: Research, Theory and Epistemology in Feminist Sociology* (London, Routledge, 1990); and A Oakley, *Experiments in Knowing: Gender and Method in the Social Sciences* (Cambridge, Polity Press, 2000).

[11] See B Hooks, *Feminist Theory: From Margin to Center* (Boston, MA, South End Press, 1984)..

The concern with ethical issues in this chapter is characteristic of feminist research. Some feminists believe that ethnography, even with the informed consent required in some countries by ethical review boards, must always be unethical. This is because the researcher always has more power than the group being studied, and it is impossible to be completely honest with interviewees about the objectives of the project or how information will be used.[12] One way of addressing, if not resolving this problem, is that feminists are more open than most qualitative researchers in acknowledging these issues, and are expected to be 'reflexive' in writing about their own role in the research process. Bano notes, for example, that even though she belonged to the same religion and ethnic group, she was quizzed about whether she was a proper Muslim. One interviewee was pleased that she was married since 'being married is important for Muslim women'. Although Bano does not fully explore the issue in this chapter, one can imagine that she had different values as a middle-class academic with progressive beliefs to the women she was interviewing.

Griffiths is an anthropologist, and it is worth noting that in this discipline there are specialist literatures about feminist methods, and obviously also about conducting ethnographic fieldwork. The chapter, as one might expect, is partly an argument for the value of spending a long period of time observing, and developing ties with a particular social group: she carried out fieldwork in a village in Botswana over a period of seven years with the aim of understanding how women experience and are governed by family law. The chapter argues that one can only address the experiences of these women through using fieldwork methods, and recording their life-histories. This kind of 'contextual approach' can address aspects of 'the relationship between law and power' in a way that is unavailable to 'formal legal discourse'.

The chapter makes an important contribution to our understanding of legal relationships in Botswana by providing background information about the economic and social position of women, obtained over many years of fieldwork, but also rich detail on the experiences of particular people. In telling the story of Ninika, she is engaging in what feminists call standpoint research by presenting her experience, and relating this to the structural forces that oppress women. She concludes that married women are just as vulnerable as unmarried women: 'in most cases, it is men's enhanced ability to draw on all forms of resources for a family base that places them in a stronger position than women to accumulate what is necessary to form a household, and thus to elevate their power and social status in terms of the social world in which they live'.

---

[12] See J Stacey, 'Can There Be a Feminist Ethnography?' (1998) 11 *Women's Studies International Forum*, 21.

Scheffer's chapter and these two feminist ethnographies are each power-ful and interesting examples of what ethnography can achieve in the sense of investigating how law is understood and experienced in society. One major difference is that Scheffer does not consider moral or evaluative issues that arose during his fieldwork: by focusing on the careers of docu-ments or 'paper trails', he is not concerned with the fairness of law, or in assessing the versions presented in court by different parties. In the same way as Erving Goffman, he can be accused of a cynical or playful attitude towards human beings, of stepping back from their political conflicts.[13] One can contrast this to the engaged moral tone of feminist ethnography. The objection here, however, might be that, in siding with women as an oppressed group, other voices are not heard. Men in particular are not paid much attention, and one can argue that Griffiths rather too quickly dismiss-es the accounts, both by the husband and mother-in-law, that do not suit her political sympathies.

There are all kinds of approaches and theoretical traditions in ethnogra-phy, and we have only touched on a few issues and debates in this introduc-tion. Extended fieldwork of the kind Scheffer used in studying a law firm, and Banio and Griffiths employed to address the experiences of women, is a method that is still not widely used in law and society studies. It allows one to address lived experience in a way that is not open to surveys or even qualitative interviews. It also opens up rich possibilities for theoretical and political debate. To give one example, a poststructuralist might want to question the assumption informing each of these chapters that it is possible to arrive at a determinate account of what really happened.[14] Sociology still sometimes attracts adverse comment from outsiders for being highly self-conscious and reflective about method. We would argue that the level of methodological self-consciousness in these chapters is precisely what makes sociology worth doing.

---

[13] See E Goffman, 'The Interaction Order' (1983) 48 *American Sociological Review* 1.
[14] See M Travers, *Qualitative Research Through Case Studies* (London, Sage, 2001) ch 8.

4

Courses of Mobilisation: Writing Systematic Micro-Histories of Legal Discourse

THOMAS SCHEFFER

Mobilize:

1 *a*) to make mobile, or movable *b*) to put into motion, circulation, or use
2 to bring into readiness for immediate active service in war
3 to organise (people, resources, etc) for active service or use in any emergency, drive, etc.
4 to become organised and ready, as for war

INSIDE THE OFFICES, paper-workers produce and combine documents. Their desks are covered with paper: with files, bundles and briefs. And the production goes on. Solicitors dictate notes, secretaries type letters, and the legal clerks compile sets of evidence. It is exactly through these paper-trails that things are set into motion for the day in court. In other words: statements, arguments, narratives and their human carriers are mobilised to make a case.

The ordinary case-work seems to a large extent a face-to-file interaction. The mounting dossier indicates what needs to be drafted, collected, posted *next*. It gives the 'full picture' as well as the missing links. At this site of the legal machinery, the socio-legal ethnographer faces, however fascinated by courtroom dramas, a writing culture.

Legal mobilisation, however, includes face-to-face work: people need to stand and speak out for the case in court. They need to articulate the written, to stage it, to bring it across to an audience. The day in court requires an ensemble set to co-enact the matter 'here and now'. The case, therefore, involves a whole bond of players, props and materials. The socio-legal ethnographer deals, however infected by 'archive fever' (Derrida), with an impressive performative culture.

And there is more: the interplay, the competition, the terror of failure. At least two social projects and individual ambitions are at odds here, putting the respective other under pressure and tension. The cases unfold, and are elaborated in the contest between defence and prosecution, both ready to challenge, weaken and undermine the opponent's case in front of a deadly quiet jury. The socio-legal ethnographer faces, however fascinated by the means, formats and methods of case-construction, a contingent and risky power-game. Competitive mobilisation.

What can sociologists learn from legal proceedings and the ways that they are conducted? And how can they organise this learning? In the following, I suggest a number of methods and frames that can be used to reveal what happens in legal practice or, to be more precise, the craft required to present a criminal case.[1] The methods are designed to stress the temporal and sequential features of legal work. They link what is commonly held apart: pre-trial and trial,[2] preparation and event, text and talk, evidence and law.[3] By doing so, they introduce the socio-dynamics of legal proceedings and the ways the defendant's or witness' view is translated into legally-relevant arguments.

How can one address these different sites and materialities[4] of legal discourse empirically? This paper proposes a sequential analysis of mobilisation that is capable of connecting what usually remains separated. The concept

---

[1] These are employed in a research-project titled 'Comparative Micro-Sociology of Legal Proceedings', funded by the German DFG. This has enabled four fieldworkers—Kati Hannken-Illjes (Germany), Alex Kozin (US), Livia Holden (Italy), plus the author (UK)—to conduct case-studies. The chapter presented here stems from the author's two year pilot-study. See www.law-in-action.de.

[2] D McBarnet, 'Pre-trial Procedures and the Construction of Conviction' in P Carlen, (ed), *The Sociology of Law* (Keele, Sociological Review Monograph 23, 1976) provides one of the few early socio-legal studies concentrating on the pre-trial. She notes that 'interactionist detail cannot provide a total explanation [!] of the processes of conviction. In the first place, it under-states the structural influences of the legal system's rules, checks and definitions on the con-struction of reality. In the second place, it underplays how much the events and information observed in court have been shaped long before the stage of public trial is reached' (175); my exclamation mark. Despite her short-cuts in describing the structures within which lawyers work, I take McBarnet's critique seriously. The interactionist problem is, indeed, that there is no concept for the procedure and the role of the pre-products accumulated over a period of time. It is, however, no solution just to ascribe agency to 'the law'. McBarnet cannot show *how* the law gets enrolled in criminal pre-trials and trials. She does not provide a praxeology show-ing how 'the law' co-produces social situations. For studies of legal preparation, see also A Sarat and W Felstiner, *Divorce lawyers and their clients* (London, OUP, 1995); and A Konradi, 'Too little Too Late: Prosecutors' Pre-Court Preparation of Rape Survivors' (1997) 22 *Law and Social Inquiry*; M Travers, *The Reality of Law: Work and Talk in a Firm of Criminal Lawyers* (Aldershot, Dartmouth, 1997) analyses how lawyer-client relations evolved during meetings before trial.

[3] There is, of course, a large amount of research on the relationship between text and talk. For an overview, see M Mulkay, 'Conversations and Texts' (1986) 9 *Human Studies*; or D Smith, 'Textually Mediated Social Organization' (1985) 99 *International Social Science Journal*. See also the author's study on the entanglements of text and talk in the German asy-lum procedure, T Scheffer, *Asylgewährung. Eine ethnographische Analyse des deutschen Asylverfahrens* (Stuttgart, Lucius&Lucius, 1999).

[4] See T Scheffer, 'Materialities of Legal Proceedings' in (2004) 26 *International Journal for the Semiotics of Law*.

of mobilisation allows us to see the 'open' phases before conflicts are settled. It can address the legal groundwork in a case and the difficulties of
actualising this in court.

A. DE-CENTRING SOCIAL SITUATIONS

Goffman's question of 'what goes on here?' is at the heart of micro-sociological research. Many sociolegal scholars started with similar curiosity:
What goes on in court? What is all the paper-work about? What happens
in client-barrister conferences? Interpretative approaches argue that 'what
goes on' is hard to pinpoint since the participants do not attribute the same
meaning to what took place. By focussing on mobilisation, 'what goes on'
appears in a different light. It does not come into sight by interpreting utter-
ances *within* the focal situation, but by weighing them in the course of pre-
ceding and succeeding situations.

As a micro-sociologist, one can distinguish between closed and open
interaction systems.[5] Closed ones rely greatly on the elements that come
about during their course, while open systems are greatly dependent on and
shaped by pre-fabricated entities. Micro-sociologists seem rather occupied
with closed systems like face-to-face interaction. They have less to say
about open systems and the ways in which they hinge on and contribute to
extended projects such as political campaigns, research processes or legal
case-work.[6]

The nature of interaction analysis changes fundamentally when one
addresses this wider context. It moves closer to what participants are confronted with and achieve in each new situation. The participants of Crown
Court hearings, for instance, are confronted with statements and interviews
they have given at earlier stages of the case.[7] They rely on these prior statements ('materialities') when constructing their court-performances. In this
way, the counsel and witnesses in court resemble 'consumers'[8]: they pick
up, mix and modify legal 'products' in the course of their inventive manoeuvres. Actors, in this view, turn out to be creative and tactical, rather than
passively responding to each new situation. This relation of products and

---

[5] See T Scheffer, 'Jenseits der Konversation. Zur Konzeptualisierung von Asylanhörungen
anhand der ethnographischen Analyse ihrer Eröffnung' in (1998) 24 *Schweizerische Zeitschrift
für Soziologie.*

[6] See for an overview M Travers and J Manzo, (eds), *Law in Action: Ethnomethodological
and Conversation Analytical Approaches to Law* (Aldershot, Ashgate, 1997).

[7] See T Scheffer, 'Materialities of Legal Proceedings' (2004) 17 *International Journal for
Semiotics of Law.* The position developed here refers back to Foucault's concept of the state-
ment in M Foucault, *The Archaeology of Knowledge and the Discourse of Language* (London,
Tavistock, 1972).

[8] M de Certeau, *The Practice of Everyday Life* (Berkeley, CA, University of California Press,
1984).

their consumption might equally characterise participants in court hearings: they rely on products and use them for all practical purposes. Not everything that surfaces and gains meaning in the social situation is created within its course.

A similar, but more categorical version of this can be found in Luhmann's distinction of different communicative layers or modes. For Luhmann, it is misleading to regard legal proceedings as consisting of just face-to-face interaction.[9] Through closed interaction-systems any wider spatiotemporal effects could not be reached. Luhmann argues generally that nowadays 'the gap between interaction and society has become unbridgeably wide and deep. (...) At no other time has it been less possible to view the societal system as composed of interactions and to consider adequate theories that conceive society as "commerce", exchange, dance, contract, chain, theatre, or discourse'.[10]

At this point, one can discuss further consequences of the suggested move. Decentred situations not only demand new frames of meaning, but also challenge the heuristics connected to the scheme of closed interaction-systems. These heuristics are systematically spelled out in ethnomethodological Conversation Analysis (CA). CA considers everything—roles, sex, gender, formality etc—as being locally and sequentially accomplished by co-present participants. By analysing turn-by-turn exchanges in ordinary and institutional conversation, CA aims to 'preserve the details of local order production "over its course" for the analyst'[11] and provides a useful 'way of seeing'.

The heuristic of proximity triggers further effects: it disciplines the researcher. It binds the analysis to empirical data and encourages reflection on what we normally take for granted. The radical localism in CA challenges the manner in which most social scientists make uncontrolled inferences from their data. As Garfinkel has argued, what matters should be *observable* in situ within the 'phenomenal field'.[12] Accordingly, no structural,

---

[9] N Luhmann, *Social Systems* (Stanford, CA, Stanford University Press, 1995): 'Writing and printing make it possible to withdraw from interaction systems and nevertheless to communicate with far-reaching societal consequences. By deciding to use the communicative form of writing, one can reach more addressees over longer periods of time, but this decision suggests that one withdraw from interaction, if it does not force one to do so. The differentiation of this mode of communication from interactional nexuses has more than quantitative significance: it enables a mode of working that could not be attained within interaction and thereby an augmentation of the difference between society and interaction to which the societal system and interactional systems can orient themselves' p 427.

[10] *Ibid*, p 430.

[11] A Rawls, 'Editor's Introduction' in H Garfinkel, (ed), *Ethnomethodology's Program: Working Out Durkheim's Aphorism* (Lanham, Rowman & Littlefield, 2002) 6.

[12] 'It is Garfinkel's primary commitment that meaningful social orders do not, cannot, occur at a conceptual level. They must be empirically witnessable, and the analyst must preserve these witnessable aspects of practice'; in A Rawls, *ibid*, p 8.

allegedly omnipresent variable can be just taken for granted as significant for the business at hand (not even the three classics: class, gender and race). Everything that matters is taken up in the turn-by-turn processing of meaning. It takes place on the (observable) surface of social interaction.

The heuristic underlying the analysis of mobilisation, while agreeing with some essential features of ethnomethodology (such as observability, sequentiality, interactivity), differs in some respects concerning the unit of analysis. Firstly, it questions the frame of analysis (closed interaction systems) and therefore the status of proximity and localism. By asking *what goes on* the analysis of mobilisation includes 'necessary' pre-products and their circulation across time and space. Secondly, by tracing statements or narratives through projects of representation one does not presuppose whether they succeed or fail or how far they make it. They are, for vast periods, unfinished and contingent entities, not ready yet to be fully exposed to the focal discourse. Thirdly, this kind of analysis transgresses as well as links several sites of case work, such as the police station, the law firm and the court itself.

B. PARTIAL ACCESS

Addressing this wider context creates several methodological problems. To give one example: the complete legal case-work is impossible to record. The work of mobilisation is, to a large extent momentary, short-lived and passing. Given the multi-sitedness of mobilisation, the ethnographer can only get in touch with a small portion of the work. The contributions by the client, for instance, remain hidden while the lawyer's part seems well-documented and, therefore, prominent in the analysis.

Tracing mobilisation has to cope with what Marcus calls, a 'multi-sited field'.[13] Casework takes place at the client's home, in the law firm's offices, and right outside the courtroom. It takes place as well in barristers' chambers and the interview rooms at court. The mobilisation of cases takes place via correspondence, telephone talks and frequent meetings. While tracing statements on their way to court, one can get lost in the intertextuality of legal discourse.

Fortunately, it is not just researchers who are confronted by such problems. The lawyers have to deal with the sheer complexity of unfolding proceedings as part of their everyday work. Despite the piles of incoming calls, letters or documents, they need to ensure that no important details, no potential trump card, no official deadlines are left out. They try to keep

---

[13] G Marcus, *Ethnography through Thick and Thin* (Princeton, NJ, Princeton University Press, 1998).

track of the circulating statements through check lists, sketches or dia-grams.[14] Solicitors try to control the statement's career: its weight for the case; its distribution inside and outside the defence ensemble. The lawyers' management of complexity turns out to be a focal issue for the study of mobilisation.

Statements need to be delivered right on time and presented in standard-ised but nonetheless shifting and tricky circumstances.[15] The duality of courtroom-performance[16] and case-preparation generates certain modes of planning (loose, flexible, multi-optional scripts) on the one hand and a whole range of speech/writing acts. Case-delivery and case-preparation are not at all appropriately grasped as homogenous writing and talking.[17] They are better captured as hybrid forms (as written speech and spoken texts) supporting, exercising and anticipating one another.

Facing these entanglements, one gets the impression that preparation *and* enactment, pre-trial *and* trial, plan *and* event have been wrongly kept apart. Both sides are better understood as co-constituting facets that cannot be reduced to one another. Preparation, in this view, appears not only as help-ful investment prior to the case-delivery, but as well a source of the event's complexity. The defendant, for instance, is prepared for and at the same time confronted by prepared opponents. To take the floor 'here and now' means for her/him to address an intertextual field (of prior statements, statements by others, one's own testimony and the others' testimonies) that easily turns into a minefield full of mobilised trumps *and* traps.

C. FOCUSED HISTORIOGRAPHY

How can one investigate extended and multi-sited projects? One way is to focus on its focal products 'in the making': the statements, pieces of evi-dence, and line of defence. From this perspective, I approach *becomings* as

[14] L Suchman, 'Making a Case: "Knowledge" and "Routine" Work in Document Production' in P Luff, J Hindmarsh and C Heath, (eds), *Workplace Studies: Recovering Work Practice and Informing System Design* (Cambridg, CUP, 2000).

[15] See P Drew, 'Contested Evidence in Courtroom Cross-Examination: The Case of a Trial for Rape' in P Drew and J Heritage, (eds), *Talk at Work: Interaction in Institutional Settings* (Cambridge, CUP, 1992) 470; and S Harris, 'Fragmented Narratives and Multiple Tellers: Witness and Defendant Accounts in Trials' (2001) 3 *Discourse Studies*.

[16] See M Atkinson and P Drew, 'Order in court: The Orgazation of verbal *interaction in judi-cial settings* (Atlantic Highlands, N.J.: Humanities Press, 1979).

[17] See D Zimmerman, 'Record-Keeping and the Intake Process in a Public Welfare Agency' in S Wheeler, (ed), *On Record: Files and Dossiers in American Life* (New York, NY, Russell Sage, 1969).

concrete/mobilised singularities rather than as abstract/dispersed collectives[18]: the mobilisation of an alibi[19] for instance. This analysis of mobilisation tracks down single features that travel through situations and are marked by their various involvements.[20] Through mobilisation, becomings gain weight, impact, force—and join together to configure new events.

This focus on becomings is meant to sharpen how 'law-in-action'[21] proceeds at a local level—but complements this with an appreciation of its translocal entanglements.[22] At this point, I would like to recommend a kind of manual to guide the investigation of legal mobilisation. The manual will emphasise methodical implications of the perspective and how it translates into a series of research activities:

(1) *The expert's presentation of the case:* In my research on English criminal proceedings, the solicitor's introduction of single cases-initiated by 'What are you working on right now?'—was a useful starting point. My informants provided brief and pointed stories of 'what the case is about'. This account often focused on a key incident that was understood differently by the prosecution and defence. The solicitor's presentation was usually divided into a factual and a legal section. He or she described 'what happened' and 'some technicalities' that were relevant to the casework at that point in time. It is important to note when exactly this narration occurred in the legal process.

(2) *Selecting single issues:* These often quite brief and concentrated narratives convey what my solicitors call the 'heart of the case' or the 'crucial point'. From the solicitor's point of view, this is what one uses to determine 'now' whether this is a winning or losing case, or a case that should or should not go to court. The 'heart of the case' may well be a medical attestation,

---

[18] G Deleuze and F Guatarri, *A Thousand Plateaus: Capitalism and Schizophrenia* (London, Athlone, 1988).

[19] T Scheffer, 'The Duality of Mobilisation: Following the Rise and Fall of an Alibi-story on its Way to Court' (2003) 33 *Journal for the Theory of Social Behaviour*.

[20] This is similar to Latour's concept of immutable mobiles. For the legal context see B Latour, 'Scientific Objects and Legal Objectivity—Portrait of the Conseil d'Etat as Laboratory' in A Pottage, (ed), *Making Persons and Things* (Cambridge, CUP, 2004).

[21] M Travers and JF Manzo, (eds), *Law in Action: Ethnomethodological and Conversation Analytic Approaches to Law* (Aldershot, Ashgate, 1997).

[22] A rich line of reference to approach becomings is provided by the laboratory studies in Science and Technology Studies (STS) examining work/research processes. See especially B Latour, *Science in Action: How to Follow Scientists and Engineers through Society* (Cambridge, MA, Harvard University Press, 1987) B Latour, *Pandora's Hope: Essay on the Reality of Science Studies* (Cambridge, MA, Harvard University Press, 1999); and B Latour and S Woolgar, *Laboratory Life: Social Construction of Scientific Facts* (New York, NY, Sage, 1979). By opening the black boxes of scientific practice ethnographers face the assembly of things and people. They turn back to the uncompleted bits and pieces in order to unfasten the complex, knotty, multifaceted nature of the later tidied, orderly and black-boxed 'facts'.

the eye-witness' identification of the perpetrator, or a psychological report on the accused' liability. It may be something seemingly minor that the researcher could fail to notice when studying the file on her own. To different extents, the heart of the case will possibly attract the attention of both parties, the prosecution and defence. This, again, depends on the stage of the matter: in the final stages, certain circumstances are presented as having dictated the case right from the beginning; during preliminary investigations, in contrast, certain foci are presented that may entirely vanish from the agenda in due course.

(3) *Tracing issues through paper trails*:   How can one trace issues through the files on their way to court? It is important here to identify when an issue is initially recorded (which does not mean that one gets to its origin) and how. Is it in an official letter, an internal memo, in one of the solicitor's to-do-lists or 'just' in a scribbled—not even filed—memo?

The counter-accusation: In a burglary case, I found the first entry of the 'self-harmer'-hypothesis in a file note on a telephone-conversation that the solicitor conducted with the co-accused partner of the client. During this telephone conversation, the young woman mentioned a talk with a neighbour. The neighbour made allegations about the complainant. She might have inflicted the reported/photographed injuries (deep cuts under her left eye) on herself. The co-accused was advised to inform her solicitor right away and to instruct him to take a statement from this neighbour. This piece of information, she added in the note, seems 'really important'.

From this point, the issue can be followed all through the file. Does it occur again? Where is it mentioned again and how? How is the issue fostered from one entry to the next? Every single file-entry is to be noted!

(4) *Activities related to the schedule of the proceeding*:   I gained a better overview of an issue's 'social career'[23] by placing it in the time-line of the proceeding in question. The date of the charge, of the indictment, of the Plea and Direction Hearing, of the deadlines for disclosure or the trial hearing provide vital contex-

---

[23] This metaphor is used in a wide range of studies. See, for example, A Cambrosio, C Limoges and D Pronovest, 'Representing Biotechnology: An Ethnography of Quebec Science Policy' in (1990) 20 *Social Studies of Science*; H Doering and S Hirschauer, 'Die Biographie der Dinge: Eine Ethnographie musealer Repräsentation' in K Amann and S Hirschauer, (ed), *Die Befremdung der eigenen Kultur: Zur Ethnographischen Herausforderung Soziologischer Empirie* (Frankfurt aM, Suhrkamp, 1997); and I Koptytoff, 'The cultural biography of things: commodification as process' in A Appadurai, (ed), *The Social Life of Things: Commodities in Cultural Perspective* (Cambridge, CUP, 1986).

tual orientation. When, relative to these stages in a case, does the issue arise? This background helps the researcher to get an idea of how arguments are channelled, adjusted and stimulated in the course of a case.

Time for preparation: The Pre-Direction Hearing took place two weeks ago. Today the matter is listed for an application by the defence asking for the full disclosure of the medical notes, reporting the medical history of the complainant. The prosecuting barrister applies for another adjournment: 'The medical report can be served within a month's time, my Lord'. The Counsel for the defence complains about the further delay and then accepts. In fact, nobody is really upset about the extra three weeks until the trial hearing—obviously apart from the defendant who is awaiting the trial in custody. Still, the defence has got plenty to do until the day in court. The account in the defence statement, for instance, was still not backed by any additional witness.

(5) *Reconstructive interviews*: How something becomes a key issue is not just a matter of file-analysis. The trusted researcher regularly faces instances of case- and file-work. Sometimes the issue to track down is a topic in a solicitor-client meeting or a conference with barrister (and whatever pre-trial meetings there are in other jurisdictions). Interviews with caseworkers are also useful: one could call these interviews as well biographical, although they do not deal with the biography of the interviewee but with the biography of a statement or narrative. The researcher can ask those involved about how a point did come about and was worked out.

(6) *Data-sheets*: In order to trace the career of a becoming through the course of the pre-trial procedure, I put the following information together. In the aforementioned case of burglary, my log entry took the following shape:

Date	Participants	Incident	Content	Function for case
12/6/03	Solicitor—co-accused	Telephone conversation	Neighbour claims that 'victim' is self-harmer	New line of argument + potential evidence for the defence-case

The log: The 'becoming' in this case can be described as the 'self-harmer statement'. Its trajectory commences with a telephone conversation, in which the co-accused mentions a rumour regarding her neighbour (the potential witness) and what he once claimed about the accuser ('Self-harmer'). According to this potential statement, she could have injured herself as she allegedly did several times before. It takes a lot more case-work (and entries) until the neighbour is enrolled as witness and until his statement is available as element of the defence. The rumour, for instance, needs to be documented in order to involve others. At a later point, it needs to be authorized or connected to an actor and his/her social credit. In court, the statement needs a human voice in order to be staged in front of a jury.

The career of this witness statement was traced through the whole case file and the related encounters. Each mentioning or reference triggered new entries in the data-sheet. The sheet, therefore, gathered together the traces left by the casework. The traces represent, as well as perform, this 'becoming' and the activities necessary to fully mobilise it.

D. FORMALISING COURSES OF MOBILISATION

Tracing mobilisation will not lead to singularised stories. As in the example above, the recruitment of witnesses can easily be put side by side with the recruitments in other cases. Such perspective across single cases requires some kind of formalisation. Here are some formal themes one can find in the logs which make possible further inquiries into the spatio-temporal characteristics of mobilisation.

> *Involvement and circulation:*   Who gets involved in the course of mobilisation? How, for instance, is a statement distributed within the defence ensemble before it is disclosed to the prosecution?[24] Who is excluded from the exchange? By following the log entries, one encounters a sequence of different circles: from one-to-one consultation to complex divisions of labour.
>
> *Rhythm and frequencies:*   How fast do statements circulate? What is the frequency of exchange in relation to the procedural stages? These queries led the researcher to examine pauses and clusters of case-work. They hint at lawyer's decisions on how to allocate and prioritise work. They reveal what participants might experience as the routine or thrilling phases of a legal case.

---

[24] As I noticed during my fieldwork in a law firm, the defence fosters its narratives and legal arguments throughout the pre-trial in a protected environment. Here, they collect valuable points, draw them together as one coherent case, pre-test the outcomes and repair the remaining weak links. The opponent is left out from the exchange of not yet presentable pre-products: first ideas, gossip, blueprints and tactics.

Social Careers: The 'becoming' has a social career in terms of its rise
(and perhaps fall) and its growing (or shrinking) weight and impact.
Applying this insight, the researcher can identify several stages of
acknowledgement and status attribution: from when it was just an
item of gossip, to a hopeful line of enquiry, up to a vital component
of the case in court. Most careers, however, are brief: statements stay
on the level of 'just ideas', neither fixed nor disputed.

The transformations of statements: Throughout the course of
preparation, the ways in which statements are delivered change.
Statements are not just written and spoken, but whispered, drafted
and read out. These shifts keep statements flexible and adjustable to
local purposes. They also trigger the 'returns and turns'[25] of voices
together with risks of incoherence. Statements are contingent in that
it is hard to account for all their future applications. Representational
projects are under threat especially by 'impulsive' statements, which
explains why lawyers insist on drafting statements before they turn
into public speech.

The unsaid: At the end of rather successful careers, the analyst
might become aware of statements that were on the one hand carefully chosen to represent the case in court, but on the other hand did not
make it to the witness box. This might call for some ethnographic
interviewing about the concrete circumstances, and those who took
the decision not to use this 'ready' piece of evidence in court.

Micro-functionalism: Each entry can be re-specified as solution for
certain problems that occur during mobilisation. A completed log,
read in this way, implies inventive queries for related projects of
mobilisation. Does the problem that is worked on during mobilisation
A occur in mobilisation B? If so, how is it solved (differently) in both
cases?

The analysis of courses of mobilisation provides some potentials for a cross-
comparative perspective. Crucial here is the hypothesis generating inven-
tiveness of the researcher. Beyond case-related story-telling, there is the need
to create analytical devices that open up the micro-perspective. The data
logs suggested above are just a starting point on the way to formalisation
and generalisation.[26] It remains the most challenging task to change from
the single-case perspective to a cross-case or even cross-cultural perspective.

[25] De Certeau, 1984, above, n 8, at 156.
[26] See as well the three-dimensional maps invented by time-geographers and discussed in
Giddens' theory of structuration.

E. THE SPECIFICITY OF THE DATA-BASE

These methodical instructions are, unfortunately, not without problems. They were developed for an English context—and based, therefore, on the body of data produced by this particular legal discourse. It is already clear that documented case-work varies considerably according to the level of court-systems (in this case, there were big differences between files for cases heard in the Magistrates' and Crown Courts). It also seems unlikely that another court-system will provide the same kind of inscriptions and files. This appears, from a comparative point of view, highly problematic. A study that looks at another legal setting will have to develop its own data-sheets and ways of completing them. There is no such thing as a standard method for all legal proceedings.

Mobilisation refers to an inscription apparatus that produces specifically formatted statements, such as the records in a case-file. It is worth asking why the English defence file provided such a 'rich resource' for the purpose of tracing mobilisation. How did the researcher's purpose meet with the lawyers' determination to organise, order, document, and report her/his ongoing case-work? Are there, to modify Garfinkel's study of record-keeping in hospitals, any 'good reasons for *good legal records*'?[27]

A few observations can be made about defence files in Crown Court cases:

> *Accounting:*   In the defence file, the solicitor in charge of the case employs a standardised system of book-keeping to ensure the accounting of the law firm's expenses and the granting and calculation of legal aid. According to this system, solicitors are asked to document all casework that takes longer than six minutes. These units—of telephoning, reading and writing letters, perusing the file and drafting statements—are recorded and later quantified for billing purposes. For this reason, one finds also work documented that does not lead anywhere: such as investigating offhand rumours or dirty gossip, or making careless presumptions in an early assessment.
>
> *Time-management:*   The lawyer in charge uses the file to reconstruct *what* is done so far and *what* needs to be done in the near future. Work that needs to be done is prompted by solicitors' diary notes, printed out and delivered every morning by the secretary. (The solicitor relies on these probably more than on his or her own memory.) The file's order and transparency are supposed to guarantee that the lawyer meets the many expectations, deadlines and duties that go along with defending a Crown Court case.

---

[27] H Garfinkel, '"Good" Organisational Reasons for "Bad" Clinic Records' in H Garfinkel, (ed), *Studies in Ethnomethodology* (Englewood-Cliffs, NJ, Prentice-Hall, 1967) 186.

Accumulation: The file is the object and source of casework. It secures, organises and pays out earlier investments. Day-to-day casework is principally about 'keeping the file in order' and 'doing what the file asks for (or requires)'. Before the trial, defence work largely takes place as interaction between the file and solicitor indicating the further transactions to be taken (with the client, witnesses, barrister and CPS). From this, strings of correspondence come together in the solicitor's office, the ensemble's centre of collaboration. They build up the case's archive guiding the next decisions to take.

Division of labour: Crown Court cases are handed over by the solicitor to a barrister, hired and instructed by the law firm to represent the defence in court. The barrister receives the main information for court through the 'brief to Counsel'. The division of labour (between solicitor and barrister) creates more transparency of the case related tactics, inquiries and decisions. The legal file is, in many ways, a semi-public object, very different from the ethnographer's field-notes. It is assembled and kept for a whole team conducting the case-work and accounting for it.

Will to completeness: 'Incompleteness' was a usual complaint or problem made about files, although they seemed to me—when compared to my own notes and narratives—amazingly comprehensive. However, solicitors are never fully satisfied. They complain: 'Where is the response to our letter?', 'Why is the statement still not signed?', 'When do I need to finish this brief?' Files are constantly accused of being 'incomplete' and therefore 'bad', which stimulates further work on the case.

The specificities of the data base raise a more general (methodological as well as political) problem that has been described by Star and Strauss as 'hidden work'.[28] There is a lot of 'private' work done by clients, witnesses or their peers that, due to the files' system of accountability, never finds its way into the legal records. The researcher may find glimpses of this hidden work in the all-too apparent tensions, concerns and fears raised during a legal case, and in the 'emotional' work of taking risks, overcoming worries, staying cool or restraining rage and anger. From the files, one can only imagine what it means for the client to get involved in the legal process.

Clusters and tension: Shortly before trials, one can witness the rising tension even amongst the professionals: a tighter schedule, an increasing assiduousness, an escalating busyness, a higher rate of correspondence, meetings and telephone consultations. Workdays become breathless before

---

[28] S Star and A Strauss, 'Layers of Silence, Arenas of Voice: The Ecology of Visible and Invisible Work' in (1999) 8 *Computer Supported Cooperative Work*.

the 'day of reckoning'. My own lists to fill in the circulation of messages show clusters before and during the days in court. The same 'clustering' of activities and tension might be true for defendants. They are unable to sleep the night before, because of the hard work of recalling their testimony. They have been told by their lawyers: 'Make sure you remember all of it! Do not confuse the dates!' In this way, the client is increasingly captured by the details of his or her own case.[29]

Performances in court are, hence, not just in danger of, in legal and technical terms, being badly prepared, but of being thwarted by, so to speak, the 'human factor'. In these ways, mobilisation hinges on partially unknown, mysterious qualities of allies, lying beyond the realm of the documented file. The achievements depend on aspects that are forcefully kept out, excluded, denied or rejected. In this way, legal work relies on 'hidden' dependencies and alliances, which can sometimes become 'weak links' of mobilisation, and undermine a carefully prepared case.

F. SOME CONCLUSIONS

Tracing mobilisation is by no means a new approach in social science or discourse analysis. Many of the ideas presented here stem from the empirical work done in interactionist ethnography, ethnomethodology and Actor Network Theory. Here, I would like to finish with some observations on the significance of this research methodology for socio-legal studies. How can it profit from this perspective?

The proposed research design, first of all, implies a critical reflection on socio-legal studies and its dominant research foci. How is it that either talk or text, either the drama in court or the rules of the books occupied socio-legal attention?[30] Does one, in the text-book manner, need to declare the primacy of either oral or written language in legal discourse? The analysis of mobilisation allows one to transcend these debates.

Despite the affinities with workplace studies, ethnomethodology, and Actor Network Theory, the analysis of mobilisation is not identical to these fields of research. Tracing mobilisation does not directly aim to grasp the social organisation of the law firm, the solicitor's workplace, or the legal

---

[29] This resembles Luhmann's observations on the increasing entanglement of the accused in the legal procedure and the rules that go with it. He or she buys, one might say, into the game and builds up a specific procedural history full of self-made decisions, victories and losses for which she/he will be held to account. See N Luhmann, *Legitimation durch Verfahren* (Frankfurt aM, Suhrkamp, 1989).

[30] See J Conley and W O'Barr, *Just Words. Law, Language and Power* (Chicago, IL, University of Chicago Press, 1998). For the active role of texts in a legal setting see M Lynch and D Bogen, *The Spectacle of History—Speech, Text, and Memory at the Iran-Contra Hearings* (Durham, NC, Duke University Press, 1996).

apparatus. It, moreover, focuses neither solely on local events, nor on the institutional talk. But what then does it offer? As I understand it, tracing mobilisation makes accessible representational projects in their socio-material course. The course includes various sites and layers of social praxis such as accumulative file-work, extended correspondence, or relatively self-driven events. This multi-sitedness directs the formation of legal discourse, and the involvement of subjects and objects.

As a micro-sociologist, I was firstly interested in how court hearings are interactively accomplished. This ethnomethodological query opened up 'regular' legal practice as contingent craftwork. It, furthermore, opened up the formation of (public) legal discourses in time: court hearings are achieved due to a temporal and personal division of labour; they are pre-configured but only partially predictable. One can go even further, stating that trials rest on the simultaneity of assorted temporalities and stabilities/flexibilities: from CA's turn-taking-machinery, to the pre-established narratives, to the accumulative files, to the court's manuals and the law codes. The analysis of mobilisation teaches about conditions of participation and involvement, and how voices are tuned on the way.

The temporal sensitivity of the proposed research design will contribute to a better understanding of the practical relation of pre-trial and trial, preparation and performance[31] in different jurisdictions. Mobilisation informs socio-legal studies about the diverse statuses of adversarial or inquisitorial, and lower or higher courts within projects of representation. Used in this way, the analysis of mobilisation provides useful frames, data and analytical tools for grounded socio-legal comparison.

---

[31] Preparation continues during the hearing. For example, the barrister takes notes that help in preparing the upcoming cross-examination or closing speech.

5

'Standpoint', 'Difference' and Feminist Research

SAMIA BANO

Building more inclusive ways of seeing requires scholars to take multiple views of their subjects, abandoning the idea that there is a singular reality that social science can discover.
(Margaret L. Andersen 1993:43)[1]

While a fair amount has now been published about relationships in the actual interview situation, much less has been written about researcher negotiation with people that they want to be in a study and about how participants themselves feel about being involved in particular pieces of research.
(Ann Phoenix 1994:50)[2]

THERE IS A growing feminist literature which seeks to understand the relationship between the experiences of women as complex, multiple and dynamic and which can only be understood in interaction with other identities and social structures. This intellectual strategy in feminist social research derives from the 'standpoint' of women and seeks to produce a 'feminist' subjectivity. With regard to understanding the complex lived experiences of women, standpoint theory draws upon feminist critiques of power to highlight the differential position women occupy within social, familial and legal life. More recently, however, standpoint theory has been criticized by black feminists, who argue that such approaches remain imbued with simplified and unqualified understandings of culture, religion, identity and community and hence subsequently fail to adequately engage

---

[1] ML Andersen, 'Studying Across Difference: Race, Class and Gender in Qualitative Research' in JH Stanfield and RM Dennis, (eds), *Race and Ethnicity in Research Methods* (Newbury Park, CA, Sage, 1993) 127–38.

[2] A Phoenix, 'Practising Feminist Research: The Intersection of Gender and "Race" in the Research Process' in M Maynard and J Purvis, (eds), *Researching Women's Lives from a Feminist Perspective* (London, Taylor & Francis, 1994) 49–72.

with the multiple positions women occupy in relation to race, ethnicity, class, family and community. Indeed, it is this complex reality that leads black feminists to draw upon the categories of 'difference' and 'translocational positionality', with the intersection of race, gender and class subordination to gain a more fuller understanding on the specificities of black women's lives.

This chapter draws upon these debates to explore the methodological dilemmas faced by the socio-legal researcher while collecting fieldwork data in the area of 'religious personal law' in Britain.[3] In doing so, it explores the methodological dilemmas in accessing, collecting and analysing data in an area of study that is confined to the 'private' sphere, is traditionally defined as non-legal and remains largely under-researched. Moreover, it questions whether these issues raise a specific set of ethical and methodological challenges for the feminist socio-legal researcher. Seeking to explore the ontological and epistemological tensions presented by feminist standpoint theory with cultural difference, it addresses the need to develop a multifaceted approach to conducting feminist social research that recognises complexity, difference and diversity within its analyses.

The chapter addresses three main issues. The first draws upon observational research to explore issues of 'access', 'consent' and 'disclosure' in undertaking empirical research with Shariah Councils in Britain. In doing so, it questions whether traditional research methods need to be used in specific ways when faced with a particular set of methodological issues.[4] This issue also relates to questions surrounding the centrality of privacy, the relationship between public and private 'space' and the situation where the researcher has little control over the research process.[5] The second issue draws upon debates on 'reflexivity' and the 'self' to analyse the role of the feminist researcher in conducting in-depth qualitative interviews. Here we draw upon debates on identity and cultural difference to consider how 'differences' may affect the research process and to question whether sharing a gender, ethnic or religious commonality with the interviewee leads to any difficulties and/or advantages.[6] It draws upon the concept of 'positioning(s)' to consider the limitations of categories such as 'insider/outsider' that fail to

---

[3] Personal laws are defined as 'customs' which, like English common law, are allowed as long as they do not conflict with English statutory law. Thus Muslims can get married in an Islamic way as long as the marriage is registered with the state. For an overview see SM Poulter, *Ethnicity, Law and Human Rights*, (Oxford, Clarendon Press, 1998).

[4] For an interesting discussion on the problems of conducting fieldwork on sensitive topics see MR Lee, *Doing Research on Sensitive Topics* (London, Sage, 1999).

[5] What has been deemed the 'politics and ethics' of social research. See P Atkinson and D Silverman, 'Kundera's Immortality: The Interview Society and the Invention of the Self' (1997) 3 *Qualitative Inquiry* 304–25.

[6] In particular it draws on the work of M Song and D Parker, 'Commonality, Difference and the Dynamics of Disclosure in In-depth Interviewing' (1998) 6 *Qualitative Research* 112–26.

capture not only the complex and varied experiences within the various groups under study but also obscures the richness and diverse experiences between the researcher and the researched.

The final part of the chapter addresses the issue of the researcher 'leaving the field' and explores ways of managing the personal relationships formed with one's informants.[7] If we take the view that the decision of the informants to participate in the research project may be conditional then we must also consider the implications that this may have upon the interpretation and presentation of data. In this way, questions can be raised about the interpretive process, and the chapter concludes by briefly considering the social and political implications of writing up research deemed 'politically sensitive'.

A. MUSLIM FAMILY LAW IN BRITAIN

Muslim family law, like other South Asian religious and customary corpuses of law defines the position of women in relation to marriage, divorce, child custody, dowry and inheritance.[8] It is often referred to as personal law as there have been some voices within the Muslim community in the UK demanding that a 'personal regime of law' be adopted for the Muslim community as a whole within the area of family law.[9] In the case of Islam, Muslim Family Law is subject to interpretation by different religious leaders and communities as there is no one comprehensive Islamic legal system but varieties exist according to ethnic or religious backgrounds.[10] There are two main groups of Muslims in Britain, Sunni and Shi'a Muslims, and the practice of Islam within these groups varies in accordance with the different Shariah schools of thought. There are also many class and sectarian divisions, operating according to different Islamic codes of laws; for example, Ismaili Muslims are part of the wider Shi'a group but practice distinct laws applicable only to them. It is, therefore, difficult to speak of 'Muslim family law' in Britain when it varies so widely according to ethnic and sectarian affiliation.

---

[7] See SJ Taylor, 'Leaving the Field: Research, Relationships and Responsibilities' in D Sliverman, (ed), *Qualitative Research, Theory, Method and Practice* (London, Sage, 1998) 274–82.

[8] For an overview see S Ali, *Gender and Human Rights in Islam and International Law: Equal before Allah? Equal before Man?* (London, Kluwer Law International, 2000).

[9] This demand was first made by a group of religious scholars in Birmingham 1977 to Home Office ministers and was rejected. For an interesting discussion on the nature of these demands see JS Nielsen, 'Emerging Claims of Muslim Populations in Matters of Family Law in Europe' (1992) 13 *Research Papers: Muslims in Europe*.

[10] For example, the Islamic personal laws which exist in the Indian subcontinent vary greatly in comparison with those which exist in Iran or Iraq.

Existing literature presents the socio-legal reality of Muslims in Britain as a complex scenario whereby official and customary laws interact to produce a new set of hybrid laws.[11] In attempting to develop a conceptual framework, which both adopts a 'postmodern approach' to the study of law and recognises pluralism and diversity in social life, Menski employs the analytical framework by the jurist Masaji Chiba[12] and constructs a legal model that he defines as 'Angrezi Sharia'. According to Menski, Asian Muslims in Britain have not simply given up Islamic law but combine Islamic law and English law to form 'Angrezi Sharia'. As part of this complex process, redefined Muslim laws in Britain have become 'hybrid' and thus 'all ethnic minorities in Britain marry twice, divorce twice and do many other things several times in order to satisfy the demands of concurrent legal systems'.[13] This complex socio-legal reality of Muslims in Britain also raises fundamental questions of whether, in a multicultural and heterogeneous society, there must be a commitment to cultural diversity and pluralism in the area of family life, just as in other areas, and whether the state should uphold and support a diversity of family arrangements. This raises a number of important conceptual and theoretical questions regarding the relation between individual and groups rights, how these are distinguished and how clashes between individual and group rights may be reconciled. Embedded in these is the key question of what makes a community a community of rights? Does the state, in granting individuals the right to enjoy their culture, have an obligation to foster that culture and ensure its survival? These issues also raise questions on what we mean by the term 'community'. Communities nest within one another: local, national, and global. They also intersect: British Muslims belong to the global Muslim *umma*, for example. Some individuals may regard the recognition of a cultural/religious practice as a 'right' and by other members of the same community as a means of oppression. A particular cause for concern for liberal feminist theorists has been whether the practice of personal laws within the familial context leads to the unequal treatment of women within these communities. This area of work has been couched within the context of tensions between multiculturalism and feminism.[14]

---

[11] There is emerging literature in this area. See D Pearl and W Menski, *Muslim Family Law* (London, Sweet & Maxwell, 1998); SM Poulter, *Ethnicity, Law and Human Rights*, (Oxford, Clarendon Press, 1998); I Yilmaz, 'Muslim Law in Britain: Reflections in the Socio-Legal Sphere and Differential Legal Treatment' (2001) 20 *Journal of Muslim Minority Affairs* 353–360.

[12] See Pearl and Menski, 1998, n 11; and M Chiba, *Asian Indigenous Law in Interaction with Received Law* (London, Kegan Paul International, 1986).

[13] See above, n 11, at 75.

[14] Moller Okin argues, such tensions become especially clear when we consider a controversial proposal endorsed by some multiculturalists: to provide cultural minorities with 'group rights' as a way to preserve those minorities from undue pressure on their ways of life. See SM Okin, *Is Multiculturalism Bad for Women?* (Princeton, NJ, Princeton University Press, 1999).

It is within this context of liberal multiculturalism that we have seen the emergence and development of unofficial non-statutory bodies identified as Shariah Councils in Britain. Framed as sites upon which family law matters are resolved according to Muslim family law, they have developed frameworks that are characterized by specific cultural and religious norms and values. This mobilisation of communities challenges the hegemonic power of state law and unsettles the multicultural project in its attempt to reconfigure social and legal discourse in matters of family law. Most interestingly, for the socio-legal scholar, this process opens up the conceptual space in which to see in evidence the multiple legal and social realities in operation, within the larger context of state law, liberal multiculturalism and rights discourse.

B. DEFINING THE RESEARCH QUESTION(S)

The central methodological questions for this study relate to formulating ways to observe how Shariah Councils operate in practice, and to encourage British Pakistani Muslim women to speak about their experiences of using Shariah Councils to obtain a Muslim divorce. The first method, which comprised observation of Shariah Council 'proceedings', was chosen for a number of reasons. As discussed earlier, existing research documents the development of Shariah Councils in Britain as evidence of an emerging parallel legal system. Thus the socio-legal reality of Muslims in Britain is presented as a complex scenario whereby official and customary laws interact to produce a new set of hybrid laws.[15] The present study attempts to problematize this approach by examining the gendered nature of the informal legal sphere(s). In doing so, it deconstructs the binary oppositions of 'state law' and 'customary law' and seeks instead to explore the contested 'space(s)' that Shariah Council's occupy as an empirical reality rather than a theoretical construct. Observational research included observing counselling and mediation sessions, interviews with Shariah Council scholars and observation of 'court' proceedings when a religious divorce certificate was issued.

The second method comprised in-depth qualitative interviews with 25 Pakistani Muslim women. The interviews sought to elicit the experiences of women using Shariah Councils to obtain a Muslim divorce. It is the 'voice' of the women that the research seeks to bring out and hence a feminist

---

[15] See I Yilmaz, 'Law as Chameleon: The Question of Incorporation of Muslim Personal Law into English Law' (2001) 21 *Journal of Muslim Minority Affairs* 297–308.

approach to interviewing is adopted.[16] In particular, it explores their motivations for using the Shariah Councils, drawing upon their experiences of marriage and analysing strategies to obtain a religious divorce. In doing so it considers how women balance social expectation based on cultural duties with religious obligations and how gender frames the relations of power on which negotiations may be based within the family and unofficial decision-making bodies.[17]

C. OBSERVATION RESEARCH ON 'SHARIAH COUNCILS'

Shariah Councils operate as unofficial legal bodies specialising in providing advice and assistance on Muslim family law matters. They are neither unified nor represent a single school of thought but instead are made up of various different bodies representing the different schools of thought in Islam.[18] In essence, the Shariah Council has three main functions: mediation and reconciliation; issuing Muslim divorce certificates; and producing expert opinion reports on matters of Muslim family law and custom to the Muslim community,[19] solicitors and courts. In addition to providing advice and assistance on matters of Muslim law, Shariah Councils have also been set up to promote and preserve Islam within British society.[20] The process of dispute resolution, therefore, is produced through various discursive practices. That is, Shariah Councils must be understood in relation to the locus of power in which they are embedded. Similarly, the emergence of Shariah Councils in Britain can be traced to a diverse set of social processes. According to Yilmaz[21] there are four conditions under which Shariah Councils emerge in Britain. Firstly, under Muslim tradition, family issues

---

[16] Qualitative feminist studies explore women's accounts through in-depth interviewing, open questions and qualitative analysis. See for example S Reinharz, *Feminist Methods in Social Research* (Oxford, OUP, 1992); L Stanley and S Wise, *Breaking Out Again* (London, Routledge, 1988).

[17] For a fascinating study on the relationship between gender relations, power, family and legal relations see A Griffiths, *In the Shadow of Marriage: Gender and Justice in an African Community* (Chicago, IL, University of Chicago Press, 1997).

[18] The four ancient Islamic schools of Sunni thought can be broadly categorized as Hanafi, Maliki, Shafi'i and Hanabali. For an in-depth analysis on the historical development of these schools see NJ Coulson, *A History of Islamic Law* (Edinburgh, EUP, 1964).

[19] Shariah Councils also issue fatwas which can simply be translated as a ruling from a religious scholar to members of the Muslim community over a contested issue. Observation research reveals that at some Shariah Councils the scholars spend considerable time deliberating on whether to issue fatwas. The outcomes of these fatwas are not known but this certainly raises interesting questions on how the community attempts to deal with local conflicts within the boundaries of the 'Muslim community' and the extent to which these processes may conflict with state law.

[20] Bunt provides a fascinating account on the role of unofficial decision-making bodies within Pakistani Muslim communities in Birmingham. See G Bunt, 'Decision Making Concerns in British Islamic Environments' (1998) 19 *Islam and Christian-Muslim Relations* 103–13.

[21] See above, n 15.

are purposively left to 'extra judicial' regulation and diasporic communities continue this tradition and resolve disputes within this sphere. Secondly, Muslims do not recognise the authority and legitimacy of western secular law on par with Muslim law and, therefore, deliberately choose to resolve disputes through a non-adversarial process. Thirdly, the familial notions of honour and shame prevent familial disputes from being discussed in the 'public sphere' and subsequently religious laws are given greater potency and legitimacy within the communities. And finally, the failure of the state to recognize these plural legal orders has led to the development of these 'alternative' dispute resolution processes within the private sphere. In short, what we see in this analysis is the development of a parallel legal system in opposition to state law.

D. RESEARCH ON 'SENSITIVE' TOPICS

Conducting research on 'sensitive' issues raises a specific set of ethical and methodological challenges. Sieber and Stanley define sensitive topics as those studies in which there are 'potential consequences or implications, either directly for the participants in the research or for the class of individuals represented by the research'.[22] This can include topics that involve taboos for the local community, for example sex or death or topics which may be sensitive in relation to the socio-political context in which the research is undertaken.[23]

Research on Shariah Councils can be deemed 'sensitive' for a number of reasons. Firstly, issues of marriage and divorce embody notions of familial honour and shame and consequently remain confined to the private spheres of family and home. The implications of discussing private matters through what is ultimately viewed as a public forum can have detrimental effects for the women and their families. In the observation of Shariah Councils, a number of scholars voiced concern about the implications of discussing personal matters of marriage and divorce 'in public' with a complete stranger. It became apparent that my presence was deemed an 'intrusive threat' by some Shariah Councils since I was attempting to gain entry into areas deemed 'private' by respondents, their families and the communities to which they belonged. One religious scholar explained,

> You must understand confidentiality is of utmost importance in our work. It is very difficult for our people to discuss these issues and we spend a lot of time and effort convincing them to seek our help. Divorce is shunned in our communities

---

[22] Quoted in Lee 1999, above, n 4, at 49.
[23] Quoted in Lee 1999, above, n 10. See JD Brewer, 'Sensitivity as a Problem in Field Research: A Study of Routine Policing in Northern Ireland' (1990) 33 *American Behavioural Scientist* 578–93.

and rightly so. It should not be given the air of respectability but that doesn't mean we condemn those who want to divorce. Divorce is permitted in Islam and we work with Muslims to achieve the best possible situation ... to allow someone they don't know to sit through our sessions would mean they would lose our trust and confidentiality.

A further issue concerned the rise of Islamaphobia and the perception of 'risk' associated with collaborating with the research project.[24] Again discussions with religious scholars revealed concern about the possibility of such research contributing to the demonisation of Muslims and what one scholar described as 'the growing climate of fear and discrimination against Muslims'. One Muslim female worker at a Shariah Council voiced concern about the possibility of the research contributing to existing stereotypes of Muslim women as passive victims of archaic religious traditions.

> It's quite understandable why Muslim women don't want to contribute to research projects because mostly we're presented as some kind of alien species, especially if we choose to practise our faith. For example discussion normally is confined to why we would choose to wear the hijab ... well if we're Muslims why shouldn't we? And also you must remember that its not that many of us are reluctant to discuss issues such as marriage and divorce in a public space but it's the lack of tolerance, and understanding in this space that makes us reluctant to engage.

There were also concerns from religious scholars on the presentation of data. One scholar informed me, 'We discussed your request at our weekly meeting and a number of us are concerned about what will happen to the material once you've completed your project.'

When access to observational research was permitted it was made clear that it was on the basis that as a Muslim researcher I was expected to present that data in a fair and accurate way. What then can be said about the ethics of conducting research under such conditions? Perhaps not surprisingly, this link between private experiences and public discourses on Islamaphobia raises questions regarding the theoretical framework upon which the research is undertaken. For example, Lee suggests that the researcher must provide a 'framework of trust' based upon confidentiality and a non-condemnatory attitude that in turn allows them to encourage those under study to confront issues that may be perceived as 'personally threatening and potentially painful'.[25] Moreover, we must remind ourselves

---

[24] The emergence of a new form of cultural racism directed at Muslims has been identified as Islamaphobia. In 1997 The Runnymede Trust in their report on Islamaphobia cited the stereotypical assumptions on the position of women within Islam, arranged marriages and the defining of Muslims and Muslim leaders as inherently 'fanatical' as examples of this new form of racism. See Runnymede Trust, *Islamaphobia: A Challenge for us All* (London, Runnymede Trust, 1997).

[25] Lee, 1999, above, n 4, at 98.

that 'sensitive' research can only be understood as 'sensitive' according to the context and conditions under which it is situated. In this way, the necessity presents itself for all researchers to address their own religious, moral and political beliefs.

In this study, gaining access to some Shariah Councils for observation research proved difficult, lengthy and problematic. It is well documented that the aim of observation fieldwork is to provide a rich insight into the organisation under study. Yet this process can be limited when access to private organisations is controlled and in some cases blocked by its 'gatekeepers'.[26] Some writers point out that the 'access processes' need to be more fully explored. For example, Lee complains that 'neither has much attention been paid to patterns of access and non-access across studies, or to the potential consequences of differential accessibility to some settings rather than others'.[27] In this study, the absence of direct measures—a result of restricted access to Shariah Councils—meant that comparisons between the bodies could not be sufficiently drawn.

This raises the question of the ways in which gatekeepers may exercise their power to curtail or prevent access. Form[28] points out this unequal relationship leads to the researcher 'bargaining in the access situation'. He identifies this as the 'politics of distrust' that can only be overcome if there is trust between the gatekeeper and researcher, even though there may be differences of opinion. In Morrill, et al,[29] the researchers found that identifying gatekeepers acts as a useful analytic device for learning about the vocabularies of structure in an organization, and that successfully managing gatekeepers requires that one understands the vocabularies of structure in use in an organization. For other scholars, the issue of 'mistrust' can only be overcome if the boundaries of the research relationship are clearly demarcated prior to the start of fieldwork. For example, Lofland and Lofland[30] devise a series of questions which the researcher must address before the research begins. These include, 'am I reasonably able to get along with these people? Do I truly like a reasonable number of them, even though I disagree with their view of the world? Why did I pursue research when it became obvious that it was going to be difficult to maintain in the long run?' These questions provide a useful criterion to explore the issue of ethics in fieldwork research but we must also remain aware of a new and different set of ethical questions arising during the course of the fieldwork.

---

[26] See M Punch, *The Politics and Ethics of Fieldwork* (London, Sage, 1986).

[27] Lee, 1999, above, n 4, at 121.

[28] See K Form, *Approaches to Social Enquiry* (Cambridge, Polity Press, 1983).

[29] See C Morrill, 'Towards an Organizational Perspective on Identifying and Managing Formal Gatekeepers' (1999) 22 *Qualitative Sociology* 51–72.

[30] J Lofland and L Lofland, *Analyzing Social Settings* (Belmont, CA, Wadsworth, 1994) 94.

In this study, observational research revealed a number of women report-ing incidences of domestic violence. At one Shariah Council, the women who did request professional help were given little guidance as to the avail-able services. Paradoxically my previous work had been in the area of domestic violence and hence I was in a position to advise them. Yet I was acutely aware that access to this particular Shariah Council had been grant-ed on the basis that there would be no direct contact by me with any of the women using its services. In this instance, I decided to approach the reli-gious scholar offering a list of relevant agencies for the women to contact. I was politely informed that my advice was not required.[31] This example illustrates the ethical issues concerning responsibility towards the respon-dents. For Mason, the researcher has a 'moral duty' to overcome potential difficulties that can be achieved if the researcher is aware of which groups or individuals may be affected by framing the research in a particular way.[32] The issue of trust is, therefore, central to gaining both consent and access into private organisations. Hammersley and Atkinson[33] explain,

> Whether or not people have knowledge of social research, they are often more concerned with what kind of a person the researcher is than with the research itself. They will try and gauge how far he or she can be trusted, what he or she might be able to offer as an acquaintance or a friend, and perhaps also how eas-ily he or she could be manipulated or exploited.

One of the interesting aspects of observational fieldwork is the exploration of the role of the researcher in the field. Coffey describes 'the marginality and presence' of the researcher as critical to exploring, 'how identities are constructed, reproduced, established, mediated, changed or challenged over the fieldwork process'.[34] The identity of the researcher raises questions on how the researcher may affect the outcome of observational research.

In this study, the ways in which the dynamics of gender, race, culture, class and religious identity interacted with the social setting under study was an important focal point of analysis. For example, did my gender affect the behaviour of the subjects (religious scholars and users) during observa-tional research? In her research with Kenyan informants, Oboler found that being pregnant increased her rapport with the informants.[35] Yet the process

---

[31] In the study only one Shariah Council adopted this approach whereas the other 3 Shariah Councils informed me that they contacted local Muslim women's organisations when con-fronted with the issue of domestic violence.

[32] J Mason, *Qualitative Researching* (London, Sage, 1996) 30.

[33] M Hammersley and P Atkinson, *Ethnography: Principles in Practice* (London, Tavistock, 1983) 78.

[34] See A Coffey, *The Ethnographic Self: Fieldwork and the Representation of Identity* (London, Sage, 1999) 22.

[35] See RS Oboler, 'For Better or Worse: Anthropologists and Husbands in the Field' in TL Whitehead and ME Conway, (eds), *Self, Sex and Gender in Cross-Cultural Fieldwork* (Urbana, IL, University of Illinois Press, 1986) 28–51.

of 'identity construction' is complex and at most times subtle. Prior to field-work, very little thought had been given to how I should negotiate my presence. It had been assumed that my religious and cultural background as a Pakistani Muslim woman would grant easier access to Shariah Councils. My assumptions proved to be both real and misleading. Over the course of the fieldwork, it became apparent that some scholars were happy for me to observe mediation sessions as they believed that Muslim women would be sympathetic to a Muslim woman conducting such research. And in some instances this was clearly the case. For example, on two occasions female clients requested that I sit next to them for support. On other occasions, however, I was asked to leave the sessions when the client was visibly uncomfortable in revealing private matters in the presence of a stranger. The 'self' in the field, therefore raises complex issues.

In this study access, though limited, was granted on the basis of privacy, trust and confidentiality and only with the informed consent of clients. For example, prior to each mediation session the client was informed of my presence and, if any objections were raised, I was refused permission. Finally, it was agreed that all feedback of the study and copies of interview transcripts would be made available to the Shariah Councils.

E. INTERVIEWING PAKISTANI MUSLIM WOMEN

Feminist ethnographic research emphasises notions of 'reflexivity' and 'situated knowledge(s)' where the relationship between the respondent and the interviewer is acknowledged and recognised and thus becomes part of the data and not external to it.[36] It contests the traditional constructions of 'knowledge' and 'society' defined within a structuralist paradigm and underlined by patriarchal norms and values. The feminist approach emphasizes the personal and subjective experiences of the researched subject, that can produce invaluable data. Here the researchers are encouraged to place themselves in the position of the researched in order to understand the dynamics of the relationship between the two and locate all research within a historical and contextual setting. Using her research on 'motherhood', Oakley[37] argues that a feminist subjective approach to interviewing is central to establishing a 'rapport' with female respondents, gaining their trust

---

[36] See for example S Harding, (ed), *Feminism and Methodology* (Bloomington, IN, Indiana University Press, 1987). Such issues are central to the research. It allows the researcher to structure an interview schedule in such a way that the researcher is in a position to ask probing questions which may elicit fuller answers. The respondent may also feel that they are in a position to think about their responses and they are given the time and the space to do so. They may answer a question, move on and later decide they want to return to that particular question and they are able to do so.

[37] See A Oakley, 'Gender, Methodology and People's Ways of Knowing: Some Problems with Feminism and the Paradigm Debate in Social Science' (1998) 32 *Sociology* 707–31.

and thus enhancing their willingness to take part in the research. Reinharz[38] puts forward a participatory model of research that aims to produce non-hierarchical, non-authoritarian and non-manipulative research relationships. This approach has led to the development of 'standpoint theories' whereby the focus of the research is on the experiences of women from the perspective of women themselves. Such research is located within a historical and political context, which gives it the space for potential social and political change in the lives of women. Given the diversity of this approach, we are able to explore the experiences of Pakistani Muslim women using Shariah Councils within a wider socio-political framework.

More recently black feminists have drawn on the concepts of 'difference' and 'translocational positionality' to inform a feminist approach to social research. The concept of difference emerged in response to the essentialism of much thinking on race and ethnicity. Hall[39] celebrates difference through the construction of new ethnic identities while interrogating traditional understandings of culture and ethnicity. For feminists, the notion of difference has been articulated around the concept of 'situated knowledges' and 'situatedness'[40] where female subjectivity introduces alternative narratives.

Yet this epistemological position of difference has been subject to extensive critique. Anthias points out that the debates on difference have ignored the dynamics of gender and class inequalities.[41] The focus on difference between groups risks the perils of cultural relativism which homogenise cultural difference in opposition to otherness. Instead, Anthias reformulates difference in terms of 'imaginings around boundaries' and 'hierarchical difference'.[42] This reformulation of difference re-evaluates the ways women are situated within different and often conflicting categories of race, gender, class and within the institutions of family, home and community. It recognises the existing power relations within these spheres that give rise to a complex interplay of values. Therefore, the concept of difference in this study is employed as a conceptual tool to challenge the existing patterns of domination and exclusion within social and legal processes.

In her work Anthias introduces the notion of 'translocational positionality' which provides the potential to recognise the importance of context and location in relation to shifting positions and identities: 'A translocational positionality is one structured by the interplay of the different locations and their (at times) contradictory effects. The "translocational" acts to fissure

---

[38] Reinharz 1988, above, n 16.

[39] S Hall, 'The Multi-Cultural Question' in B Hesse, (ed), *Un/settled Multiculturalisms* (London, Zed Books, 2000).

[40] See above, n 16.

[41] F Anthias, 'Beyond Feminism and Multiculturalism: Locating Difference and the Politics of Location' (2002) 25 *Women's Studies International Forum* 275–86.

[42] Anthias, 2002, above, n 41 at 279.

the certainties of fixed singular locations by constructing potentially contradictory positionalities.'[43]

On a practical level, this involves recognizing women may be in a position of dominance or subordination at particular times and contexts. In this way, individuals are actively engaged in the process of cultural contestation, renewal and change.

This analysis is useful for it reminds us that we need to draw upon theoretical approaches that recognise contradictions and ambiguities in women's positions within families and communities. In this way, the binaries of insider/outsider become destabilised where one may be an insider and an outsider simultaneously in relation to different dimensions of power and hierarchical difference. The purposefulness of this approach is recognizing the complexity and difference of women's lives but also understanding how their positions within the family and community may be fragile and potentially exploitative. This complements the 'intersectional' approach, developed by the writers Crenshaw[44] and Volpp[45] who point out that race, class, gender and other systemic oppressions work through rather than alongside each other.

F. RESEARCHING ACROSS GENDER, ETHNICITY AND RELIGION

There has been much discussion over the issue of race matching in conducting interviews. The argument is rooted within 'realist epistemology', which holds that there is some kind of 'unitary truth' which interviewers should obtain. It is believed that a black researcher is more able to blend in with a black interviewee and, therefore, get an insight that may otherwise not be possible. Constructivist theories differ from this perspective, arguing instead that all accounts from interviews can only be understood in the context of the interview and any information given cannot be taken to mean the 'truth'. This raises the question of whether there are unique methodological obstacles in conducting research among minority communities. In particular, questions have arisen in relation to the unequal power relationship of a white researcher conducting research on non-white communities. It is argued that white scholars can only produce incomplete data as interviewees view them with distrust, hostility and exclusion. This view has, however, been challenged by a number of theorists.

---

[43] Anthias, *ibid*, at 278.
[44] See K Crenshaw, 'Demarginalising the Intersection of Race and Sex: A Black Feminist Critique of Antidiscrimination Doctrine' in K Crenshaw, *Feminist Theory and Antiracist Politics* (Chicago, IL, University of Chicago Forum) 139.
[45] See L Volpp, 'Talking "Culture": Gender, Race, Nation and the Politics of Multiculturalism' (1996) 96 *Columbia Law Review* 1573–617.

Among them is the feminist writer Hill-Collins[46] who develops the notion of 'outsiders within' where white researchers are deemed capable of conducting research on minority communities but in doing so must ensure that they recognise the influence of institutional racism in shaping and developing their research. Therefore, the question becomes not whether white researchers should conduct research on minority communities but whether their interpretation should be considered the most authoritative. Indeed, there can be both advantages and disadvantages. In her research on Black women, Andersen writes that she was aware that the women might not have reported the same things to her as they may have done to a black interviewer and that her data may, therefore, have been impartial and incomplete.[47] She goes on to argue that her data also revealed women telling her that they were able to speak to her openly and freely without barriers, whereas they may not have been able to do this with a black interviewer. She thus adopted a self-reflexive approach where her role in the research was pivotal in gaining the trust of the respondents in order to elicit data that was not imbued with problems of power. She notes that:

> Developing analyses that are inclusive of race, class and gender also requires that discussions of race, class and gender be thoroughly integrated into debates about research process and the analysis of data. This requires an acknowledgement of the complex, multiple and contradictory identities and realities that shape our collective experience.[48]

G. NEGOTIATING PARTICIPATION

In this study, a very specific group of British Pakistani Muslim women were investigated. All the women were from Birmingham, Bradford and London and aged between 25–40 years old and from a variety of socio-economic backgrounds. I developed an interview method, which allowed women to raise and discuss issues that were important to them, and not only those in which I was interested. All the women were offered anonymity for their accounts and have been given pseudonyms.

The logic of why a sample of British Pakistani Muslim women was chosen for research as opposed to 'Muslim women' as a general category is two-fold. Firstly, as a result of the complex and changing nature of identity this approach provides the opportunity to explore the subtleties of cultural difference between Muslim women. In this way, we are also able to provide an insight into the dynamics, representation and practice of power

---

[46] PH Collins, 'Learning from the Outsider Within: The Sociological Significance of Black Feminist Thought' (1996) 33 *Social Problems* 14–32.
[47] Andersen, 1993, above, n 1.
[48] Andersen, *ibid*, p 137.

within Muslim communities. To categorize all British Pakistani Muslim women as belonging to an homogenous Muslim community presumes the primacy of a universal religious Muslim identity. It prevents one from exploring ambivalence and antagonism outside the binaries of insider/outsider, Muslim/non-Muslim and subordinate/dominant.[49] This does not mean, however, that some British Pakistani Muslim women do not embrace this unifying identity that homogenizes cultural and religious difference. Evidence also suggests, however, that there are also unique differences between and within the category of 'Muslim women', and by focusing upon one group of women we are able to explore the conditions under which they develop strategies to obtain a Muslim divorce and participate in family and community mediation. Hence, we can explore how identities may be ambivalent, situational and strategic.

Negotiations with female respondents were long and difficult. Matters concerning marriage and divorce are largely confined to the private sphere of the family and home and women are often involved in lengthy and complex negotiations. They may, therefore, be reluctant to discuss such personal issues in a 'public forum' as epitomised by a research project. It is also important to remember that women are seen as carriers of 'collective honour' in the family and community and they play a central role in the symbolic reproduction of 'community' and its survival.[50] Matters concerning marriage and in particular divorce are closely tied to the honour of the family and the implications of private details becoming public maybe too great for the women. Existing research literature fails adequately to address this issue of the specific methodological obstacles faced when conducting research with diasporic communities in Britain. For example, it is commonly believed that respondents agree to take part in a study once they meet the researcher, yet this is not always the case.[51] In this study, consent still depended upon lengthy discussions and 'assurances' on the specific ways in which the research would be used and the importance of confidentiality and anonymity. Furthermore, only 25 of the 45 women who were approached and who fitted the criteria for the in-depth study agreed to take part. The other women failed to return phone calls or said that they were not ready to share their personal experiences. I spent a lot of time thinking of how I could contact the women and once contact had been made how I could stay in touch with them. A number of women expressed their concern about participating in research that might contribute to the stereotype of Muslim

---

[49] This approach draws upon the work of HK Bhabba. See HK Bhabba, 'Cultures in Between' in D Bennett, (ed), *Multicultural States: Rethinking Difference and Identity* (London, Routledge, 1998).

[50] See for example F Anthias and N Yuval-Davis, *Racialized Boundaries: Race, Nation, Gender, Colour and Class and the Anti-Racist Struggle* (London, Routledge, 1992).

[51] Phoenix, 1994, above, n 2.

women as victims of a patriarchal cultural/religious system. Some women, therefore, refused to take part in the research as they felt that it might be more damaging to them rather than beneficial. Out of 25 women, 13 informed me that the implications of divulging private details would affect not only themselves but also their immediate families. Rubina explained, 'I have to be careful about what I say … . It's not that I don't trust you but I have to think about what will happen if what I say gets back to my family'. Assurances of complete confidentiality and anonymity were not enough to convince some of the women.

This raises the question as to *why* respondents may choose to take part in a research project. Phoenix points out that respondents have their own varied reasons that 'include simple curiosity; desire to talk and to be listened to; to help with the researcher's training or the aims of the study; [and] to complain about the aims of the study or about the specific kinds of research'.[52] In this sample, the women were asked why they had chosen to contribute to this study and their responses were both diverse and conflicting. For some women the study provided an opportunity to put across their version of events. Others were keen to challenge stereotypes of Muslim women as passive, and finally a small number of women hoped the research would hasten the introduction of Muslim family law into English law. The period of negotiation between the researcher and respondent to participate in the study is a formidable time for the researcher. It is during this time that the respondents are in the powerful position in refusing to take part and possibly curtailing the objectives of the project. Even when consent is given, however, negotiations continue. In fact, discussions with the women over how the research would proceed and develop continued once the interviews had been completed. Out of 25 women, 8 expressed concern over what would happen to the interview tapes once the research had been completed. Brannen suggests that participants respond favourably to some methods and not to others when there is an overlap between the concerns of researchers and those of participants, and 'where both parties are in search of similar explanations'.[53] Perhaps, somewhat unsurprisingly, the shared experiences of other women were important.

H. DISCLOSURE AND POWER IN INTERVIEWS: AN UNEQUAL RELATIONSHIP?

There has been much discussion in the research literature over the unequal power relations between the interviewer and interviewee. Feminist writers

---

[52] Phoenix, *ibid*, at 56.
[53] J Brannen, *New Mothers at Work: Employment and Childcare* (London, Unwin Hyman, 1988) 324.

point to the unequal relationship, with the interviewer having greater power over disclosure and instead they put forward a method which emphasizes notions of 'rapport' and 'self-disclosure' on the part of the interviewee. Through a shared gender identification, female interviewers are able to establish in the interview a 'rapport' that ultimately leads to greater disclosure. This approach has been challenged, however, for its failure to recognise that power relations transcend gender identification. Wise[54] points out that class, ethnic and religious factors must be taken into account. Similarly, in this study, I was positioned in different ways by the interviewees in terms of a perceived cultural, religious and gender identity. This raises interesting questions that challenge the traditional research orthodoxy, which argues that the researcher is in a more powerful position. For example, was the research process affected when I was perceived in ways which I found objectionable? If I felt I was perceived in an objectionable way, how did the interviewee respond to being objectified? This process of objectification is usually observed where the interviewer and interviewee are racially/ethnically different. Song and Parker point out, however, that objectification can also happen where the interviewer and interviewee share similar racial/ethnic characteristics.[55] In addition, the research process must take into account the ways in which interviewees position interviewers and how they are perceived and constructed. Researchers may feel, for various reasons, that they want to respond to positionings themselves and that this is an integral part of any interview dynamic. These positionings by both the interviewer and the interviewee are important as they may affect the research process. For example, the interviewees might withhold or disclose certain kinds of information, depending upon their assumptions about the researcher; interviewees might describe aspects of their lives and their identities and compare themselves to the researcher.

Likewise, this raises the question of the extent to which the interviewer ought to divulge personal details during the course of the interview. Jane Ribbens notes:

> It does seem to me that to talk about yourself completely openly in an interview situation might significantly shift what is said to you, in fairly unpredictable ways. We need more work on the various advantages and disadvantages of such different approaches. Perhaps what we should be sensitive to, is to take our cue from the person being interviewed.[56]

This approach can make an important contribution to the research process. In spite of the obvious difficulties concerning confidentiality, the interviewees in this project did directly and indirectly ask me questions, and I

---

[54] Stanley and Wise, 1988, above, n 16.
[55] Song and Parker, 1998, above n 6.
[56] J Ribbens, 'Interviewing—An "Unnatural Situation?"' (1996) 12 *Women's Studies International Forum* 579.

responded as openly as I could. Sometimes the discussions went on once the tape recorder had been switched off. This may be important not only for the research but also for the researcher in order to make clear their own contribution and commitment to the research.

I. COMMONALITIES AND DIFFERENCES

Prior to and during the interviews the respondents discussed at great length their own religious identity, often in relation to me. For example, prior to the interview Safia explained that she was willing to take part in the research because of its focus on Muslim women and Islam. Being Muslim was of central importance to her and she referred to this throughout the interview. Drawing upon her experiences Song explains she was put into a position whereby she found herself having to decide how far she would respond to the way she was 'positioned' by her interviewees.[57] Similarly, I found myself in a comparable position and pondered long and hard as to whether I should discuss my religious identity with the interviewees. I was concerned about the effect that this discussion would have upon their responses. This intriguing position resonates with the role of the researcher as insider/outsider in the research process. For example, what are the advantages and/or disadvantages of a Muslim woman conducting research on a Muslim community? How does this type of matching affect the interview process itself? Are the accounts any fuller or more complete than in those situations where 'matching' is not involved? In her research, Edwards discusses the expectations of the interviewees.[58] In the first meeting the interviewer may challenge expectations, and the interviewee may not know where to place the interviewer. Given the similarities in ethnic and religious background, it is perhaps not surprising that interviewees would often begin answers with 'being a Muslim woman yourself ...' The response to this standpoint indicates the importance some women attached to my religious background. This was most vivid, however, when on one occasion an interviewee describing her family's reaction to the breakdown of her marriage suddenly stated, '... actually I don't feel comfortable discussing this with you'. When probed further she explained, 'cause you know what goes on in the community ... you're Muslim ... and ... well ... I just don't feel comfortable discussing it with you'. It is of interest that this respondent considered myself as an 'insider' and was, therefore, unable to divulge intimate details to me. I was struck by the way that this perception, one that I did not immediately accept, had led to limited feedback from this interviewee.

---

[57] Song and Parker, 1998, above, n 6, at 117.
[58] D Edwards, *Discourse and Cognition* (London, Sage, 1990).

My being British Pakistani also bought up issues of commonality and difference. For example, Salma spoke at length about the different attitudes between 'Pakistanis and the English' towards marriage. She explained, 'We do things differently don't we? Our families have expectations of us and we have to do certain things, English people don't understand that do they? Some of them they think we're all forced into marriages but it's not like that'. More significantly, differences were discussed in the context of how far I identified myself as 'Pakistani'. Which part of Pakistan did my family originate from? Could I speak any language apart from English?

I was also asked a series of personal questions. Interviewees asked whether I was married and had children. Once I explained that I was married and had children it was interesting to note how some of them related this fact to their own situation. For example, Mina informed me, 'being married is important for Muslim women. I don't think women are recognised in the community unless they're married'. When probed further on what she meant, she explained, 'well when I was married I was accepted more ... you know like what I said and did seemed to have more authority with the elders of the community and family. Divorce is really shunned upon and that's why I think a lot of women will only get divorced as a last resort'. On more than one occasion I felt my being married was a commonality, a space in which the interviewees felt at ease with discussing their experiences of marriage and marriage breakdown.

My dress code and appearance also raised questions of difference and commonality. While a few women queried my not wearing the headscarf most women shared similar tastes in clothing and dress. Hina commented, 'I like your scarf ... you're like me, I don't wear it on my head but I always have a scarf around me'. Through this commonality, I was able to share personal experiences with some of the interviewees.

J. LEAVING THE FIELD

We discussed earlier the ways in which relationships with informants may impinge upon the research process. Similarly, once the research has been completed, we must consider whether this relationship should proceed. This raises questions on the possible repercussions for participants divulging private details and the responsibility of the researcher in protecting their participants. In my study, it was clear from the outset that participants were prepared to contribute only if all transcripts of interviews remained anonymous and if pseudonyms were used in the study. A total of 7 women requested that the interview tapes be destroyed once the research had been written up and all the other women questioned what would happen to the tapes. A final request from all the religious scholars of Shariah Councils and some of the female interviewees was that they are kept informed of any policy implications the research might generate.

K. CONCLUSION

In this chapter I have explored the relationship in social research between a feminist standpoint theory and cultural difference to consider how the researcher's positionality shapes the structure and substance of the research study. The question posed was how to explore and present complexities and tensions in data based upon cultural and religious difference within the context of feminist research. Drawing upon the concepts of standpoint and difference we found that this approach allows us to interrogate what we understand as culture, community and identity as fluid, changing and contested entities that are open to social and cultural contestation within minority ethnic communities. Furthermore, instead of denying the importance of the standpoint of the researcher in the field, this approach demands a critical analysis of their engagement in the research process. The usefulness of this approach lies in the fact that it provides the means by which we are able to interrogate the power relations upon which the research is based.

The concern of conducting research deemed 'sensitive' within local communities raises the importance of identifying the local context in which the communities are constituted. In this study, bearing in mind the difficulties of access to participants and the role of 'gatekeepers', the rising number of attacks on Muslims meant that the benefits of contributing to the research that addresses difficult questions was not always viewed as benefiting the community. As a consequence, access to some material was withheld, research observation limited and access to the female users of the Shariah Councils chosen denied. Nonetheless, with the material made available, I have been able to provide an insight into how these bodies resolve family disputes.

I found that the gendered experiences and realities of Muslim women's lives' mean a multi-faceted approach to conducting feminist social research must be adopted. Further, the influence of the religious and gender identity of the researcher on the research process is subtle and complex. Mccarthy, Holland and Gillies[59] ask, 'how do we place ourselves as researchers, with our own sympathies and particular perspectives, within such multiplicities?' The dichotomies of 'insider/outsider' are too limiting and fail to capture issues of difference and commonality when the researcher shares similar ethnic/cultural and religious identity.

Do we need a radically different approach to conducting socio-legal research on 'sensitive' issues within minority diasporic communities?

---

[59] JR Mccarthy, J Holland and V Gillies, 'Multiple Perspectives on the "Family" Lives of Young People: Methodological and Theoretical issues in Case Study Research' (2003) 6 *International Journal of Social Research Methodology* 1.

Research findings suggest we need to incorporate notions of difference and diversity into the feminist analytical approach. As Hall points out:

> The temptation to essentialize 'community' has to be resisted—it is fantasy of plentitude in circumstances of imagined loss. Migrant communities bear the imprint of diaspora, 'hybridization' and difference in their very constitution. Their vertical integration into their traditions of origin exists side by side with their lateral linkages to other 'communities' of interest, practice and aspiration, real and symbolic.[60]

The concept of 'standpoint differences' allows us to draw upon different theoretical approaches while recognising the complexity of 'individual histories, shared family lives and standpoints of gender, generation, class and ethnicity ... all interwoven in these related but individual accounts'.[61] This approach allows us to interrogate what we understand as culture, community and identity as fluid, changing and contested entities, which are open to social and cultural contestation within diasporic communities. As a feminist researcher, I was able to draw upon these multiplicities and move away from the traditional dichotomy of Muslim women as subordinated and oppressed within local Muslim communities.

Finally, I must pay tribute to all those women who contributed to this study and chose to share their experiences, often in difficult circumstances. As one interviewee reported:

> I was the shameless one who wanted a divorce ... . My mum would meet someone in the shop who would say your daughters a whore because she did this, this and this and people would invite themselves to my family home uncles of mine and say you know you should now disown her and have nothing to do with her and all this kind of stuff. So my family had that for many, many years.

Pursuing this type of research depends on women placing sufficient trust in a researcher to share these experiences with wider audiences, both within their own ethic and religious community, and in society more generally. The political and ethical challenges are many, but it is important that socio-legal researches engage with the issues raised by feminist standpoint research.

[60] S Hall, 'Conclusion: the Multi-cultural Question' in B Hesse, (ed), *Un/settled Multiculturalisms* (London, Zed Books, 2000) 209–241.
[61] Mccarthy, Holland and Gillies 2003, above, n 59, at 19.

6

Using Ethnography as a Tool in Legal Research: An Anthropological Perspective

ANNE GRIFFITHS

THE POWER OF law in regulating the social, economic and political life of society is widely acknowledged. Both lawyers and social scientists are concerned with the relationship between law and power—where it is located, how it is constituted and what forms it takes. They address these questions, however, from different perspectives with the result that they provide very different insights into legal analyses and the ways in which law works. Conventional legal theorists limit the scope of their inquiry to an analysis of law-as-text through a rigorous exposition of doctrinal analysis founded on a specific set of sources, institutions and personnel that gain their authority and legitimacy from a formal model of law derived from the nation-state. In contrast, social scientists pursue a broader remit which extends beyond the study of formal legal institutions to take account of the social basis upon which law operates. Anthropology of law falls within this latter category providing a contextual analysis of law that highlights the effects that economic, social and political processes have in establishing differential legal relations among individuals and social groups.

This approach provides an alternative vision of law from the one promoted by conventional legal theory and discourse.[1] In promoting another viewpoint anthropological perspectives have made a major contribution to the study of law by challenging Western notions of what constitutes a legal

[1] This theory and discourse forms part of a formalist or centralist model of law. For a discussion and critique of this legal model see A Griffiths, *In the Shadow of Marriage: Gender and Justice in an African Community* (Chicago, IL, University of Chicago Press, 1997) 29–38.

domain[2] and by extending the concept of law beyond rule-based formulations to incorporate views of 'law as process'.[3] In adopting actor-oriented perspectives that interrogate who is 'inside' and 'outside' law[4] these approaches have highlighted the frontiers of legality.[5] Through pioneering a methodological approach based on ethnography that has focused on local, specific, micro-studies, issues about race, class and gender have been highlighted in ways that expose the inadequacies of legal systems in dealing with them both in theory and practice.

My chapter explores an ethnographic approach to law and the advantages of such an approach when documenting people's experiences of law in daily life. It is based on fieldwork carried out in southern Africa, among Bakwena[6] in Molepolole village, between 1982–89.[7]

This research focused on women's procreative relationships with men and their access to family law in Botswana. In pursuing this research agenda, which was aimed at developing the foundation course on family law at the University of Botswana,[8] I not only worked with conventional legal sources such as legislation, court records, and court proceedings, as well as interviews with court officials, but also extended my research data to include village members discussions of everyday life, including women's and men's life histories and extended narratives of dispute. The life histories

---

[2] KN Lewellyn and EA Hoebel, *The Cheyenne Way: Conflict and Case Law in Primitive Jurisprudence* (Norman, OK, University of Oklahoma Press, 1941); M Gluckman, The *Judicial Process Among the Barotse of Northern Rhodesia* (Zambia), 2nd edn, (Manchester, MUP, 1955); P Bohannan, *Justice and Judgment Among the Tiv* (London, OUP for the International African Institute, 1957); L Pospisil, *Kapauka Papuans and Their Law* (New Haven, CN, Yale University Publication in Anthropology, No 54, 1958).

[3] SF Moore, 'Law and Social Change: The Semi-Autonomous Social Field as an Appropriate Subject of Study' (1973) 7 *Law & Society Review* 719–46; SF Moore, *Law as Process: An Anthropological Approach* (London Routledge and Kegan Paul, 1978); L Nader and B Yngvesson, 'On Studying Ethnography of Law and its Consequences' in J Honigman,(ed), *Handbook of Social and Cultural Anthropology* (Chicago, IL, McNally, 1973); JL Comaroff and SA Roberts, *Rules and Processes: The Cultural Logic of Dispute in an African Context* (Chicago, IL, University of Chicago Press, 1981).

[4] O Harris, (ed), *Inside and Outside Law: Anthropological Studies of Authority and Ambiguity* (London, Routledge, 1996).

[5] B de Sousa Santos, *Toward a New Common Sense: Law, Science and Politics in the Paradigmatic Transition* (London, Routledge, 1995).

[6] In Setswana, one of the official languages in Botswana. The prefixes 'Ba' and 'Mo' is the plural and singular modifiers of nouns designation persons, so 'Bakwena' is the plural form of Kwena, that is Kwena people or persons.

[7] For a detailed account of this research see Griffiths, above, n 1.

[8] Edinburgh University had long established links with the universities of Botswana, Swaziland, and Lesotho and at that time provided two years of undergraduate training in law in Edinburgh out of their five year programme. In 1981 Sandy McCall Smith and myself assisted in setting up an independent law department at the University of Botswana.

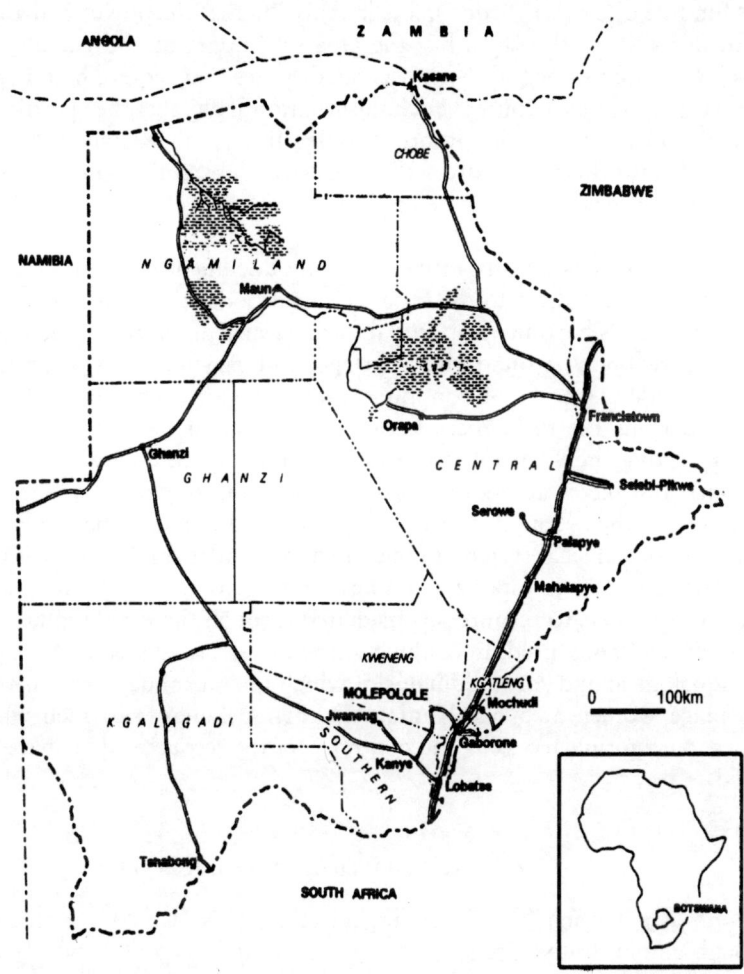

were gathered from members of Mosotho kgotla which represented 1 of 73 such social units that made up the village in 1982.[9]

These life histories and discussions of everyday life were crucial in revealing village people's perceptions of law, the circumstances under which they do or do not have access to formal legal forums, and in particular, the conditions under which individuals found themselves silenced or unable to

---

[9] These life histories collected in 1984 and 1989 expanded on unpublished data gathered by Issac Schapera in 1937 which he kindly gave me. This material included genealogies of Mosotho kgotla which made it possible to trace the descent of people associated with the kgotla in 1984 back to 1937 and to develop a historical profile of the kgotla's development.

negotiate with others in terms of daily life. The latter is especially important for, like other jurisdictions, it is in daily life that the power and authority to negotiate with others has the greatest impact on individuals' lives. This is because few negotiations become disputes that require handling in a legal arena, such as a court.[10] Such information highlights the specific, concrete, lived-experiences that inform people's lives, a dimension that is often missing from official narratives that focus on substantive and procedural aspects of the legal system as well as its more abstract claims to equality and neutrality.

The life histories and narratives not only document individuals' experiences but connect them to the broader social polity to which they belong, one that extends beyond institutional forums, such as courts, to incorporate networks revolving around kin, marriage, and varying forms of resources. They provide a picture of continuity and change across two generations that underpins the differences between and among the sexes as well as demonstrating how membership of different family networks shapes women's and men's access to resources, including the power to negotiate with one another. How this power is constructed remains unarticulated so far as the formal legal system is concerned, but understanding how it is created and operates is especially important for women given the ways in which their access to resources is mediated through the gendered networks of family and household, in conjunction with the broader economic, political, ideological and social domains of which they form part. For these factors place women at a disadvantage in their dealings with men when it comes to acquiring access to and control over the resources that shape their world.

A. THE HOUSEHOLD AND THE KGOTLA

As with any Tswana village, the organization of Molepolole is structured through administrative units, known as wards and dikgotla,[11] which derive from households. It is through households that the political structure of the morafe or polity maintains itself. Kwena society, like other Tswana merafe (polities), revolves around a tightly organized hierarchy of coresidential administrative units. Their political community is conceived of as a hierarchy of progressively more inclusive coresidential and administrative groupings,

---

[10] See M Galanter, 'Justice in Many Rooms: Courts, Private Ordering and Indigenous Law' (1981) 19 *Journal of Legal Pluralism and Unofficial Law* 1–47; H Genn, *Paths to Justice: What People Do and Think About Going to Law* (Oxford, Hart Publishing, 1999); H Genn and A Paterson, *Paths to Justice Scotland, What People in Scotland Do and Think About Going to Law* (Oxford, Hart Publishing, 2001).

[11] Dikgotla represent more than one kgotla that make up the plurality of units that give rise to the Kwena polity.

beginning with households, and extending through kgotlas and family groups, to wards which represent major units of political organization. These are presided over by men. The Chief's kgotla which is the most senior and powerful ward in the morafe, represents the apex of the administrative and political structure through which the kgosi ('chief') exercises his power. When I began my research in Molepolole in 1982, with Mr Masimega who acted as my interpreter,[12] there were 6 main wards[13] and 73 kgotlas.

B. PROPERTY AND RESOURCES

When it comes to property and resources in Botswana, Kerven has noted that 'Tswana livelihoods are made within the minimal core of the family and the maximal universe of the southern African economy'.[14] Families depend on a combination of 'crops, cattle and wages' for their existence which 'are combined according to a family's class position and stage in the life cycle'.[15] Migration forms an integral part of family life and has done ever since the founding of the Bechuanaland Protectorate in 1885. This has continued into the post-independence period from 1966 but the forms have shifted towards a greater degree of internal rather than external migration, due to development taking place within the country, as well as South African policies now geared to restricting the numbers of external migrants working in South Africa. Most families in Molepolole are dependent on a mix of subsistence agriculture, livestock and cash for their existence and on family members acting co-operatively to pool their resources. This interdependence among family groups based on the foregoing gives rise to what Parson has termed the peasantariat[16] who represent the majority of families in Botswana today. However, there are a small group of those who have been able to focus on other activities and to form part of an elite, referred to as the salariat.[17] Their focus on education (often to university level) has enabled them to acquire skilled and stable forms of employment, as bureaucrats or government civil servants, which provide access to a whole range

---

[12] Mr Masimega, who was nearing seventy when I started my research was affectionately know in the village as 'Mr Commonsense' and assisted generations of researchers in their studies of Botswana.

[13] These are Kgosing, Maunatlala, Mokgalo, Ratshosa, Ntoloedibe and Borakalalo.

[14] C Kerven, 'The Effects of Migration on Agricultural Production' in *Migration in Botswana: Patterns, Causes, and Consequences* (*Final Report National Migration Study* vol 3) (Gaborone, Government Printer, 1982) 544.

[15] *Ibid,*, p 545.

[16] J Parson, 'Cattle, Class and State in Rural Botswana' (1981) 7 *Journal of Southern African Studies* 236–55.

[17] DM Cooper, *An Overview of the Botswana Class Structure and its Articulation with the Rural mode of Production: Insights from Selebi-Phikwe* (Cape Town, University of Cape Town, 1982).

of benefits. Examples of both family types exist in Mosotho kgotla through the descendants of Makokwe and Radipati.[18]

C. ACCESS TO RESOURCES AND THE ROLE OF GENDER

Within families gender operates to constrain women's access to, and control over, resources. Although most women have access to land their ability to utilize it is dependent upon their raising cash to buy the necessary seedlings and other items necessary for its maintenance and mobilizing the labour necessary for its cultivation. In these activities women, especially from the peasantariat, tend to be dependent on men because of the structure of Kwena society and poor employment prospects compared with those of men.

Kwena society is based on households which form the basis for the political structure of the kgotla and customary law. Authority is based on age and status but women do not have comparable authority with that of men for although they may act as heads of households,[19] they can never become headman of a kgotla.[20] In addition, material and social circumstances combine to create a situation where it is the households of married men and women that prove the most effective in agricultural production as they have a greater command over the resources required for such production compared with others, such as female-headed households.[21]

Women also find themselves at a disadvantage when it comes to acquiring livestock. This is due, in part, to succession laws that favour cattle being handed down from father to son, referred to as estate cattle. Although

---

[18] The men Makokwe and Radipati both share the same father Koosimile, but have different mothers. For more detailed information see Griffiths, above, n 1, p 62–105.

[19] The National Development Plan for the years of 1985–1991, *National Development Plan (NDP6) 1985–1991* (Ministry of Finance and Development Planning Central Statistics Office Gaborone, Government Printer, 1985) notes that 'women predominate among young adults and as heads of households' p 8. It also comments, that 'Females head a third of the households in urban areas and half in the rural areas' p 11.

[20] In the past women have very occasionally acted as regent for the morafe but in these unusual circumstances they were seen to be fulfilling a male gender role. However, since my study was concluded Mosadi Seboko has been installed as a Kgosi for the Balete of Ramotswa.

[21] My data and that of others shows that it is these households that have the necessary livestock to plough and thus command the labour of other family members, or who can afford to hire whatever is necessary. See, for example, C Kerven, *Urban and Rural Female-Headed Households' Agricultural Productivity in Botswana* (Gaborone, Ministry of Finance and Development Planning, Central Statistics Office, 1979). Female-headed households, however, which exist without any male contributions to the household tend to have an income that is less than half that of male-headed households and are among the poorest in the country. See, *National Development Plan (NDP7) 1991–1997* (Ministry of Finance and Development planning Central Statistics Office Gaborone, Government Printer, 1991) 17; UNICEF, *Children, Women and Development in Botswana: A Situational Analysis* (Gaborone, Government of Botswana/UNICEF, 1989) 58.

daughters can and do acquire some beasts (where such cattle exist), their share is rarely on a par with that of their brothers, especially their eldest brother who takes over responsibility for the family group on his father's death.[22] Women may inherit livestock from their mother, but a mother's opportunities for acquiring her own beasts are limited, as these can only derive from certain sources of labour. These include produce from their own (and not their husband's) land, which may be exchanged for livestock, or which may be used to make beer, which in turn is sold to provide the cash to purchase livestock. Surplus produce rarely exists as most of what is grown is consumed in house and is susceptible to drought, making it extremely hard to acquire livestock in this way. Acquiring money to buy livestock is also difficult for women given poor employment prospects and rates of pay. Even where successful women have to cede control over such livestock to the boys and men who run the cattle posts where they are quartered.

Employment is one of the most important factors affecting the social and economic position of women in Botswana today.[23] This is because the money it provides, that is essential for survival, is generally less available to women for a number of reasons. In the formal sector, women are excluded from employment that many men engage in the mining and construction industries. Other jobs, requiring a certain degree of education, are beyond both sexes although women in Botswana, as elsewhere in Africa, are more likely to lack these qualifications than men are.[24] The kind of employment open to the majority of women involves domestic service or working as a barmaid or shop assistant. There is competition for such work which is insecure and poorly paid. In this situation women find it hard to negotiate or enforce their terms of service even where these are laid down by law. Men also experience difficulties but they have more options regarding potential employment.

---

[22] This is situation has been documented elsewhere in Africa, although recent research by W Bikaako and J Ssenkumba, 'Gender, Land and Rights: Contemporary Contestations in Law, Policy and Practice in Uganda' in L Muthoni Wanyeki, (ed), *Women and Land in Africa: Culture, Religion and Realizing Women's Rights* (London, Zed Books, 2003) 31–65; and C Nyamu-Musembi, 'Are Local Norms and Practices Fences or Pathways? The Example of Women's Property Rights' in A An-Na'im, (ed), *Cultural Transformation and Human Rights in Africa* (London, Zed Books, 2002) 126–50 notes a change in practice that is to women's benefit.

[23] See B Brown, 'The Impact of Male Labour Migration on Women in Botswana' (1983) 82 *African Affairs* 367–88; C Kerven, 'Academics, Practitioners and all Kinds of Women in Development: A Reply to Peters' (1984) 10 *Journal of Southern African Studies* 259–68; UNICEF, *Children, Women and Development in Botswana: A Situational Analysis* (Gaborone, Government of Botswana/UNICEF, 1993) 12–20.

[24] See HL Moore, *Feminism and Anthropology* (Minneapolis, MN, University of Minnesota Press, 1988) 104.

The informal sector provides a supplemental or alternative means of raising income on which many women depend.[25] However, as studies elsewhere have shown,[26] investment in this sector does not guarantee returns and where it involves illegal activities, such as prostitution, puts the women concerned at risk. Among Bakwena experience indicates that the returns women receive are insufficient on their own to provide for capital accumulation or personal enrichment.

D. DIFFERENTIALLY SITUATED SOCIAL NETWORKS

Many women do not have marital status in Botswana but it is important to note the social contexts in which marriage occurs and the implications that this has for both married and unmarried women. For the peasantariat, representing a substantial proportion of the population in Botswana, marriage still play an important role in providing access to the broader networks of supra-household management and cooperation on which they rely for their subsistence. This is true of Makokwe's family from Mosotho kgotla where there has been a relatively high rate of kin marriage among members of the older generation and whose access to land has been acquired through their wives' maternal relatives.

Among the salariat, however, there has been a tendency to limit kin recognition[27] in order to circumscribe obligations adhering to these relationships. Among this group women more frequently express negative views on marriage.

Membership of different networks has implications for women and for their power to negotiate their relationships with men. Women within the peasantariat find their choices mediated through their position in relation to male networks and structures of authority which provide the mainstay for their existence. So for example, through male sibling support, some women find themselves with the power of choice which is not available to other women who lack access to this type of network.

Within Mosotho kogtla, Olebeng, who is Makokwe's youngest child and only daughter, has had several children with different fathers. She has five adult brothers who have all married and had children. In her case, however, neither she nor her family ever had any interest in marriage for her. Among women within this group she is relatively well supported by her siblings who have given her control of the natal household and who plough

---

[25] W Izzard, 'The Impact of Migration on the Roles of Women' in *Migration in Botswana: Patterns, Causes and Consequences*, above, n 12, p 654–707.

[26] See above, n 21.

[27] EM Kocken and GC Uhlenbeck, *Tlokweng, A Village Near Town* (Leiden, Leiden University Institute of Cultural and Social Studies, ICA Publication No 39, 1980).

Genealogical relations of Mosotho Kgotla

for her and provide her with food and cash when they can. Other women from the same background are not so fortunate. Diane, for example, who is of the same generation and roughly the same age as Olebeng has not only been abandoned by her brothers but they have expropriated land given to her by her mother. Without her brothers' support she has found herself unable to negotiate marriage and has had to rely on a series of male partners who have only intermittently provided support for her and her nine children. She represents one of the poorest female-headed households associated with the kgotla.

In contrast, women within the salariat, have a greater degree of power and control over the choices that are open to them. This is the case with Goitsemang. Her father, Radipati, was Makokwe's half brother but his family have experienced a very different life trajectory from Makokwe's descendants. Unlike his contemporaries, Radipati was an educated man who educated his children, including his three daughters (at a time when many women received only a nominal education). This helped them acquire formal employment. The eldest unmarried daughter, Goitsemang worked as a nurse in South Africa and then in a management capacity for a construction company in Botswana, enabling her to build a house in the capital city, Gaborone. Her younger unmarried sister, Olebogeng, has also acquired a plot of land in Gaborone by working for the same company. Radipati's sons were also educated and two of them even went on to acquire university degrees. Through their access to education and skilled, stable employment, the family fits the kind of profile associated with the salariat in that they no longer centre their activities around subsistence agriculture and migrant labour.

Within this family group Goitsemang has had children with two different fathers. But unlike Diane, her relationships had the potential for a customary marriage from which she withdrew and she has now has no interest in marriage as it 'just brings quarrels'.

Olebeng, Diane, and Goitsemang are within the same generation and age group yet their lives vary considerably. Taking account of the specificity of their lives is important for government planning and policy development related to 'female headed households'[28] as it has been the subject of great controversy surrounding the definition and basis upon which such households *as a group* should be the recipient of government aid.[29]

The life histories demonstrate that women's access to resources is shaped by the type of network to which they belong. So, women within the peasantariat, who operate within the matrix of domestic, agricultural and unskilled labour, find themselves heavily reliant upon the male networks and structures of authority which provide them with support. Women, within the salariat, however, who have stable employment of another king are less reliant on male networks and so experience a greater degree of independence. Not only that, but some of these women have been able to reshape the normative considerations that pertain to women's dealings with men within a familial context.[30] Thus Goitsemang was able to challenge her brother David over control over the natal household by reconfiguring the terms of the discourse in a way that would not have been open to Olebeng or Diane.[31]

E. ASYMMETRICAL POWER RELATIONS AMONG SPOUSES

The life histories demonstrate how access to resources is intimately bound up with familial and household ties and how individuals, particularly women, are located within kin and social networks that control their distribution and utilisation. While some unmarried women, like Goitsemang, are able negotiate control over their resource base the majority of women remain dependant on their relationships with their fathers, brothers, male partners, or husbands for their support. This poses a particular problem for unmarried women like Diane whose male kin have abandoned her. While marriage may enable women to improve their access to resources and enhance their status they still find themselves located in unequal power relations with their husbands which are highlighted on divorce. These inequalities arise from the different positions men and women occupy in the family hierarchy, which not only involve access to and authority over resources and the gendered division of labour within the family, but are also due to the different social conceptions that attach to the roles of husband and wife.

---

[28] National Development Plan (NDP7) 1991–1997, above n 19, p 242.

[29] E M Kocken and G C Uhlenback, above, n 27; P Peters, 'Gender, Developmental Cycles and Historical Process: A Critique of Recent Research on Women in Botswana' (1983) 10(1) *Journal of Southern African Studies* 100–22; C Kerven, above n 21.

[30] For more detailed information on this see A Griffiths, 'Reconfiguring Law: An Ethnographic Perspective from Botswana' (1998) 23 *Law & Social Inquiry* 587, 603–11.

[31] For more detailed information on this see A Griffiths, 'Mediation, Gender and Justice in Botswana' (1998) 154 *Mediation Quarterly* 335–42.

What is at stake in the public dissolution of a relationship and distribution of property under customary law is displacing the burden of fault onto the other spouse.[32] Thus both parties seek to escape blame for marital breakdown and to secure their share of property. The claims that are open to them, however, differ, and it is particularly hard for a wife to displace the burden of fault. This is because a wife is expected to defer to her husband's authority as head of the household. So, for example, she is not permitted to leave home without his consent or without cause (eg, a death in the family or domestic abuse). Where she does so, she will have to overcome the appearance of negative conduct before she can assert any claim to marital property. Men's conduct, however, is not viewed in the same way. So, for example, where a husband is having an affair with another women, it is considered inappropriate for a wife to complain unless he is failing to support her and the children or is using their family property to support the other woman. Even where a wife is able to establish good conduct, she still confronts the problems posed by the structure of family property.

Under Kwena customary law[33] it is the husband who maintains control and ownership of the family property because he is the one who is publicly accredited as head of the household and the person who is regarded as their children's custodian. In this context he is awarded most of the property because he is responsible for handing it on to the next generation. Among Bakwena, children's inheritance is a major consideration when it comes to division of property. On divorce, children remain affiliated with their father's family, and where there is property, their interests often effectively restrict or subordinate women's claims to property as wives. Thus wives find themselves doubly disadvantaged compared with their husbands when it comes to making property claims.

F. NINIKA (WOMAN) AND MOAGISI (MAN) BAKWENA

I first met Ninika Bakwena in Mokgalo ward in 1982 where kgotla members were dealing with an ongoing dispute between Ninika and her mother-in-law. On this occasion, Ninika complained that her mother-in-law had locked her out of the dwelling that her husband, Moagisi, had built for her. The tension between them arose from the fact that Moagisi's mother regarded Ninika as an unsuitable wife and did all she could to disrupt the marriage. Mr Bakwena Kgosidintsi, the headman of Mokgalo ward, observed 'Moagisi fell in love with Ninika but his parents wanted him to marry another woman who was half deaf. He refused and went to live with

---

[32] For a more detailed discussion of this see Griffiths, above, n 1, p 134–82.
[33] The national legal system of Botswana incorporates both customary and common law that includes statutory law. For details see Griffiths, above, n 1, p 53–57 and 184–85.

Ninika at her parents' home. He eventually married her by special licence at the DC's [District Commissioner's] office in 1975.[34] Patlo was not done.[35] His parents reluctantly accepted the marriage. They disapproved because when he became involved with her she already had a child by someone else. There was a formal marriage but it was vulnerable because patlo, a crucial aspect of familial approval (involving relatives and kin on behalf of both families) was lacking. In fact Moagisi's family's disapproval was well known. Without the family's support Ninika was at risk because her own family connections were less powerful than those of Moagisi who is related to the headman of Mokgalo ward and to the royal Kgosidintsi family. Moagisi not only has the benefit of those connections, but his status is enhanced by perceptions that his family is well off because its' members are in government employment. Moagisi's two sisters are teachers, and he himself, unlike many in his generation, has been employed since 1972 in Molepolole as a messenger for the Veterinary department.

Ninika, however, comes from a poor family in Thato ward. Ninika's bargaining position is further weakened by the fact that her father divorced her mother years ago and distanced himself from his daughters when they had children out of wedlock. In contrast with Moagisi's sisters, Ninika and her sister, have only a minimal education. Both work only intermittently, picking up odd domestic or agricultural labouring jobs from local people or institutions. They operate on the fringes of the peasantariat.

Both women had children young. Ninika's sister had three children with three different fathers, only one of whom provides any support. Both women were close to their mother who died in 1988 but their male relatives ignore them and their children, and do not provide any support. A Thato ward headman observed 'Ninika and her mother lived under very poor conditions' and that they had no cattle. When Ninika and Moagisi met she already had a child by a man whom she had met in domestic service in Gaborone. She returned to Molepolole and had three children aged 14, 12 and 9 with Moagisi. Moagisi maintains that the father of the youngest is Ninika's lover and that she was conceived when Ninika was moving between Mokgalo to her mother's home in Thato ward (or as Moagisi alleged to her lover's place in Borakalalo).

At the beginning the families attempted to mediate the couple's problems in the normal manner. These attempts proved unsuccessful. Over the next

---

[34] In Botswana parties may marry according to civil or religious rites under s 7 of the Marriage Act 1970 [Cap 29: 01] and such a marriage is registered. Parties may also marry, however, according to customary law which is exempt from the provisions of the 1970 Act.

[35] Unlike a registered marriage, a customary marriage is a process which may take many years and which does not necessarily involve any particular identifiable occasion. However, Bakwena place great emphasis on a ceremony called patlo which for them is a definitive marker of a customary marriage, even although they may recognise a relationship as a customary marriage without it having been performed.

two years there were subsequent hearings in Mokgalo ward where Ninika complained of being denied access to her home and of lack of support. Though the kgotla ostensibly supported Ninika no progress was made over these issues. In these types of disputes relatives and kin attempt to get parties to reach consensus. Where this fails the dispute works its way up through the kgolta system until it eventually arrives in Kgosing, the chief's kgotla. As the Bakwena's dispute demonstrates this process may take many years.

When disputes are processed in the kgotla they take the following form. The party with a grievance initiates the hearing. S/he presents his or her account of the grievance and is questioned by kgotla members present who include the third party hearing the dispute, eg, the headman, wardhead (or Kgosing personnel) and the other party to the dispute. The process is then reversed and the other party is likewise subject to questioning by all the foregoing. No legal representation is permitted in the kgotla, including Kgosing. Finally, the third party asks the disputants to state their claims and where they fail to reach agreement asks kgotla members for their views. After consultation with them he gives his decision.

Ninika and Moagisi went through this process on numerous occasions during their married life. Their dispute eventually arrived in Kgosing in 1984. Here Ninika not only raised the issue of neglect but of her husband's lover. This was one of the rare times that a hearing was adjourned to bring the other woman, Kgomotso, into the process. During the hearing Kgomotso admitted that she had had a child with Moagisi but maintained that this occurred before he married Ninika and her before own marriage. Now widowed, she explained that Moagisi visited her; his visits to her home were to see his child. But Mr Kgosiensho who was hearing the dispute found that 'Ninika is telling the truth. Moagisi, her husband, does not really take care of her. This kgotla has shown Moagisi that he is neglecting his wife and children'.

(a) Ninika's Perspective

During the years Ninika was in dispute with her husband

> I went to Kgosing and was referred back from there to the DC [meaning magistrate][36] where the case [under the Deserted Wives and Children's Protection Act 1963] has not yet been called [in 1984]. I went to Kgosing twice this year. Kgosi

---

[36] During the colonial period DC's operated as magistrates for their district as well as carrying out administrative duties. Today Magistrates Courts are staffed by magistrates but local people still refer to these courts as DC's courts. Ninika was sent to the Magistrate's court to claim maintenance.

Sebele [Senior Chief's Representative] told me to go back to the DC.[37] He phoned the DC and told me to go there. Nothing happened. I told the kgotla people (Mokgalo) and they fixed a date for the hearing. My husband was called and instructed (at Kgosing) that he should stay with me and the children and that he must support us. That was the order my husband was given but he did nothing. The matter was then dealt with once more in Mokgalo because Mr Kgosiensho referred it back to the ward. However none of my relatives were informed.

She had reached an impasse with the kgotla system and 'Mr Sebele said it was better to claim support through the Magistrate's court. He explained that it would be easier than to keep on discussing the matter in the kgotla when the kgotla men order Moagisi to support and he does not'.

After the hearing in 1984 Ninika received some minimal support including sorghum flour, flour to make bread, a small tin of coffee, some sugar and a small tin of powdered milk but this was all that she received between 1982 and 1984. During this period she was still waiting for the magistrate to call her case. Support was hard to come by. The self help project in which she was involved was a failure. 'We reaped very little because the vegetables burned [due to the severe drought]. The soil was poor and they got scorched by the sun. We stopped cultivating after that'. Ninika was reduced to begging in order to survive. 'I live by begging food from other relatives, mostly my husband's sister'. Sometimes I go to the clinic (health) and they give me some mealy meal for me and the children. She has become dependent on others for her existence. In 1984 she commented 'It is a problem living from day to day'.

(b) Moagisi's Perspective

Moagisi presented a very different account of their marital history. He maintained that the problems began when Ninika left him taking the children to stay at her mother's home. 'We had not quarreled and I had not beaten her. I think it was her own idea [to move] because she was not interested in living with me'. He stated that when asked about his lack of support by Mr Kgosiensho he stressed that he would provide food only if his wife and children were living at home in Mokgalo. He was told that 'I must see to it that my wife and children come back home and that I support them'. In his view it was Ninika who caused all the problems because she returned to her parents' home every few days. He could do little as 'my wife never tells me anything, she never responds to my questions'. No mention was made of his mother's role in all of this. The constant moving, he

---

[37] This reference may be to the District Commissioner as the magistrate at that time was not present everyday in the court which shared accommodation with District Administration. The DC at that time often dealt directly with local people.

implied, was to visit her lover. She would leave the children with her mother and then take off. To his mind she was ignoring the kgotla pronouncement that they should live together, 'she is not actually doing that. At sun down she goes away to sleep at her home'. He vehemently denied allegations of non-support, explaining that as Ninika was absent so often, he bought food which his mother cooked for the children.

He firmly denied allegations about his lover, 'this is invented by my wife. When a woman's panicking or in sorrow she will say anything that will make people believe that her husband is a bad man'. He knew about the case Ninika had lodged with the Magistrate's court and commented that he had also gone to the court 'after I caught her sleeping with another man I went up to district administration and asked the clerk of [the Magistrate's] court what he would do'. He was ordered 'to go home and support her and the children'. The case in the Magistrate's court was finally heard and Moagisi was ordered to pay support. Moagisi supported for two months and then filed for divorce in the High Court.[38] Ninika did not know this at the time. He asked her to sign a form which she did, unaware that this was connected with divorce proceedings.

Shortly after, Moagisi presented her with a paper from the High Court saying that they were now divorced. He stated that he had been granted a divorce and custody of the children. Ninika was shocked and went to the DC who explained that the case was now over, that custody had been awarded to Moagisi. She opposed this, but when visiting Moagisi's mother the children were detained by his family and she has not seen them since.

1. Divorce and its Consequences

Moagisi divorced Ninika for desertion and adultery with another man in Borakalalo with whom he alleged that she had had two children. He maintained that she was already living with this man in 1984 when she claimed support. Moagisi stressed 'I made arrangements for her to stay in Mokgalo. She did not stay, but went back on her own to the man in Borakalalo with the children'. That Ninika did have a lover seems to have been common knowledge in the community, but whether this was due to Moagisi's neglect was unclear. The allegations of the affair with Kgomotso in the 1984 hearing proved to be valid. In 1989, he openly admitted to living with her. Kgomotso is regarded as a much more suitable partner for Moagisi because she is a teacher and is related to him.[39]

---

[38] As the parties were married under the Marriage Act 1970 their marriage had to be dissolved by divorce under the Matrimonial Causes Act 1970 (Cap 29: 07) which is modelled on English divorce law.

[39] There is a preference for marriage among kin, especially for cousins or for cross-cousin marriage. See Griffiths, above, n 1, p 41–44.

For the divorce Moagisi hired a lawyer from Gaborone. Ninika had no legal representation. Moagisi observed that Ninika did not defend the divorce, 'she did not even appear. The judgment was in my favour'. The fact that she knew nothing of what was happening did not concern him. He interpreted her lack of response as admission of the facts submitted in his pleadings. Although the High Court awarded Moagisi custody of all the children,[40] he has allowed Ninika custody of their youngest 'because she is still small'. Nothing was said about property and the matter was not raised at Kgosing.[41]

Moagisi confirmed that he did not have any cattle or livestock. He even observed 'we have never had a field to plough'. Ninika never considered division of property as 'nobody told me that there was any property to be divided'. However she recalled 'a bedstead, a table, [and] four chairs' at home which had remained with Moagisi. She was less concerned about these items than the loss of her clothes. In 1984, she claimed that Moagisi changed the locks on their door so that she had to go and stay with her mother. When she went to collect her clothes which were in a tin trunk she was told that Moagisi had taken them to the headman's house. She went to collect them, but the trunk was nowhere to be found.

From 1984 onwards, Ninika tried to gain support through a series of temporary jobs. She worked as a labourer in the drought relief scheme until that ended, and then took on a temporary job as a cleaner for district administration. After that she went from place to place wherever short-term labour was needed. Her liaison with the man from Borakalalo ended and since 1987 she and his offspring have been living with another man (in 1989), with whom she also has two children. They find it hard to survive living off subsistence agriculture and the occasional odd job.

Ninika attributed the kgotla's lack of interest in her case and that of her own relatives (who stopped attending hearings early on in the process), as being due to the fact 'my marriage with Moagisi was not founded properly [as patlo had not been done]'. She believed that 'Moagisi had no intention of living with me permanently as his wife. The Kgosing people wouldn't do anything because he had no intention of living with me'. In her view, 'Moagisi planned to divorce me for a long time. He wanted to get rid of me long ago'.

In the disputing process it was hard for Ninika to gain access to hearings, and when she did so little was achieved. She was clearly disadvantaged, not

---

[40] In making a custody award the High Court operates on the basis of what is in 'the child's best interests'. However, fathers' applications for custody are often uncontested because of the general social view that marriage has the effect of affiliating children with the husband's kin group, a proposition that is upheld under customary law.

[41] Although the parties were required to divorce in the High Court as Africans their property would devolve according to customary law unless certain exceptions applied.

only by her family background and inability to mobilize kin in her support, but also on account of her lack of knowledge. Unlike some women who have found themselves in conflict with their husbands over divorce[42] she lacked knowledge about the system that she faced and this acted to her detriment particularly where divorce proceedings were concerned.

It is clear that women operate within a gendered environment As a result women who are married find themselves in unequal power relations with their husbands. This is because in most cases it is men's enhanced ability to draw on all forms of resources essential for a family base that places them in a stronger position than women to accumulate what is necessary to form a household, and thus to elevate their power and social status in the social world in which they live. However, the effects of gender hierarchy not only apply where women make claims against their husbands but may also have an effect on their relations with other women.[43] So, for example, married women who are in receipt of regular income (generally acquired through their husbands and adult children) may exercise a degree of power over other women who lack a regular source of income and who, therefore, find themselves dependent on these married women (whose households are generally the best resourced) for employment in the agricultural or domestic sphere. As a result, differential status not only attaches itself to the spousal relationship, but also has an impact on women's relationships with one another in ways that contribute to the growing social stratification that is in evidence in Botswana today.[44] In Ninika's case she not only experienced problems with Moagisi but also faced an uphill struggle when she tried to call her mother-in-law to account for her actions. As a daughter-in-law she was in a less powerful position compared with her mother-in-law who had age, more senior status, and a closer affiliation with Moagisi's family operating in her favour.

Women who are married not only face the constraints of motherhood and limited economic opportunity (in some cases due to their husband's dissipation of assets) but also have to contend with their role as wives. Such a role situates women in a different position from that of their husbands in the family hierarchy, due to the different social conceptions that inform the roles of husband and wife. In this context, it is not just control over resources that is important, but also the ideological component that attaches to spousal roles which generally operates to the detriment of women in their dealings with men. For this reason, Kwena women exercise care in the

---

[42] See Griffiths, above, n 1, p 175–76; A Griffiths, 'Gendering Culture: Towards a Plural Perspective on Kwena Women's Rights' in JK Cowan, MB Dembour and RA Wilson, (eds), *Culture and Rights: Anthropological Perspectives* (Cambridge, CUP, 2001) 102, 115–19.

[43] See A Griffiths, 'Siblings in Dispute over Inheritance: A View from Botswana' (2002) 49(1) *Africa Today* 61–82.

[44] See above, n 19, NDP6 at 8, 19 and 21.

kinds of issues that they choose to make public in confrontations with their spouses and in the ways they present them. Given their vulnerable position, this involves establishing credibility over the long term by building on a series of family consultations and hearings over a number of years. Under accusations of neglect and lack of support—which are only too real—wives often seek to pursue a larger agenda concerning the preservation of present and future rights to their family property if this has come under threat from their husbands' relationship with and behaviour toward other women and their families. While Ninika attempted to do this she was singularly unsuccessful in acquiring any real support for her position due to the factors outlined earlier.

G. AN ETHNOGRAPHIC PERSPECTIVE AND ITS CONTRIBUTION TO THE STUDY OF LAW

These findings, based on an ethnographic study of law derived from life histories, interviews, participant observation and extended case studies of dispute, highlight the specific circumstances under which people have access to resources and how this shapes their power to negotiate with one another in daily life as well as in a legal forum. They provide another perspective on the relationship between law and power from that promoted by formal legal analyses, through a contextual approach that moves beyond the confines of conventional legal discourse. Such an approach, that situates law in relation to other bodies and agencies that construct social relations, such as families, households, and economic and political institutions, opens up for discussion aspects that remain unaddressed by formal legal discourse, namely:

a) the conditions that facilitate or impede access to legal forums;
b) the factors that underpin the power and authority of narratives in social and legal settings, including the role of gender, that lead to the empowerment of some individuals while silencing others;
c) alternative strategies for those who are excluded or silenced by the formal legal system in seeking redress;
d) the gap between law in theory and in practice; and
e) the broader question of how law is constituted and reconfigured through social processes that frame both its continuity and transformation over time.

Such discussion extends the remit of what constitutes a legitimate focus for legal inquiry by drawing together the threads of 'public' and 'private' dimensions of social life to reveal what underpins the relationship between power, law, and discourse that governs people's daily lives. In doing so, a more grounded view of law is acquired, one that is freed from the traditional 'top down' model of law in which legislators and judges are accorded hierarchical superiority in the production of authoritative legal meaning. Adopting a grounded view of law in analysis is especially pertinent for Kwena women, for it highlights the ways in which their power to negotiate their intimate relationships with men is shaped by the gendered construction of the world in which they live, one that also frames their relationship with other women. The ethnographic character of this form of analysis, derived from detailed field studies, also allows for a more finely tuned analysis of how individuals' membership of differentially situated networks, such as those associated with the peasantariat and salariat, shapes their access to resources with varying consequences for individuals' life trajectories. Thus the life histories not only mark the differences that arise between the generations, and the sexes, but between members of the same sex. They not only provide important information on specificities of the local that may be used to flesh out the more abstract understandings of law that are promoted by conventional legal discourse but also provide an opportunity for analysing the conditions under which change or transformation might be brought about. For studying the factors that give rise to local differences (as well as the continuities or patterns that such life histories provide) creates an understanding of how differential power relations among persons and social groups are constructed and their effects. This in turn fosters insight into the potential for change through an analysis of the conditions under which power and its discourses may alter or be transformed over time.

This gives rise to a more sophisticated analysis of law, one that recognizes and takes account of social differentiation and inequality, something that is absent from discussion within traditional legal discourse.[45] In making these factors visible and opening them up for discussion, ethnography provides an opportunity of exploring in detail how class, ethnicity, gender and age contribute to relations of inequality that impact on individuals and families, especially women's access to and control over resources such as law. It also provides a more grounded approach for pursuing strategies for legal change and thus redressing the current inequities that exist.

---

[45] See above, n 1.

Section Three

Studying Legal Texts

REZA BANAKAR AND MAX TRAVERS

N O MATTER HOW we view the legal system, whether we describe it as a system of rules and decisions, as a set of institutions or repeated patterns of practices, we have to recognise its linguistic make-up. We have to take into consideration law's dependence on forms of communicative action, ie, law, its processes and institutions are produced and reproduced through written and spoken words. Trivial as this observation might be, the dependence of law on language poses fundamental questions for the ideology of legal positivism.[1] This ideology has traditionally regarded legal language as an internally developed system of legal meanings and values which should be employed as a neutral instrument for realising law's intentions. The positivist ideal of legal decision-making is, thus, presented as a neutral, objective and dispassionate process of ascertaining and applying the content of law to the facts of a case. However, the linguistic indeterminacy in law,[2] which is brought about by the open texture of law and the fluid and contextual nature of language, disturbs this objective and somewhat mechanical image of legal decision-making.

This problem has been the object of much jurisprudential reflection, research and debate by scholars specialised in law and linguistics.[3] The focus of this section is, however, not so much on the philosophical issues and debates on the linguistic properties of law, but on legal communication

---

[1] Biochemistry uses language too, but as Timothy Endicott points out 'there is nothing about biochemistry that can be best said by saying something about language'. TAO Endicott, 'Law and Language' in *Oxford Handbook of Jurisprudence and Philosophy of Law* (Oxford, OUP, 2003).

[2] The indeterminacy thesis maintains that laws do not determine legal outcomes, thus, challenging the ideal of the rule of law that forbids arbitrary decision-making and requires that like case be treated alike.

[3] For different perspectives on studies of law and language see P Goodrich, *Legal Discourse: Studies in Linguistics, Rhetoric and Legal Analysis* (London, Macmillan, 1986); B Bix, *Law, Language, and Legal Determinacy* (Oxford, OUP, 1996); and A Phillips, *Lawyers' Language: The Distinctiveness of Legal Language* (London, Taylor & Francis, 2002).

as recorded in textual representations. We understand the use of legal language as a form of social practice and argue that legal texts necessarily reflect this practice and reveal how law is socially organised.[4]

A significant part of communications constituting the law and legal practice is either conducted through written documents or recorded in textual forms such as in statutes, cases, opinions, commentaries or law reports. For example, those aspects of legal reasoning, which aim to identify the valid law and establish the content of that law on a given issue are dependent on the documentation of previous decisions and are documented in turn for future references. As a result of law's dependence on texts, legal scholars have adopted and developed techniques of interpretation which were originally devised by theologians for the study of religious scripture. The traditional methods of reading, interpreting and applying legal texts imply that the centre of gravity of the legal system rests on an esoteric body of knowledge, primarily of formal character, which may be accessed by those who possess the necessary exegetical skills. According to this point of view, law becomes essentially concerned with interpretation of acts and case readings, expounding legal doctrines, and constitutes itself through textual manifestations of legal decisions, judgements, opinions and so on. The understanding of legal texts and interpretation which underpins doctrinal studies of law and black-letter scholarship, places the law beyond the direct reach of the laity and strengthens law's position among other disciplines and forms of knowledge. By doing so, it also neglects law as a field of *social* practice which we shall explore in chapter 10, and overlooks its role as an instrument of social organisation. Although law and legal practice are often presented in terms of daily struggles with statutory interpretation and law reports, the reality of legal practice is often formed by reference to institutional facts of the law, which is captured more by the procedural aspects of law (how things are done) rather than by knowledge of substantive law (which requires legal interpretation). Also, law is frequently used out of courts, and often without the involvement of lawyers and judges, as part of the efforts of ordinary men and women to organise their everyday life.[5]

The chapters in this section each challenge the traditional approach of law, legal interpretation and legal texts by arguing that legal discourse and forms of knowledge are intimately linked to, and dependent on, other forms of discourse and knowledge. More importantly, they use legal texts not to

---

[4] Law and language has also been a topic of ethnographic studies, which often examine the relationship between law and language by analysing conversational exchanges in legal setting. For an overview see M Travers, 'Understanding Talk in Legal Setting: What Law and Society Studies Can Learn from Conversation Analysts' (forthcoming) *Law and Social Inquiry*.

[5] For discussions of law as a form of social organisation see P Stjernquist, *Organised Cooperation Facing Law: An Anthropological Study* (Stockholm, Almqvist & Wiksell International, 2000); and ch 7 in R Banakar, *Merging Law and Sociology* (Berlin, Galda & Wilch, 2003).

establish the content of law, but to study how such legal institutions as the ombudsmen are organised, how ethnicity and race are legally constructed and how certain EU directives are negotiated and implemented.[6] In other words, they employ legal texts as empirical indicators of various institutional, organisational, racial or gender specific properties of law, which are either ignored or neglected by the traditional methods of legal studies.

The first chapter in this section is by Reza Banakar, who makes use of legal documents to study the office of the Swedish Ombudsman against Ethnic Discrimination. Banakar views legal texts as a source of sociological data, which can enable researchers to shed light on how institutional facts regarding the ombudsman and anti-discrimination Act are constructed. He is, however, conscious of the limitations that this type of data imposes on sociological studies of law. The cases he uses consist of written complaints on unlawful discrimination and legal records of how these complaints were processed and how discrimination cases were decided by the ombudsman. These cases are, on the one hand, valuable sources of empirical data in so far as they register the interaction between the perspectives of various social actors who are involved in legal processes and their perception of the law. He also maintains that this interaction ultimately creates a legal case and determines its outcome, ie, it describes the reality of law in action. On the other hand, the empirical data provided by the study of cases are sociologically restricted, because law registers this interaction on its own terms to address its own concerns and not those of the sociologists. Then, through its functionaries and institutions, law constructs its images and perceptions of society and social relationships in its own limited and formal language. The formal articulation and documentation of events in the legally restricted vocabulary of law, almost by definition excludes extra-legal factors, ideas, experiences and arguments which might be of paramount importance to a sociological inquiry. That is why Banakar concludes his chapter by questioning if one could rely solely on data extracted from legal cases in a sociological study of law which is concerned with social action, behaviour and agency. To counterbalance the empirical shortcomings of legal documents as a source of empirical data he argues that they need to be complemented with other forms of data gathered through other methods of inquiry such as interviews and observations.

Mary Seneviratne overcomes the limits of legal cases, which were described by Banakar, in the second chapter of this section, which also concerns the study of ombudsmen, by employing a variety of methods in her

---

[6] Legal texts are also used frequently by feminist scholars to investigate the legal construction of gender. For examples of such studies of legal texts see C Smart, *Feminism and the Power of Law* (London, Routledge, 1995); and P Smith, (ed), *Feminist Jurisprudence* (Oxford, OUP, 1993).

work, including textual analysis, interviews and surveys. At the same time, Seneviratne provides a lucid and useful guide to how UK ombudsmen can be studied, for example as individual schemes or as part of the legal system's mechanism of dispute resolution. Not surprisingly, her study relies heavily on the study of legal documents which include statutes, annual reports, investigation reports, complaints statistics, articles by ombudsmen and ombudsmen's files. Despite this reliance, she maintains that her approach should not be confused with the method of discourse analysis, which approaches texts and other forms of discourse in their own right. Instead, her study uses texts and discourses to access attitudes and events which lie beyond the texts. Our understanding of Seneviratne's argument is that while discourse analysis, particularly as it is used within legal studies, is normatively tuned to discover (or construct) the meaning of a text in an attempt to examine or clarify the implementation of legal rules, her use of texts is sociologically tuned to discover (or construct) institutional facts regarding ombudsmen. As she explains, her research can be described as 'an investigation into what ombudsmen actually do and how they and others perceive what they do'.

Seneviratne's study could have also been presented in Section Six of this volume as an example of socio-legal research in the UK. Her general approach is theoretically informed, yet in the final analysis engages with such policy issues as the internal effectiveness of ombudsmen schemes. Banakar, on the other hand, studies ombudsmen not so much because he is specifically interested in evaluating them or describing how they operate, but as a means of investigating how law creates its images of ethnic relations and copes with ethnic discrimination. Despite their different objectives, both Banakar and Seneviratne study legal texts, partly because legal documents constitute records of legal communications about previous communicative actions, which in turn reveals how ombudsmen organise themselves and execute their tasks. Both these methodological approaches are therefore concerned with different structural and functional properties of law. The focus on the organisational features of law distinguishes them, however, from interpretative methods of discourse analysis, which also study texts and other forms of written, visual or verbal communication. Discourse analysis often aims at discovering how social identities such as gender and race, (power) relations and systems of knowledge are signified, constituted and constructed.

These two methods of textual analysis are combined in the final chapter of this section. In her chapter, Bettina Lange uses a combination of a discourse analysis and other quantitative approaches to study 'the key obligations under the EU directives on Integrated Pollution Prevention and Control'. She acknowledges the difficulty inherent in distinguishing discourse analysis from qualitative approaches in general because both these methods recognise the significance of language for the construction of social life and human relations. By way of clarification, Lange notes that discourse analysis is not necessarily a form of qualitative research method; it can in fact make use of quantitative methods. More importantly, discourse analysis and quantitative methods work with different concepts of agency, social action and the relationship between discursive and non-discursive elements in the social world.

However, as illustrated by Lange, discourse analysis can be used within the framework of other theories, such as Anthony Giddens' structuration theory, which help us not to lose sight of the problem of structure/agency.[7] Using this framework, we can examine how discursive 'resources' are employed by the agency in relation to structural (power, economic or cultural) relationships and how these structures, in return, impact on and position the agency and restrict or enable him/her to construct social meaning. This chapter provides us with an excellent example of how one can combine discourse analysis and interviewing to capture both the discursive and non-discursive factors used in the construction of social reality.

The chapters presented in this section do not claim to cover all the theoretical and methodological implications of studying legal texts and documents. Yet, we hope that they highlight three central methodological problems associated with the textual analysis of legal texts. Firstly, we hope that the chapters illustrate how legal texts can be *interpreted* using methods significantly different from those which are traditionally adopted by legal scholars. The studies presented in this section could be read as examples of how legal texts can be studied as empirical indicators of the way law organises itself internally, interacts with its social environment and constructs its images of social relations. Secondly, we hope that these studies draw attention to the limitation of legal texts as a source of empirical data. Legal texts might be empirical indicators of the relationship between legal and social factors and relationships, but they reflect the social reality with great selectivity. Finally, we hope that the following chapters demonstrate how textual analysis of legal texts may be combined with other methods of data gathering to enrich socio-legal research.

---

[7] Structuration theory rejects the duality of individual and society and maintains that there is a recursive relationship between structural properties of social organisation and the purposive actions and interactions of human agency. Actions produce and sustain structures, while structures enable and constrain actions. Rules and resources are another pair of concepts which link structure and action and correspond to the enabling and constraining properties of structures. Rules make actions recognisable and determine their normative content. Resources are the structured material, symbolic, biological or cognitive properties of the social systems which provide the knowledgeable actor with some means of realising his/her objectives. For a critical assessment of the shortcomings of the 'Structuration Theory', see D Held and JB Thompson, *Social Theory of Modern Societies: Anthony Giddens and his Critics* (Cambridge, CUP, 1989); and R Collins, 'The Romanticism of Agency/Structure "Agency/Structure" Versus the Analysis of Micro/Macro' (1992) 40 *Current Sociology* 77.

7

Studying Cases Empirically: A Sociological Method for Studying Discrimination Cases in Sweden

REZA BANAKAR

T HIS PAPER USES two previous studies of unlawful discrimination, which I carried out in Sweden in 1992 and 1996, to develop a more comprehensive sociological method for studying anti-discrimination laws.[1] The initial question asked in these studies concerned the impact of the Swedish Act against Ethnic Discrimination (hereafter the AED), ie, how the legal system dealt with unlawful discrimination and to what extent it counteracted discriminatory practices using the AED. The data used comprised official studies of various aspects of immigrants' and ethnic minorities' conditions in employment and occupation, open interviews with various groups such as lawyers and immigrants, a study of the discourse on ethno-cultural relations in Sweden, and discrimination cases. The focus of this chapter will be on the limitations of discrimination cases which were used in the studies of ethnic discrimination in Sweden.

The following is divided into two sections. Section One provides a brief account of how the first two studies were conducted by focusing on the communicative practices through which the cases were processed and decided. The experience of conducting these studies is then used to discuss the limitations of legal documents as empirical data. In Section Two, I propose a new approach to the study of unlawful discrimination, which uses the experiences gained from the previous studies to argue that each case has

---

[1] See R Banakar, *Merging Law and Sociology: Beyond the Dichotomies of the Socio-Legal Research* (Berlin, Glada and Wilch Verlag, 2003); R Banakar, *The Doorkeepers of the Law: A Socio-Legal Study of Ethnic Discrimination in Sweden* (Aldershot, Dartmouth, 1998); R Banakar, *The Dilemma of Law: Conflict Management in a Multicultural Society* (Swedish title: Rättens Dilemma: Om konflikthantering i ett mångtkulturellt samhälle) (Lund, Bokbox, 1994).

its own specific social structure.[2] The social structure of each case can be explored by highlighting the interaction—conceptualised in terms of communicative action—between the perspectives of various actors, ie, parties to the dispute, officers of the court, judges, or ombudsmen, who together create the case. The focus then becomes how the perspectives of various actors and their perceptions of law, interact with each other to bring about a specific outcome. The actor's perspective varies in accordance with his/her standing in relation to the law and his/her involvement in legal processes. My approach moves from a mere concern with the impact of law on unlawful discrimination to a more fundamental concern with how legal rules, doctrines, legal decisions, institutionalised cultural and legal practices work together to create the reality of law in action.

A. TWO STUDIES OF THE AED

1. Background

The Swedish Parliament enacted its first piece of legislation specifically designed to counteract ethnic discrimination in 1986.[3] This legislation did not contain provisions prohibiting ethnic discrimination in recruitment and/or employment.[4] Instead, it created the Office of the Ombudsman against Ethnic Discrimination (hereafter the Ombudsman)[5] and entrusted

---

[2] In D Black, *Sociological Justice* (Oxford, OUP, 1989), Donald Black outlines a theory of legal cases, which aims to predict and explain variations in the application of law. Black argues that each case has a specific social structure 'relevant to every kind of legal behaviour, including the likelihood of a telephone call to the police "police", a visit to a lawyer, an arrest, a prosecution, a lawsuit, a victory in court, the severity of a disposition, and the likelihood of a successful appeal' (Black 1998, *ibid*, p 8). These are 'variations in the quantity of law', or to put it differently, 'the amount of governmental "authority" brought to bear on a person or group' (*ibid*). Although Black's conceptualisation of the social structure of legal cases is sociologically informed, it nonetheless falls short of a full engagement with law as an institutionally constructed normative system of rules and practices. The approach presented in this chapter has been developed independently of Black's theory. For a critique of Black's theory see Banakar 2003, above, n 1.

[3] See Swedish Legislation SFS 1986: 442.

[4] Prior to the enactment of this legislation, statutory provisions against various forms of unlawful discrimination did exist, but they were scattered across various areas of Swedish law ranging from the Constitution to the Criminal and Labour Law.

[5] The institution of ombudsman 'Ombudsman' is part of Sweden's tradition of constitutional democracy and a tool for preserving and enhancing 'the rule of law'. The Swedish Parliament adopted the idea of appointing a special officer, the Parliamentary Ombudsman (or the PO), for the first time in 1809 to supervise the compliance of judges, civil servants and military officers with laws and ordinances. The modern PO scrutinises the administration of justice and draws attention to the shortcomings of laws by reporting and making recommendations on individual cases and administrative procedures to Parliament. Everyone is entitled to lodge a complaint with the PO and, in fact, in the vast majority of cases, an inquiry is set in

the Ombudsman with the task of counteracting discrimination through information—ie, by informing public opinion of what ethnic discrimination was—and by scrutinising the actions of employers. The law gave the Ombudsman the necessary legal power to demand from employers against whom a complaint was lodged explanation for their alleged discriminatory treatment of job seekers or employees. However, it did not provide sanction against ethnic discrimination in the labour market and working life. The AED (1986) was heavily criticised for neglecting ethnic discrimination in recruitment and employment, as a result of which it was revised and amended after eight years.[6] The amended AED[7] gave the Ombudsman greater powers to counteract ethnic discrimination legally and became Sweden's first anti-discrimination legislation to protect ethnic minorities (primarily immigrants) in the labour market. The AED (1994) did not, however, cover the entire recruitment process. The employers could simply evade short listing applicants with foreign names or backgrounds and in this way exclude them from being considered seriously for a job opening, without the risk of being sued. Also, the Act fell short of making any impact on indirect discrimination, which meant that employers could use seemingly objective procedures to exclude certain ethnic groups from participation in the labour market. For example, they could demand proof of proficiency in Swedish for jobs which required limited verbal or written skills, which would exclude some immigrant groups. Finally, the AED (1994) placed the burden of proof on the claimant, making it extremely difficult to demonstrate that direct discrimination had actually taken place. As a result, and despite the fact that the necessary legal powers to take cases to the Labour Court were conferred on the Ombudsman by the AED (1994), the Ombudsman succeeded in taking only one case to court, which, incidentally, he lost.[8]

---

motion as a result of a complaint made by a member of the public. Swedish ombudsmen may (unlike their counterparts in other countries such as the UK) start investigations on their own initiative, but they cannot enforce legal decisions or reverse administrative actions, for which they remain dependent on the courts. They should, therefore, not be confused with judges or tribunals who have such powers. Besides the PO, there are a number of other ombudsmen in Sweden, each with a specialised task and a specific jurisdiction, 'Jurisdiction' which is considerably more limited than that of the PO. The Consumer Ombudsman, the Equal Opportunities Ombudsman, the Ombudsman Against Ethnic Discrimination, the Ombudsman against Discrimination on the basis of Sexual Orientation, the Office of Disability Ombudsman, Ombudsman for Children, and the Press Ombudsman are also appointed by the Parliament and are subjected to the PO's supervision (but they may not monitor each other). Unlike the courts these ombudsmen are capable of conducting lengthy and in-depth investigations with a procedural flexibility which often lies far beyond the scope of the courts.

[6] See Banakar, 1994, above, n 1.
[7] Swedish Legislation SFS 1994: 134.
[8] See Banakar, 1998, above, n 1. I shall refer to the Ombudsmen as 'he' because the first two ombudsmen who were appointed and processed the cases used in this study were men.

At the same time, the plight of certain immigrant groups in the Swedish labour market was highlighted in the mass media and public political debates.[9] Various studies also showed that many immigrants felt that they were being discriminated against.[10] A range of factors gave empirical weight to immigrants' claims regarding relatively widespread ethnic discrimination in Sweden. Previous studies demonstrated that immigrants had *significantly* higher unemployment rates, *significantly* lower incomes and inferior working conditions compared with a comparable Swedish group.[11] Their mobility in the labour market, and consequently their upward mobility, was considerably less than those of native Swedes.[12] Among certain immigrant groups, such as Latin Americans and second-generation immigrants, a downward mobility in the labour market had been observed.[13] Social scientists who had studied the relationship between immigration, the economic development of Sweden and the status of immigrants in the Swedish labour market pointed out that two separate labour markets, one for ethnic Swedes and one for immigrants, existed in Sweden. The latter consisted mainly of low-paid jobs that require working in shifts or in harmful working environments with no prospect for career advancement.[14]

Not surprisingly, criticism against the AED (1994) soon mounted and a proposal for a new AED with further amendments was submitted to Parliament and enacted in 1999. The AED has, therefore, gone through three distinct stages in its transition from an anti-discrimination law without

---

[9] This point is further discussed below in ch 10.

[10] See, for example, A Lange, *Invandrare om Etnisk Diskriminering* (Stockholm, Stockholm Universitet, CEIFO, 1996). In this study, which was conducted on behalf of the Ombudsman in order to highlight the relation between immigrants and Swedes, it was shown that a large portion of Sweden's immigrant population had been subjected to discriminatory, degrading, threatening or violent behaviour during their stay in 'Sweden'. The investigation was carried out by the Swedish Bureau of Official Statistics (SCB) and was based on interviews with 1008 African, Arab, Latin American and Polish immigrants who had come to Sweden between 1971 and 1991. One of the questions asked was if they had applied for a job over the last five years for which they were qualified, but failed to obtain the position in question because of their ethnic, national or religious background. Among those who responded to this question, 33.7% of Africans, 38.5% of Arabs, 24.8% of Latin Americans and 24.8% of Poles reported being discriminated against in their search for employment. A considerably larger percentage reported encountering threatening behaviour in public places. Fifty-one percent of all Africans queried, 45.5% of Arabs, 45% of Latin Americans and 12% of Poles reported that they had been threatened or insulted because of their ethnic origin.

[11] Source: Swedish Immigration Authorities, *På tal om invandrare* (Regarding the Immigrants) (Norrköping, SIV, 1994).

[12] J Ekberg, *Yrkeskarriärer under 1970–Talet* (Stockholms läns Landsting, Regionplanekontoret, Rapport, 1985); Swedish Official Investigation (SOU, 1989) 111; *Invandrare i storstad* (Underlagsrapport från Storstadsutredningen, 1989) 38.

[13] W Knocke, *Invandrare möter facket–Betydelsen av hemlandsbakgrund och hemvist i arbetslivet* (Stockholm, Arbetslivscentrum, 1982) 66; and J Ekberg, *Inkomsteffekter av Invandring* (Högskolan i Växjö, Centrum för ArbetsMarknadspolitisk Forskning, 1983).

[14] C-U Schierup and S Paulson, *Arbetets Etniska Delning* (Stockholm, Carlsson, 1994).

specific provisions prohibiting unlawful discrimination in working life to a law with sanctions against direct and indirect discrimination. Although it might be of interest to consider each of these stages separately, this task falls outside the present undertaking. Instead, we shall limit our discussions to the first two stages of the development of the AED.

To sum up, although the AED (1986) created a starting point for preventing ethnic discrimination in public and private services, it nonetheless fell short of providing explicit sanctions against ethnic discrimination in the labour market. This law also set up the Office of the Ombudsman against Ethnic Discrimination and entrusted it with the task of eradicating ethnic discrimination from all walks of life including the labour market, which the legislature ironically left unregulated in this regard. One of the initial questions motivating this research focused on the Ombudsman's ability to counteract unlawful ethnic discrimination in the labour market, which is arguably the most damaging form of racial discrimination. This question was of special interest because the Ombudsman lacked a legal instrument empowering him to force employers to comply with a non-discriminatory policy. In the first of the two studies mentioned above, I used cases from 1990, when the AED had not yet provided sanctions against unfair treatment of job applicants and employees on ethno-cultural grounds. In the second study, I used data collected after the enactment of the amended AED in 1994, which did contain such sanctions.[15]

The empirical data used in these studies consisted of cases processed by the Ombudsman and were collected in two separate phases in 1990 and 1995. The first set of data was based on a qualitative study of all cases lodged with and processed by the Ombudsman in 1990. In that year the Ombudsman registered 736 cases, of which roughly half were complaints about ethno-cultural conflicts. The second set of data is from 1995, reflecting the amended AED of 1994 in action. The Ombudsman registered about 1000 cases during 1995, more than half of which concerned ethnic discrimination. From these cases I selected 78, of which 73 were directly related to discrimination in the labour market. These cases were chosen primarily to examine the amendment which recognised the need to protect ethno-cultural minorities in the labour market by prohibiting ethnic discrimination in working life. The question was whether the amendments, which gave greater power to the Ombudsman did, in fact, help to curb unlawful ethnic discrimination against job applicants and employees. At the time when these 73 cases were selected (at the end of 1996) they constituted all the major *processed* cases on discrimination in the labour market that were

---

[15] An unabridged version of the part of this chapter, which draws on data from 1990, was published in Swedish in Banakar, 1994, above, n 1.

registered during 1995 by the Ombudsman. (A handful of cases which had been lodged during 1995 were still being processed in 1996.) This choice of data allowed the study to focus on labour-related ethnic discrimination. It also made it possible to explore the changes which were brought about as a result of the amendments to the AED (in 1994) that directly addressed ethnic discrimination in the labour market for the first time.

Although, as pointed out above, most of the selected cases concerned ethnic discrimination in working life, I nonetheless included examples of cases that did not concern strictly ethno-cultural disputes and did not directly have a bearing on the problem at hand. These were chosen to provide an insight into the diversity of the cases lodged with the Ombudsman.

2. The Method of Investigation

The two studies mentioned above followed three methodologically distinct but interrelated stages. These stages can be briefly described as: 1) gaining an overview of the empirical data in order to formulate a number of working hypotheses; 2) constructing a preliminary conceptual apparatus to conduct a systematic substantive analysis of the empirical data; and 3) attempting to develop the theoretical basis of the investigation. The theoretical framework of this study was, therefore, developed in view of the available data. As pointed out above, the bulk of the material used in this study consisted of ethnic discrimination cases. The cases ordinarily contained two types of information: 1) a letter of complaint which provided the complainant's account of a dispute with a second party; and 2) a record of how the dispute was processed by the Ombudsman. Occasionally, an account of the Ombudsman's correspondence with the second party and/or of the response from the second party towards whom the allegation of discrimination was directed was also included. The cases were systematically registered and kept at the Ombudsman's archive in Stockholm. Going through all the cases which were processed by the Ombudsman during 1990 constituted the first phase of the analysis of the empirical material.

This initial stage of the study was carried out in an inductive manner and aimed at describing the properties of these cases. The result indicated that the cases contained sufficient information to answer socio-legal questions on issues such as conflict resolution, policy implementation, regulation of public administration, discretion, the rule of law and legal decision-making. However, the information contained in the files was limited from a sociological point of view in the sense that it revealed little or nothing about the social psychological mechanisms of ethnic discrimination. The data contained in the files did not provide clues of causal relations between racial attitudes and discriminatory practices, which meant that they could not be used to examine, for example, why certain ethnic groups were systematically excluded by employers while others were recruited.

As pointed out above, the files mainly contained two types of documents: letters of complaint (and occasionally responses from the party who was accused of discrimination) and records of measures taken by the Ombudsman. Such content introduced two sociological limitations. First, regarding the complaints, each one was ordinarily a (written) narrative based on a one-sided account of an ethno-cultural dispute. As such, it was at best proof of *experienced* discrimination, which might or might not have been caused by *intended* discriminatory action. The second limitation, emerging from the transcripts of legal measures taken by the Ombudsman was linked to the selective nature of legal processing, where only the legally relevant aspects of the dispute (but also how it was investigated by the Ombudsman) were recorded.

In interpreting the complainants' written presentations (and also any second party's responses) attempts were made to follow the so-called 'literal rule' according to which words that are reasonably capable of only one meaning must be given that meaning whatever the result.[16] Where possible, I tried to let the texts of the complaints 'speak for themselves'. I do not, however, claim that a pure literal interpretation is possible, but I used this method in an attempt to contain certain side-effects of textual analysis. In other words, this method of interpretation helped to an extent to avoid *attaching* to the texts and words meaning that transcended their everyday usage and was not intended by the author of the texts.

However, a different interpretative approach was employed to analyse legal records. The legal documents produced by the Ombudsman and other authorities were interpreted broadly and in a teleological fashion.[17] This was because many aspects of laws, directives and guidelines, which were used by the Ombudsman to decide cases, were formulated broadly and resembled policy declarations.[18] These laws and directives left leeway for the Ombudsman to process each case by taking into consideration its social and legal properties. This approach also enabled me to take into account the social functions of the Ombudsman as envisaged by the legislature.

[16] The so-called 'literal rule' is a method developed *inter alia* for statutory interpretation.

[17] Teleological construction of a statute, which in Sweden is associated above all with Per Olof Ekelöf, is an interpretation of the statute in view of its *purpose*. It is often used when there are some ambiguities embedded in the makeup of the statute or the Act in question. For a detailed discussion on this mode of reasoning see P O Ekelöf, 'Teological Construction of Statutes' in F Schmidt, (ed), *Scandinavian Studies in Law* (Stockholm, Almquist & Wiksell, 1958); and A Peczenik, *On Law and Reason* (Dordrecht, Kluwer, 1989) 404–25.

[18] To give an example, according to the AED the Ombudsman is to try to ensure that ethnic discrimination does not occur in the labour market in employment or in other areas of social life. By advice and in any other ways that the Ombudsman sees fit, he shall assist anyone subjected to ethnic discrimination to safeguard his or her rights. The Ombudsman shall, by means of consultations with other authorities, companies and organisations and by influencing public opinion, information and other similar means initiate measures against ethnic discrimination.

Diagram 1 illustrates the types of document and methods adopted to interpret their contents.

Diagram 1

Content of the Files	The Structure of Documents	Empirical Property	Method of Interpretation
1. Letters of Complaints	Extra-legal	Narratives	The Literal Rule
2. Records of Measures Taken by Ombudsman	Legal	Records of Rational Procedural Measures	The Teleological Rule

The initial analysis of cases demonstrated that they provided a valuable source of information on various types of disputes related to ethnicity. The contents of the files also depicted the legal and extra-legal strategies developed by the Ombudsman to process these conflicts and the way in which the legal system subsequently dealt with them. However, as pointed out above, despite the fact that most of the complaints were concerned with ethnic discrimination, the files could not offer a reliable basis for investigating the social psychological causes of ethnic discrimination. As a result, the scope of the analysis was restricted to questions on which the empirical data could throw light. Thus, research questions were formulated concerning 1) the types of conflicts presented to the Ombudsman, 2) the strategies which were adopted by the Ombudsman to deal with them, and 3) the subsequent socio-legal effects that were brought on by the application of these strategies. These effects revealed how such concepts as discrimination, ethnicity, race or racism were reproduced within the legal system and used for legal decision-making and how law's understanding and definitions of these concepts impacted on ethnic discriminatory behaviour and race relations.

The objective of the initial stage was to gain an overview of the material in order to formulate a number of working hypotheses. The second stage aimed to devise a theoretical instrument. A conceptual apparatus was needed which could facilitate a substantive examination of the contents of the cases and provide us with plausible answers to the research questions. Again going back to the empirical material, three major areas were identified which needed to be addressed theoretically. These were: 1) communication, 2) conflict or dispute, and 3) modes of dispute resolution.

I defined the *process* of lodging a complaint with the Ombudsman and the Ombudsman's subsequent handling of it in terms of *communication*. In order to develop this idea further, I used the theory of communicative action as my main theoretical framework to grasp and analyse the legal system's application of procedural processing of complaints.[19] Thus, the method of investigation used here was developed through a close interplay between the available empirical data, the research questions posed and the relevant theoretical constructs within the sociology of law.

Stage three, using cases filed in 1995, was conducted in accordance with the initial research questions. It was, moreover, concerned with assessing the possible impact of the amended AED on ethnic discrimination and developing the theoretical basis of this investigation further. The remaining part of this section is devoted to presenting some of the insights gained by the initial investigation of the cases. These insights concern the strategies used by the Ombudsman to deal with conflicts and the types of disputes brought before the Ombudsman.

3. Processing Complaints and the Ombudsman's Gate-keeping Techniques

The Ombudsman reviews complaints brought before him/her by deciding: 1) if the complaint concerns ethnic discrimination or is related to ethno-cultural issues; 2) if the dispute as it is expressed and presented by the complainant is *bona fide*, in the sense that it provides adequate grounds for legal action, or to put it differently, if some aspects of the dispute can be subsumed under a legal rule and therefore can be brought within the domain of legal regulation; and 3) in cases where there is a *bona fide* dispute, what further legal measures may be taken to process the case successfully. In this sense the Ombudsman acts as the first 'gatekeeper' of the law on ethnic discrimination, selecting the cases which may enter the normative sphere of legal meaning.

This model depicts a rather simplified picture of the way in which the Ombudsman processes discrimination complaints. Any decision to include or exclude a complaint involves statutory interpretation, which in turn involves making value judgements on many issues. Some of these issues are legally pertinent and concern fundamental principles underlying the due process and the rule of law. Other issues involve social psychological factors or political values, which are not recorded in the cases and are, therefore, difficult to isolate empirically in the available data.

I should add here that the procedure underlying this gatekeeping technique is far from unique to the Ombudsman, and is also employed by other legal authorities. The procedural model below closely reflects the process of subsumption used by the functionaries of the legal system. Scholars as diverse in their sociological orientations as Ronon Shamir and Niklas Luhmann have grappled with and theorised this process. Shamir argues that

---

[19] J Habermas, *The Theory of Communicative Action*, (Boston, MA, Beacon Press, 1987).

Diagram 2

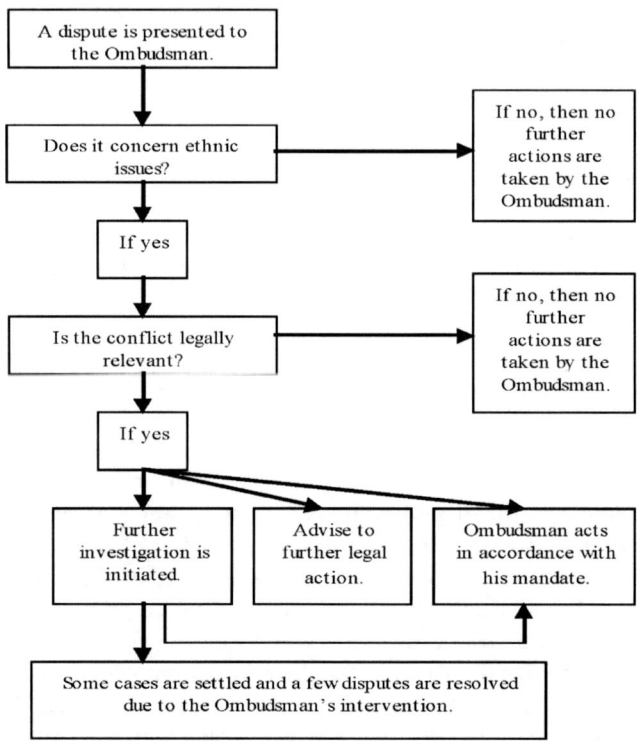

The procedure used by the Ombudsman to process complaints

we need to understand the role of law in terms of its *modus operandi*, which is driven above all by the need to reproduce its own identity. Law achieves this by 'conceptualising' the disputes and issues brought before it, in effect imposing its own limited formal categories on social life. According to Shamir, the imposition of these categories, which lawyers often regard as part of the method of establishing the 'facts' of a case, amount to:

> A mode of cognition based on the belief that the most accurate and reliable way of knowing reality (hence 'truth') depends on the ability to single out the clearest and most distinct elements that constitute a given phenomenon. Conceptualism is a praxis of extraction and isolating elements from the indeterminate and chaotic flow of events and bounding them as fixed categories.[20]

---

[20] R Shamir, 'Suspended in Space: Bedouin Under the Law of Israel' (1996) 30 *Law and Society* 231, 235.

At the most fundamental level, this operation is dependent on the ability of law to impose a conceptual grid on space and time. In this way it controls the space and orders the time in accordance with its own narrow conception of social reality, thus excluding all social, cultural and historical experiences that do not fall within its own limited vocabulary. In this way law confirms the normality of its own categories and reconstructs the society in its own image.

Luhmann, whose interpretation of law is fundamentally different from that of Shamir, explains the same process using the concept of 'complexity reduction' through which law as a *meaning* system (ie, a system which in contrast to biological systems is capable of self-reflection) creates a normatively closed, yet cognitively open and dynamic, autonomous system.[21] Complexity reduction indicates a mode of operation based on creating and sustaining a fundamental difference between law as a system and law's environment. By recursively referring to its own operations law creates for itself the components of which it consists. This idea was also central to Hans Kelsen's definition of the sources of law (through self-reference law becomes the source of its own reproduction, thus gaining autonomy and developing an identity of its own[22]). In the same way that Shamir's conceptualisation excludes alternative meanings which cannot be located easily within the framework of law's categories, Luhmann's autopoietic systems constitute themselves by excluding the diversity of their environment, hence reducing their own complexity in relation to their environment. This operation is conducted by normatively closing the system, a process which requires a system to refer simultaneously to its own internal components and to its external environment.

Let us take a look at four different types of cases, which demonstrate how the model described above operates. These types would also give us a general idea about the efficacy of the AED and the office of the Ombudsman.

4. Four Categories of Complaints

Cases processed by the Ombudsman fall under four general categories indicating the stages shown in diagram 2. The first category includes cases which

---

[21] N Luhmann, 'The Self-Reproduction of Law and its Limits' in G Teubner, (ed), *The Dilemma of Law in the Welfare States* (Berlin, Walter de Gruyter, 1986); and N Luhmann, 'Meaning as Sociology's Basic Concept' in N Luhmann, (ed), *Essays on Self-Reference* (New York, NY, Columbia University Press, 1990).

[22] See H Kelsen, *Introduction to the Problems of Legal Theory* (Oxford, Clarendon Press, 2001) 63–64.

do not concern ethnic discrimination and are not legally relevant, which means that the ombudsman has no alternative but to terminate them without taking any action. The second category consists of cases which articulate types of ethno-cultural conflicts for which the law has not provided any remedy. The Ombudsman leaves these also without further action. However, the Ombudsman recognises and reports to Parliament the importance of these cases, which signal the shortcomings of law and policy in the area of race relations. The third category relates to cases which lend themselves to legal action, but fall outside the Ombudsman's jurisdiction. In these situations the Ombudsman passes the case on to the appropriate authority for further legal action, but continues to monitor its progress through the legal system. Finally, the fourth category contains of cases which are processed by the Ombudsman successfully and where a form of settlement is reached through his/her intervention.

(a) Category One

Sometimes the complaints made to the Ombudsman can be related neither to ethnic discrimination nor to ethnic issues. A typical example is that of a man who writes to the Ombudsman accusing his colleagues of discriminating against him by not allowing him to smoke at the office. There are also Swedes who write to the Ombudsman claiming that they are being discriminated against because they are Swedes. Such complaints fall outside the jurisdiction of the Ombudsman and his terms of office as described by the AED and are thus rejected. Some of these complaints are based on a misunderstanding of the role of the Ombudsman and the concept of ethnic discrimination. However, some of them have a distinctly racist undertone and appear to be intended as agitation by racists who, by presenting their point of view in the form of a complaint, question the legitimacy of the Ombudsman. This category of complaint does not concern us here, but there is no reason to take its value as socio-legal material lightly. The least one can say about these 'misplaced' complaints is that they express dissatisfaction with the organisation of society in general and ethno-cultural relations in particular. One can also see that many citizens feel a need to express their grievance in the public arena, even when it regards their smoking habits as viewed by others.

Also, in some cases a complaint is made without any demand of redress. The complainant writes to the Ombudsman not because he/she intends to take any legal action, but simply because of the need to express frustration publicly with some unfulfilled expectations. In such cases we can postulate that the Ombudsman fulfils an important 'latent' social function by helping some citizens to cope with certain types of disappointments, in particular those caused by (unfulfilled) expectations that are out of tune with their social environment.

(b) Category Two

A second category consists of complaints which, although pertaining to ethnic relations, are nonetheless classified as legally irrelevant. An immigrant, for instance, writes to the Ombudsman accusing Swedish State Television of ethnic discrimination.[23] The complainant makes his case in the following way:

> The television is a visual medium, which means that the picture itself and not what is actually discussed in various programmes constitutes the main message; the images are, in other words, the message communicated.

> Among the elements that shape this message are the appearances of those on the television screen: those who read the news, compère, and so on. Even their very appearance and posture is a message. Today there are people belonging to many races living in Sweden, each with its specific skin colour and facial features etc. However, because of the racial policy of Swedish State Television, these diversities are not reflected on the television screen. There is not one person among those appearing on the screen with an Asian or African appearance. The message communicated is that there are only Swedes living in Sweden ...[24]

This complaint is now 14 years old and the television screen has somewhat adjusted itself to the existing ethnic diversity in Sweden. A handful of those who have appeared on the screen more recently do have non-Swedish facial features.

The point made by the complainant is highly pertinent to the regulation of race relations in Sweden, in so far as it accuses one of the main organs of the establishment of institutionalised race discrimination (or even of institutional racism). He argues that as long as only personnel with northern European facial features appear on the television screen, Swedish State Television in effect ignores Sweden's multiethnic diversity. Furthermore, one may wonder if this policy does not set the standards for what is to be regarded as 'normal' implying that Asian and African features are to be regarded as ethnic aberrations.

No matter how interesting the content of this complaint might be, it provides no grounds for taking legal action. It is based on an allegation or, to put it differently on a hypothesis concerning the alleged consequences of the racial policy of Swedish State Television. At the time these complaints were made there were no laws against the type of indirect discrimination alleged here. The problem as it was presented could not be regarded as legally relevant and the Ombudsman closed the case without any further action.

---

[23] The complaint refers to Sweden's public television channels.
[24] The Ombudsman's Case Number (Diarienummer) 75/90.

(c) Category Three

A parish clerk writes to the Ombudsman complaining about a radio programme that is regularly transmitted on one of the Stockholm local radio stations. According to the clerk, the person presenting the programme expresses racist and extreme right-wing views. The presenter warns the listeners about immigrants in general, who, according to him, not only cost the Swedish society a great deal in economic terms, but also rape Swedish girls and so on. The complainant encloses a tape with recorded samples of the programme in question and asks the Ombudsman if the recordings could be used as grounds for indicting the radio station in question on criminal charges. The Ombudsman sends the written complaint and the tape enclosed to the Office of the Chancellor of Justice for further examination regarding the breach of the Freedom of Expression Act.[25] In this way, the Ombudsman paves the way for other authorities to investigate the complaint originally brought before him.[26]

(d) Category Four

The complainant (we shall call him C) is an immigrant who has fallen out with his Swedish neighbours.[27] The neighbours have complained to the Tenants' Society (*bostadsförening*) concerning C's disorderly conduct. According to the neighbours, C disturbs them 'through pounding and running in the flat until late at night'. The district manager of the Tenants' Society at C's housing area sends C a letter of warning and points out that:

> the complaints made show that your conduct in the flat is in breach of the rules you agreed to follow when you moved in.... In accordance with the Tenement Act, if further complaints are received the housing corporation will write to inform you once again that your conduct must be corrected. This will be the last warning before your tenancy contract is terminated.[28]

C sends the letter of warning issued by the Tenants' Society to the Ombudsman and emphatically maintains that he has not disturbed the neighbours. C points out in his letter that this strategy is being used to terminate his contract.

On the basis of C's complaint, the Ombudsman contacts the Tenants' Society and asks the following questions:

---

[25] The Act is applicable to radio, television and other similar transmissions, films, video programmes and other recordings of moving pictures as well as sound recordings (gramophone records etc.). The Chancellor of Justice (JK) is responsible for examining complaints regarding possible offences against this Act.

[26] The Ombudsman's Case Number 28/90.

[27] The Ombudsman's Case Number 16/90.

[28] *Ibid.*

1. Has the Tenants' Society made any effort to reconcile the neighbours, settle their problems and harmonise their relations?
2. Have the complaints that were made to the Tenants' Society been examined in accordance with the principle that no one is to be condemned until found guilty?

As it transpires the district manager of the Tenants' Society has not made any effort to investigate the problem and the neighbours' allegations are simply accepted as true. Furthermore, the only reasonable and effective solution to him is to work for the termination of C's contract.

A week later the Ombudsman receives a reply from the district manager who explains that he has now talked to the neighbours who made the complaint and gets the impression that they are 'a bit touchy'. Furthermore, he informs the Ombudsman of a meeting that he has arranged at his office to which all the neighbours are invited. The purpose of this meeting is to give everyone the opportunity to air their feelings and talk to each other as adults. Finally, he assures the Ombudsman that he gets the impression that the neighbours are really going to try 'to meet each other half way ...'. The Ombudsman closes the case with a letter to the Tenants' Society in which he points out:

> In your opinion the complaining neighbours are a bit touchy. Then, on the basis of information provided by them, one ought not to issue letters of warning as the final measure. We must try to uphold the protection provided by the law for our tenants who are exposed to unjustified complaints from neighbours. You are welcome to comment on my views on this matter.[29]

This case is an example of the way the Ombudsman can, by investigating a complaint, bring about a settlement which is acceptable to parties in dispute. The Ombudsman appears here as an officer of the law whose words carry weight and who can act decisively towards the resolution of disputes. However, the Ombudsman is using the symbolic force of the law and much of what he does in this case may be described as *extra-legal*. In a sense, the Ombudsman's actions are not strictly supported by any particular legal rule. Furthermore, in this example, the element of coercion is absent. The manager of the Tenants' Society did not have to comply as he did with the instructions communicated to him by the Ombudsman.

This case also exemplifies the role of communication in resolving disputes. Such conflicts can be resolved only if the parties to the dispute willingly consent to negotiate their differences with each other. At the same time, the Ombudsman demonstrates that he can contribute to creating a forum for such a discourse by using the authority conferred on him by law. It does not of course mean that C's dispute with his neighbours is resolved,

[29] *Ibid.*

but if a resolution can be reached it is through open dialogue. In such a situation, the law can only create favourable conditions for the resolution of conflicts.

The above case is from 1990. The Ombudsman successfully processed a similar complaint in 1995.[30] This second case was not about a dispute between neighbours, but a housing association's decision to rent its houses to immigrants or refugees only under 'exceptional circumstances'. The housing association promptly reconsidered its rental policy once the Ombudsman contacted and questioned their policy to exclude immigrants and refugees.

B. THE SOCIAL STRUCTURE OF DISCRIMINATION CASES

1. Actors' Perspectives on Law

The first two studies described above explored the impact of the AED by highlighting some of the main communicative practices through which the law was enacted and enforced. In a more recent study which compares the AED with the Swedish Equal Opportunity Act I have extended this enquiry into the role played by the interplay of the distinct perspectives of different actors, such as the complainant's, the Ombudsman's or those of other authorities or parties to the dispute.[31] An actor's perspective is viewed in the context of his/her *standing* in relation to law, which is conceptualised in terms of his/her knowledge and experience of law, on the one hand, and interest and involvement in legal processes, on the other. This action theoretical approach was developed using two related theoretical assumptions. Firstly, by making a distinction between the perspectives of 'insiders' and 'outsiders' to law, and secondly, by regarding law as 'a participant-oriented discipline', which prioritises definitions, assumptions and approaches which are based on 'practical insider attitudes'.[32] These two assumptions bring into consideration the notions of 'observation' and 'participation' in relation to law's processes, thus helping us to examine the actors' perspectives on law and how these perspectives interact with each other to create, present, process or resolve a dispute or a legal case.[33]

Since the inside and outside of law do not exist independently of each other and the boundary between them is re-negotiated from case to case,

---

[30] The Ombudsman's Case Number 545/95.

[31] Banakar, 2003, above, n 1.

[32] W Twining, *Globalisation and Legal Theory* (London, Butterworths, 2000) 129.

[33] The notion of perspective was developed in a previous study inspired by George Gurvitch's sociology of law. See R Banakar, 'Integrating Reciprocal Perspectives: On Georges Gurvitch's Theory of Immediate Jural Experience' (2001) 16 *Canadian Journal of Law and Society*.

any absolute distinction between them amounts to introducing a false dichotomy. Law, whether defined as a sphere of social action, as a field of practice, as a form of discourse or as a system of rules, is continually in flux. That is why the inside and outside of law are used here not as absolute and immutable entities, but as *variables* indicating two relative forms of experience, ie, experience-near and experience-distant manifestations and perceptions of the law, which an actor can develop in relation to law and legal processes. These experiences are shaped by the social context, which defines the inside and outside of law in relation to those people and circumstances that reproduce the law and its institutions at any given *time* and *place*. An individual (such as a policeman or an academic lawyer) or an organisation (such as the police or the law faculty) could be insider in one relationship and, at the same time, outsider in another relationship or social context. An arresting officer could be regarded as an insider to the law from the point of view of a detainee, but as an outsider from the point of view of the prosecutor, the defending attorney or the magistrate. A solicitor can be regarded as an insider when advising his or her clients, but as an outsider in the Inns of Court. A lower court judge is an insider when residing his/her court, but an outsider to the court of appeal.

Focusing on the specific position adopted by various actors in respect to law and the degree to which they participate in legal processes, we can distinguish at least four standpoints each capable of producing specific forms of legal knowledge and interest. The first standpoint belongs to insiders who participate in and reproduce legal processes and various institutional practices associated with law (the inside participants). The best example of this group is practising lawyers such as ombudsmen, arbiters, judges or barristers, who play indispensable roles in bringing to bear the values and methods internal to law and legal reasoning on a dispute. More importantly, they participate in the actual process of legal decision-making. The second standpoint belongs to insiders who observe legal processes without participating in them (the inside observers). A legal scholar systematising and expounding legal decisions and cases belongs to this second category. Actors taking these two standpoints are 'insiders' in so far as they share a practical insider attitude towards law, which is in turn dependant on their experience-near knowledge of law and legal institutions. What distinguishes them from each other is their involvement, or lack thereof, in the actual process of legal decision-making. To make matters more complicated most insiders play a double role. Solicitors, for example, act as inside observers when providing legal advice to a client on how to initiate a case or make a claim and as inside participants by representing clients in legal proceedings. To give another example, Lord Chancellor is the president of the Supreme Court, but he/she is also a cabinet minister responsible for advising the government on all judicial appointments and promotions. He/she acts as an inside participant when presiding the Supreme Court or participating in the judicial sessions of the House of Lords, but acts as an inside observer when advising the government. The ombudsman too can, and in fact regularly does, act as an 'inside observer'. He/she not only advises complainants on how to take their cases further, but also monitors the performance of the AED and reports back to Parliament. In this sense the Ombudsman can act as an inside participant in one case and as an inside observer in another.

The third standpoint belongs to outsiders to law, who temporarily participate in legal processes (outside participants). Examples of this group are plaintiffs, defendants, juries, lay judges and witnesses. The complainants who lodge cases with the Ombudsman come under this category if the Ombudsman takes up their case. The fourth standpoint belongs to those who observe legal processes and institutional practices of the law from the outside without participating in legal processes (the outside observers). Sociologists studying law's effects or journalists reporting on trial proceedings can belong to this fourth category. This group, too, interacts with and influences the law and legal institutions. These last two standpoints belong to actors who often have experience-distant knowledge of law and its institutions and are not committed to upholding the practical insider attitude of the first two groups.

Diagram Four illustrates the relationship between the inside and outside of law, on the one hand, and the factors of participation and observation, on the other.

Diagram 3

	Participation	Observation
Insider's Perspective	1. Inside Participant ——Judges ——Barristers	2. Inside Observer ——Legal Advisors ——Legal Scholars
Outsider's Perspective	3. Outside Participant ——Juries ——Plaintiffs	4. Outside Observer ——Journalists ——Sociologist

To sum up, the notions of inside/outside help us to highlight the actor's knowledge and experience of law. The inside participants, such as judges, and the inside observers, such as legal scholars are distinguished from outsiders, such as juries or journalists, by sharing practical inside attitudes and legal know-how, which the outside participants and outside observers usually (but not always) lack. Not only are insiders versed in substantive and procedural law, but more importantly, they also have a tacit knowledge of how legal institutions are organised and work. In other words, insiders are those who are socialised in the internal culture of law and its institutions. The notion of participation, on the other hand, draws attention to the actor's interest. In a legal setting the two participant categories can influence the law in different ways and to different degrees. Moreover, their interest in law is different and in some cases they might, in fact, be pursuing opposite goals. A plaintiff, a witness or a juror do, indeed, participate in legal processes and form an experience-near understanding of the law. Yet, the reasons for their participation and the ends they seek remain different from those of the inside participants, in general, and the judiciary, in particular. Finally, the notion of observation indicates a relative form of theoretical distance from legal processes, which the participant insiders, who are engaged in reproducing these processes, can find hard to maintain.

The standpoints described above form the basis for actors' perspectives on law and exist independently of the sociological characteristics of the actors in the sense that the same person can entertain more than one such perspective in a day's work. This means that the perspectives should be attributed to 'agents' rather than to individual actors. A lawyer, for example, can act as an inside participant in one social setting by making a judgement and as an outside observer in another setting by providing legal advice. In the same day's work, the same lawyer might even act as an outside participant by appearing before a court as a plaintiff or defendant. The important characteristic of these perspectives is that they *interact* with and inform each other. The totality of what we perceive as law is the outcome of the interaction of such perspectives at any given time and place.

In the remaining part of this chapter I argue that we can analyse the social structure of each case by studying the way in which various actors, or their perspectives on law, interact with each other. Here, I limit the analysis to two main perspectives, which initially interact to structure discrimination cases: that of the Ombudsman and the complainant. But it should be noted that there might be other perspectives, such as that of a third party who is accused of discrimination, other authorities such as the police, or even journalists, which might also come into play and influence the processing and subsequently the outcome of certain cases.

In the earlier studies of the AED I compared a number of cases processed by the Ombudsman during 1990 and 1995 in order to describe how the AED of 1994 functioned in practice. Looking back at the cases that I used as the basis of my empirical investigation I can also observe several distinct perspectives on, and subsequently realities of, the AED. One perspective is that of the ombudsman as an inside participant (ie, when he/she participated in the process of investigating and deciding cases) or inside observer (when his/her input was limited to providing advice to the complainants). The ombudsman's view and perception of the AED and the measures that he took and the choices that he made were, however, in the first instance, a function of how the law was constructed internally. This meant that the

Ombudsman's perspective on law and the decisions that he took were constrained by a host of internally constructed factors such as the jurisdiction and terms of his office as they were defined in the AED or by the existing body of other legal rules and doctrines described in other laws and legal decisions. This also means that the Ombudsman had to consider how other authorities, such as the labour courts and other Ombudsmen, viewed and evaluated his legal opinion and decision on how to process cases. For example, the Ombudsman had to act primarily as an impartial and legally competent investigator of complaints, and ensure that all parties viewed him in that light.

The second perspective was that of the complainant as an outside participant to law, who very often viewed the ombudsman as the champion of his or her cause and a legal bulwark against racism, discrimination and social injustice. In this context the AED became no more or less than an instrument to realise justice and to eliminate ethnic discrimination. Most importantly, the perspective of the complainant was in most cases free from the internal normative constraints that the law and the legal system placed on the Ombudsman. At the same time, the perspective of the complainant was formed in relation to, and was concerned with, social and economic factors. For example it was instead informed by how formal and informal norms of organisation were employed and exercised by employers. In this context, a third perspective belonging to the accused party also became pertinent to the formation of the law.

Although these perspectives are distinct in their empirical manifestations, and in certain respects do not overlap, they are nonetheless interacting with one another. The specific social structure of each case is a product of this interaction. The outsider's view of the AED expressed in the complaints which are lodged with the ombudsman were often based on personal and subjective experience of ethnic discrimination, and neglected the importance of providing evidence of unlawful discriminatory practices which could stand up in court. No matter how inadequate this outsider's view on law and legal practice might be, it still constitutes the starting point for the ombudsman, whose actions are constrained by the imperatives of the law and its institutions. It is also a basis for if, and how, the third party's perspective is shaped and brought to bear on the case.

This study demonstrated that the social functions and efficacy of the AED were ultimately the result of the interplay between these perspectives, which produced and reproduced the internal and external realities of the AED in relation to each other.

C FINAL COMMENTS

I touched on the limitation of legal cases above, brought on by legal reasoning as it informs legal decision-making, which can exclude from documentation much of what is sociologically interesting. There are, however, other important limitations which I have not discussed. For example, it is doubtful that one could conduct a sociologically informed empirical study solely on the basis of legal cases. The studies presented above were complemented with other types of data, such as secondary data on the living conditions of immigrants (including income, education, health, employment and occupation) and ethnic minorities (as compared with those of the native Swedes), open interviews with lawyers interested in combating racism and with lawyers who worked at the office of the Ombudsman and assisted in processing of the cases. In addition, I conducted a parallel study on race discrimination by examining the discourse on ethno-cultural issues in Sweden.[34] These other types of related data together created a context in which discrimination cases were studied. Without these supporting studies, the empirical data collected from the cases would hardly have thrown light on the sociologically interesting aspects of processing of discrimination cases. When used independently of supporting empirical data, discrimination cases will at best provide a record of how the Ombudsman has organised his office and his various activities overtime.

Keeping in mind the limitations of legal cases as a source of empirical data and a basis for sociological analysis, the general approach to the study of discrimination cases, as described above, could also be of use to the study of other types of legal documents and cases.

[34] The studies were published separately. See R Banakar, 'Det offentliga samtalet om ethnokulturella frågor' (Public Discourse on Ethno-Cultural Issues) (1993) 1–2 *Häften för kritiska studier* (The Swedish Critical Studies Review).

8

Researching Ombudsmen

MARY SENEVIRATNE

T HE GROWTH OF ombudsmen schemes in the public and private sectors in the United Kingdom has been a feature of modern life. First
appearing in Sweden 200 years ago, ombudsmen were unheard of
outside Scandinavia until 50 years ago, since when they have proliferated
all over the world.[1] In the UK, schemes originated in the public sector, with
the establishment of the Parliamentary Ombudsman in 1967.[2] Since then,
ombudsmen for local government[3] and the health service[4] have been introduced, together with systems for investigating police complaints,[5] and the
prisons and probation service.[6] In the 1980s and early 1990s, the ombudsman concept was adopted by the private sector,[7] mostly on a voluntary
basis,[8] covering a variety of industries. A more recent development is the

---

[1] It is now estimated that over ninety countries have ombudsman offices, operating on a
national, state, regional or municipal level. R Gregory and P Giddings, 'The Ombudsman
Institution: Growth and Development' in R Gregory and P Giddings, (eds), *Righting Wrongs:
The Ombudsman in Six Continents* (Amsterdam, IOS Press, 2000).

[2] Parliamentary Commissioner Act 1967.

[3] Local Government Act 1974.

[4] National Health Service Reorganisation Act 1973, now replaced by the Health Service
Commissioners Act 1993.

[5] The Police Act 1976 established the Police Complaints Board. This was replaced by the
Police Complains Authority, established under the Police and Criminal Evidence Act 1984,
which was itself replaced by the Independent Police Complaints Commission in 2004, as a
result of changes made to the system by the Police Reform Act 2002.

[6] In 1994, a non-statutory ombudsman scheme was introduced to deal with complaints
from prisoners about the prisons service. It was extended to cover complaints about the probation service in 2001.

[7] Here they were established as consumer redress mechanisms, by the insurance industry,
banks, building societies, estate agents, investments, funeral services (this ombudsman has now
ceased to exist), and social housing.

[8] The building society scheme was established by statute. The Legal Services Ombudsman,
established to deal with complaints about legal services is also a statutory scheme, as is the
Pensions Ombudsman. These latter two schemes are probably best described as hybrid
schemes, as they are publicly funded, but have jurisdiction over private sector bodies.

'nationalisation'[9] of the private sector schemes operating in financial services, which have been integrated to produce the statutory Financial Ombudsman Service.[10] There are now few non-statutory ombudsmen schemes remaining in the UK, although there has recently been established an ombudsman for telecommunications,[11] and there are proposals for an ombudsman scheme for dealing with the removals industry.

The title of 'ombudsman' is not strictly defined, and, moreover, definitions are not easy, as there are 'significantly different interpretations of what exactly the Ombudsman's functions are in the world community'.[12] In general, ombudsmen are independent persons, who receive complaints, investigate them, directing or recommending a remedy where the complaint is justified. They are complaint-handlers, providing an impartial, accessible, informal, speedy and cheap way of resolving complaints. However, this simple definition masks the fact that ombudsmen world-wide have a variety of remits and functions. In the UK, the focus of the public sector ombudsmen is on maladministration, whereas in some countries, the emphasis is on human rights. In the private sector, the ombudsmen are not limited to maladministration, and their remits cover issues that could be the subject of litigation.

Moreover, those bodies that perform ombudsman functions are not always called 'ombudsmen'. Indeed, in the UK, the statutory term for the public sector ombudsmen has traditionally been 'commissioner',[13] although they are commonly and semi-officially referred to as 'ombudsmen'. In the world community, sometimes these offices are called 'ombudsmen', sometimes 'commissioners', sometimes 'defenders' or 'protectors'. It is therefore clear that researching ombudsmen is not confined to those bodies bearing that title.

A. WHY STUDY OMBUDSMEN?

Ombudsmen present a fascinating area of study for socio-legal researchers. As indicated, ombudsmen are independent persons, who receive complaints, investigate them, directing or recommending a remedy where

---

[9] See R James and P Morris, 'The New Financial Ombudsman Service in the UK' in CEF Rickett and TGW Telfer, (eds), *International Perspectives on Consumers Access to Justice* (Cambridge, CUP, 2002).

[10] Financial Services and Markets Act 2000.

[11] The non-statutory Office of the Telecommunications Ombudsman (OTELO) was established in October 2002.

[12] K Friedman, 'Realisation of Ombudsman Recommendations' (1988) *Fourth International Ombudsman Conference Papers*.

[13] The new public sector ombudsman scheme in Scotland does however use the term 'ombudsman' in the statutory title.

the complaint is justified. They are thus an important mechanism for redressing grievances against both public bodies and private sector industries, providing alternative dispute resolution mechanisms[14] to the courts, and thus access to justice. Empirical research into the work of ombudsmen provides an opportunity to evaluate their role, not only in their ability to solve disputes, but also in relation to their impact on system reform. They can thus be studied in relation to legal procedure, legal institutions, dispute resolution, regulation, access to justice and human rights.

One of the reasons for the development of ombudsmen in the private sector was dissatisfaction with the courts as a means of ensuring redress for consumers in dispute with large organisations. In terms of procedure, ombudsmen provide 'soft' or informal mechanisms of dispute resolution.[15] They are an easily accessible, low-cost alternative to the courts.[16] The methods that they use are inquisitorial rather than adversarial, and many ombudsmen make decisions based on written representations rather than oral hearings. They are 'a form of privatisation of dispute resolution',[17] providing consumer redress mechanisms, and thus playing a significant role in the civil justice system. It is thus important to evaluate them to ensure that they are able to provide similar guarantees of justice as the courts. The study of ombudsmen can therefore compare and contrast the procedural aspects of this remedy with those of the courts, and evaluate the claims ombudsmen make for their procedures.

In the public sector, where they originated, ombudsmen were not intended to provide an alternative dispute resolution mechanism to the courts. They were established to deal with grievances where no remedy was available in court, because the matter was not justiciable, as no legal right was infringed. The Parliamentary Ombudsman was originally established as an adjunct to Parliament, and thus part of the political and administrative regimes. The remit of the public sector ombudsmen is essentially to provide remedies for maladministration, rather than to adjudicate legal claims or appeals against the merits of discretionary decisions. Ombudsmen thus provide an interesting area of study in terms of their

---

[14] It could be argued that this 'alternative' is still 'juridification', a law-like intervention which is thus spreading to wider social fields. A Hunt, 'The Problematisation of Law in Classical Social Theory' in R Banakar and M Travers, (eds), *An Introduction to Law and Social Theory* (Oxford, Hart Publishing, 2002) 29.

[15] See P Nonet and P Selznick, *Law and Society in Transition: toward responsive law* (New York, Harper & Row, 1978); G Teubner, 'Substantive and Reflexive Elements in Modern Law' (1983) 17 *Law and Society Review* 1443–62.

[16] Ombudsmen schemes are free to the users of the schemes, and legal representation is neither required nor advantageous. In terms of the numbers of cases they deal with, they are probably more cost-effective than the courts. See M Seneviratne, *Ombudsmen: Public Services and Administrative Justice* (London, Butterworths, 2002) 11–12; R James, *Private Ombudsmen and Public Law* (Aldershot, Dartmouth, 1997) 207–9.

[17] R James, *Private Ombudsmen and Public Law* (Aldershot, Dartmouth, 1997) 2.

constitutional role and significance, and in relation to the other mechanisms that exist for resolving disputes with, and checking the abuse of power of, public bodies. The study of complaints is an accepted part of social science, and important in its own right, but, as well as examining how complaints mechanisms are working, such studies provide a 'useful point of entry for researchers and policy makers to monitor some aspects of the general functioning of public administration *vis-a-vis* the public'.[18]

The interface of ombudsmen with the courts also provides an interesting area of study for socio-legal scholars. Despite the view that the 'more that is done to enhance access to the courts, the less the public will be interested in wasting time in ... alternative dispute resolution processes',[19] there is no sign that the ombudsman remedy is on the decline. On the contrary, ombudsman schemes 'continue to evolve and flourish',[20] offering a flexible mechanism for dispute resolution. 'Access'[21] is not the only problem with the court process, and it may be that the ombudsman remedy is more appropriate for some types of dispute. Rather than the courts and ombudsmen being seen as rivals, they should perhaps be seen as partners in the system for resolving disputes. Ombudsmen should thus be studied in order to explain their place in the civil justice and administrative justice systems, and to suggest means of making these systems more coherent.

In conclusion, ombudsmen are of interest to socio-legal researchers because, although concerned with conflict resolution, and despite the fact that many ombudsmen are lawyers,[22] 'the law and ombudsman practice are far from the same'.[23] Despite their rapid rise in number over the past 50 years, there is still widespread ignorance and confusion about their work, confusion that is exacerbated by the fact that no two ombudsman schemes are the same. They can be usefully studied by those interested in accountability mechanisms,[24] regulatory systems, human rights and civil procedures.

---

[18] B Danet, 'Toward a Method the Evaluate the Ombudsman' (1978) 10 *Administration and Society* 335, 338–39.

[19] H Genn, *Paths to Justice: What People Do and Think about Going to Law* (Oxford, Hart Publishing, 1999) 263.

[20] N O'Brien, 'Ombudsmen and the Courts: Time for Dialogue' (2002) 19 *The Ombudsman* 15.

[21] Access to the courts is problematic because of procedural complexity, delay and expense. See H Genn, *Paths to Justice: What People Do and Think about Going to Law* (Oxford, Hart Publishing, 1999) 1–2.

[22] It should be noted however that the Legal Services Ombudsman (and Scottish Legal Services Ombudsman) cannot be legally qualified. This bar is a statutory requirement.

[23] N O'Brien, 'Ombudsmen and the Courts: Time for Dialogue' (2002) 19 *The Ombudsman* 15.

[24] The Select Committee has highlighted the role of ombudsmen in this respect, noting that the Ombudsman 'is a key component of the mechanisms which hold government to account' (Third Report of the Select Committee on Public Administration, Ombudsman Issues (HC 448 (2002–3) para 33).

B. HOW TO STUDY OMBUDSMEN

Researching ombudsmen can take a number of forms. Ombudsmen can be studied as individual schemes,[25] or as part of a total system for dispute resolution, with their place at the apex of that system.[26] Individual schemes can be compared and contrasted with other mechanisms for dealing with similar complaints, or with similar schemes in different jurisdictions.[27] Ombudsmen can be studied in order to describe their work, and evaluate their effectiveness as alternative mechanisms to the traditional methods for resolving disputes. They can be studied in order to find the range of types of ombudsmen available, in order to produce taxonomies, although there are problems of classification, because of the wide range of remits and functions of ombudsmen world-wide. In the UK for example, they have been classified into public and private, although these categories are becoming blurred with the advent of statutory ombudsmen, which may or may not be publicly funded, and which have jurisdiction over private sector organisations and private individuals.[28] The modern ombudsman concept fulfils a variety of roles, as it has been adapted to suit local conditions, with varying operating methods and objectives. Classifications are also difficult because not all those who fit the definition of an 'ombudsman' are called one.[29]

Moreover, there are difficulties with conducting evaluations of ombudsmen schemes. One problem is that individual schemes may be found to be effective, but the complaints system in which they operate may not. For example, evaluations of ombudsman schemes for legal services have found

---

[25] There are some impressive and comprehensive studies of individual ombudsmen schemes, for example: the New Zealand Ombudsman, see LB Hill, *The Model Ombudsman: Institutionalizing New Zealand's Democratic Experience* (Princeton, NJ, Princeton University Press, 1976); the UK Parliamentary Ombudsman, see R Gregory and P Hutchesson, *The Parliamentary Ombudsman: A Study in the Control of Administrative Action* (London, Allen & Unwin, 1975); R Gregory and P Giddings, *The Ombudsman, the Citizen and Parliament* (London, Politico's Publishing, 2002); the European Ombudsman, see K Heede, *European Ombudsman: redress and control at Union level* (The Hague, Kluwer Law International, 2000); the Scottish Local Government Ombudsman, see JG Logie and PQ Watchman, *The Local Ombudsman* (Edinburgh, T & T Clark, 1990).

[26] See M Seneviratne, *The Legal Profession: Regulation and the Consumer* (London, Sweet & Maxwell, 1999).

[27] See M Seneviratne, 'Joint Regulation of Consumer Complaints in Legal Services: A Comparative Study' (2001) 29 *International Journal of the Sociology of Law* 311–30.

[28] These include, for example, the Legal Services Ombudsman, the Pensions Ombudsman, and the Financial Ombudsman Service.

[29] This is true in the UK, where the statutory term for the public sector ombudsmen has traditionally been 'commissioner', although the new ombudsman scheme in Scotland uses the term 'ombudsman' in the legislation. They are however commonly and semi-officially referred to as 'ombudsmen'. In some countries they are known as citizens' or people's defenders, or citizens' protectors. Some countries use the word 'commissioner', but emphasise the human or civil rights aspects to their role, for example 'Parliamentary Commissioner for Human Rights' (Hungary), and 'Commissioner for Civil Rights Protection' (Poland).

that they are effective in terms of certain criteria, but that the professional bodies' systems for dealing with complaints are not.[30] As ombudsmen are used as a last resort, there is then some query as to whether it can be said that the ombudsman system is really effective. It is also difficult to make comparisons across jurisdictions, as much depends on the extent to which procedures exist for the resolution of disputes before a complaint is made to an ombudsman. Another issue is the question of against what criteria the evaluation will be made. Evaluation research has been described as in essence 'the analysis of a set of activities to test whether they contribute effectively toward the pursuit of some goal or goals'.[31] However, unlike some evaluation research, the goals of ombudsmen can be vague, making it difficult to specify criteria to evaluate their effectiveness.

The goals of ombudsmen have been said to include: righting individual wrongs; making bureaucracy more human; lessening popular alienation from government; preventing abuses by acting as a bureaucratic watchdog; vindicating civil servants when they are unjustly accused; introducing administrative reforms.[32] Some of these goals are more amenable to measurement. It will be very difficult, for example, to measure the goal of delivering justice for citizens of public services. Even when the researcher decides on certain measures, for example the independence or accessibility of an ombudsman system, it has to be acknowledged that there are no objective measures of such criteria. These have to be constructed. In addition, ombudsman schemes may have been established with one set of goals, but these may have changed over time because of the changing context in which the scheme operates.[33]

My work on ombudsmen is conducted within the context of public law, and involves two levels of inquiry. At the institutional level, the concern is whether the structure of a scheme guarantees that the minimum conditions for an adjudicative body are ensured. Thus the scheme will be examined to evaluate its independence and jurisdictional coverage. The other level of inquiry concerns the internal effectiveness of the scheme as a grievance

---

[30] See R James and M Seneviratne, 'The Legal Services Ombudsman—Form versus Function' (1995) 58 *Modern Law Review* 187–207; M Seneviratne, *The Legal Profession: Regulation and the Consumer* (London, Sweet & Maxwell, 1999); M Seneviratne, 'Joint Regulation of Consumer Complaints in Legal Service: A Comparative Study' (2001) 29 *International Journal of the Sociology of Law* 311–30.

[31] B Danet, 'Toward a Method to Evaluate the Ombudsman' (1978) 10(3) *Administration and Society* 335, 340.

[32] These goals were identified by LB Hill, *The Model Ombudsman: Institutionalizing New Zealand's Democratic Experience* (Princeton, NJ, Princeton University Press, 1976). See also, B Danet, 'Toward a Method to Evaluate the Ombudsman' (1978) 10(3) *Administration and Society* 335, 341.

[33] This is true of the public sector ombudsmen in the UK, especially the Parliamentary Ombudsman. It may have been fit for the purpose for which it was established in 1967, but what about its fitness for the 21st century.

handling mechanism. This involves an examination of its independence, fairness, openness, and accessibility. In the studies that I have conducted, individual schemes are evaluated according to the criteria established by the British and Irish Ombudsman Association.[34] These criteria, aimed at ensuring that schemes are effective, are as follows: independence, adequate powers of investigation and wide jurisdictional coverage, effective remedies, accessibility.

Independence is, of course, a crucial factor for ombudsmen. An ombudsman scheme must offer impartial investigation of grievances, and an ombudsman must be independent of the executive and any partisan influence. The independence of a scheme can be tested in a number of ways. For example, the jurisdiction, powers and method of appointment of an ombudsman ought to be a matter of public knowledge, and these aspects of the system can be evaluated. Research will reveal whether those appointing the ombudsmen are independent of those who will be subject to investigation, and whether the appointment can be subject to premature termination in the absence of incapacity, misconduct or other good cause. Statistical information can be gathered to ascertain whether the office is adequately staffed and financed.

Research will reveal whether the powers of investigation of the ombudsman are adequate, in order for the system to be effective, and whether the jurisdictional coverage of the scheme is sufficiently wide. Ideally, in the public sector, there should be an ombudsman to cover all types of administrative agencies and all levels of government. The powers of the ombudsman must be sufficient to ensure the production of relevant information and documents to enable thorough examination of the complaint. Effective remedies must be available where the complaint is upheld. Where decisions are not legally binding, there should be a reasonable expectation that there will be compliance.[35] In order to be effective, the ombudsman must be accessible. This will normally require the service to be free for complainants, with easily accessible procedures. There should be no need for legal representation. The service must also be widely known, and thus should have adequate publicity.

There is an implicit assumption in these evaluations that these criteria represent a shared set of values, both for the effective functioning of a democratic system, and for a system which purports to be one of resolving

---

[34] This was formed in 1993, originally as the United Kingdom Ombudsman Association, the name being changed in 1994, following the inclusion of three ombudsman schemes from the Irish Republic as members. It is a self-regulatory organisation, established with the main aim of ensuring that the currency of the title 'ombudsman' should not be devalued.

[35] Ombudsmen in the private sector can make legally binding decisions. The public sector ombudsmen however do not do so, but only make recommendations. This is not out of line with ombudsmen world-wide, who rarely make decisions that can be legally enforced.

disputes. The assumption is based on a belief in the effectiveness of law in a wider arena.[36] However, there is an element of subversion, in the sense that the ombudsman remedy presents a challenge to the orthodox tradition of the legal system, by providing an alternative method of dealing with disputes.

C. METHODS FOR STUDYING OMBUDSMEN

Ombudsmen can be studied by using a range of techniques and methodologies. In my own work I have used a variety of methods,[37] including documentary analysis, interviews, and surveys. Ombudsmen studies have also been conducted using ethnographic techniques[38] and even 'mystery shoppers'.[39]

For documentary analysis, the documents used can include statutes, Parliamentary debates, annual reports, investigation reports, complaints statistics, articles by ombudsmen, ombudsman's files, as well as secondary sources. The documents can include the ombudsman's annual reports and investigation reports. Complaints statistics are also useful, revealing the volume of complaints, their subject matter, the proportion investigated and the outcomes. The annual reports and statistics can reveal important measures about the operation of the office, including the staff workload, throughput times, the number of justified complaints and whether the matter was rectified. All this information assists in evaluating the effectiveness of the ombudsman as a grievance redress mechanism.

When examining statistics, one must always be wary of concluding that low numbers of complaints indicate that all is well within an organisation. They are not always 'a sign of bureaucratic health',[40] but could reflect the fact that there are insurmountable barriers to complaining. Indeed, on the contrary, large numbers of complaints may reflect a more open, responsive

---

[36] See R Cotterrell and B Bercusson, 'Introduction: Law, Democracy and Social Justice' (1988) 15 *Journal of Law and Society* 1, who note that law 'is a primary means by which institutions are defined and protected, established policies are turned into state structures of guiding principle, strategies implemented through the elaboration of rules and regulation'.

[37] M Seneviratne, *Ombudsmen: Public Services and Administrative Justice* (London, Butterworths, 2002) documentary analysis of annual reports, other studies of the ombudsmen, academic and professional articles, decided cases, legislation, Hansard, together with interviews of ombudsmen and their staff were used in order to conduct the research.

[38] This is not a technique I generally use, but the study into the operation of the Legal Services Ombudsman is one example, see R James and M Seneviratne, 'The Legal Services Ombudsman—Form versus Function' (1995) 58 *Modern Law Review* 187–207.

[39] For example in one study, student researchers were sent into bank and building society branches to see what publicity was being given for ombudsmen schemes, see C Graham, M Seneviratne and R James, 'Publicising the Bank and Building Societies Ombudsman Schemes' (1993) 3(2) *Consumer Policy Review* 85.

[40] See F Stacey, *The British Ombudsman* (Oxford, Clarendon Press, 1971).

and positive attitude to complaints by an organisation. Such an attitude reflects the view that complaints are a part of systems control, which should therefore be encouraged. It should also be noted that, in ombudsman systems, the proportion of complaints that result in a formal investigation with a written report is often very small. This does not mean that the other complaints have no merit, but that other, more appropriate means may be found to resolve them. This then prompts an investigation of the methods used by ombudsmen, for example, mediation, arbitration, conciliation and local settlement in general, in order to evaluate their effectiveness. In other words, the published statistics do not present the whole picture. Ombudsmen investigations can also result in outcomes which are different to the remedies provided by the courts. If a complaint is found to be justified, not only can compensation be recommended or awarded, there can also be a recommendation that decisions be changed, and other action be taken to put complainants back into the position they would have been in had the fault not occurred. In addition to compensation for actual financial loss, awards can be given for distress, inconvenience, and the time and trouble involved in bringing complaints.

Interviews are also important in order to investigate in more detail the information found in the documents, and to discover perceptions of the system. They can reveal any gaps in the documentation, and the underlying motives and assumptions of the ombudsmen and their staff. In my studies of ombudsmen systems, I have interviewed ombudsmen and their staff, civil servants, and staff operating in the lower level complaint handling process. Interviews give atmosphere and colour to a study, sometimes revealing entirely new information, and thus offering another dimension of understanding.[41]

Questionnaire surveys can also be used in researching ombudsmen, whether they are surveys of the ombudsmen themselves, the bodies subject to their investigations, the consumers of their services, or the public in general. Surveys of ombudsmen can give valuable insights into how ombudsmen see their role. Surveys of organisations within the jurisdiction of an ombudsman scheme can reveal their perceptions of the scheme and their views of the ombudsman as an influence on good practice, and as a dispute resolution mechanism.[42] Surveys of complainants can be difficult, because of problems of access and confidentiality, and even when ombudsmen are happy to co-operate with the research, methods must be found of maintaining

---

[41] See F Brookman, L Noakes and E Wincup, *Qualitative Research in Criminology* (Aldershot, Ashgate, 1999) 137.

[42] See M Seneviratne, R James and C Graham, 'The Banks, the Ombudsman and Complaints Procedures' (1994) *Civil Justice Quarterly* 253–68; R James and M Seneviratne, 'The Building Societies Ombudsman Scheme' (1992) *Civil Justice Quarterly* 157–74; R James, C Graham and M Seneviratne, 'Building Societies, Customer Complaints and the Ombudsman' (1994) *Anglo-American Law Review* 214–48.

confidentiality.[43] Surveys of the public may often require the assistance of market research organisations, but can provide valuable information about the use of, and perceptions of, ombudsmen.[44]

Ombudsmen can thus be researched in a variety of ways, for a number of purposes. Individual schemes might be examined, to discover, for example, why they were set up and how they measure up to their objectives. Studies can be undertaken to examine the impact of a scheme or schemes on a particular industry or public authority, for example in terms of raising standards and having an impact beyond individual cases. This is an important aspect of research into ombudsmen, as it is not just their ability to right individual wrongs that is important, but also the impact of their decisions on administrative and organisational processes. Similar systems in different countries can also be compared and contrasted.[45]

D. ANALYSIS OF DISCOURSE AND TEXTS

My work on ombudsmen is mainly qualitative. It is concerned with the analysis of text and discourse. Discourse includes all forms of talk and writing, and the way in which talk is meshed together.[46] Discourse also refers to much broader, historically developing linguistic practice[47] and is closely connected to semiotics, which is concerned with the study of any human realm to which meaning is systematically applied. This method of analysis is now being recognised as useful in the study of law and socio-legal studies. There are, of course, very good reasons why lawyers should be interested in language and meaning. Language provides the framework for the law,[48] and language interprets that framework.[49] The data on which the analysis of discourse is based are familiar to all social scientists. They include interviews, focus groups, documents, records, media representation, and policy statements. The textual sources used by socio-legal scholars are similarly well-known, comprising constitutions, statutes, precedents, and

---

[43] My research has included studies where it was possible to conduct postal questionnaire surveys of complainants: see M Seneviratne and S Cracknell, 'Consumer Complaints in Public Sector Services' (1988) 66(2) *Public Administration* 181–93; M Seneviratne, 'Estate Agents, the Consumer and the Ombudsman for Corporate Estate Agents' (1997) *Consumer Law Journal* 123–33.

[44] See M Seneviratne and S Cracknell, 'Consumer Complaints in Public Sector Services' (1988) 66(2) *Public Administration* 181–93.

[45] This has been done in relation to legal services, see M Seneviratne, 'Joint Regulation of Consumer Complaints in Legal Services: A Comparative Study' (2001) 29 *International Journal of the Sociology of Law* 311–30.

[46] J Potter and M Wetherell, *Discourse and Social Psychology* (London, Sage, 1987) 6.

[47] See M Foucault, *The Archaeology of Knowledge* (London, Tavistock, 1972).

[48] For example, Acts of Parliament, court judgments.

[49] For example, Parliamentary debates, court judgments, official papers, discussion documents.

commentaries. All these are central to a developed system of law, and the interpretation of such texts is a highly important element in adjudication, legal practice and legal scholarship.

My study of ombudsmen is not discourse analysis,[50] but the analysis of discourse and texts. Discourse analysis, as a method, approaches discourses in their own right, and not as secondary routes to things beyond the text, like attitudes and events. Discourse analysis is concerned with how the discourse is put together, and its construction in relation to its function.[51] Although discourse analysis is a 'very broad church', whose central concepts are 'contested' and its 'boundaries loosely defined',[52] it is different to text analysis. Text analysis is concerned with what the text means, whereas discourse analysis is concerned with 'why and how the text comes to mean various things to various readers'.[53] Text analysis involves an interpreting of texts,[54] and an exploration of how the participants understand their own actions. It is an examination of the implementation of legal and administrative rules. It is an investigation into what ombudsmen do and how they and others perceive what they do. My method for the study of ombudsmen uses documentary evidence, supplemented by interviews, in order to explore the research question. I am examining texts in order to answer questions, rather than using the texts in their own right to explore their construction in relation to their function.[55] The texts are being used as secondary routes, to discover matters beyond the text, like attitudes and events.

I conduct evaluations, using certain criteria, which I consider are worthy ones. I base my studies on the assumption that there is a shared understanding of the meaning of these criteria, and a shared belief in their value. Of

[50] Discourse analysis, simply put, is analysing talk and text in context. It is the study of the use of language and communications, see J Black, 'Regulatory Conversations' (2002) 29 *Journal of Law and Society* 163. It has been used as a generic term for virtually all research concerned with language in its social and cognitive context, and to cover developments from structuralism and semiotics.

[51] J Potter and M Wetherell, *Discourse and Social Psychology* (London, Sage, 1987) 160. Socio-legal scholars can use discourse analysis in this narrow sense, and records and documents can be used to do so. For example, there can be discourse analysis of Hansard, which would identify MPs construction of their own version of the social world and how they undermine their opponents. Interviews can be done, but interviews are used differently in discourse analysis than in other types of social research. Discourse analysts focus on how the talk is constructed, and what it achieves, rather than whether it is an accurate description of the participant's viewpoint.

[52] J Black, 'Regulatory Conversations' (2002) 29 *Journal of Law and Society* 163, 165–66.

[53] R Coulon, 'Discourse Analysis versus Text Analysis: The Reading of Ideology in Foreign Language Texts' (1988) 1 *International Journal for the Semiotics of Law* 195.

[54] This includes all written material, and notes and transcripts of interviews.

[55] This is not to say that discourse analysis cannot be used for ombudsman studies. The texts (eg investigation reports, annual reports) can be examined in their own right to analyse their construction in relation to their function. There may also be interesting work to be done in relation to Independent Housing Ombudsman scheme, for example, which has introduced a new oral hearing method for dispute resolution.

course, all this can be contested. For example, the concept of 'independence' has a different meaning for regulators and those regulated. In relation to the legal profession, it can be argued that government intervention is necessary in order to ensure that the complaints systems for consumers of legal services operate independently. This is a different meaning of independence to that adopted by the profession itself, which sees self-regulation as the hallmark of a profession and a necessary safeguard of independence. The concept of 'justice' too is conditioned by our social structure, our history, culture, and ideology. Even the very word 'ombudsman' could be deconstructed, to unravel its significance in relation to the function that the institution is designed to serve.

E. CONCLUSION

Despite the rapid growth in ombudsman schemes over the past 50 years, there has until recently been little systematic research which tests the effectiveness of this increasingly popular remedy. Recent research has evaluated their effectiveness as alternative dispute resolution mechanisms. Using a variety of research methods, various schemes have been investigated in order to assess whether the mechanisms for processing complaints are adequate, and whether the outcomes of the process are satisfactory. In general, the research has concluded that particular schemes operate satisfactorily within their remits, and that they operate well as alternative dispute resolution mechanisms. The research has also recognised that ombudsmen have another function, that of improving practice, and thus the evaluations have also considered how successful a particular scheme has been in monitoring central and local administration or a particular industry. Again, the general conclusion is that ombudsmen have had a salutary effect on administrative agencies and organisations.

As more ombudsmen schemes are created, and as existing schemes change their focus, similar research into the effectiveness of individual schemes can be conducted. There is also scope for wider evaluations of the place of ombudsmen within systems of administrative justice and civil justice. In this respect, studies of the appropriate relationship between ombudsman schemes and the courts is necessary. Research needs to be conducted on the appropriate role for ombudsmen, in the context of both dispute resolution and accountability mechanisms. Assessments need to be made about whether the proliferation of ombudsman schemes is desirable, or whether 'super' ombudsmen like the Financial Ombudsman Service[56] is

---

[56] See R James and P Morris, 'The New Financial Ombudsman Service in the UK' in CEF Rickett and TGW Telfer, (eds), *International Perspectives on Consumers Access to Justice* (Cambridge, CUP, 2002).

more effective. Comparative research is necessary in order to discover the models of ombudsmen systems available, and their relative drawbacks and merits. The ombudsman remedy is evolving, and research is needed to assess its ability to adapt to new social and political structures.

Like other topics for socio-legal research, ombudsmen can be researched using a variety of research methods. The methods chosen will of course depend on the research questions been asked. As indicated, my research questions have centred around a concern about the effectiveness of this type of dispute resolution mechanism, and the methods of inquiry have been primarily qualitative, with some quantitative material. Whatever methodology is used, it is clear that theory is inseparable from the research process. All empirical work is based on certain theoretical assumptions, and it is important that the socio-legal researcher makes them explicit. As a lawyer, my concern is that the law and legal systems operate effectively. In order to assess this, legal institutions, which include ombudsmen and other dispute resolution mechanisms, must be researched in ways that are theoretically grounded and methodologically sound. My research is conducted on the assumption that the legal system can be used effectively to address issues of participation, social inclusion, justice and human rights. I see ombudsmen as part of the legal system, and as another avenue of access to justice.

9

Researching Discourse and Behaviour as Elements of Law in Action

BETTINA LANGE

THIS CHAPTER CRITICALLY examines and advocates the combination of a discourse analytic and a qualitative approach to socio-legal research.[1] It aims to contribute to the literature on socio-legal research methods by telling the behind-the-scenes story of how a research method emerged through the process of engaging in real-life, messy and mundane research activities. It suggests that practical research design can not be separated from an engagement with fundamental social science questions about the relationship between ideas and practices, and postmodernist and modernist perspectives on these. The chapter also highlights the importance of methodology for substantive socio-legal debates. It suggests that combining qualitative and discourse analysis may generate new insights into European Union (EU) law in action.

The first section of this chapter briefly introduces the research project, while the second section discusses reasons for the combination of a discourse analytical and qualitative approach in this specific study. Section three further explains how some approaches to discourse analysis and qualitative research can be considered as distinct. The fourth and main section of this chapter shows—also on the basis of a data extract and introductory analysis—how in practice a discourse analytical and a qualitative approach were combined.

A. THE RESEARCH PROJECT

What can be understood as 'law' and how normativity is constructed have been key concerns for socio-legal researchers[2]. These questions need

[1] I would like to thank Dave Cowan for comments on a previous draft of this paper.
[2] BZ Tamanaha, *A General Jurisprudence of Law and Society* (Oxford, OUP, 2001).

further exploration in the context of EU law. Theories of EU integration have emphasised the role of law in the integration process, but have often relied on formal, autonomous, *quasi*-state law conceptions of normativity.[3] For instance, formal EU law has been considered as moving integration forward when political initiatives among Member States have been waning.[4] Hence, the research project explores the meaning of EU law in action and its contribution to integration processes. The study analyses the key legal obligation under the EU Directive on Integrated Pollution Prevention and Control.[5] Under this Directive Member State regulatory authorities have powers to require operators of mainly industrial installations[6] to employ the 'best available techniques' (BAT), in order to prevent and reduce their emissions to all three environmental media, air, water and land.[7] Article 2. Nr. 11 of the IPPC Directive provides a rudimentary definition of 'best available techniques':

> BAT shall mean the most effective and advanced stage in the development of activities and their methods of operation which indicate the practical suitability of particular techniques for providing in principle the basis for emission limit values designed to prevent and, where that is not practicable, generally to reduce emissions and the impact on the environment as a whole.[8]

Annex IV to the Directive spells out further criteria for the determination of BAT. Some of these address environmental considerations, such as waste minimisation, energy efficiency of regulated processes and the principles of prevention of damage to the environment and precaution. Others refer to the 'costs and benefits of a measure'.[9] Finally, Member State regulatory authorities must take into account, but are not bound by, BAT Reference Documents (BREFs) when determining BAT for a specific plant.[10] These BREFs are the result of an EU-wide information exchange between representatives of industry, Member State regulatory authorities and—upon invitation of the EU Commission—environmental non-governmental

---

[3] AM Burley and W Matti, 'Europe before the Court: A Political Theory of Legal Integration' (1993) 47 *International Organization* 41–70; G Garrett, 'The Politics of Legal Integration in the EU' (1995) 49 *International Organisation* 171–81.

[4] J Weiler, 'Community, Member States and European Integration: Is the Law Relevant?' (1982) *Journal of Common Market Studies* 39–56.

[5] IPPC–96/61 OJ L 257, 10 October 1996, pp 26–40.

[6] Installations subject to the obligations of the Directive are listed in Annex I They cover activities from the energy industry, the production and processing of metals, the mineral industry, the chemical industry, waste management activities, pulp and paper production, textile pre-treatment and dying, tanning, slaughterhouses as well as intensive pig and poultry rearing. Furthermore surface treatments, carbon and electro graphite production as well as food production are covered.

[7] J Scott, 'Flexibility, "Proceduralization", and Environmental Governance in the EU' in G De Búrca and J Scott, (eds), *Constitutional Change in the EU: From Uniformity to Flexibility* (Oxford, Hart Publishing, 2000) 260.

[8] IPPC Directive, 96/61 OJ L 257 10 October 1996, p 29.

[9] Annex IV, first sentence IPPC Directive.

[10] Annex IV Nr 12 IPPC Directive.

organisations.[11] Implementing the Directive requires determining in more detail what constitutes BAT. At the EU level this occurs mainly during the BREF writing process. At the national and local level this happens during the drafting of national implementing legislation and when licences for specific plants are issued. I refer to the various BAT options which different social actors advance as 'BAT law in action' and to the final legally authoritative choice of one particular BAT definition in implementing legislation or licences as 'state law BAT'.[12] But how can 'BAT law in action' and its interaction with state law be researched?

B. REASONS FOR COMBINING A QUALITATIVE AND DISCOURSE ANALYTICAL APPROACH

Three criteria informed the choice of methodology for the IPPC project. The methods had to be able to answer the specific research question asked and they had to fit the characteristics of the BAT determination process and help to manage restrictions on access to data. The combination of a qualitative and discourse analytical approach fulfilled all three criteria. I use the term discourse analysis here to refer to an examination of discourse in both its linguistic and Foucauldian dimension. A linguistic notion of discourse refers to 'informal and formal, including institutionalized, spoken interaction and written texts'.[13] Foucault's concept of discourse, in contrast, is more comprehensive and complex. First, it comprises speech acts and any system of signs, not just language. These are taken to represent knowledge about 'a topic at a particular historical moment'.[14] Second, Foucault's concept of discourse covers not just statements but also the regulated practices which account for statements.[15] Hence, groups of statements on a particular topic, such as the discourse on what constitutes 'best available techniques' is captured, as well as the—sometimes hidden—rules and structures which produce this discourse.[16] Discourses can generate exclusion when certain statements are kept in circulation while others are marginalised. Hence, discourse is an essential aspect of relations of power. In fact, discourse can be an instrument and effect of power as well as a starting point

---

[11] NGOs—Art. 16(2) IPPC Directive.

[12] In order to study EU law in action this project draws on three case studies. The first case study covers BAT determinations during the BREF writing process at EU level. The second and third case studies deal with BAT determinations at the national implementing and local licensing stage in Germany and England.

[13] J Potter and M Wetherell, *Discourse and Social Psychology* (London, Sage, 1989) 7; M Wetherell, 'Part Three: Minds, Selves and Sense-Making: Editor's Introduction' in M Wetherell, *et al*, *Discourse Theory and Practice: A Reader* (London, Sage, 2000) 193.

[14] S Hall, 'Foucault: Power, Knowledge and Discourse' in M Wetherell, et al, *ibid*, p 72.

[15] M Foucault, AM Sheridan, (tr), *The Archaeology of Knowledge and the Discourse of Language* (London, Tavistock, 1972) 80.

[16] S Mills, *Michel Foucault* (London, Routledge, 2003).

for resistance.[17] According to Foucault, expert status is an important resource for the production of discourse, since its successful circulation depends on whether statements will be judged as 'true' rather than 'false'. Discourse relies on the idea that there will be limitations on who will be considered to speak authoritatively.[18] Hence, discourse analysis pays attention to the discursive resources which social actors use, such as 'category systems, narrative characters and interpretative repertoires'.[19] It also examines the distribution, exchange and control of discourse.[20]

In contrast to this, qualitative research analyses a whole range of social interactions, including non-verbal behaviour. Participant observation and unstructured interviewing are often considered as its key data collection techniques.[21] Qualitative research assumes that actors create social life through a range of interpretative practices. Definitions of situations are key to how people act and can thus produce real consequences.[22] Qualitative researchers attempt to understand these through entering the social actors' behavioural world and becoming familiar with its perspectives.[23]

Combining a discourse analytical and a qualitative approach allows us to shift the emphasis from behavioural to discursive aspects of the 'law in action' and thus to depart from the classical sociology of law literature and contemporary studies influenced by it. For instance, Ehrlich defines the living law through reference to patterns of behaviour from which a rule can be deduced.[24] These can be empirically identified through observations of further behaviour, such as the experience of informal social sanctions by those who do not comply with the living law.[25] Similarly, Pound's concept of the law in action, though different from Ehrlich's, also considers social actors', in particular law makers' and law enforcers', behaviour, as key.[26] It is an evaluation of their activities—in the light of the normative benchmark of state law—that helps to identify the law in action that they generate. Hence, some contemporary studies of the law in action have focused on behaviour by asking how legal actors make discretionary decisions, how

[17] *Ibid*, p 54.

[18] *Ibid*, p 58.

[19] J Potter and M Wetherell, 'Discourse Analysis' in JA Smith, (ed), *Rethinking Methods in Psychology*, (London, Sage, 1995) 81.

[20] M Shapiro, 'Textualizing Global Politics' in M Wetherell, *et al*, above, n 13, p 323.

[21] G Allan, 'Qualitative Research' in G Allan and C Skinner, (eds), *Handbook for Research Students in the Social Sciences* (London, Falmer Press, 1993) 177.

[22] A Bryman, *Quantity and Quality in Social Research* (London, Routledge, 2000) 52, 53.

[23] Allan, above, n 21, p 208.

[24] E Ehrlich, *Principles of the Sociology of Law* (Cambridge, MA, Harvard University Press, 1936) discussed in D Nelken, 'Law in Action or Living Law? Back to the Beginning in Sociology of Law' (1984) 4 *Legal Studies* 163.

[25] Ehrlich, *ibid*.

[26] R Pound, 'Law in Books and Law in Action' (1910) 44 *American Law Review*, discussed in D Nelken, above, n 24, p 165.

they receive state law in regulated and regulatory organisations, how they avoid law and what alternative social norms they create.[27]

A shift to discursive aspects of normativity is not new. Conversations, for instance, have been perceived as helping to solve problems raised by regulating through legal rules.[28] Conversations, however, are seen here as separate from rule formation and are analysed after formal legal rules have been defined and established.[29] In contrast to this, the discourse analytical approach in the IPPC project aims to analyse how law in action feeds at an earlier stage into the creation of state law. It works with a broad definition of discourse, including text, not just conversations. By combining a discourse analysis and qualitative approach the project aims at a full explanation of BAT discourse. This should also address how discourse is shaped by non-discursive aspects of the social world, which can be accessed through a qualitative approach. The combined approach also allows us to ground BAT discourse in the social *process* of accounting for BAT. This avoids characterising BAT—in an abstract and reified manner—as a discursively constructed norm *concept*. Participants in the BAT definition process do not invoke a BAT *concept*. Instead they are engaged in a process of describing BAT in which the meaning of BAT appears to be elusive.

Research methods should also fit the actual characteristics of the social process being studied. Two impressions from the initial fieldwork phase seemed to suggest that combining a qualitative and discourse analytical approach would be fruitful. The BAT determination process gave rise to alliances which crossed traditional interest group boundaries. Sometimes, the BAT discourse seemed to suggest that individual social actors influenced significantly BAT determinations. Hence, this process could not be fully captured through reference to pre-given interests and lobbying by distinct social groups, such as 'regulators', 'industry' and 'environmental NGOs'. Furthermore there was an opaque and labyrinthine system of consultations over a period of time which provided a number of formal and informal opportunities for various actors to express what they considered as BAT. Hence, the exercise of political power in the BAT determination process seemed complex and more fully captured through Foucault's notion of the microphysics of power. One of the key aspects of this concept

---

[27] K Hawkins, *Environment and Enforcement: Regulation and the Social Definition of Pollution* (Oxford, Clarendon Press, 1984); B Hutter, *The Reasonable Arm of the Law? The Law Enforcement Procedures of Environmental Health Officers* (Oxford, Clarendon Press, 1988); HL Ross, 'Housing Code Enforcement as Law in Action' 17(2) Law and Policy 133–60; B Hutter, *Regulation and Risk: Occupational Health and Safety on the Railways* (Oxford, OUP, 2001); K Hawkins, *Law as Last Resort* (Oxford, OUP, 2002).

[28] J Black, 'Talking about Regulation' (1998) Spring Issue, *Public Law* 77–105; J Black, 'Regulatory Conversations' 29(1) *Journal of Law and Society* 163–96.

[29] J Black, 'Talking about Regulation' (1998) Spring Issue, *Public Law* 77, 103, 104.

of power is that it departs from the idea that power can be possessed, for example by the state or various social actors. Instead power is best understood as a strategy and its effects arise from 'small-scale manoeuvres, tactics, techniques and functionings'.[30] Not conscious intentions, the interests of groups or individuals, but detailed practices are fore grounded in this analysis of power.[31] In fact categories, such as 'individual', 'group' or 'social actor' are perceived as effects of power. Hence, Foucault's concept of power helps to move away from ideas of power as institution or social structure. It even considers various points of resistance as an integral part of power. An understanding of the microphysics of power, however, is not restricted to a ground level perspective on power. It can also assist analysis of macro-level manifestations of power by rendering visible how small-scale tactics of power can be appropriated for its more large-scale exercise.[32]

While discourse is clearly central to the construction of BAT normativity, initial fieldwork also suggested that social life—beyond the words—seemed to matter for understanding BAT law in action. Surprisingly, some important sources of BAT discourse, such as written records, contained few references to the costs and benefits of technologies and their cumulated effect upon all three environmental media, land, water and air. According to the text of the IPPC Directive, these were, however, key criteria for defining BAT. Hence, it seemed important to consider a broader conception of the social world—accessible through qualitative methods—in order to explain this silence of the BAT discourse.

Thirdly, the idea of combining qualitative and discourse analytical perspectives also developed in response to access opportunities and problems.[33] A focus on selected elements of BAT discourse helped to compensate for restrictions on traditional qualitative observational data about oral BAT negotiations in technical working group meetings (TWG). In these meetings delegates from EU Member State regulators, industry and environmental NGOs would debate what should be considered as BAT for a specific industrial sector. I was refused access to these meetings, but was provided with an official audiotape recording of a past TWG meeting which, in transcribed form, provided a rich source for discourse analysis. So far I have argued that the combination of a discourse analytical and qualitative approach is particularly suited to answering the research questions of the IPPC project. It needs to be further explained, however, in what way I consider these two approaches as different.

---

[30] B Smart, *Michel Foucault*, rev edn, (London, Routledge, 2002) 77.
[31] Smart, *ibid*, p 78.
[32] Smart, *ibid*, p 79.
[33] R Banakar, 'Reflections on the Methodological Issues of the Sociology of Law' (2002) 27 *Journal of Law and Society* 273–95.

C. DISCOURSE ANALYSIS AND QUALITATIVE RESEARCH AS DIFFERENT METHODS?

Conventionally the research methods literature does not clearly distinguish between discourse analysis and qualitative research. The important role of language in social life is recognised in both approaches. Some textbooks even consider two approaches towards discourse analysis—conversation analysis and the ethnography of speaking—as a form of qualitative research.[34] Discourse analysis, however, is not necessarily a form of qualitative research. One variant of it—content analysis—relies on quantitative methods.[35] Furthermore some discourse analytical and qualitative methods work with different concepts of agency, social action and the relationship between discursive and non-discursive elements in the social world.

Especially qualitative approaches informed by hermeneutics perceive social actors as 'conscious, individual, meaning-giving subjects'.[36] They are independent language users and language facilitates their agency. Social actors can be 'speakers', 'hearers' and unaddressed third parties—'bystanders'—in a conversational encounter.[37] In contrast to this, discourse analysis perceives social actors as constructed through discourse.[38] Subjects can not be outside discourse and they have little control over it.[39] Descriptions of social life can 'become established as solid, real and independent of the speaker'.[40] Hence 'subjects' in discourse analysis personify the particular forms of knowledge which the discourse produces: 'the human voice is conceived merely as another means for registering differences'.[41] These two different conceptions of agency have implications for the two perspectives' respective concepts of social action.

---

[34] G Miller, 'Introduction' in G Miller and R Dingwall, (eds), *Context and Method in Qualitative Research* (London, Sage, 1997) 6; D Silverman, 'The Logics of Qualitative Research' in G Miller and R Dingwall, (eds), *Context and Method in Qualitative Research* (London, Sage, 1997) 24.; A Bryman, *Quantity and Quality in Social Research* (London, Routledge, 2000) 53.

[35] SJ Taylor, 'Locating and Conducting Discourse Analytic Research' in M Wetherell, *et al,* (eds), *Discourse as Data* (London, Sage, 2001) 10; A Bryman, *Social Research Methods* (Oxford, OUP, 2001) 178.

[36] HL Dreyfus and P Rabinow, *Michel Foucault: Beyond Structuralism and Hermeneutics* (Brighton, Harvester Press, 1982) 57.

[37] E Goffman, 'Footing' in M Wetherell, *et al,* (eds), *Discourse Theory and Practice: A Reader* (London, Sage, 2002) 97.

[38] Dreyfus and Rabinow, above, n 36, at xxii, xxiii; M Wetherell, 'Part Three: Trends, Selves and Sense Making: Editor's Introduction' in Wetherell, *et al,* above, n 13, p 188.

[39] S Hall, 'Foucault: Power, Knowledge and Discourse' in Wetherell, *et al,* above, n 13, p 78; M Wetherell, 'Themes in Discourse Research: The Case of Diana' in Wetherell, *et al,* above, n 13, p 16.

[40] J Potter and M Wetherell, 'Discourse Analysis' in JA Smith, (ed), *Rethinking Methods in Psychology,* (London, Sage, 1995) 81.

[41] J Wertsch, 'The Multivoicedness of Meaning' in Wetherell, *et al,* above, n 13, p 222 referring to Holquist.

From a discourse analytical perspective discourse itself accomplishes social action.[42] It can 'order, request, persuade, accuse, take sides and disclaim responsibility'.[43] When discourse generates social action it acquires a material quality and no longer exists just in a realm of ideas. From a qualitative perspective language fulfils merely a representational function. Texts can 'open the door to an understanding of the social world', but can not be equated with it.[44] Whether language is seen as constituting or as merely representing the social world also influences these two approaches' different views of the relationship between discursive and non-discursive aspects of the social world.

Qualitative approaches see discursive and non-discursive elements as linked through a process of interpretation. From a hermeneutical perspective, discourse can be understood and explained through reference to a 'horizon of intelligibility', a field of shared social practices.[45] Social actors, including researchers, look for what is 'underneath' the use of language, in order to understand how meaning in the social world is achieved. Hence, the non-discursive world becomes an important resource for understanding discourse.[46] For qualitative researchers the discursive and non-discursive world can also be linked through a process of causation. Non-discursive factors, such as pregiven, separate interests are sometimes considered as explanations for linguistic phenomena.[47]

In contrast to this, Foucault does not intend to explain discursive elements in terms of non-discursive ones.[48] A Foucauldian approach describes the surface details of a discourse.[49] It does not assume that discourse could only be rendered meaningful through reference to exterior shared social practices.[50] There is no 'deep truth behind experience' and hence interpretation is considered as an arbitrary and groundless process.[51] Discourse becomes decontextualised.[52] Non-discursive social practices, however, still inform discourse: '[...] what gets said depends on something other than itself, discourse, so to speak, dictates the terms of this dependence'.[53]

---

[42] M Wetherell, 'Themes in Discourse Research: The Case of Diana' in Wetherell, *et al*, above, n 13, p 15; M Wetherell, 'Part One: Foundations and Building Blocks: Editor's Introduction' in Wetherell, *et al*, above, n 13, p 12; H Mehan, 'The Construction of an LD Student: A Case Study in the Politics of Representation' in M Wetherell, *et al*, above, n 13, p 346.

[43] J Potter and M Wetherell, *Discourse and Social Psychology* (London, Sage, 1989) 32.

[44] G Kress, 'From Saussure to Critical Sociolinguistics: The Turn Towards a Social View of Language' Wetherell, *et al*, above, n 13, p 35.

[45] Dreyfus and Rabinow, above, n 36, p 51.

[46] J Carabine, 'Unmarried Motherhood 1830–1999: A Genealogical Analysis' in M Wetherell, *et al*, (eds), *Discourse as Data* (London, Sage, 2001) 276.

[47] M Wetherell, 'Themes in Discourse Research: The Case of Diana' in Wetherell, *et al*, above, n 13, p 25.

[48] Dreyfus and Rabinow, above, n 36, p 82–3.

[49] M Foucault, 'Politics and the Study of Discourse' (1978) 3 *Ideology and Consciousness* 12.

[50] Carabine, above, n 46, p 276.

[51] M Foucault, AM Sheridan, (tr), *The Archaeology of Knowledge and the Discourse of Language* (London, Tavistock, 1972) 202.

[52] Dreyfus and Rabinow, above, n 36, p 51.

[53] Dreyfus and Rabinow, *ibid*, p 64.

Hence, the non-discursive sphere can provide the conditions of existence for a discourse and form the objects of discourse.[54] But it is discourse, rather than non-discursive elements, which generate real, material effects in the social world. In fact, Foucault suggests that there is a circular and complex relationship between the non-discursive and discursive world. He distinguishes between primary and secondary relations. Primary relations occur between institutions, techniques, social forms and other elements which make up the non-discursive world. Secondary relations describe how 'practising subjects reflectively define their own behaviour'.[55] Foucault calls relationships between primary and secondary relations discursive practices. They determine 'who has the right to make statements, from what site statements emanate, and what position the subject of discourse occupies'.[56] Foucault also suggests that relationships between a discursive and a non-discursive sphere vary with the organisation of a particular discourse.[57] Hence, the archaeological method of discourse analysis searches for the way in which discourse is 'articulated' with the non-discursive world.[58] Given these different perspectives which underpin discourse and qualitative research the question arises how the two approaches, and in particular their criteria for what constitutes 'good' data and analysis procedures, can be combined in practice.

D. COMBINING A DISCOURSE ANALYTICAL AND QUALITATIVE APPROACH IN PRACTICE

1. Constructing Criteria for What Constitutes 'Good' Data

Validity is a key criterion for evaluating any research data. Do the data shed light on the research question accurately? Sample size can influence the validity of the data and for qualitative researchers sample size matters more than for discourse analysts. From a qualitative perspective data refer to a separate, external social realm. It therefore needs to be considered how much and what type of data are needed in order to generate a valid description of this world. In contrast to this, discourse analysis focuses on a detailed, in-depth analysis of the construction of the discourse itself and hence only a small sample can be entirely sufficient.

The scope of the BAT discourse sample in the IPPC project is limited in two main ways. First, it is a 'snapshot' of BAT determinations during a specific

---

[54] Foucault, above, n 49, p 10,15.
[55] Dreyfus and Rabinow, above, n 36, p 63.
[56] Dreyfus and Rabinow, *ibid*, p 68.
[57] B Brown and M Cousins, 'The Linguistic Fault: The Case of Foucault's Archaeology' in M Gane, *Towards a Critique of Foucault* (London, Routledge and Kegan, 1986) 36.
[58] A Hunt and G Wickham, *Foucault and Law: Towards a Sociology of Law as Governance* (London, Pluto Press, 1994) p 10.

time period. I interviewed all those eleven BREF authors which were present in the EIPPC Bureau during the two months that I spent there. Before and since then different staff have worked on BREFs. Second, the BAT discourse sample has a specific geographical focus. Data about BAT determinations in specific licences are derived from one each among a large number of local permitting authorities in Germany and the UK. An examination of BAT discourse from case studies located in two countries should help to understand which features of BAT are specific to a national setting and which reflect a broader notion of EU law in action which transcends national characteristics and potentially reflects an EU integration process. Since my data also contained repeated themes, it appears that from a qualitative perspective, too, the sample is big enough to allow inferences to be drawn about the social world narrated in the data. From a discourse perspective the sample is sufficient in order to examine micro interactions in BAT communication as generating BAT law in action.

Reliability is another criterion which can be referred to in order to identify 'good' research data. Data are reliable if the same data could be obtained in a replication of the original study. In the case of several researchers collecting data, reliability requires that they can achieve some agreement on their observations and understandings.[59] Hence, reliability means that there should be limits to the extent to which the research data are constructed. This criterion matters, though in different ways, to both qualitative and discourse researchers. From a qualitative approach 'good' data should report truthfully about the social world researched and the way in which it is constructed by social actors. Thus, qualitative researchers sometimes involve participants in the validation of research data, for instance by making interview transcripts available for comments by interviewees.[60] Discourse researchers also strive for 'naturalistic' data, but this means that the discourse which is analysed should reflect as closely as possible the research participants' own discourse as it occurs in real-life situations. Interference with the research participants' natural discourse through data collection procedures should be minimised. Whether the discourse itself is actually 'truthful' or not, is irrelevant for discourse researchers, since they do not assume that there is a separate social world which can be accessed through the discourse. Discourse itself is a site of social action.

In order to evaluate the reliability of the data for the IPPC project it is important to consider how and to what extent written documents—which are one of the key data sources for the project—were constructed. From a qualitative perspective their reliability is enhanced because they are complemented by interview and some observational data. Moreover, the German Land environmental ministry records on the TA Luft drafting

---

[59] A Bryman, *Social Research Methods* (Oxford, OUP, 2001) 270–71.
[60] S Taylor, 'Locating and Conducting Discourse Analytic Research' in M Wetherell, *et al*, (eds), *Discourse as Data* (London, Sage, 2001) 321–22.

process[61] were compiled as this process was unfolding. They also appeared to be truthful because they included photocopies of the submissions from various interested parties. The background files for the BREFs varied in their completeness and detail. The truthfulness of the written records may also have been enhanced by the fact that they were constructed in order to support the staffs' own drafting process and, in the case of the German files, also to inform other staff about the progress of the drafting of the 'TA Luft'. But for wider organisational purposes these records could also be harnessed to portray BAT determinations as rationally ordered, legal and open. From a discourse analysis perspective both written records and the transcript of the audiotape recording are sources of 'naturalistic' data. If criteria for 'good' data from a qualitative and discourse analysis perspective can be reconciled, does this also apply to analysis procedures?

E. RECONCILING ANALYSIS PROCEDURES

Both discourse and qualitative researchers share a commitment to rigour in their analysis procedures. For instance, both approaches advocate carrying out deviant case analysis which involves seeking out and accounting for parts of the research data which do not fit the main hypothesis or interpretation.[62] Discourse and qualitative researchers, however, may read, code and theorize data differently. Qualitative researchers tend to read data 'for gist', in order to identify the main themes, while discourse researchers often conduct a more fine grained reading, in order to understand the full interpretative repertoire which language users employ in the construction of the discourse. Hence, for qualitative researchers consistency in the data usually indicates that a social phenomenon exists 'out there' in the social world or that an internal state can be ascribed to a research participant.[63] For discourse researchers consistent language patterns are not linked to an external social world. They only reveal insights into the construction and function of the discourse itself, while rupture and discontinuities are—also from a Foucauldian perspective—just as important features of discourse.[64]

Discourse researchers' interest in variation has implications, in turn, for coding. Qualitative researchers code in order to aggregate large amounts of unsystematic data into categories which help to manage the data. In contrast to this, discourse researchers do not usually apply extensive coding to

---

[61] The TA (= Technische Anleitung) Luft is an ordinance, a 'Verwaltungsvorschrift'. It is based on para 48 Nr 1 and para 51 of the German Federal Immission Law (Bundesimmissionsschutzgesetz). It comprises detailed, technical tertiary rules which implement key aspects of the IPPC Directive into German national law.

[62] Taylor, above, n 60, p 320; Carabine, above, n 46, p 306.

[63] J Potter and M Wetherell, 'Unfolding Discourse Analysis' in Wetherell, *et al*, above, n 13, p 200.

[64] J Potter and M Wetherell, *Discourse and Social Psychology* (London, Sage, 1989) 164.

the discourse because they do not want to lose sight of its variation. Moreover, some discourse researchers would perceive coding as constructed categories, which themselves should be subject to discourse analysis.[65]

Discourse and qualitative research also have different views about how theory is generated from the data. Some discourse analysis involves reference to preconceived theoretical concepts, for instance from Foucault's work. In qualitative research, however, data are often analysed from a 'grounded theory' perspective. This means that small-scale and medium range theory is developed out of the data themselves, without reference to external 'grand theory' concepts.[66] So, how can these different emphases in qualitative and discourse analysis procedures be reconciled in practice?

F. BLENDING QUALITATIVE AND DISCOURSE DATA ANALYSIS—A PRACTICAL EXAMPLE

The data analysis addresses initially two questions: what is BAT law in action and how is it achieved?[67] How do social actors distinguish BAT from non-BAT and how do they arrive at views about what they consider as BAT? I attempt to answer these questions through a two-stage analysis procedure. The first stage draws on a qualitative approach and blends this with some elements of discourse analysis. During this stage I read through the data for gist in order to identify themes. Themes relate, for instance, to the argumentation strategies employed for describing certain technologies and operating procedures as BAT, as well as organisational and procedural features which shape their views of BAT. I look for consistency in the data in order to identify key themes, while trying to remain sensitive to detecting variation.

From a discourse analytical perspective I then code the data into larger chunks, in order not to lose a feeling for the BAT discourse as a whole. I also interrogate the themes about their function. What tasks does the talk accomplish? These coding categories can later be linked and thus can help to detect patterns in the data which contribute to answering the research question. Finally, general propositions can be formulated which can be tested against the data and thus the data—from a qualitative perspective—are treated as 'evidence'.[68] During this first stage of reading through the data I also identify a limited number of clear 'BAT stories'.

---

[65] *Ibid*, p 137.

[66] BG Glaser and A Strauss, *The Discovery of Grounded Theory, Strategies for Qualitative Research* (New York, NY, Aldine de Gruyter, 1967).

[67] The analysis also addresses a third question of whether and how BAT law in action contributes to EU integration in the field of standards for emissions to air, water and land from the installations covered by the IPPC Directive.

[68] N Alexiadou, 'Researching Policy Implementation: Interview Data Analysis in Institutional Contexts' (2001) 4(1) *International Journal of Social Research Methodology* 65.

These are self-contained episodes in the data which allow us to trace how specific BAT definitions are achieved.

During the second stage of data analysis this limited number of BAT stories is then more intensively analysed from a discourse analytical perspective. I call these data extracts 'BAT stories' because they are each a coherent unit of text which allows us to explain the discourse as a whole. At this stage I am asking how is the story about what is BAT constructed? Through what discursive techniques are arguments built in order to affirm that one particular technology or operating procedure is BAT? In the following section I will provide an introductory application of these analysis procedures to a BAT story.

1. DATA EXTRACT

The following is a non-representative extract from the transcript of the official audiotape recording of the second TWG meeting for the Iron and Steel BREF.[69]

About 46[70] delegates, mainly from Member State environmental ministries and regulatory authorities, from industry and environmental NGOs, are assembled in a meeting room in the EIPPC Bureau in Seville.[71] The discussion is chaired by the EIPPC Bureau co-ordinator, while the author for the Iron and Steel BREF takes the meeting through comments from TWG members on a first draft of the BREF.[72]

[BREF author]:

Another comment tells us that we did not consider top layer sintering and it should be described as a BAT candidate and even it represents BAT. First, my question is, should we describe it, is it BAT and third who can provide me with the full description of a BAT candidate called 'top layer sintering' if we agree with the first two questions.

[Bureau co-ordinator]:

Mr [name of industry delegate] seems to have some answers. Mr [name of industry delegate]:

---

[69] These recordings are routinely produced for all TWG meetings by the EIPPC Bureau. For each BREF there are two TWG meetings for the determination of what constitutes BAT for a particular sector. While the first meeting is usually more concerned with agenda setting and planning the work for the group, the second meeting often deals with discussion of an already written draft BREF and the firming up of BAT conclusions. For more detail see B Lange, 'From Boundary Drawing to Transitions: The Creation of Normativity under the EU Directive on Integrated Pollution Prevention and Control' (2002) 8 *European Law Journal* 246–68.

[70] This is the number of members of the Technical Working Group for the Iron and Steel sector which appears on the EIPPC Bureau's website at http://eippcb.jrc.es/(site last visited 25 February 2005).

[71] Present at the meeting were also one member of staff from the Directorate General Enterprise and one member from the Directorate General Environment of the EU Commission.

[72] English is not the native language for a number of people who speak during this extract. This explains some speakers' unusual grammar and style constructions.

[Industry delegate]:

No, I have no answers, but I have some questions. Ah, why is two, ahem, top layer sintering introduced, because it is in existing plants, practically an impossibility to install it. Ah, you have second conveyor belts, you have second dowsing equipment, an ignition hood, everything and it is impossible to install it in existing plants. It is just not feasible. So, I see difficulty, how it could be BAT, even a candidate BAT. So, what is the reason, why is it used, if it is used somewhere. I think it is one in Austria. So, why is it used in Austria?

[Bureau co-ordinator]:

First of all, we might put that question to our Austrian colleague, but I would suggest that just because a technique is very difficult to install on an existing installation that is no reason to exclude it, if it is possible, if you were to build a new sinter strand now, it is a technique that is perhaps there. It is putting a marker down, it is one beautiful case, where it may not be implemented or seen for a very long time, but at least it is information, which is, that is a technique. [BREF author's first name], how do you feel about that?

[BREF author]:

As far as I know this technique has been introduced in order to manage residues with a high content of oil. So they have the first layer, the sinter feed itself and a second layer, with residues containing a high amount of oil. So, this was, is a technique to lower the hydrocarbon content in the off-gas, as far as I know and it is applied in one plant of [name of the company] in [location of the plant] in Austria. So, I take it that you really have doubts that it could be BAT. This is, ahem, would be an answer to question number two, but the question number number one, should we then even describe it as a candidate. Maybe the conclusion then is, that it is not BAT, it is just a candidate.

[Bureau co-ordinator]:

Mr [name of industry delegate] please.

Mr [name of industry delegate]:

Now, to reduce the content of hydrocarbons there exists other techniques. We also reduce it, we have very low input of hydrocarbons in our sinterplant. So we have to get rid of the hydrocarbons elsewhere in an integrated steel plant. So, that is not, there is no necessity to introduce this technique.

[Bureau co-ordinator]:

Mr [name of industry delegate] please.

[Bureau co-ordinator]:

With the microphone, Mr [name of industry delegate] please.

[Industry delegate]:

I just have a general question. How many installations do we need to have to call it BAT? One, two, three, four, is there a cut-off value to accept the techniques as BAT or not? Just a general question.

[Bureau co-ordinator]:

I will give you a general answer. And again this was coming from the debate we had last week and I am sure we will have it next week. Ahem, I would remind you of the words in the Directive, which simply says that, ahem, it is something capable of being implemented in a sector, so you could say, it does not have to be implemented, it is developed to a scale which is capable of being or allows implementation. So, I don't think there is any cut-off, indeed I believe actually, you could if the group were to agree as such the concept that something is BAT, even though it is not yet implemented in a sector. Otherwise, how on earth do you introduce a new technology? [First name of industry delegate], please.

[Industry delegate]:

Do you talk about candidate BAT or BAT?

[Bureau co-ordinator]:

Now there I am talking about the (*hesitation*) definition in the Directive.

[Industry delegate]:

Now, in the Directive I quote, wait a moment, best available techniques shall mean the most effective and advanced stage in the development of activities and their methods of operation which indicate the practical suitability of particular techniques for providing in principle the basis for emission limit values. And in that case, I think, if there is only one situation in the world where a certain technique is used, it is almost by definition is not BAT.

[Bureau co-ordinator]:

Actually, I am also quoting from the Directive in terms of the definition of available, which says, it shall mean those developed on a scale which allows implementation in the relevant industrial sector. And of course the debate is, is it working in another sector. And it is clearly a case of technology transfer from one sector to another sector. And then can you associate any particular emission level with it. There seems to be a clear opportunity there to transfer technology, in this case techniques, from one sector to another sector, if it is considered that it has been developed to a stage that it allows implementation in the new sector.

[Industry delegate]:

Alright, but if we, for instance, name a certain sector and there is SCR[73] implemented over there as a rule and they reach emission values of, ahem, 20 mg Nox. Does not necessarily mean that if you have got another plant that you can use SCR for it and have an emission limit value of 20 mg. That is what EUROFER[74] is afraid of will happen if you use this references.

---

[73] This is the abbreviation for selective catalytic reduction. It helps to abate NOx and N2 emissions through NH3 and a catalyst at temperatures of about 300–400 degree Celsius. It is used, for instance, for NOx emissions abatement in coal-fired power stations and waste incinerators.

[74] This is the abbreviation for the European Confederation of Iron and Steel Industries which lobbies on behalf of the European steel industry the EU institutions and international organisations (http://www.eurofer.org/organization/index.htm—site last visited 1 December 2004).

[Bureau co-ordinator]:

I would, ahem, accept what you say quite readily. It is one thing saying it is an available technology because it has been developed elsewhere and can be transferred, quite often the associated emission limit, or emission value would be different for good reason. If you talk about particulates, you got resistivity of the dust, you got the chemicals of the dust, you got the particle size and with SCR you got similar technical considerations. And I think the door is open, at least, to start considering. You may not gonna say what it will achieve. That is clear, I think.

[Industry delegate]:

So, do I understand it right that, for instance, SCR in the Iron and Steel industry is considered as BAT but there are no concentrations connected to it. In that case I can agree.

[Bureau co-ordinator]:

Ahem, I have not got anywhere near, to the concept of looking at, [first name of BREF author], that SCR is BAT, I thought that was a later stage. If that were the case, that the group said, we think SCR is applicable in this case. We just don't know what it will achieve, that may be the result, that people think, yeah, there is no technical or economic reason why it should not work. We don't know quite how it will work. [First name of Member State delegate], were you ... please.

[Member State delegate]:

I do not want to interfere in this discussion, because I thought this was already solved elsewhere, to put it again into this point, well, my impression was, that what is applied today, yeah, on an industrial scale, is potentially BAT candidate. And the number of plants is not of importance. Of importance is the industrial scale, where that is really industrial scale and proven technology and its only one plant that is as good as 10. That is not the question of the number of plants. But, certainly, we could continue this discussion, but I wanted to come back to the issue here, and when we were seeing this on the list of issues, we were wondering about data about this top layer sintering. There are no data available and I wonder now whether we can decide whether or not this is a BAT candidate without having any data. Will there be data provided for the technique?

[BREF author]:

There is one publication available. I have this publication from this company which can potentially provide this system and who has developed this kind of technology in one plant at [company name] in [location name]. So, thank you for coming back to this topic. I think, if you can provide a full BAT candidate within reasonable time, that means for me within two weeks, we could implement it, even I have personally also doubts, that it could end up in the conclusion that it is BAT, because no new installation, I think, would adapt to a top layer sintering because it is a very special case for this plant, as far as I know because of the oily residues and to manage them and of course we have other possibilities to reduce the oil content in the residues. So, that means I will leave it with you, because you have submitted this proposal. O.K.

[Bureau co-ordinator]:

You seem to be concluding there, [BREF author's first name], that top layer sintering is a particular technique which could in a particular instance here solve a problem and be therefore BAT. Does anyone wish to speak for or against that? [Industry delegate first name] would and then [Member State delegate first name] please.

[Industry delegate]:

I interpreted a different conclusion. I thought what Herr [BREF author's name] was saying was in this specific circumstance this technique is being applied so we must consider it as a candidate BAT, but in general it was unlikely, in his view anyway, to be BAT.

[BREF author]:

This is my feeling so far, yes.

[Bureau co-ordinator]:

O.k. [first name of Member State delegate] please.

[Member State delegate]:

I don't know details of the process, but I think there is, the Directive does require a certain hierarchy to be applied. And if my understanding of what has been said about this process, ahem, it is an end of pipe approach. What we should be looking at is, preventing rather than minimising. So, if this process were to be applied at a new plant and it is applying an end of pipe approach, rather than looking at alternative process modifications then it would not be BAT.

[Bureau co-ordinator]:

You seem to have two things there ...

[BREF author]:

We have already concluded already. If it will be provided it will be considered as a candidate and as far as I take it even, also from this round it seems to be we cannot consider it as BAT. So we can come to the next.

2. An Introductory Analysis of the Data Extract

First, I identify key themes in this extract, such as 'procedure'. On the one hand, BAT determinations are seen to be the outcome of an open, deliberative, reasoned discussion process,[75] while, on the other hand, BAT seems to be determined by external factors, partly beyond the control of the TWG, such as time constraints. Upon closer analysis it appears that there are even two procedures here for determining BAT. Firstly, there is

---

[75] For instance, the EIPPC Bureau co-ordinator invites TWG members to speak 'for or against' the proposal that top layer sintering is BAT.

a discussion—mainly between the EIPPC Bureau co-ordinator and industry delegates—which seeks to define BAT in general and abstract terms. It discusses, for instance, how widely a technique needs to be applied in order to be considered as BAT. A key resource for this debate is interpretation of specific terms in the text of the IPPC Directive. BAT seems to derive from a prescriptive principle[76]: technology transfer from one industrial sector to another. Assent by the TWG, rather than a detailed technical discussion, is the key decision criterion for BAT here. Group consensus is achieved through power brokerage, such as the compromise not to specify associated emission levels with SCR, rather than through persuasion based on technical arguments. Hence, what appears to the EIPPC Bureau co-ordinator as a surprisingly quick agreement is achieved, by dispensing with a time-consuming data gathering, scrutiny and discussion process.

But there is also a second procedure for BAT determinations invoked in this extract. This focuses on the more specific question, whether top layer sintering can be described as BAT for the iron and steel sector. This debate is conducted mainly between the delegate from a Member State regulatory authority and the BREF author. Very specific technical 'data', in fact one publication from an equipment supplier, are considered as crucial for determining BAT. The detailed description of an existing technology, rather than an abstract, prescriptive principle, such as 'technology transfer', is the starting point here for a BAT determination.

Themes, such as 'procedure', can be further broken down into sub-themes, such as 'social relations'. Various aspects of the procedure for determining BAT establish and structure social relations between the EIPPC Bureau co-ordinator and the BREF author, as well as between the EIPPC Bureau and TWG members. For instance, different degrees of social distance are indicated through the use of formal addresses or first names for speakers by the EIPPC Bureau co-ordinator.

In the next step of the analysis I ask about the functions of the talk which has been categorized into various themes. For instance, talk about the procedure negotiates an organisational structure for BAT determinations which complements the formal, but rudimentary structure set up by the IPPC Directive and DG Environment. This organisational structure provides roles for its various members. For instance, the IPPC Bureau co-ordinator asks TWG members for 'answers', but they decline the role of providers of answers and instead opt for the role of questioner. Establishing organisational structures and allocating roles is part and parcel of the exercise of power by the participants in the BAT determination process. This extract seems to suggest that BAT determinations are the outcome of a subtle balance of power between BREF author and EIPPC Bureau

---

[76] See, for example, the statement by a TWG member that '[...] there is SCR implemented over there *as a rule*' (emphasis added).

co-ordinator on the one hand, and the TWG on the other hand. The BREF author determines the procedure by putting a sequence of questions to the TWG and by finally setting a deadline which will decide whether top layer sintering will be considered as BAT. In contrast to this, some of the TWG members cast themselves in the role of participants who 'just ask questions'. This appears to be less directive than the BREF author's and IPPC Bureau co-ordinator's steering, but it still allows TWG members to exercise power by holding to account those who are being asked questions. Most importantly, however, talk about procedure can by itself produce BAT determinations. For instance, reference to time restraints for the provision of information about top layer sintering may displace substantive criteria for the BAT determination.

In the second stage of the analysis I ask in more detail through what discursive techniques BAT determinations are achieved. Four discursive techniques seem to matter here. First, the participants in the debate frequently resort to interpretation of text, like the IPPC Directive and oral speech, such as their contributions to the debate. Interpretations are mobilised in order to attempt to close down the discourse to a specific meaning of BAT. By its very nature, however, this interpretative process reopens the debate by drawing attention to various different meanings which can be attributed to statements about what BAT is.

Secondly, speakers attempt to fix the meaning of BAT by drawing distinctions between various terms. In Foucauldian terminology this is a process of normalization through which power is exercised.[77] Distinctions are drawn, for instance, between 'BAT' and 'candidate BAT' as well as between 'new' and 'existing plants'. Given the fact that these key terms are not clearly defined, distinguishing these terms from each other becomes especially important for constructing their meaning.

Thirdly, the BAT determination in this extract is facilitated through a discourse which is not a unified narrative, but works through parallel stories and ruptures. This is illustrated through the two unconnected debates about what constitutes BAT for abating emission from iron and steel plants. These refer, on the one hand, to SCR and, on the other hand, to top layer sintering. Furthermore, some elements of the BAT discourse, such as the suggestion that end-of-pipe approaches can not be considered as BAT, remain isolated and are not picked up in the discussion and some questions asked by TWG members are not answered, but receive an evasive reply.[78]

---

[77] Carabine, above, n 46, p 277.

[78] When an industry delegate asks the EIPPC Bureau co-ordinator whether he talks about 'BAT or candidate BAT', the EIPPC Bureau co-ordinator replies that he is talking about 'the definition in the Directive'. The text of the Directive, however, does not refer to the term 'candidate BAT'.

Fourthly, the EIPPC Bureau co-ordinator, the BREF author and some TWG members refer to 'we', 'us' and 'the group' in their statements. This discursive technique can furnish the BAT determination process with a greater claim to democratic legitimacy. It gives the impression that a unified and significant number of members of the technical working group are involved here in BAT determinations, while in actual fact—apart from the BREF author and the EIPPC Bureau co-ordinator—6 out of 46 TWG members speak in this extract.

G. CONCLUSION

To conclude, through combining a qualitative and a discourse analytical perspective, insights should be generated which could not be obtained by focusing on either one of these two perspectives. The approach discussed in this chapter aims to transcend postmodernist—modernist methodological dichotomies. The qualitative approach captures the surface of the discourse—the meaning of the words—as well as non-discursive factors— social actors' behaviour beyond the words—which shape the construction of the discourse. The qualitative approach sees BAT determinations through the eyes of the participants and focuses on the meaning which the participants construct in their discussions. This first layer of analysis, however, needs to be complemented by an examination of the discursive techniques through which BAT is established in order to develop further a critical investigation of how BAT discourse constructs the microphysics of power which inform EU law in action.

Section Four

Structural Approaches

REZA BANAKAR AND MAX TRAVERS

THE ORIGINS OF structural theories which were advanced by sociologists such as Emile Durkheim, Talcott Parsons, Niklas Luhmann, Anthony Giddens and Pierre Bourdieu, to name a few, can be traced back to works of the 19th century sociologists such as Hebert Spencer and Auguste Comte.[1] Spencer drew an analogy between society and living organisms, while Comte stressed the systematic character of society.[2] Spencer's analogy was, admittedly, not new and had been used previously by various thinkers since Plato. Yet, the way he applied it to explain how different types of society evolved from lower to higher levels of differentiation and complexity was new.[3] Using this analogy, social life was viewed and studied as a complex system or an organism composed of interdependent, interconnected and differentiated parts or relationships. Comte's sociology was also based on evolutionary assumptions similar to those of Spencer, paid little attention to the role of individual actors and instead focused on larger social units such as family. This emphasis has through Durkheim's work influenced much of the later sociological theorising.

---

[1] H Spencer, *On Social Evolution: Selected Writings* (Chicago, IL, Chicago University Press, 1972). For references to Comte, see the discussions on positivism and objectivity in ch 1.

[2] Structuralism refers also to a certain theoretical perspective which became fashionable during 1960s and 1970s within linguistics, social anthropology, psychoanalysis and psychology. Ferdinand de Saussure, who is generally regarded as the founder of structural linguistics, distinguished between the study of language as *parole* (speech, that is language as produced by a speaking individual) and of language as *langue*, as a system of signs. The *langue* is essential in the sense that it is a condition for speech act and, thus, is given priority over *parole* which is contingent. Attributing priority to *langue* over *parole* suggests Saussure's familiarity with the works of Emile Durkheim, which were very influential in Saussure's time. Saussure's structuralism directly and indirectly influenced the development of social theory, most notably through the structural anthropology of Claude Levi-Struauss. See F de Saussure, *Course in General Linguistics* (London, Fontana, 1974); and A Giddens, 'Structuralism, Post-Structuralism and the Production of Culture' in A Giddens, *Social Theory and Modern Sociology* (Cambridge, Polity Press, 1987).

[3] Hein Andersen argues that such concepts such as social institutions, differentiation, complexity, integration and social structure, which are current currency within structural functionalism and systems theory, were employed by Spencer. H Andersen and H Spencer, H Andersen and B Kaspersen, (eds), *Classical and Modern Social Theory* (Oxford, Blackwells, 2000).

Within structural functionalism, the constitutive elements of a system are never considered in isolation from each other or from the *totality* of the system, which is in turn regarded as more than the sum of its constitutive parts. That is why structural approaches often study the relationships between the constitutive elements of the system, on the one hand, and the totality of the system, on the other, to unravel the mysteries of social life. This also means that they share a general methodology: they try to throw light on the normative features of social life by examining the relationship between the micro elements of social systems such as norms, roles, human agency, practices or communicative action and their macro manifestations such as social institutions, structures, systems or fields. In the earlier versions of structural theories, like in those of Marx and Durkheim, the latter often carried more sociological weight than the former, ie, the focus of analysis was on how structural or macro social relations formed micro relations.[4] Legal forms of behaviour or organisation are, thus, explained as 'the result of the *structure of the relationships* existing in the larger society and the legal system itself'.[5] The other shared commonality of structural approaches, which was discussed in some detail in section one, is the belief in the possibility of objectivity in social research. Structuralists believe in sociology's ability to analyse social behaviour and relationships *objectively* by examining how social systems are constituted through patterns of meaningful action or processes.

Sociology of law has been heavily influenced by positivism, in general, and by structural functionalism, in particular, from its inception in the latter part the 19th century.[6] The forerunners of legal sociology and anthropology, such as Durkheim, Ehrlich, Pound and Malinowski,[7] were all proponents of the 'scientific method' and viewed law at the level of social organisation and in terms of the functions it performed in the wider society. The focus on structural and functional make-up of the law was taken for granted by many later sociologists. Adopting a structuralist approach was convenient for at least two reasons: 1) It conformed to the rules of sociological methods and theory as expressed by two closely related major sociological paradigms, ie, structural functionalism and systems theory, and 2) it found itself in resonance with how law was viewed and defined by legal scholars, policymakers and legislators alike. As Norberto Bobbio

---

[4] Later sociologists such as Giddens and Bourdieu have tried to link these two levels of analysis. For a brief description of Gidden' structuration theory see n 7 in the introduction to Section 3.

[5] RL Kidder, *Connecting Law and Society: An Introduction to Research and Theory* (New Jersey, Prentice Hall, 1983).

[6] There is close affinity between positivism, scientism, the application of quantitative methods and a concern with structural functional analysis, which will be discussed in ch 14.

[7] See R Banakar, 'Sociological Jurisprudence' in R Banakar and M Travers, (eds), *An Introduction to Law and Social Theory* (Oxford, Hart Publishing, 2002).

explains, 'the legal science has always had a tendency to study structures, to conceive of law as a structure, as a system, a complex totality ...'.[8]

The problem with taking the structural descriptions of law as the starting point for sociological analysis is that one might, unwittingly be (mis)led into reproducing the ideology of law, which underpins law's self-descriptions and self-presentations, as empirical (objective) observations. Paradoxically, structural functional analysis can become an effective tool for uncovering this ideology when law's self-descriptions and claims are treated as the object of analysis.[9] However, whether one adopts a critical approach towards law's claims or takes its self-presentations at face value, a study which focuses its analytical and empirical lenses only on structural aspect of law and legal institutions is bound to overlook the non-structural elements which constitute law and legal behaviour.[10]

The structuralist approaches dominated the development of the sociology of law after the Second World War, were further developed during 1970s and 1980s,[11] and continue to be a major theoretical and methodological force in socio-legal research. Today, on the one hand we have a growing number of studies which are influenced by various attempts to bridge the structure/agency and macro/micro divide, as attempted by Giddens, Bourdieu and Habermas to name a few. On the other hand, we have studies which are informed by systems theory, which emphasises the self-regulatory properties of social systems.

This section contains two chapters which exemplify the structural functional tradition in its more recent and theoretically sophisticated forms. The first of these applies ideas developed in Pierre Bourdieu's sociology to the study of law and legal institutions. The second chapter adopts a systems theoretical approach, which was discussed earlier in section one. These two chapters share a fundamental concern with the structural features of society, but differ on their conceptualisation of the structural relations. Bourdieu's sociology belongs to the tradition of critical theory, which views social development in terms of *conflict* and highlights how agents and

---

[8] Quoted from a letter written to André-Jean Arnaud in 1969, see AJ Arnaud, 'Structuralist Theories of Law' in P Amselek and N MacCormick, (eds), *Controversies about Law's Ontology* (Edinburgh, EUP, 1991).

[9] Post-structuralist approaches which are informed by Foucault's methodology have also proved successful in this regard. For an example see C Smart, *Feminism and the Power of Law* (London, Routledge, 1995); and A Hunt and G Wickham, *Foucault and Law: Toward a Sociology of Law and Governance* (London, Pluto Press, 1994). Forms of post-structuralism are not discussed here because although they emphasise macro aspects of social life, they nonetheless adopt interpretative methods.

[10] For a discussion see M Travers, 'Putting Sociology Back into Sociology of Law' (1993) 20 *Journal of Law and Society* 443–44.

[11] For an overview of structural functional research during the period following the Second World War see WM Evan, (ed), *The Sociology of Law: A Social-Structural Perspective* (New York, NY, Free Press, 1980).

groups produce and reproduce structural relations through their social practices of struggling for 'stakes'. Systems theory, on the other hand, has its roots in the consensus sociology of Parsons and Durkheim, which is more concerned with *functional* stability of social institutions. It also means that systems theory pays greater attention to how the system as whole is integrated and little attention (if any at all) to social actors or social action.[12]

The first chapter in this section is by Ole Hammerslev, who uses Bourdieu's sociology to analyse the biographical data on Danish judges. The aim of this study is to examine the social and legal position of judges in Danish society. Hammerslev explains that there is a tradition of collecting this type of information in Denmark, which goes back to 1736. This is a valuable source of sociological information, which can be used to describe and analyse the field of law, and what Hammerslev calls the field of judges. A 'field' is a socially constructed symbolic space consisting of 'objective' relations between individual positions and institutions. It accommodates one or several social groups and is, at the same time, structured by forms of patterned activity or 'practices' of these groups. In a sense a social group is constituted in virtue of its location within the field, which as a rule involves competitive relations with other groups in the field. Hammerslev refers to sources such as *Who's Who*, *festschrifts* written by jurists and official and ministerial reports about courts in his attempt to describe the development of field of judges and the trajectories of judges as a group. More significantly, Hammerslev views the field and its internal relations with the theoretical conviction that they have an 'objective' existence lending themselves to 'a scientific understanding'. He feeds the biographical data available to him on judges' background, such as the occupation of their parents, place of birth, material status, educational patterns, membership of various boards and commissions etc, into a data base, so that he can analyse them in order to describe the field of judges and the strategies that the judges use to consolidate and expand their power.

In short, Hammerslev uses Bourdieu's sociology as a guide to conduct empirical research and ultimately to gain access to the self-description of agents-a description which transcends a biographically ordered life story based on the self-centred logic of those agents who are engaged in playing the game in the field of law. He is ultimately concerned with how agents-and their collective relational biographies-reveal the structural development of the field of law.

The second chapter in this section, by John Paterson and Gunther Teubner, starts by asking why theory and empirical research in law and society is divided by 'a structural hiatus', 'which renders theory rather

---

[12] For Luhmann the unit of social analysis is communication and not social action. See section one for a presentation of Luhmann's systems theory.

empty and empiricism rather blind'. Their chapter has some similarities to Klaus A Ziegert's chapter in section one in arguing for the value of autopoiesis theory, although it also shows how this can be used in addressing a substantive socio-legal topic: the regulation of the health and safety in the off-shore oil industry. Like many other structural or 'synthetic' traditions, they believe that most other kinds of sociology can be incorporated into their own project. They argue, for example, that the future of autopoiesis looks bright and promising 'for all kinds of historical analysis, for genealogical and archaeological digging in historical texts, and for qualitative research techniques, case studies of formal organisation, ethnomethodological types of socio-legal interaction, discourse analysis, and for "critical empiricism"'. All of these can be brought within the autopoiesis framework! However, they are less friendly towards variable analysis or correlational studies. Whether, of course, an ethnomethodologist, qualitative researcher or critical discourse analyst would welcome, or see the need for incorporation, seems doubtful, and one should not expect autopoiesis to be any more successful than previous attempts to produce a unified social science.[13]

Paterson and Teubner then move on to outline a framework for their research by questioning the causal chains of regulation which are often assumed to exist and used to guide socio-legal studies of regulation. According to this traditional model, policy-makers identify and define social problems, which they then translate into legislative acts and legal norms. These acts, then, motivate and guide the administrative staff (the regulators in this case) to implement the policy goals crystallised in the acts. By implementing the acts, the regulators impact on and motivate actors in the field influencing their incentives, attitudes, behaviour and so on. Somewhat oversimplified, this means that the actions of social actors or processes taking place within the sphere of politics causes developments in the sphere of law, which in turn set the regulators in motion, who impact on the behaviour of social actors bringing about social change.

Paterson and Teubner suggest a new understanding of social regulation by replacing this horizontal causal model of regulation with 'a multitude of autonomous but interfering fields of action'. Their suggested framework attaches no importance to the role played by policy-makers or administrative staff as individual social actors who interact with and influence other social actors. In addition, it assumes that there are no input-output relationships between different spheres such as politics, law, administration and the area targeted for regulation. Each of these should instead be viewed and studied as a self-steering spheres of action or processes. As they explain: 'regulation is possible only as self-regulation within each of these recursive processes'. This does not mean that regulatory attempts produce no effect,

---

[13] See, for example, the comments about structural sociology by John Flood in section one.

but that these effects cannot be properly understood using the causal relationships used by traditional theories. Instead, the researcher needs to describe how self-regulation is realised within several spheres of action and whether these self-regulatory attempts diverge causing regulatory failure, or travel together for a time in a common direction bringing about regulatory success.

Paterson and Teubner's critique of the traditional causal analysis of regulation is, arguably, not new in substance and articulates the type of critique that other sociologists of law have been directing towards the ideology of legal instrumentalism.[14] However, no matter what we think of the ability of autopoiesis to unify social sciences, capture the complexity of social life, or bridge 'the structural hiatus' mentioned earlier, Paterson and Teubner show that there are good reasons to revisit, if not indeed to reconsider, much of the discussions traditionally used to explain the relationship between law and legal change (or legal reform).

The general approach adopted by Paterson and Teubner shows certain commonalities with some of the theoretical concepts discussed in Hammerslev's chapter. The very notion of 'system' which they use resembles Bourdieu's 'field' in that it signifies a socially constructed space consisting of a set of objective relations. The fundamental difference between a 'system' and a 'field' lies in what Paterson and Teubner, on the one hand, and Hammerslev on the other, regard as the constitutive elements of this social space. There are also other differences, which concern the sociological roots of these two approaches. While systems theory is concerned with the *functional* stability of social systems, Bourdieu focuses on the *power* relations and how groups and individual agents struggle over the 'stakes' in the field (this distinction is somewhat blurred in the study of the Danish judges).

However, both approaches are concerned with objectivity and claim to be scientific. But Paterson and Teubner go further than Hammerslev by quite categorically maintaining that the researcher cannot select his or her 'system' arbitrarily to satisfy a research interest or certain theoretical assumptions. Researchers can treat an entity as a 'system' only if it demonstrates an 'objective' empirical reality of its own. To put it differently, 'autopoietic systems are produced by self-organising processes in the social world and not by scientific observers'.

The underlying assumption of this last statement appears in different guises in many theories concerned with structural or functional relations

---

[14] Legal instrumentalism understands the law as 'an independent agency of social control and social direction'. See R Cotterrell, *The Sociology of Law: An Introduction* (London, Butterworths, 1992) 44. For a critique of legal instrumentalism, which articulates some of the concerns of Paterson and Teubner in a less abstract fashion see J Griffiths, 'Legal Pluralism and the Theory of Legislation: With Special Reference to the Regulation of Euthanasia' in H Petersen and H Zahle, (eds), *Legal Polycentricity: Consequences of Pluralism in Law* (Aldershot, Dartmouth, 1995).

and reveals one of the guiding principles of structural functionalism. This assumption was conceptualised by Durkheim as 'social facts', which according to him had an existence of its own, external to the individual, and yet influenced social actions and ultimately the way structural relations were shaped. This belief in the objectivity of certain patterns of action and forms of social relations, which is in part the sociological heritage of Durkheim, continues to inform what many researchers regard as empirical data and how they go about collecting and analysing this data.

Finally, structuralism should be seen as a paradigm capable of encompassing a variety of approaches. The two chapters presented in this section to exemplify structuralism are not the only studies in this volume which are influenced by this tradition. Leaving aside chapter 3 by Klaus A Ziegert, which was written in defence of systems theory, Reza Banakar's study of Swedish anti-discrimination laws, Bettina Lange's study of an EU Directive in the previous section, and Marina Kurkchyian's study of socio-legal transformation in Russia which will be presented in the section 5, are also influenced to difference degrees by structuralism. In addition, Michael Adler's chapter on constructing a typology of administrative justice, which is presented in section six, could have also been presented in this section as an example of structuralist analysis. This shows that despite the growing theoretical diversity within socio-legal research, forms of structural functionalism continue to influence the way many researchers study the law.

10

How to Study Danish Judges

OLE HAMMERSLEV

I N THIS CHAPTER I will use Pierre Bourdieu's sociological theory to discuss how to examine the social and legal position of judges in Denmark.[1] Using my study of Danish judges,[2] I will try to explain how this can be done by focusing on the biographies of individual agents in the field, and how through the records of individuals' biographies we can write a collective biography of the field.[3] Although, as Bourdieu notes, it is not the individual who is the focus of the research, we nonetheless cannot understand the social world but through the individuals, since the information necessary to generate relevant data is attached to individuals.[4] As Bourdieu explains, his concepts are analytical tools designed to help the researcher to do empirical research. They are not predefined concepts, but developed in relation to the specific field under examination. The important point is to make the concepts work, to 'put them in motion', rather than use them rigidly 'in themselves and for themselves'.[5] I will develop Bourdieuian

---

[1] The social position of the legal profession in general and judges in particular has been viewed and conceptualised differently by different researchers. See for example T Mathiesen, *Ideologi og Motstand* (Oslo, Pax Forlag, 1979); T Parsons, *Essays in Sociological Theory* (New York, NY, Free Press, 1954); C Guarnieri and P Pederzoli, *The Power of the Judges: A Comparative Study of Courts and Democracy* (Oxford, OUP, 2002); M Bertilsson, (ed), *Rätten i Förvandling: Jurister mellan stat och marknad* (Stockholm, Nerenius & Santerus Förlag, 1995); RL Abel and PSC Lewis, (eds), *Lawyers in Society: The Common Law World* (Berkley, CA, University of California Press, 1988); RL Abel and PSC Lewis, (eds), *Lawyers in Society: The Civil Law World* (Berkley, CA, University of California Press, 1988); RL Abel and PSC Lewis, (eds), *Lawyers in Society: Comparative Theories* (Berkley, CA, University of California Press, 1989); and V Aubert, 'The Changing Role of Law and Lawyers in Nineteenth and Twentieth Century Norwegian Society' in DN MacCormick, (ed), *Lawyers in Their Social Setting* (Edinburgh, Green & Son, 1976) 1-17.

[2] See O Hammerslev, *Danish Judges in the 20th Century: A Socio-Legal Study* (Copenhagen, DJØF-Publishing, 2003).

[3] See Y Dezalay and BG Garth, *The Internationalization of Palaces War: Lawyers, Economists, and the Contest to Transform Latin American States* (Chicago, IL, University of Chicago Press, 2002).

[4] P Bourdieu and LJD Wacquant, *An Invitation to Reflexive Sociology* (Chicago, IL, University of Chicago Press, 1992) 107.

[5] *Ibid*, p 228.

notions as tools to identify and label differences between individuals in the field, showing how it becomes possible to differentiate between judges using their hierarchical rank and geographical position by means of a relational database. I will then go on to discuss how to examine the legal position of judges. I shall pay special attention to the double role played by judges in society. Besides holding legal positions which are decisive for the internal structure of the law, judges also hold social positions outside the legal system.

Law works internally as a symbolic system, which means that it fosters its own specific way of thinking, perceiving and viewing social life and relations. Having said that, it is important to remember that law exists through, and is formed by, the people who act within it and in relation to it, ie, by the social agents who create law as a social field. And judges' internal legal positions matter in terms of the legal power that they enjoy, which is why we also need to determine their legal position in relation to other positions in the field.

According to Bourdieu, and historical sociology in general, it is difficult to understand the social and legal position of judges in society without describing the emergence, transformation and continuities in their social and legal position during previous historical periods. Therefore, one of the aims of this chapter is to show how a historical perspective can be employed as part of the general method to conduct a study of this type. However, before developing a method suitable for this kind of examination, let me describe some characteristics of the field, and my own experiences when I began my study of judges in different courts in Denmark.

A. CHARACTERISTICS OF STUDYING A FIELD OF JUDGES

The advantage of studying judges is that a considerable amount of information exists regarding their background, career, prominence, independence, etc in the public domain. However, researchers who are new to this area may find it difficult to gain access to the legal field, and the field of judges in particular. In order to be granted access to the field and the wealth of information available in it one often needs personal contacts with agents who are willing to facilitate the researcher's entry into the research area.

There is a great deal of material on this subject, collected for different reasons. First, legal historians have already scrutinised courts and judges, mapping the development of the court system and positions of judges, providing statistics on cases tried in court and examining the backgrounds of previous judges. Second, judges have been the subject of much biographical research and reporting. In Denmark, for example, biographical information exists from 1736 in reference books such as *Who's Who*.[6] Third, jurists in general have made many analyses of the social and legal position of judges. Not only have legal scholars examined the legal position of judges, but judges and court systems have also been celebrated in many *Festschrifts* (this is at least the case in Denmark) written by jurists for, and addressed to, other jurists. In addition, there are, of course, many consultant and ministerial reports about courts in modern times. With so much documentation, one should be able to conduct a socio-legal study of judges from a historical point of view relatively easy.

It is important, however, to break away from many of the established discourses, categories of visions and divisions in the field, as well as being reflexive about adopting and importing the problems and issues existing in the field into one's main research questions. Many of these issues are social products that have emerged out of the previous struggles of, and competition between, the social actors over the stakes of the fields. Thus, they refer to social struggles and are not necessarily social scientific problems *per se*. Moreover, many of the understandings in the field may mask hidden structures, which can be of relevance to the researcher. From a Bourdieuian perspective, many of the categories, differentiations, and analytical objects existing *in* the field as mental structures are a part of a social struggle, where agents in the field try to strengthen their positions vis-à-vis other agents, and the field tries to strengthen its position vis-à-vis the field of power. This also relates to another difficulty, namely to the presentation of the research to agents in the field. As Bourdieu points out regarding different fields, resistance to accept alternative discourses and descriptions—objectivations—of issues are normally monopolised by the field itself: 'Among the strategies used to resist scientific analysis, one of the most infallible consists in destroying the very purpose of the enterprise of objectivation by reducing the distanced description ... to the status of "critique" in the everyday sense, if not to that of satire or gossip.'[7]

The problem for the sociology of law becomes significant because it studies a field, which is characterised by a claim to a monopoly of its own objectivation. The agents of the field project their partial observations, problems and concerns based on their and the field's specific trajectories to real concerns and descriptions of the field, which hinders the interference of alternative objectivations.

Due to the central position of the highest ranking judges in the field of power throughout the legal history of Denmark, and due to the fact that the people involved in the strategic work of the field are reflexive about what they are doing and what the world looks like, very strong discourses and

---

[6] The Danish version of *Who's Who* is called *Kraks Blå Bog*. Also it is worth noting that in the UK many biographies have been written about the Law Lords and other judges, with the backgrounds of the highest ranking judges in the court hierarchy again reported in *Who's Who*.

[7] P Bourdieu, *The State Nobility* (Cambridge, Policy Press, 1996) 395.

categories have emerged about what is interesting and how the world should be perceived. Issues such as independence and the idea of the centrality of the judge in the legal system are, for instance, defined from a legal point of view but can in practice work very differently in different countries. In that sense, law is related to a broader field of power.

Having said that, it is naturally legitimate to use pre-existing material for one's own purposes. (What else can you do conducting historical research?) Ironically, it can be difficult to obtain access to this information, particularly if you are examining the power of judges and question their discourses and issues connected to their relation to the field of state power as well as the general field of power.

B. STUDYING THE HIDDEN STRUCTURES BEHIND THE FIELD OF JUDGES

When examining the social position of judges, it can be useful not to see them as a coherent unit and instead adopt a relational approach to get beyond the common sense understanding that judges are equal and only divided by means of internal legal structures. As Bourdieu explains the concept of profession is a dangerous concept, as it has:

> ... all appearance of neutrality in its favour ... . To speak of 'profession' is to fasten on a true reality, onto a set of people who bear the same name (they are all 'lawyers' for instance); they are endowed with a roughly equivalent economic status and, more importantly, they are organized into 'professional associations' endowed with a code of ethics, collective bodies that define rules for admission, etc. 'Profession' is a folk concept which has been uncritically smuggled into scientific language and which imports into it a whole social unconscious. It is the *social product* of a historical work of construction of a group and of a *representation* of groups that has surreptitiously slipped into the science of this very group.[8]

This means that categories such as 'profession' or 'lawyers' are socially constructed and include both mental and social structures. They conceal differences and contradictions between the competing individuals including their social, economic, ethnic, sexual, etc status. But how is it possible to get beyond the type of categories like 'professions' and 'lawyers'?

Here the Bourdieuian research tools can become helpful in empirical research. They can identify, label and explain differences between individuals in the field. By focusing on the logic of everyday practice, Bourdieu has devised analytical tools which link objective structures with everyday interpretations. In this way he demonstrates how modes of domination tend to be reproduced through everyday interactions. Applying these tools and relating them to Bourdieu's theory of practice, it becomes possible to

---

[8] Bourdieu, above, n 4, p 242f.

explain how patterns of domination are produced and reproduced by *different* individuals in the field.

C. GRASPING THE RELATIONAL

In order to focus on the differences between legal professionals—and go beyond the existing discourses on the positions of judges—it is necessary to construct a field. In contrast to the notion of system (and much institutional theory), the notion of field has the advantage that it allows for the understanding that participants involved in the field do not form a coherent body, but are defined by their relation to other participants in the field. The Bourdieuian approach throws light on the *relationships* between different individual participants in the professional groups.[9]

Hence, the focus should be on *differences within the field*—be they sexual, ethnic, economic, educational, social relations, etc (forms of capital). A field is a net of objective relations between individuals or institutions that make up a structured system with its own activities. The field is defined as 'a field of struggle', that is a space in which the individuals struggle to gain monopoly on exerting legitimised violence in the field. Understood in a legal context this means that different (groups of) jurists struggle over the *right to* determine what law is.[10] As specific legal modes are adopted in a legal habitus they seem obvious, and therefore law becomes a form of symbolic (hidden) power. Using the concept of 'field' for 'a field of judges' implies that the field is a subfield, a part of a larger legal field where the different agents struggle over the power of the law.[11]

The differences in the forms and contents of *capital* of the individuals create the objective relations and determine their place in the field. It is by way of the differences between the individual's possessions of capital that the power structures surface. The amount of power a person exerts in the field thus depends on the amount of capital the person possesses and on the person's position in the field. Capital, be it economic, social, cultural or symbolic, is the property or form of power the individuals carry. It works as 'admission fees' to different fields and can improve the owner's position in the field. Capital exists and functions only in relation to a field. Therefore, it is necessary to examine individuals' possession of capital.

---

[9] This addresses the question from a different perspective based on much of the previous research on the legal profession, found in convergence and conflict traditions, *see* for instance V Aubert, *Rettens Sosiale Funksjon* (Oslo, Universitetsforlaget, 1976); Aubert, above, n 1; and Mathiesen, above, n 1.

[10] P Bourdieu, 'The Force of Law: Toward a Sociology of the Juridical Field' (1986) 38 *Hastings Law Journal* 814-53.

[11] My concept of field is related to research on professions, whereas the strict Bourdieuian application of the term refers more to a field of interests—such as a field of judicial conflict resolution. However, using the field notion forces you to think relationally in an analysis of the position of the judiciary, which makes it a useful tool.

The relational possession of capital can be found by constructing the *trajectories* of individuals. The notion of trajectories means, in the Bourdieuian sense, the continuous succeeding positions individuals occupy in a space with other individuals. The notion draws our attention away from 'the biographical illusion',[12] that is people's self-representations of their own lives. Biographical research normally adopts common sense understandings of life stories, and this gives the impression that life constitutes a form of coherent totality. In much biographical research, life is seen as a coherent unity understood as a figuration of an 'intention' or 'project', and it is thus *meaningfully* narrated with cause, purposes and means.[13]

In particular, avoiding the 'biographical illusion' is important when examining fields such as the legal field, in which strong discourses and universal understandings of how the field functions are embedded. But how is it possible to construct a field by way of individuals' trajectories? And how is it possible to construct the legal field over longer time periods by focusing on individuals' trajectories? I will now discuss how it is possible to construct a field by means of a relational database.

D. CONSTRUCTING A FIELD

In order to construct the field it is important to have empirical material from which the field can be constructed. Citing Bachelard, Bourdieu stresses that scientific facts are 'won, constructed, and confirmed'. Facts are never given but are created or won in the breaking with common sense understandings and immediate appearances. The constructed analytical object which can be analysed from a system of relations emerges from the scientific work.[14] In the following I will discuss how reference books like *Who's Who* can be used to conduct historical research on the development of the field of judges, with selected parts of judges' trajectories often listed.[15]

In these types of books information about the following can usually be found: the parents' occupations, place of birth, marital status, career and education, membership of boards and commissions and involvements in other fields, such as the cultural, political, religious and academic fields.

---

[12] Bourdieu 1986, above n 10.

[13] P Bourdieu, 'L'illusion biograpique' in (1986) XII *Actes de la recherche en sciences sociales* 69-72. This is also one of the problems of accepting the knowledge of the agents in the field, as the field history is written as such.

[14] P Bourdieu, *et al*, *The Craft of Sociology: Epistemological Preliminaries* (Berlin, Walter de Gruyter, 1991) 11.

[15] Reference books like *Who's Who* are found in many countries, and contain much of the same information despite the nationality of the books. Of course, these books contain only the information which their editors regarded as valuable and important, and in that sense they reflect specific understandings of categorisations of social life. *Cf.* for a discussion about information and sources of errors in reference books like *Who's Who* in P Bourdieu, *Homo Academicus* (Cambridge, Policy Press, 1988) 227ff.

These types of information can be used in the construction of the trajectories of the individuals. However, the data can only be used as indicators of social structures and not of mental structures.[16] Reference books contain similar data about individuals' trajectories over longer periods of time, and this makes them valuable as sources of data.

We are now able to construct a field on the basis of biographical information generated from what Bourdieu calls 'empirical individuals'.[17] That is, it is necessary to construct a statistical matrix of judges with different, but comparable and specifically chosen, properties (forms of capital) which exist in the field and are employed by the judges to advance their careers. The 'empirical individual'—the judge we have information about—is transferred to a constructed position in a space characterised by the system of differences established between the finite set of '... relevant properties in the theoretical domain considered, and the whole set of finite sets of properties attached to the set of other constructed individuals'.[18] The constructed individual's position in the social space is defined by the properties related to other individuals' properties, properties that are constructed in accordance with the same explicit principles. These different properties are necessary in order to analyse the social space and to transform the empirical individual into a constructed object. In order to carry out such a transformation, one must be able to identify the judges. In other words it is necessary to know their names in order to be able to look them up in reference books.[19] When studying a field of judges, it should not be a problem to identify who is a part of the field. On the contrary, it is relatively easy to limit the analyses, as judges are in possession of the objectified form of capital such as a title.

The usual way of conducting this form of research is by, what the social mobility tradition calls, 'inflow analyses' instead of 'outflow analyses'. Inflow analyses examine the background of persons who take a specific position whereas outflow analyses examine where persons with the same background arrive at. Although the conclusions of the two ways are normally different, inflow analyses are dominating. This means that the analysis of the fields is generated by focusing on persons who are in the fields and their previous and contemporary relations and backgrounds. The reason for this is that the material is more accessible when doing inflow analyses,

---

[16] Bourdieu, above n. 7 differentiates between 'social' and 'mental' structures. It is worth noting that the information I discuss here only captures the social structures.

[17] Bourdieu, above, n 15, p 21f.

[18] *Ibid*, p 22.

[19] This is not difficult in Denmark, since the names of the judges are all listed in the *Hof-og Statskalenderen*. Doing this kind of research in the UK, for example, is more difficult because there is no similar book about judges. However, one way to find the names of the higher court judges is to look at the law reports from different courts in different years. At the beginning of the reports, all the names of the judges are listed. Today, it is also possible to find the names via the Lord Chancellor's home page on the internet. It is still not possible to get the names of the lower court judges who do not necessarily have a university degree.

as the field is constructed from persons you can first identify through their positions, and then get access to information about their trajectories.

The constructed judge is singled out by a set of specific properties, constructed in accordance with the same specific properties as the rest of the judges. In other words, it is necessary to focus on the differences between the same sets of properties of judges. Judges are thus differentiated on the basis of the same forms of properties. However, it is not enough simply to look the judges up in the reference books, it is also necessary to analyse the data. We need to devise methods which help us to analyse the data and to distinguish between different positions in the field over time. These methods should enable us to differentiate between judges from different levels of the formal legal hierarchy—ie, between higher and lower court judges—as well as, for instance, different geographical positions. We need tools which are able to distinguish between judges and thus construct the field on the basis of the forms of capital of judges and not on the basis of pre-existing understandings of the organisation of the field.

For the actual analysis a relational database is a useful tool. Before up-to-date computer technique it was very difficult—and time consuming—to make these kinds of analyses. Scandinavian convergence and conflict studies, for instance, either examined judges as a coherent unit or only looked at smaller groups of judges, namely judges in higher positions.[20] This is also the case with many comparative studies.[21] A database can be defined as an integrated repository of data, and it serves two primary purposes: to provide information, and to capture data about entities and relationships. It is a tool that makes it possible to analyse large amounts of data relationally and to make enquiries into different positions in the field, as well as enabling analyses of the generative and transforming processes of the field.

Focusing on social, educational, residential, and career backgrounds as well as the relation to other fields such as academic, economic and religious fields, indicators of forms of capital and of the strategies that the judges use in order to reproduce their power become apparent. Strategies are understood in the Bourdieuian sense: the individuals' strategies are conscious and unconscious practices which tend to reproduce the conditions of their own production. They are intuitive practices of everyday life that are structured within the boundaries of habitus. Wacquant explains Bourdieu's notion of strategies:

> By strategy, he [Bourdieu] refers not to the purposive and preplanned pursuit of calculated goals ... but to the active deployment of objectively oriented 'lines of action' that obey regularities and form coherent and socially intelligible patterns, even though they do not follow conscious rules or aim at the premeditated goals posited by a strategist.[22]

---

[20] Aubert, above, n 1; and Mathiesen, above, n 1.
[21] See for example Abel and Lewis, above, n 1.
[22] Bourdieu and Wacquant, above, n 4 p 25.

In a Bourdieuian framework, *habitus* is the notion which combines objectivism with subjectivism, structures with subjective meaning. It integrates individuals' accumulated experiences and determines future possibilities for action, norms etc. Habitus is the precondition for co-ordination of practices. Practice is a feeling about how to behave and how to act in different fields, where agents act within the limits of perceived possibilities of the habitus within conscious and unconscious limits. It is from this point of view that the notion of *strategies* is defined.

The database is a tool for analysis, helping to reveal more easily strategies, differences and similarities in the field regarding capital possession. However, before it is possible to analyse the data, it is necessary to design the database for the specific topic as well as transfer the information from the reference books to the database. In the following, I will discuss how it is possible to work with a relational database.

E. ENTERING DATA INTO THE DATABASE

The database should be designed so that most of the information from *Who's Who* can be entered unmodified, which means that the exact data are entered in an almost non-codified way. In order not to bias the information that is transferred from the biographical reference books to the database, the information should be entered without being categorised. The database should be designed to grasp the information relevant for the study and information that can be provided.[23] In line with the reflexive sociology, once entered the data can provide categories more differentiated than if categories had been created before entering it which would have forced the data into preconstructed understandings of the field. Thus, by using the database relationally, it is possible to avoid what Bourdieu calls a 'pre-existing list' or 'operational definitions'. This is because the categorisation is part of the research object.[24] This means that the researcher should avoid common sense as well as preconstructed notions in his/her scientific understanding of the world, because they blind you and link you to a preconceived understanding of the world. Given the jurists' deep understandings of the legal reality and organisation of the legal field, as previously discussed, this is even more relevant. In the analytical process, the data can be transferred to statistical programs from the database.[25]

When examining the capital formation in the field over time, it is operationally necessary to choose certain judges employed during certain years.

---

[23] See for a detailed introduction how to design the database in appendix 3 in Hammerslev, above, n 2.

[24] Bourdieu, *et al*, above, n 14.

[25] Here it is possible to make correspondence analyses or other form of statistical analyses. See for example S Clausen, *Applied Correspondence Analysis: An Introduction* (London, Sage, 1998); and MJ Greenacre, *Correspondence Analysis in Practice* (London, Academic Press, 1993).

In my study, I conducted a detailed analysis of Danish judges of the 20th century by focusing on 25 year intervals in order to follow Geiger's principles. He finds that: 'Within a 25 year period it is not necessary to allow for major social structural shifts. The methodological essence of this procedure is that you do not group the material according to preconceived historical ideas of a period ...'.[26] Within 25 year intervals it is possible to examine changes and continuities over time without being biased by preconceptions of history

F. EXAMINING THE EMERGENCE AND DEVELOPMENT OF THE FIELD

According to Bourdieu the field should be examined from its genesis in order to observe the emergence of structures forming or, in the language of Bourdieu, structuring the field, internal differentiation of different groups and development vis-à-vis the field of power.[27] In my own study, I analysed the emergence and development of the field by means of legal history and by using statistical material about the number of different parts of the professions. By focusing on the development of the number of members of the profession seen through a Bourdieuian theoretical perspective, overall developments of the fields can be examined. Moreover, with such data it becomes possible to examine how successful members of the profession have been over time vis-à-vis other professional groups.[28] This is relevant, as the agents of a field are not only struggling with each other, but also with other fields in order to preserve or even to extend their areas of power. It is a struggle between different professional groups armed with different forms of professional (and other) capital. Focusing on these kind of statistical developments combined with biographical information about the professions it becomes possible to examine developments of the fields over a longer period. Not only can we reveal forms of capital within a single field, but also examine the field's relation and development against the general field of power. Thus, by using statistical information about the positions of jurists in different fields related to the general field of power and the field of state power, it is possible to examine the development of the overall position and organisation of professional knowledge. The different professional groups are singled out by their practical and educational forms of capital. The relevant statistics should be relatively easy to find by means of national statistical sources.

---

[26] T Geiger, *Den Danske Intelligens fra Reformationen til Nutiden* (Copenhagen, Ejnar Munksgaard, 1949) 33. My translation.

[27] Bourdieu and Wacquant, above, n 4.

[28] In this way it is possible to follow the approach of convergence studies, where the numbers of members of different professions are indicators of coherence and success. See for example Aubert, above n 1; and N Luhmann, *Ausdifferenzierung des Rechts: Beiträge zur Rechtssoziologie und Rechtstheorie* (Frankfurt aM, Suhrkamp Verlag, 1981).

However, it is important to note that this form of 'outside' information does not show how forms of capital are internalised and how they work and are invested via habitus. It merely helps to describe how the field is constituted and draws attention to certain structures which can be examined in more depth through interviews or questionnaires.

G. EXAMINING THE LEGAL POSITION OF JUDGES

Material regarding the social position of the legal profession does not provide information about the professional groups' position within law. Again, taking judges as an example: they play a vital role in legal processes and decision-making, both as it regards deciding cases and identifying, constructing and developing the sources of law, which are then used to make other legal decisions in the future.

In a Bourdieuian perspective, law is a historical and social construction produced by (legal) agents. Law is a discourse of power, which contributes to the legitimacy of the state. The understanding behind this is that law is not merely a matter of techniques, but must be understood in relation to power structures, and thus in relation to the core of the construction and reproduction of the field of state power. Law is a kind of symbolic power, which agents struggle to determine. Therefore, by revealing the legal position of judges—and the jurists that are participating in legal constructions—it is possible to examine the development of law. The question is how we can determine the symbolic power of judges.

In my study of Danish judges, I have examined the development of the logic of the legal field, the internal structures of legal thinking, and the symbolic struggle between the legal field and the field of politics. In order to reveal the symbolic power of judges, I chose to examine how these legal structures appear in the field. I asked how do judges consider legal methods, and how jurisprudence considers and legitimises the limits of the interpretation of judges. I tried to reveal the direction of the development of law regarding the distinction between common law and civil law. That is, if the idea of the logic of law—in the language of Weber—reflects lawmaking rather than the application of law. In the idea of law, the judiciary makes law when the decisions, in the words of Cotterrell, 'constitute the law itself',[29] whereas judges merely apply law when they are strictly bound by legal texts. The idea was to reveal the logic of law and the legitimised legal domination of judges, and hence to show the range of the legal power of judges. Or, in other words, to determine the legal position of judges. The focus is thus on how the field considers the range of judges' legal power, differentiated on different ranks of judges, as well as the directions of legal argumentation for certain decisions.

[29] R Cotterrell, *Sociology of Law: An Introduction* (London, Butterworths, 1992) 205.

In order to examine these questions, I consulted legal textbooks on constitutional law, human rights law, and legal methods among other topics. Moreover, I examined how philosophy of law considers judges' involvement in the legal processes as well as how judges, jurists in general, and policy-makers argued about the position of judges in interviews and public statements. These areas were chosen because they are significant in the legal determination of the position of judges. As with the analysis of the outside perspectives, the legal development should also be examined over time in order to focus on how changes appear.

H. CONCLUSION

In this chapter I have tried to show that to study Danish judges we need to break with the self-understandings of the field which is a product of the objectivations and discourses that have been developed over time concerning the role and importance of judges in society. These self-understandings are brought about through social struggles between different individuals in the legal field and between the legal field vis-à-vis other fields. In addition, the field has often determined how questions about the formal organisation of the field and how the field should develop are formulated. I have also argued that the conceptual tools provided by the reflexive sociology of Bourdieu show how to break with these objectivations and categories which emerge out of them.

Since the focus of this chapter was on Danish judges, I excluded references to other sections and groups within the legal profession. However, information about other parts of the Danish legal field (and other fields) can also be found in reference books, as well as in other historical and biographical sources. So it is possible to examine other parts of the legal field and other fields using a similar relational database. It is, however, important to note that such an analysis only concerns social structures and not mental structures. The data do not show how forms of capital are internalised and how they work in the fields via habitus.

Neither do these types of data provide information about the symbolic position and power of judges in law. In order to understand how law is used to legitimise the position of judges it is necessary to examine the symbolic struggles between different fields to learn how the internal structure and the logic of law is produced, developed and exercised. In order to take the internal logic of law into consideration, one needs to focus on legal practice and legal decision-making, on the one hand, and the internal discourse of law, as reflected in legal theoretical debates and legal writing, on the other. Finally, different areas of law develop differently, which means that we need to pay great care when generalising about the symbolic position and power of judges in society.

11

Changing Maps: Empirical Legal Autopoiesis

JOHN PATERSON AND GUNTHER TEUBNER

A. INTRODUCTION

THE IDEA OF self-organisation was invented simultaneously in different fields of knowledge, in the natural as well as in the social sciences. Theories such as self-referential processes,[1] autopoiesis[2] and second-order-cybernetics,[3] among many others, spontaneously emerged and began to influence each other in a trans-disciplinary discussion and to form a common web of theoretical constructs. And in due course these theories stimulated empirical research. But while such projects have flourished in areas as diverse as economy, psychotherapy and flamenco, in 'law and society' there has so far been a paucity of empirical research on self-organisation. This anomaly can perhaps be traced back to certain peculiarities of legal sociology as a field of knowledge. It seems that the long-lasting and deep hiatus between theory construction and empirical research is actually deepened by the emergence of theories of self-organisation and autopoiesis. This is our first thesis. Secondly, if we look more closely at concrete, detailed, historical research carried out in the name of autopoiesis, we can discern clear discontinuities with 'normal' practices of empirical research. Autopoiesis calls for a redefinition of empirical work and requires different empirical tools—tools that are capable of analysing *the transformational dynamics of recursive meaning processes*. As a consequence, everything changes: research questions, the phenomena to be identified, the concepts to be made operational and the analytical instruments. And there are even stronger anomalies in the socio-legal relationship between the empirical and the theoretical. The constructivist orientation of legal autopoiesis, we submit in our third thesis, works against the fantasies

---

[1] DR Hofstadter, *Gödel, Escher, Bach: An Eternal Golden Braid* (New York, NY, Basic Books, 1979).
[2] HR Maturana and FJ Varela, *Autopoiesis and Cognition* (Boston, MA, Reidel, 1980).
[3] H von Förster, *Observing Systems* (Seaside, CA, Intersystems, 1981).

of omnipotence inherent in the process of empirical falsification. Legal autopoiesis is not anti-empirical, but it does suggest a role for empirical research that is different from straightforward Popperian theory-killing. It suggests, instead, a *quasi*-therapeutic relationship between the speculators and the data collectors. But who, then, is the therapist and who is the patient?

B. THE GREAT HIATUS

Why is there a structural hiatus between theory and empirical research in law and society? In the classics of legal sociology, Marx's historical methods, Durkheim's *choses sociales* and the ideal-typical method in Weber's interpretive sociology were guarantees of the unity of empirical research and grand theories of law. But the introduction of modern empirical methods signalled problems for theory.

'The dissolution in data and their recombination with the help of newly developed methods of data analysis destroyed the high level of theorising which had been built up in the classics without being able to substitute it adequately.'[4]

Today, the field is still suffering from this deep hiatus, which renders theory rather empty and empiricism rather blind. Or to put it more mildly, empirical research in law and society has developed a highly sophisticated methodology which is, however, based on poor and rather *ad hoc* theorising, while theorising about law and society has become more and more philosophical and speculative relying, however, on poor and rather *ad hoc* empirical support.

And today the hiatus is deepening. Empirical legal sociologists are giving in to the temptation of trying economic models and theories for their data with the predictable result that they are losing their sociological identity. Meanwhile, legal theorists are tempted to follow the famous 'linguistic turn' in sociology and thus to question the validity of systematic data collection and patient data analysis.

Usually it is the micro-macro problem that is held responsible for the empirico-theoretical gap. Empirical methods are good at gathering individual data at the micro level of legal action and aggregate data at the macro level of socio-legal relations. But they fail when it comes to analysing law's 'organised complexity' which good theory regards as central to understanding law as a social phenomenon. Without denying the importance of the micro-macro difference, we prefer to identify another famous *petite différence* as responsible for the great hiatus: the difference between law as operation and law as observation,[5] which has sharply divided socio-legal

---

[4] N Luhmann, *Die Wissenschaft der Gesellschaft* (Society's science) (Frankfurt aM, Suhrkamp, 1990) 410.
[5] von Förster, above, n 3.

theoreticians and empiricists. Empirical analysis has opted for first-order observation of the law. It takes legal action as simple operations, as spatio-temporal events, which can be correlated in empirical models with other social events. This drives empirical analysis of law in two directions: towards models of logical and mathematical formalisation on the one hand and towards attempts at causal explanation and prediction on the other.[6] In contrast, ambitious sociological theories of law are usually second-order observations. They see legal action itself as observation, as a trinity of utter-ance, information and understanding, as the recursive transformation of differences, as constructing a special space of meaning and an autonomous world of knowledge. This drives socio-legal theories deeper and deeper into the hermeneutic tradition, which allows for sophisticated analyses of the 'operation called *Verstehen*', but which ridicules attempts at formalisation, causal explanation and prediction. And attempts to combine both tradi-tions are sucked into the black hole bounded by formalisation, causal explanation and hermeneutics.

If this is an adequate sketch of the intellectual map, how does self-refer-ence and autopoiesis change the somewhat desperate outlook for law and society? At first sight it looks like Columbus's egg, as François Ewald has called it.[7] It nourishes hope for a recombination of both the empirical-ana-lytical and the normative-hermeneutic traditions. It seems to promise a bridge between law as operation and law as observation since it compels us to combine first—and second—order analysis. Since law is defined as a closed system of self-reproductive observing operations, legal action is seen as being at the same time both operation and observation. This requires the normative tradition to leave Popper's World III and to search for 'law in action' as its social base, and it requires the empirical tradition to include in its observations the complex chains of normative observations of the 'law in the books'.

But a closer look reveals that autopoiesis offers no easy synthesis. It burdens the three traditions—the hermeneutic, the formal and the causal orientation—with an almost unbearable task. How to cope with self-refer-ence? Hermeneutics, with its long tradition of dealing with self-referential relations, reflexivity, paradoxes and hermeneutic circles, is obviously in the best position. This explains the rapid development of autopoiesis in hermeneutically oriented theories of law. In a view of law as a concatena-tion of communicative events based on a code which deparadoxifies a basic self-referential relation autopoiesis has strong (s)elective affinities with dis-course analysis as developed by the *maître-penseurs* of poststructuralism: Foucault, Lyotard and Derrida.

---

[6] D Black, *Sociological Justice* (Oxford, OUP, 1989).
[7] F Ewald, 'The Law of Law' in G Teubner, (ed), *Autopoietic Law: A New Approach to Law and Society* (Berlin, de Gruyter, 1987) 36.

The tradition of formalisation in legal theory has much greater difficulties with autopoiesis. The reason is that the paradoxes of self-reference pose an enormous challenge for a formal calculus. It is true that Hofstadter's famous book on the enigmas of reflexivity and self-reference has had a certain impact on legal theory.[8] However, sophisticated attempts to come to terms with self-reference, such as Spencer-Brown's *Laws of Form*,[9] the development of a multi-value logic by Günther[10] or 'A Calculus for Self-Reference' by Francisco Varela[11] have up to now only found one resonance in legal sociology which is Niklas Luhmann's discussion of the legal paradox and the binary coding of law.[12]

However, the situation for causal explanation and prediction, the precious hope of orderly empirical work in law and society that would transform it into a real science, is disastrous. For causal analysis, self-reference is an explosive. The blast comes from a theory of recursive systems and from a concept of non-trivial machines; and the blast is so strong because these explosive concepts were developed not just from the hermeneutic softies of the *Geisteswissenschaften* but also from the hard-liners of the exact sciences. According to the sociologists Krohn and Küppers, who deal with problems of the legal regulation of social fields, the results look like this:

> [i]n non-linear systems with a recursive dynamics ... there are only few cases in which prediction of the system's development is possible, even if their mechanism is known, the systems are deterministic and disturbances do not occur ... Due to recursion, even very small deviations in the initial conditions are reinforced in such a way that similar starting constellations lead after a very short time period to totally opposite system developments ... . In the case of a non-linear and recursive system dynamics ... no prediction of the system's development is possible.[13]

---

[8] Hofstadter, above n 1, p 692ff; DR Hofstadter, 'Nomic: A Self-Modifying Game Based on Reflexivity in Law' in DR Hofstadter, (ed), *Metamagical Themas: Questing for the Essence of Mind and Pattern* (New York, NY, Bantam, 1985) 70ff; P Suber, *The Paradox of Self-Amendment: A Study of Logic, Law, Omnipotence and Change* (New York, NY, Peter Lang, 1990).

[9] G Spencer-Brown, *Laws of Form* (New York, NY, Julian, 1972).

[10] G Günther, 'Cybernetic Ontology and Transjunctional Operations' in G Günther, (ed), *Beiträge zur Grundlegung einer operationsfähigen Dialektik I* (Hamburg, Meiner, 1976); G Günther, 'Life as Poly-Contexturality' in G Günther, (ed), *Beiträge zur Grundlegung einer operationsfähigen Dialektik I* (Hamburg, Meiner, 1976).

[11] FJ Varela, 'A Calculus for Self-Reference' (1975) 2 *International Journal of General Systems* 5–24.

[12] N Luhmann, 'The Third Question: The Creative use of Paradoxes in Law and Legal History' (1988) 15 *Journal of Law and Society* 153–65; N Luhmann, 'The Coding of the Legal System' in G Teubner and A Febbrajo, (eds), *State, Law and Economy as Autopoietic Systems: Regulation and Autonomy in a New Perspective* (Milan, Giuffrè, 1992); N Luhmann, 'Operational Closure and Structural Coupling: The Differentiation of the Legal System' (1992) 13 *Cardozo Law Review* 1419–41; N Luhmann, *Das Recht der Gesellschaft* (Suhrkamp, 1993); N Luhmann, 'The Paradoxy of Observing Systems' in (1995) 31 *Cultural Critique* 37–55.

[13] W Krohn and G Küppers, 'Selbstreferenz und Planung' (1990) 1 *Selbstorganisation* 101, 114ff.

And if law as a social system is correctly defined as one of these 'non-trivial machines' (that is, as one of the deterministic systems whose input-output relationship is not invariant, but is determined in a self-referring way by the machines' previous output), then, in the words of von Förster, 'for all practical reasons they are unpredictable: an output once observed for a given input will most likely not be the same for the same input given later'.[14] The only hope for causal explanation and prediction is a trivialisation of law and society, their social construction as trivial machines—something that happily coincides with the triviality of certain results of attitude and impact research, results that everyone familiar with the fields already knew in advance.

So what does this mean for the chances of empirical research in the autopoietic framework? Well, they look excellent for all kinds of historical analysis, for genealogical and archaeological digging in historical texts, and for qualitative research techniques, case studies of formal organisation, ethnomethodological types of socio-legal interaction, discourse analysis, for 'critical empiricism'. And indeed these are the research techniques that are mainly used in the empirical projects. For static correlations (of 'the more x, the more y' variety), however, the chances look rather bleak.

C. AUTOPOIESIS AND CAUSAL CHAINS

But before we get carried away, is it not the case that autopoiesis is simply incompatible with the dominant working orientation of orderly empirical research, where the task of theory is causal explanation and prediction of empirical facts, and the task of empirical research is the reality test of hypotheses derived from theoretical constructs? Indeed, it is incompatible. Viewed from the constructivist position of autopoiesis, every element of this statement about the empirico-theoretical relationship is flawed.

To put the counter-position bluntly:

1. Empirical research is by no means closer to the reality of the outside world than theory. Even from empirical experience we know that often the opposite is true. The hard facts about the external world that empirical research pretends to produce are in reality highly artificial constructs, excessively selective abstractions, mere internal artefacts of the scientific discourse that are both as real and as fictional as are theoretical constructs.
2. The real role of empirical research does not lie in dull falsification. It is in the 'surprise value' of its self-produced data. Empirical world constructions in law and society do not need to be destructive of theories. Rather, they could play a maeutic role in the birth of theories in the spirit of empiricism.

[14] von Förster, above, n 3, 201.

3. Causal explanation and prediction are grossly overestimated in law and society. They are only special cases of theoretical work, which are indeed very rare, and they by no means exhaust the potential of theoretical explanation.
4. For autopoiesis, theoretical explanation of empirical results means that the theory reformulates these artefacts of perception in new contexts in order to analyse the transformational dynamics of recursive meaning processes.

Let us take a concrete example of the social effects of legislation in order to discuss this counter-position. Occupational health and safety in Britain's offshore oil industry constitutes a well-defined area that has seen considerable regulatory development over its 40–year history. Traditional empirical research on the effectiveness of law and implementation research suggest the construction of a network of dependent and independent variables among which we can identify correlations and find out their causal connections.[15] The usual causality chain—as Renate Mayntz, for example, tells us—works like this: political goal definition → legislative act → legal norm → motivation of implementation staff → motivation of actors in the field → deviation/sanction/incentive → social behaviour → social effects.[16] In our concrete example of offshore health and safety regulation, it is possible to trace this sort of causality chain as follows.

During the early days of the offshore industry in the mid–1960s there was no detailed regulation of occupational health and safety, simply an instruction from the government that those involved should follow an industry code of practice. When a serious accident occurred in 1965, the inadequacies of this approach became evident and an Inquiry chaired by a lawyer recommended that 'a statutory code with credible sanctions' be implemented to provide for the safety of workers in the industry.[17] This recommendation was accepted by the government of the day, which introduced a Bill to Parliament that eventually became law as the Mineral Workings (Offshore Installations) Act 1971. This provided a framework for the development over a period of years of detailed regulations by the regulators (mainly the Petroleum Engineering Division of the Department of Energy) covering every aspect of the industry from the design and construction of offshore installations to the content of first aid kits. These regulations were then implemented and the oil companies they were aimed at complied with or deviated from them ultimately producing an effect on the level of safety that existed in the industry.

---

[15] For example, H Rottleuthner, *Einfuehrung in die Rechtssoziologie* (Darmstadt, Wissenschaftliche Buchgesellschaft, 1987) 54ff.

[16] R Mayntz, 'The Conditions of Effective Public Policy: A New Challenge for Policy Analysis' (1983) 2 *Policy and Politics* 1.

[17] Ministry of Power, *Report of the Inquiry into the Causes of the Accident to the Drilling Rig Sea Gem* (Cmnd. 3409) (London, HMSO, 1967) para 10.2(i).

We might summarise this on the basis of the foregoing causal chain as: political goal definition by the Ministry of Power Inquiry → introduction of a Bill to Parliament by the government → passing of the Mineral Workings (Offshore Installations) Act 1971 → development and implementation of detailed regulations by the regulators → compliance/deviation by the industry → effects on safety. In accordance with this understanding of the regulatory chain, when questions are asked about continuing safety problems in the industry, we find concern about delay in getting detailed regulations into place and about the toughness of the regulators' enforcement.[18] In other words, control of safety will be achieved when detailed regulations are in place telling the industry what it must do and when these are being enforced by the regulators.

Autopoiesis, however, forces us to break up this causal chain of events and to replace it by a multitude of autonomous but interfering fields of action in each of which, in an acausal and simultaneous manner, recursive processes of transformation of differences take place. To put it more simply, a single horizontal chain of causal relations is replaced by a multitude of vertical chains of recursions. We can indicate this shift graphically in Figure 1.

Moreover, our framework gives us a new understanding of social regulation through law. Understanding these vertical chains of recursions as operationally closed means that each constructs information internally: there are no input-output relationships between, say, the regulators and the industry. As a consequence, attempts by the regulators to steer the industry by means of prescriptive regulations backed by sanctions and incentives must be understood in a fundamentally different way. Such attempts can only ever be a multitude of *self*-steering processes. More specifically, this self-steering must be understood as the *minimisation of a difference*, an attempt to reduce the difference between the current situation and the desired one. This definition is consistent with all forms of steering but in the context of a recursively closed system of communicative operations the difference is itself

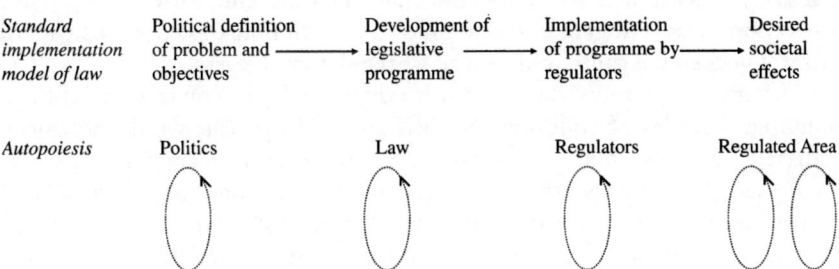

Standard implementation model of law	Political definition of problem and objectives	Development of legislative programme	Implementation of programme by regulators	Desired societal effects
Autopoiesis	Politics	Law	Regulators	Regulated Area

Figure 1: The Shift from a Horizontal Chain of Causal Relations to Vertical Chains of Recursions.

[18] WG Carson, *The Other Price of Britain's Oil: Safety and Control in the North Sea* (Oxford, Martin Robertson, 1981).

internally constructed. Thus, offshore safety regulators construct the current situation according to their own code and similarly construct a desired situation and apply their own *programme of difference minimisation* in an attempt to arrive at it. Given that the industry constructs reality according to its own code and steers according to its own difference minimising programme, the limits of regulatory ambition become clear. In other words, regulation is possible only as self-regulation within each of these recursive processes. Regulation over the boundaries of action fields is impossible. Chains of causality need to be replaced by simultaneous events of structural coupling. This is not to say, of course, that regulatory attempts produce no effects, only that those effects cannot properly be regarded as steering in the sense implied by traditional theories. Instead, these effects arise from the construction of differences by the regulators and their attempts to minimise them but depend on the internal construction of differences by the industry and its attempts to minimise them.[19]

This is a suggestive idea, but can it be made empirical? The task for empirical research in these circumstances would become one of inquiring into several chains of difference minimisation and into their interferences. We would have to retell in detail several divergent stories of self-regulation in the political arena, in the legislative chambers and courtrooms, in the offices of the regulatory agencies and in the managerial suites of corporate actors, and on the drill-floors of offshore installations. The question would be one of how, in each of these stories, the events common to them are idiosyncratically reconstructed and processed in the meaning context of their specific difference minimisation programmes. To be clear, such a division of the regulatory chain into divergent stories does not imply that autopoiesis is bound to discover regulatory failure. Autopoiesis is not in some sense the opposite of regulatory success, as Nahamowitz seems to believe.[20] Instead, understanding steering as self-steering means that the theory accounts for regulatory failure and success in ways different from theories where linear causality is assumed. So, if we find that our different stories of recursive operations travel together for a time in a common direction instead of diverging then we can readily speak of regulatory success.

The crucial question, then, is how to disentangle the connections of these multiple cascades of concatenated differences. To repeat, we do not mean causal influences, but the acausal synchronisation of ongoing parallel processes. And our theory tells us that there is not one magic formula of structural coupling; rather there are several types of synchronisation. In order to find out how the different recursive processes are interrelated we need first of all to find out how they are closed to each other. *L'ouvert s'appuye sur le*

---

[19] N Luhmann, 'Limits of Steering' (1997) 14 *Theory, Culture and Society* 41–57.
[20] P Nahamowitz, 'Difficulties with Economic Law: Definitional and Material Problems of an Emerging Legal Discipline' in G Teubner and A Febbrajo, (eds), *State, Law and Economy as Autopoietic Systems: Regulation and Autonomy in a New Perspective* (Milan, Giuffrè, 1992).

fermé[21]—this is not a matter of theoretical definition but a matter of empirical variation. Autopoiesis theory suggests a variety of closure mechanisms in the relations between meaning systems to which correspond a variety of ways in which they are open to each other: from *ad hoc* contacts to systematic linkages and long-term co-evolution. Success or failure of regulation depends— this is our guiding hypothesis—on the specific qualities of interwovenness of several recursive meaning processes, which in turn depend on the qualities of their mutual closure.

This compels us to ask a twofold question when it comes to detailed empirical research:

1. How can we identify concretely the multitude of elementary acts— meaning operations—that constitute the autopoietic closure of the various processes involved?
2. How can we identify the different types of mutual recontextualisation that are responsible for a meeting of these closed discourses?

Applying the first question to our example: are the legislative process and the implementation field autopoietic systems? Although we have so far spoken as if they are for the sake of the argument, this is not in fact a question we can answer theoretically but only by empirical observation. Autopoiesis theory does not impose a set of pre-existing systems but rather compels us to observe the concrete interactions in legislative chambers, lobby halls and the technological processes in our implementation field in order to discover the systemicity of our research object. Strangely enough, this reliance on empirical knowledge runs counter to the opinion of empirically-minded researchers who tend to treat this as an 'analytical' question, namely the identification of a 'system' as the somewhat arbitrary conceptual selection of the field of inquiry according to the concrete research interests. In contrast, the system concept of autopoiesis is much closer to empirical reality than the abstract models of empirical research.

Unlike the semi-autonomous fields, which, as Griffiths tells us, owe their systemic character only to the research designs of legal sociologists,[22] our decision about their systemicity is dependent upon observable self-organising processes in the social world. Autopoietic systems are produced by self-organising processes in the social world, not by scientific observers. We need careful empirical observation, therefore, in order to find out which operations are recursively linking up to other operations in our field so that in their concatenation they gain the autonomy of an autopoietic system. In the area of the social effectiveness of law, we researchers are by no means free to define the concrete legislative process as a 'system'. Empirical observation would rather compel us to split it up into four or five more or less loosely

[21] E Morin, *La Méthode: 3. La Connaissance/1* (Paris, Seuil, 1986) 203ff.
[22] J Griffiths, 'What is Legal Pluralism?' (1986) 24 *Journal of Legal Pluralism* 1, 35.

coupled recursive processes: the ongoing power game of the political actors, the *quasi*-scientific policy-talk of the experts, the profit-oriented calculations of the lobbyists and the doctrinal arguments and constructions of the lawyers. If we are interested in regulation we have to identify not only the concrete binary codes that are used in each of these processes and the concrete rules of the game which they have developed over time but especially the specific programmes of difference minimisation that they follow at any given moment: strategies of interest and power, reputational gains, policy objectives, risk minimisation and the reduction of deviance.

In addition, we will also have to split up our regulated field into a similar multitude of recursive processes. For example, when the object of regulation is a specific technology in economic organisations, such as offshore installations, does the concrete technology form a system? Autopoiesis would qualify the usual definitions of technology as 'man-machine-systems' as irresponsibly loose talk.[23] Can we identify in the real world elementary operations like 'legal acts', 'theoretical statements' or 'economic transactions' that would process technological differences in a binary code? Probably not. What we will find is a concrete technology as a social field in which formal organisation ties together—with varying degrees of strength—the scientific, economic and political processing of distinctions related to technical artefacts.[24] And as regards regulation, it would again be important to investigate each of these processes to discover their established difference minimisation programmes: organisational goals, accumulation of knowledge, profit orientation and so on.

D. GRAPHIC METHODOLOGIES

The question arises, however, as to just how we might go about an empirical study guided by autopoiesis. What sort of systematic observation must we carry out? What sort of tools can we use? What sort of methodology could be envisaged that could accommodate more broadly the analysis of several systems operating on the basis of different codes and steering by distinct difference minimising programmes?

It is probably the case that only through consideration of individual concrete examples can researchers decide upon a methodology that is appropriate to each case. If a narrative style seems appropriate, then perhaps techniques such as multi-voice or reflexive texts may provide an answer,[25] but the ideal would be to find something that could represent more *graphically* what it is that autopoiesis claims to offer to legal sociology.

---

[23] See N Luhmann, *Die Gesellschaft der Gesellschaft* (Frankfurt, Suhrkamp, 1997) 517ff.
[24] See R Grundmann, *Marxism and Ecology* (Oxford, Clarendon Press, 1991) 147ff.
[25] S Woolgar and M Ashmore, 'The Next Step: An Introduction to the Reflexive Project' in S Woolgar, (ed), *Knowledge and Reflexivity: New Frontiers in the Sociology of Knowledge* (London, Sage, 1988).

Santos provides us with a compelling graphical metaphor for law when he describes it as a 'map of misreading',[26] distorting reality systematically through the mechanisms of scale, projection and symbolisation. Depending on the scale employed, different features of the landscape which law attempts to map will appear or disappear; the particular projection used will emphasise some features over others; and the symbolisation will say much about the cultural background of the law and its intended purpose. Now, whereas Santos believes that laws misread reality in order to establish their exclusivity, understanding law as an autopoietic system reveals that the misreading is not calculated in this way but is rather the *inevitable* result of law's autopoietic nature—reality is constructed on the basis of the selections made by law according to its code (legal/illegal) as it seeks to achieve order from complexity. In other words, it is impossible to avoid a misreading and law can only observe what its code allows it to construct. But the map metaphor remains useful since, in much the same way, a map, because it cannot reproduce the world, must offer a selective and incomplete view of that world and consequently there is a sense in which that which is not included on the map is not real.[27] Indeed, there is in cartography an analogue of the binary code of autopoietic systems, namely the *tectonic code* 'which configures graphic space in a particular relation to geodesic space'.[28]

The map metaphor is, then, a powerful one, but its true potential is only released when the following points are taken into account.

1. Law's map is but one of a potentially very large number of similar maps arising from the selections of different recursive systems according to their own codes, their own attempts to achieve order from complexity.
2. Because law (and other recursive systems) are in a state of constant change, we must not see the map metaphor as introducing an unwarranted element of stasis but rather think of changing or evolving maps.
3. The second consideration should not, however, lead us so far away from the idea of a map that we lose the insight that maps are multiply connected; once a particular tectonic code is employed, local changes cannot easily be made without having knock-on effects globally; there are, therefore, built-in constraints limiting the extent to which changes can be made unproblematically—a fact recognised by cartographers who concentrate on redundant information thus over-determining the main features.[29]

---

[26] B de Sousa Santos, *Toward a New Common Sense: Law, Science and Politics in the Paradigmatic Transition* (London, Routledge, 1995) 456ff.

[27] D Wood, *The Power of Maps* (London, Routledge, 1993) 85–87.

[28] *Ibid*, p 124.

[29] See J Ziman, *Reliable Knowledge: An Exploration of the Grounds for Belief in Science* (Cambridge, CUP, 1978) 82.

If we can, then, see the different autopoietic systems as maps evolving through time with the codes and programmes represented by different tectonic codes, constraining by this internal multiple connectivity the changes that can be made as the maps are recursively redrawn, then we can perhaps get a first idea of what the results of autopoiesis research might look like. Such results would allow a comparison of the ways in which the same events (whether, for example, new regulations, a fall in the price of oil or a major accident) appear on the maps of the different systems in our concrete example. Equally, they would allow examples of closer communication between systems to be identified. If such results could be attained, then what Luhmann calls second-order observation would be achieved; that is, the observation of 'what others observe and what they cannot observe'.[30] But can the map metaphor be made more concrete?

One existing technique (suitably 'stripped down') appears singularly appropriate in this regard, not least because it allows us to retain the graphical metaphor of the map. More importantly, it is appropriate because it maintains an insistence on systematic empirical observation while allowing a representation of the multitude of autonomous but interfering fields of action into which autopoiesis proposes to break the causality chain: *cognitive mapping.*

This technique was developed from graph theory by Robert Axelrod,[31] primarily as a means of examining decision-making processes with a view to improving the performance of policy-makers, and it possesses many features that render it useful in the present context. The basic idea is extremely simple. In analysing, for example, a text or a series of texts, the concepts or constructs employed are represented as points, while the causal assertions used to link the concepts or constructs are represented as arrows between the points.[32] Positive and negative causal assertions are signified by the addition of a positive and negative sign respectively to the arrow concerned.[33] The basic format of the cognitive map is, therefore, as shown in Figure 2.

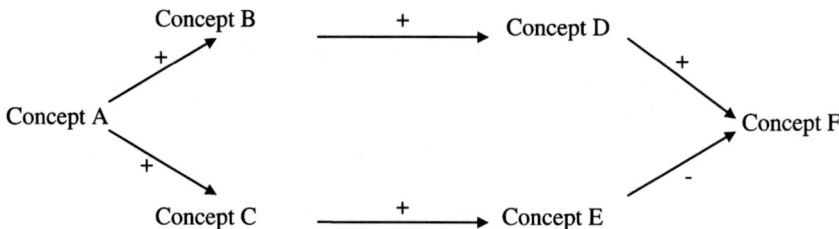

Figure 2: Format of a Cognitive Map.

[30] N Luhmann, *Risk: A Sociological Theory* (Berlin, de Gruyter, 1993) 108.

[31] R Axelrod, (ed), *Structure of Decision: The Cognitive Maps of Political Elites* (Princeton, NJ, Princeton University Press, 1976).

[32] R Axelrod, 'The Cognitive Mapping Approach to Decision Making' in R Axelrod, (ed), above n 31, p 5.

[33] R Axelrod, 'The Analysis of Cognitive Maps' in R Axelrod, (ed), above, n 31, p 60.

The cognitive map is thus for Axelrod a graphical representation of a belief system. In other words, concept or construct A is an explanation of B and is an answer to the question 'How or why did (or does) B happen?' Similarly, concept B is a consequence of A and answers the question 'What were (or are) the consequences of A?'[34] The details of the technique as developed by Axelrod (for example, the mathematical approach to the process) are not being discussed here because the value of the technique in the present context does not depend on the exact methodology proposed by him but rather on its ability to provide a graphical representation of autopoietic systems. Indeed, the mathematical element of Axelrod's methodology implies a view of information and its transferability that is at odds with that of autopoiesis.[35]

In the context of autopoiesis research, cognitive mapping provides a means of representing graphically the world which a system has constructed, the concepts its code gives it access to as well as the causal relations which complete its model of reality. In other words, it allows a picture to be produced of the order that a system has created by means of its selections from the noise of complexity. In this way, one could imagine cognitive maps being produced in our concrete example for legislators, regulators and for different sectors of the industry which would allow us to observe not only the economic and power relations which other approaches impose on the situation but rather the world construction of each system—what each can and cannot observe as a result of the application of its code. Similarly, perhaps even finer detail can be resolved in the form of the programmes by which each system steers itself, which differences it constructs and seeks to minimise. If this could be achieved then a potentially rich account of the development of occupational health and safety offshore would emerge. Our explanation of regulatory success or failure would not be restricted to the dominant rationality of more traditional empirical tools but would depend much more upon what the regulators and the regulated could and could not observe.

In this spirit, we can now understand Figure 1 above as displaying the cognitive maps respectively of traditional implementation theories of law and of autopoiesis. But what about the concrete example of health and safety in the offshore oil industry? It is to that example that we now turn.

---

[34] See M Jones and L Brooks, 'Addressing Organisational Context in Requirements Analysis Using Cognitive Mapping' (1993–94) 17 *University of Cambridge Research Papers in Management Studies* 6.

[35] See J Savelsberg, 'The Making of Criminal Law Norms in Welfare States: Economic Crime in West Germany' (1987) 21 *Law and Society Review* 529–61.

E. COGNITIVE MAPPING

The brief discussion of this topic which follows is drawn from a larger study[36] and due to the present space restrictions necessarily presents a rather truncated and incomplete picture of the subject. The intention, however, is primarily to demonstrate the usefulness of cognitive mapping in carrying out an empirical study guided by autopoiesis and to demonstrate how a more adequately complex picture of the study area can emerge in terms of different codes and individual difference-minimising programmes.

As was mentioned earlier, occupational health and safety in Britain's offshore oil industry was initially not the subject of any detailed state intervention. Only in the aftermath of a serious accident and a Public Inquiry[37] were moves made to introduce prescriptive regulations. Again as was seen previously, the Inquiry criticised the lack of a clear code of statutory authority regulating the question of safety offshore and this was precisely the issue that the government attempted to address in drafting the legislation. The process which saw the passing of the Mineral Workings (Offshore Installations) Act 1971 together with subsequent parliamentary debates provide us with a view of how politics constructed this issue and how it sought to improve safety in what it saw as a technologically complex and rapidly developing industry operating in a hostile environment.

These sources reveal that the discussions of the legislators are very much influenced by the findings of the Public Inquiry.[38] In place of the previous non-interventionist stance, a detailed enforceable code is envisaged. Requirements are to be set out clearly and penalties are to be graded. The fact that the industry is comparatively new and developing rapidly means that there must, however, be flexibility. A comprehensive set of regulations is to be made in due course within the framework of the Act. These regulations are seen as being more easily adaptable than primary legislation and can thus keep pace with technological change. They are envisaged as providing the basis for detailed inspection and enforcement by the regulators. Equally, concern is expressed that the regulations should not cramp development nor lead to excessive expenditure.

From these deliberations we can construct a cognitive map for legislators at the time of the passing of the 1971 Act (Figure 3).

From the cognitive map emerges a fairly standard view of regulation and its impact on the area of society at which it is aimed. Perceiving a need to act on this issue as determined by the political power code, legislators set

---

[36] J Paterson, *Behind the Mask: Regulating Health and Safety in Britain's Offshore Oil and Gas Industry* (Aldershot, Ashgate, 2000).

[37] Ministry of Power, above n.17.

[38] Earl Ferrers, Hansard HL (Debs) 18 February 1971, cols 741–46; Hon Nicholas Ridley (Under Secretary of State for Trade and Industry), Hansard HC (Debs) 28 April 1971, cols 645–49.

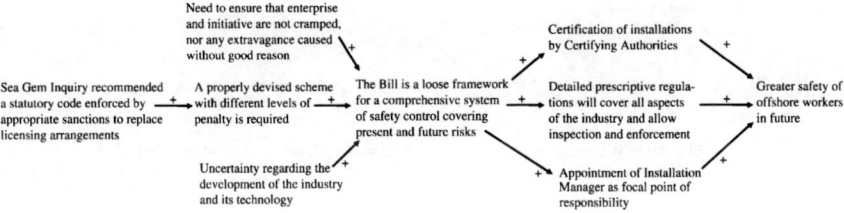

Figure 3: Cognitive Map for Politics.

up the framework for a detailed regulatory response. In other words, they deploy a programme of legal instrumentalism. A difference is constructed between the current unregulated situation where a number of accidents have occurred and the desired situation of improved occupational safety. The programme by which this difference is to be minimised, is one of detailed regulatory intervention. Regulators will develop detailed norms of action that will tell the industry what to do. Provided these norms are followed—and if they are not then the regulators can impose sanctions—the difference between the current problematic safety situation and the desired situation can be minimised.

There is nothing particularly surprising here. Not only could we expect to find this basic code and programme repeated in many legislative chambers, but they are also of course the code and programme which underlie many legal theoretical and sociological approaches. Thus, it is not surprising to find that in subsequent debates on the issue of offshore safety, legislators maintain very much the same code and programme and thus construct a relatively stable picture of the problems they confront and the range of appropriate solutions.[39]

But if this was the understanding of the legislators, what was happening when the task was passed on to the regulators? Drawing on material produced by the regulators,[40] it is possible to construct the following cognitive map shown in Figure 4.

In place of the legislators' ongoing optimism about the capabilities of a programme of detailed regulatory intervention, the regulators are aware, from the very earliest stages, of the struggle they will have in keeping up with the industry. On the one hand there is continual development of the technology, and on the other there is a lack of environmental data from the untried waters of the North Sea. Both of these factors make even the most rapidly adaptable detailed regulations difficult to achieve. Consequently, at

---

[39] For example, Hansard HC (Debs) 16 January 1974 cols 669–96 following the sinking of the Transocean 3 and the disabling of the Transworld 61 in the winter of 1972–73; and Hansard HC (Debs) 6 November 1980, cols 1472–546, following the publication of the Burgoyne Report into Offshore Safety.

[40] Especially WR Street, 'United Kingdom Regulations for Permanent Offshore Structures' (1975) 3 *Offshore Technology Conference* 731–36.

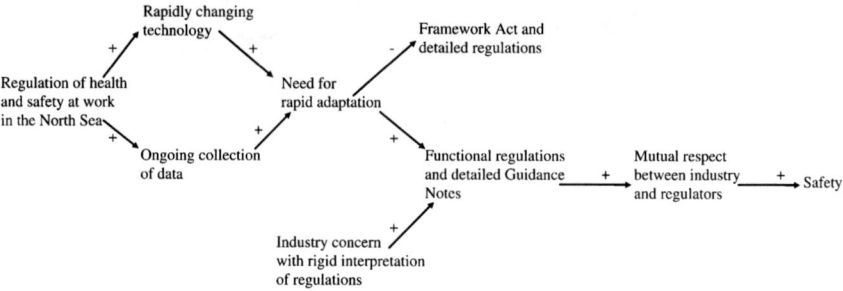

Figure 4: Cognitive Map for Regulators

a comparatively early stage, the regulators abandon the idea of providing detail at the level of the regulations as these are simply too cumbersome to adapt to new data and new technology. This is a telling point given that the regulations would be subject only to minimal negative resolution procedure, which would see them pass into law in the absence of active intervention by legislators. But instead, the regulations are described as 'functional', laying down only the broad principles, with detail being provided at the level of non-mandatory guidance notes, which can be withdrawn, replaced or amended with even less formality.

The regulators are thus operating in a way that would probably trouble the legislators. The very fact that the detail is to be at the level of guidance notes means that failure to comply with such a requirement would not constitute a breach of the law unless it could be shown that the failure to comply also contravened the broad principle laid down in the regulation. Dubious though this might appear to legislators, it can be seen to be a step that is based on the same sort of rationale that motivated them. In other words, in the same way that the legislators were unable to provide detail at the level of the 1971 Act, so the regulators, faced with a rapidly developing technological industry and ever greater refinement of models based on the ongoing collection of environmental data, found that even the relatively broad confines of negative resolution procedure did not provide the speed and flexibility they required. Their response was to develop detail at the yet lower level of guidance notes.

But the programme of legal instrumentalism envisaged by the legislators has very clearly become something quite different in the hands of the regulators. Faced with technical problems in the form of a lack of data and rapidly developing technology, the regulators are also trying to minimise the difference between two safety situations (the current and an improved one) but the programme of legal instrumentalism no longer appears appropriate. Instead, lacking the cognitive resources to develop regulations with any degree of certainty and in any event unable to keep pace with developments, they adopt a programme of fostering the respect of the industry as a means of ensuring that the requirements of guidance notes are complied with. The ongoing lament of a variety of commentators about a lack of tough enforcement of detailed regulation[41] now appears in a rather different light.

But if a shift in approach of this magnitude is evident between the legislators and the regulators, what happens when we reach the regulated area? Although the regulated area is more complex, for the sake of the current argument two dominant recursive systems will be considered, those of industry management and of engineering.

Studying the recursive system of industry management at this period, it is immediately clear just how peripheral the issue of occupational health and safety is in the context of the entire system. Nor is this as pejorative as it may initially sound. The industry does not primarily exist to carry out functions associated with the improvement of safety. It exists to explore for and produce offshore oil and it is on the basis of this fact that the entire system operates.[42] It is accordingly possible to construct the detailed cognitive map for this system shown in Figure 5.

It is not necessary here to go into this map in detail. It is sufficient to note that the system stresses certain features of the substance it seeks to produce (concealment, state ownership and fluid nature) which in turn determine the way in which it must operate (broadly: spreading the risk of failed

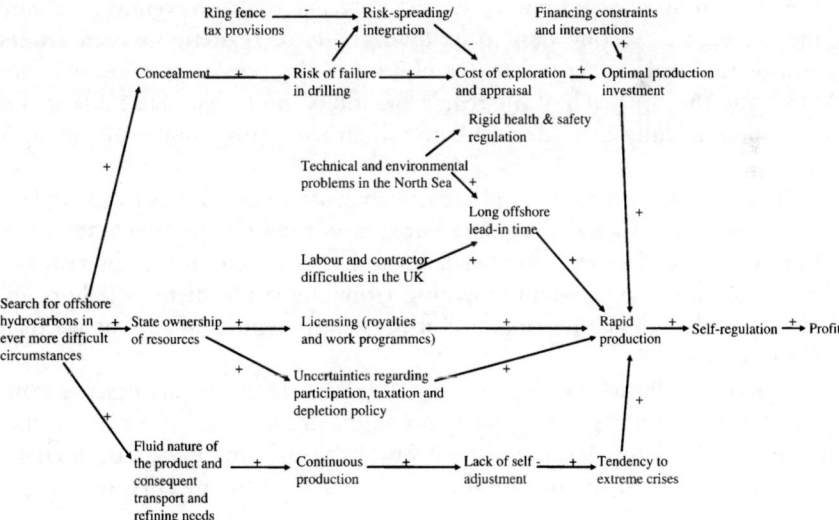

Figure 5: Cognitive Map for Industry Management.

[41] For example, Carson, above, n 18.

[42] PH Frankel, *Essentials of Petroleum: A Key to Oil Economics and Essentials Updated 1968* (London, Frank Cass, 1968).

exploration; in accordance with state licensing programmes; and continuously). These operational 'facts' combined with the added complexity of the offshore environment (long lead-in time and extremely high front-end loading of costs) mean that the industry is confronted by large economic risks. In other words, the self-steering programme of industry management is not related to two situations of occupational safety but to two situations of economic safety. But we must beware of understanding this too simplistically. This does not mean that the industry seeks first and foremost to cut costs. While profit is undoubtedly the goal, it sees this as most likely to be achieved by reducing the time between expenditure and payback; that is, by implementing a programme of rapid production. Industry management assesses operations on the basis of the net present value of money not on the gross amount it will ultimately receive. In this regard, it is worth noting that other legislative interventions (for example, regarding taxation, state participation and depletion policy) are constructed by the industry as increasing the economic risk and as necessitating the application of the same difference-minimising programme.

Now, whereas other commentators have noted the detrimental effect of speed on the occupational health and safety situation,[43] it is now possible to see why this speed occurs. It is also possible to see how *any* rigidity in health and safety regulation is constructed by industry management as being fundamentally at odds with its need to move as quickly as possible in order to minimise economic risk, and how external interventions of any kind are seen as second best to its own ability to regulate its own affairs towards this end. The regulatory ambition of the legislators takes another knock and the approach of the regulators looks somewhat better adapted if still fundamentally at odds with the self-steering programme of management.

Of course, as was mentioned previously, autopoiesis forces us to consider the possibility that the regulated area is not defined by one system but rather by many, the exact number being a matter for empirical observation. The other dominant system emerging from the study of the offshore oil industry is that of engineering, and it is to this cognitive map that we turn next (Figure 6).[44]

Despite the broad range of issues with which the regulators are concerned at this time regarding occupational health and safety, we find in the initial decade of the development of Britain's offshore oil a preoccupation in engineering with the design and construction of the installations to the

---

[43] For example, Carson above, n 18; C Wright, 'Routine Deaths: Fatal Accidents in the Oil Industry' (1986) 34 *Sociological Review* 265–89.

[44] Although a wide range of offshore engineering sources have been drawn on in the larger study, a convenient overview of its development can be found in RJ Howe, 'Evolution of Offshore Drilling and Production Technology' (1986) 4 *Offshore Technology Conference* 593–603.

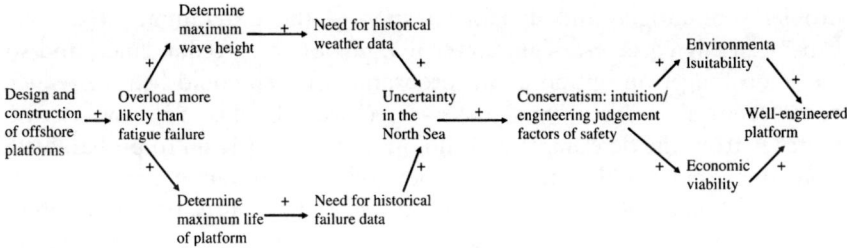

Figure 6: Cognitive Map for Engineering.

practical exclusion of other matters. For engineering, the North Sea represents the largest challenge it has ever faced but it deals with this simply by scaling up techniques developed in less hostile environments. Thus, it assumes that structural overload is the principal problem (as it was in the hurricane-prone Gulf of Mexico) and sets about design and construction on the basis of expected maximum wave height and the period that installations will be operational. Engineering is seeking a well-engineered platform—one that is both economically viable and capable of operating in its required environment. The lack of data from the new province means, however, that there is a degree of uncertainty and as a consequence a programme of scientific conservatism is adopted. In this way, it is hoped that over-design and margins for error will accommodate the uncertainty.

Two issues are of particular importance here. First of all, the concentration on installation design and construction means that engineering cannot observe other health and safety issues, notably the more mundane occupational problems that produced such a toll of death and injury during this period. Safety is constructed purely in terms of the integrity of the installation. Secondly, the assumption on which this approach is based (the primacy of the problem of structural overload) means that engineering cannot observe other factors affecting structural integrity. And indeed, this systemic blindness was exposed on two occasions during the 1970s as first fatigue and then dynamic response emerged as more significant problems in the North Sea.

In short, the difference-minimising programme of engineering (scientific conservatism) is certainly directed to safety but it is a narrower construction of that concept than that of the legislators or the regulators. Furthermore, the definition of a well-engineered platform as one that is both economically viable and suited to its environment reveals the location of engineering at the junction of science and economics. Thus, for as long as cost is not a significant factor during the initial decade of North Sea development, engineering is free to employ a programme of scientific conservatism: as we have seen, industry management at this time is happier to incur costs than to lose time. But once cost pressures increase—not least as a result of the redesign and modification necessitated by the emergent problems of fatigue and dynamic response—the programme of conservatism, involving over-design, larger margins of error, redundancy, and so on, is no longer an option and a programme which could help to reduce both technical and economic risks is required. In this way, engineering switches from the deterministic techniques of conservatism to probabilistic techniques that could rationally accommodate more factors, economic as well as technical. When that happens, the steering is in relation to different calculations of overall risk—still quite different from what the legislators and regulators observe.

This is just a brief and simplified snapshot of a larger study but it serves to demonstrate how autopoiesis reveals the shortcomings of linear-causal assumptions about the regulatory process. The legislators certainly understood their programme of legal instrumentalism in this way but in the eyes of the regulators these aims seemed hopelessly optimistic and different strategies had to be adopted. For the regulated area, regulation was at this early stage either constructed as at odds with the programme of minimising economic risk by a programme of rapid production in the case of industry management or barely constructed at all in the case of engineering.

And of course, freed from the constraints of a linear-causal approach to the regulatory process, interactions among regulated systems, for example, also become visible. Thus, the management programme of speed as the answer to all problems (which were always constructed as problems of economic risk) meant that yet more pressure was put on engineering. Furthermore, management constructed engineering solutions as final and fixed and was thus unable to observe the uncertainty which engineering was so concerned about. But of particular significance to regulators and legislators is the finding that throughout the cognitive maps of the regulated area there is simply no mention of *occupational* health and safety in any way equivalent to their concerns. What the autopoietic approach reveals is that it is no longer sufficient simply to call for tougher enforcement of detailed regulations. Implementationists would disagree, of course. If industry management is set on a course of rapid production to minimise economic risk and this is detrimental to the safety of workers then a tough stance is exactly what is needed. But it seems clear from the present approach that the codes and self-steering programmes of the industry—especially of management—are deep-seated, internally coherent and not something that can simply be pushed aside by interventionist regulation or prosecution. In other words, autopoiesis research produces something more than 'the triviality that the legislator has to take into account certain facts about the addressees of his regulations'.[45]

---

[45] H Rottleuthner, 'The Limits of Law: The Myth of a Regulatory Crisis' (1989) 17 *International Journal of the Sociology of Law* 273, 274.

F. CONCLUSION

Autopoiesis and empiricism are not, then, as mutually exclusive as might have been suspected. In conjunction with techniques such as cognitive mapping, it is possible to obtain a distinctly different view of a research area, which is potentially more adequately complex and not reduced to the dominant rationality of the analysis employed. In other words, changing our map of the regulatory process to an autopoietic view allows the study area to be taken more seriously. While cognitive mapping has been proposed here, perhaps other (more sophisticated) empirical techniques may also be useful when they are deployed within the context of autopoiesis. Only practice will tell. But equally, experience may reveal that we will have to lower drastically our expectations as to the sophistication of available instruments and be content with narratives, with storytelling, with case studies, with more or less journalistic type of inquiries. But one thing is clear: autopoiesis theory essentially depends on systematic empirical observation.

In conclusion, however, a somewhat more technical question regarding autopoietic empiricism remains to be answered: in what way does autopoiesis depend on empiricism if falsification is excluded and causal explanation and prediction marginalised? To understand the role of empirical observation in the autopoietic framework we need to enter somewhat into the nuances of the debates within the epistemology of social constructivism. The starting point is, contrary to many myths about constructivism, this: the environment exists! It is not an invention of discourse. The problem is only that the environment cannot be reached by the system's operations and, accordingly, the system is forced to invent internal constructs of the external world in order to cope with it. This is not only true for the cognitive acts of the stomach, of the brain and the mind, but also for communicative cognition and for empirical observations within the scientific discourse. They can never reach the outside world. They only produce artificial data for science as a social system to enable it to cope with the unknown outside world. And this is the point where the debate within the constructivist camp begins. It concerns the qualities of this 'coping'. Is it the mere survival of certain empirico-theoretical constructs? Is it the pragmatic use of scientific constructs for social action? Is it the resonance of the instruments of science with the music of the outside world?

Amid these turbulent waves of the epistemological debate, autopoiesis tries to steer a stable course avoiding the temptation of both sirens of constructivism: Mary Hesse's 'soft programme' as well as the 'strong programme' of the Edinburgh school of social constructivism. Bloor's 'strong programme' excludes for complex theories the possibility of a world feedback so that any science, even that of law and society, is nothing but a 'socially generated imaginative schema like other social myths'.[46] Against

---

[46] D Bloor, *Knowledge and Social Imagery* (London, Routledge and Kegan, 1976); H Collins, *Changing Order: Replication and Induction in Scientific Practice* (Beverly Hills, CA, Sage, 1985).

this, autopoiesis stresses the relevance for theory of empirical observation due to its direct structural coupling to consciousness and its indirect structural coupling to the outside world. Empirical observations are artificial constructs within science but they have real contacts with the environment insofar as they make themselves sensitive and react to perturbations from the outside world by building up new structures. They are not themselves perceptions but communications about perceptions. To be sure, this does not allow for 'correspondence' of scientific constructs with outside events, but it binds the system to its environment by self-determined constraints. Thus, autopoiesis remains a coherence theory of truth: we have to look for coherence between two types of internal constructs—theoretical concepts and empirical facts—that are constructed according to diverse procedures. But via perturbation one of these constructs—the artificial data—is closely coupled to psychic (ie, individual mental) perception of the outside world. Thus, Edinburgh's 'social idealism' with all its solipsist and monadologist threats is rejected. And perhaps it comes as a relief that on this basis we do not agree with Feyerabend's 'anything goes' relativism.

So do we agree with Mary Hesse's soft programme of constructivism: '[w]e construct the natural world in our science, but s-t [space and time reality] constrains these constructions by feedback'?[47] Our answer is a decisive yes and no. Yes, empirical research is world construction, not a reality test. Yes, empirical research constructs the environment in an internal model and simultaneously produces constraints for its constructive imagination by exposing it to the feedback of perturbations. But here the difference begins. No, the feedback does not come from the external world; it is purely internal. No, spatio-temporal reality itself does not produce any constraint. It is the cognising observer (psychic or communicative) who decides about which constraints to create and to which perturbations to expose the constructive imagination. Thus, feedback is not information from the external world, but rather is internally produced information stimulated by perturbations.

Thus, it is more than mere viability, the sheer survival of a construct that gives empirically supported theories their certainty of being in tune with the environment. It is the self-assertion of internal recursive operations that are able to develop stable eigenvalues. And they do this not only as a formal calculus, but also in close structural coupling with recursive operations of other cognitive processes and those exposing themselves to the perturbations of the outer world, which will always remain unknown to them. Thus, our highly speculative constructs do know that they are on the right track, but they do not know where they are.

Our constructs feel a resistance from the objects they produce. They expose their self-produced expectations at predefined points to outside perturbations. Everything is in the hands of the recursive operations themselves:

---

[47] MA Arbib and MB Hesse, *The Construction of Reality* (Cambridge, CUP, 1986) 3.

the expectations, the conditions under which such expectations are fulfilled or disappointed, the consequences drawn from such an experience. Only the yes and the no makes for the crucial point of contact where they lose control, where they make themselves dependent upon their environment.

Theories do not die from a falsification via independent empirical facts. We called this the omnipotence fantasies of empirical researchers, which they tend to develop when they feel disturbed by speculative theories. The only thing that empiricism can do is to create counter-irritations and compel theory to create new routinisations that may keep itself in tune with other constructed worlds or drive itself into implausibility. This is what we would call a relationship of therapy—of course, not the usual interventionist therapies but a therapy rethought in the spirit of autopoiesis. Has Marxism, for example, died from its countless empirical refutations? For decades we have witnessed successful immunisation strategies by this Grand Theory by which it moved into admirably complex constructions. Marxism's disaster had its origins elsewhere, in its loss of resonance with other cultural, political and economic operations, especially with its own communicative political and social consequences which rendered it more and more difficult to reintegrate them into the theory framework. In many respects (for example, with respect to the analysis of social differentiation, the concept of systemic autonomy, the circularity of social self-production, the totalising tendencies of social systems and human alienation), theories of social self-organisation are the legitimate heirs of Marxian theories. At the moment they seem to be in good resonance with other recursive processes in modern society. And only the future will reveal whether they survive their self-produced consequences. But, given their esoteric character, will they have any consequences?

Section Five

Studying Legal Cultures

REZA BANAKAR AND MAX TRAVERS

F EW SOCIO-LEGAL concepts are as theoretically inspiring and methodologically challenging as legal culture. On the one hand 'it raises many
of the most puzzling questions of the law and society relationship'.[1]
On the other, it is often used comparatively in an attempt to throw light on
how law is used and viewed elsewhere and/or to view one's own law and
legal practices in a *new* light. Comparative methods require taking into consideration a larger number of factors, relationships and pitfalls than what
is usually the case in non-comparative studies. At the same time, legal culture
links together a number of multifaceted concepts, some of macro character,
such as culture, law, institutions, and some of micro quality, such as perception, attitude and behaviour. The study of each of these concepts requires
precise definitions and different methods of analysis suited to the level of
social reality in which they are rooted. Seen in this light, we could argue
that legal culture should not be regarded as a concept, but as a paradigm or
a methodological approach.

This section consists of two chapters by David Nelken and Maria
Kurkchiyan which illustrate some of complexities involved in using legal culture as the basis for doing socio-legal research. Nelken's chapter uses the idea
of legal culture to compare various legal systems and practices. In that sense,
it addresses much of the concerns of comparative law from sociological and
anthropological perspectives. The second chapter also uses the concept of
legal culture, but not so much to compare two legal systems or to make sense
of foreign legal traditions, but to capture legal change and social transformation in post-Soviet Russia. Both of these studies use the notion of legal culture in a comparative manner, yet they seek different ends. It also means that
the notion of *comparative methodology* should not be limited (as is often the
case within legal and even socio-legal studies) to the comparative studies of
different legal systems.

---

[1] D Nelken, 'Comparative Sociology of Law' in R Banakar and M Travers, (eds), *An
Introduction to Law and Social Theory* (Oxford, Hart Publishing, 2002) 329.

If we define 'comparative method' broadly to include even the study of 'variables' and 'relationships' then all social scientific research is, in one form or other, comparative.[2] Emile Durkheim regarded the idea to develop a branch of sociology called 'comparative sociology' as a tautology.[3] All forms of sociology become comparative as soon as they take the step from being purely descriptive into the domain of explanation, which requires accounting for and juxtaposing facts. However, in the first chapter of this section we are clearly using 'comparative' in the narrow sense of comparing the 'familiar'—the taken-for-granted way of doing things—with the 'unfamiliar'—how other people or institutions do the same thing. It is in this latter sense that comparative legal methods are developed to study the differences and similarities between legal institutions and systems.[4]

Social scientists and lawyers use comparative methods, but in different ways and for different reasons, which are determined by the concerns of their specific disciplines as discussed in chapter 1. Social scientists employ comparative methods because comparing and contrasting variables, cases or larger units of study, such as social institutions, cultures or legal systems, increase their understanding of social life. Legal scholars, on the other hand, investigate the causes of similarities and differences between national legal systems, to answer questions ranging from policy issues—investigating, for example, which national legal system provides the best solution to a specific problem—to theoretical issues—asking, for example, if all legal systems share a common core.[5] Those scholars who focus on similarities are often searching for ideas or practices common to all developed legal orders (seeking the universal core of all legal systems). Those who study the differences among legal systems are, on the other hand, often interested in 'family' classifications, which is 'an approach that analyses a small number of legal families rather than the particularities of the numerous individual legal systems themselves'.[6] More importantly, traditional forms of comparative law examine these differences and similarities in a *formal* way, by 'contrasting or comparing selected provisions'.[7] The social sciences, on the other hand, are more interested in the behavioural and institutional environments of law and the social and cultural mechanisms underlying judicial orders. It is, therefore, not surprising if comparative socio-legal research draws more

[2] See C Ragin, *The Comparative Method: Moving beyond Qualitative and Quantitative Strategies* (CA, University of California Press, 1987).

[3] E Durkheim, *The Rules of Sociological Method* (New York, NY, Free Press, 1964).

[4] See K Zweigert and H Kötz, *An Introduction to Comparative Law*, 3rd edn, (Oxford, OUP, 1998).

[5] M Bogdan, *Comparative Law* (Stockholm, Norstedts juridik, 1994) 22.

[6] R Hyland, 'Comparative Law' in D Patterson, (ed), *A Companion to Philosophy of Law and Legal theory* (Oxford, Blackwell, 2000). One classification distinguishes seven such families: French, German, Scandinavian, English, Russian, Islamic and Hindu.

[7] M Feeley, 'Comparing Criminal Law for Criminologists' in D Nelken, (ed), *Comparing Legal Cultures* (Aldershot, Dartmouth, 1997) 93.

on the theoretical and methodological resources of legal anthropology, and the studies of globalisation and legal cultures, than on the traditional methods of comparative law.[8]

This section starts with a chapter by David Nelken who, although focusing on comparative studies of criminal justice, nonetheless reveals the depth and breadth of *comparative* socio-legal research. At the same time, he introduces us to some of the methodological issues arising out of comparative studies of legal cultures. Nelken dismisses studies which limit themselves to 'comparison by juxtaposition' and criticises the standard texts in comparative criminal justice, which typically invite the local 'experts' from different countries to provide national reports. Such studies provide no insight into what lies behind the descriptions and interpretations of experts. Comparative research will, according to Nelken, stagnate unless more explicit attention is given to clarifying what a given comparison is for and how a given aim can best be achieved.

More importantly for our purposes here, Nelken argues for the need to reflect on the aims, issues and methods of comparative criminal justice and to deliberate critically on what it means to understand, describe and analyse other (legal) cultures. He draws attention in particular to the issue, which ultimately interrogates the epistemological bases of comparative research: How can we be sure that we are comparing 'like with like' both in terms of the distinctive elements of the criminal process and its place in the larger culture? Nelken then goes on to present three methods, based on the approaches employed by various researchers to understand, conceptualise and analyse another culture. These techniques depend on whether the researcher has been 'virtually there', 'researching there', or 'living there'. In this way, Nelken sets up the scene for comparing the theoretical adequacy and methodological efficacy of the mode of investigation used by various comparative approaches. Can we do comparative research of this type without the first hand experience of the culture(s) we are studying; without, for example, being able to speak the language of, and see the world, at least momentarily, from the point of view of those we are investigating? What are the advantages and disadvantages of long-term engagement with the cultures we are studying? Although these questions are presented here in relation to criminal justice, they can be extended to debate the methodological issues of comparative studies of legal cultures in general.

The second chapter of this section is by Marina Kurkchiyan who describes her experience of researching the legal culture of post-soviet Russia. This chapter's contribution to comparative socio-legal methodology is different

---

[8] See AC Budak and V Gessner, (eds), *Emerging Legal Certainty: Empirical Studies of the Globalisation of Law* (Aldershot, Ashgate, 1998); V Gessner, (ed), *Foreign Courts* (Aldershot, Dartmouth, 1996); D Nelken and J Feest, (eds), *Adapting Legal Cultures* (Oxford, Hart Publishing, 2001); RP Appelbaum, WLF Felstiner and V Gessner, (eds), *Rules and Networks: The Legal Culture of Global Business Transactions* (Oxford, Hart Publishing, 2001).

from that made by Nelken's chapter. Instead of comparing different legal systems, which are often separated by different cultures, customs and languages, Kurkchiyan uses the traditional Russian legal culture as a yardstick to examine the transitional changes and the current status of law in Russian society. Has the expanded volume of laws and the increased number of lawyers brought more genuine legality and respect for law into Russian society? What path is Russia taking towards the development of its legal environment? How does post-Soviet transition affect Russian legal culture?

Kurkchiyan conceptualises legal culture with the help of such variables as people's attitudes to law, their expectations of how everyone else will behave towards the law, and the interplay of political institutions with the functionaries of the law. Most importantly, she writes that legal culture is determined by the professionalism of these functionaries and the institutional make-up of the law. The role of law, then, becomes dependent on the principles upon which social order is founded in society; on what its dominant values happen to be; and on the forms of problem-solving people opt for. To conduct a study of legal culture, as defined here, Kurkchiyan interprets the way in which people use language as an index of cultural meanings. She records people's perception of the law, and also what they said indirectly about it while they described their own or other people's dealings with the law. In addition, she observes common practices on matters relating to law in business and in the instinctive responses to challenging situations in everyday life.

One important issue, which is not directly connected with the study of legal cultures, but appears to create a methodological dilemma for some socio-legal researchers, is revealed clearly in Kurkchiyan's chapter. Although Kurkchiyan's approach is essentially qualitative—she conducts her study mainly through open and unstructured interviews—and concerned with 'interpretation' and 'meaning' of social action, nonetheless, she talks of 'how to *measure* legal culture', uses the notion of 'hypothesis' rather than 'research question' and worries about the 'validity' of her research.[9]

There are many ways of interpreting this 'mixing up' of methodological standards. Looking at it negatively, we could say that although qualitative research methods have proved themselves invaluable in conducting socio-legal research and are used widely, they are nonetheless viewed as less 'scientific' or as less 'reliable' than quantitative methods, even by many of those who employ them. If there is any truth in this explanation, then we have to conclude that, outside of pure interpretive approaches such as ethnomethodology,[10] the ideology of scienticism continues to hold its grip on

---

[9] For another example of this 'mixing up' of criteria belonging to positivism and interpretivism, see Bettina Lange's chapter in section 3.

[10] See R Dingwall, 'Ethnomethodology and Law' in R Banakar and M Travers, (eds), *An Introduction to Law and Social Theory* (Oxford, Hart Publishing, 2002) 227–44.

much of socio-legal research. Looking at it positively, we might say that researchers who immerse themselves in what appears to be, and is experienced as, the 'messy' process of qualitative research, find reflexive and critical relief in the concept of 'validity'. Even when their research is inductive—searching for, rather than testing, questions and hypotheses—they nonetheless use notions of 'rigour' and 'sampling' as a way to reflect critically on the *credibility* of their arguments and conclusions.

These methodological insecurities aside, the two chapters presented in this section can also be seen, as alternative ways of engaging with issues which are traditionally addressed by comparative law and studies of law and social reform. David Nelken's chapter goes beyond the formalistic and decontextualised descriptions of legal institutions, rules and procedures, which we often find within comparative law, and instead tries to provide insights into the daily practices within the legal system and how ordinary people experience and engage with legal institutions. Kurkchyian's approach illustrates that the concept of legal culture can also be successfully employed to conduct studies of socio-legal change and transformation.

12

Doing Research into Comparative Criminal Justice

DAVID NELKEN

EVEN THE BEST of current English language theorising about crime control takes much of its sense and point from background assumptions and developments which are most at home in what continental Europeans call 'Anglo-American' legal culture. David Garland's important and influential analysis of the way 'the State' is currently seeking to divest at least part of its responsibilities in this sphere,[1] has much less relevance to societies in Continental Europe where in some respects it is only now that the responsibility of the State to protect its citizens from street crime is beginning to be taken seriously. In Italy for example until recently the emphasis was always given to the relatively more serious threats facing the state from terrorism, corruption and organised crime. Conventional or street crimes, from burglary to robbery, were termed 'micro-crimes'. Matters changed only with the arrival of foreign immigrants in considerable numbers for the first time in the 1990's. Rather than the crime label serving as the means to create 'outsiders', the Italian media simply formulated the more direct equation: those who came from the 'outside' (the so called 'extra-comunitari') were to be considered potential or active criminals.

Much the same can be said for Jock Young's eloquent analysis of what he calls the 'exclusive society'.[2] Despite the many similarities at the level of practice brought about by the homogenising and converging influences of the European Union, the debate over solidarity versus exclusion takes rather different forms depending on whether it is the representatives of the State or the members of civil society who are allocated the main role in creating an integrated sense of identity and community. If 'penality' is so much

---

[1] D Garland, 'The Limits of the Sovereign State: Strategies of Crime Control in Contemporary Society' (1996) 36 *British Journal of Criminal* 445–71; and D Garland, *The Culture of Control* (Oxford, OUP, 2000).

[2] J Young, *The Exclusive Society* (London, Sage, 1999).

a matter of cultural meaning and not merely instrumental affectivity[3] it is obvious that this will vary from culture to culture. Indeed it is fair to say that many of the important points made by these leading scholars are comparative observations about the similarities and the differences they notice within Anglo-American culture.

There are many reasons for doing comparative research in criminal justice.[4] As a result of globalisation we are increasingly affected by what is done elsewhere and increasingly aware of developments in other places.[5] The literature shows a growing interest in exploring wider differences in criminal justice, especially, but not only, with respect to the slow move to legal unification or collaboration within the European Union. There are now many valuable monographs on different aspects of the criminal process, in addition to articles in both general and specialist journals. There are also the beginnings of distinct schools and approaches, whether positivist,[6] interpretivist,[7] or Foucauldian.[8] Research into comparative criminal justice also needs to take account of what is currently being produced in other disciplines: not only in sociology and anthropology but also history, political science or cross-cultural psychology. In addition, there is an obvious if under-theorised overlap with comparative law.[9]

It remains true, however, that whether the goal is understanding other systems of criminal justice as such, or only parts thereof, there is still too much reliance on what may be termed 'comparison by juxtaposition'. The standard texts in comparative criminal justice typically invite the local 'experts' from different countries to provide national reports. In collective research projects representatives of different systems say 'this is what we do in Poland, what do you do in Denmark? It is much rarer for scholars to address what lies behind their descriptions and interpretations. With few exceptions, collections of articles about criminal justice contain relatively little about the

---

[3] D Garland, *Punishment and Modern Society* (Oxford, OUP, 1990).

[4] D Nelken, 'The Future of Comparative Criminology' in D Nelken, (ed), *The Futures of Criminology* (London, Sage, 1994) 220–43.

[5] D Nelken, 'The Globalization of Crime and Criminal Justice: Prospects and Problems' in M Freeman, (ed), *Law at the Turn of the Century* (Oxford, OUP, 1997) 251–79; and D Nelken, 'Criminology: Crime's Changing Boundaries' in P Cane and M Tushnet, (eds), *Oxford Handbook of Legal Studies* (Oxford, OUP, 2003) 250–70.

[6] See for example, HG Heiland, LI Shelley and H Katoh, (eds), *Crime and Control in Comparative Perspectives* (Berlin, De Gruyter, 1992).

[7] See for example, A Crawford, 'Contrasts in Victim/Offender Mediation and Appeals to Community in Comparative Cultural Contexts: France and England and Wales' in D Nelken, (ed), *Contrasting Criminal Justice* (Aldershot, Dartmouth, 2000) 205–29; D Nelken, 'The Future of Comparative Criminology' in D Nelken, (ed), above, n4, 220–43; L Zedner, 'In pursuit of the Vernacular; Comparing Law and Order Discourse in Britain and Germany' (1995) 4 *Social and Legal Studies* 517–34.

[8] R Smandych, (ed), *Governable Places: Readings on Governmentality and Crime Control* (Aldershot, Dartmouth, 1999).

[9] D Nelken, (ed), *Contrasting Criminal Justice* (Aldershot, Dartmouth, 2000).

actual process of doing cross-cultural research.[10] At best this question is addressed briefly by the editors rather than by the contributors themselves.[11]

Comparative research will make slow progress unless more explicit attention is given to clarifying what a given comparison is for and how a given aim can best be achieved. Considerable care is also required in deciding what needs to be compared, and how significant similarities and differences are to be identified. It is not uncommon for writers to assume that there are 'functional equivalents'[12] between the stages of criminal justice in different societies.[13] But it may be a mistake to treat the concept of 'criminal justice', as a set of interdependent decision making stages, as itself a cultural universal. There are many even industrially advanced societies which do not conceive of the decisions of those responding to criminal law violations as part of an interconnected scheme and where there are few if any empirical studies of such decision-making. The same applies to taking dilemmas such as the choice between 'due process' and 'crime control' or between 'justice' and 'welfare' as universal.[14] To protect themselves against the dangers of ethnocentrism researchers need to engage in patient dialectical interchange between cultures and so become alive to their cultural biases, the problems of translation, and the pervading influence of specific histories.

On the other hand, it is also true that the effects of globalisation mean that 'national' legal cultures, or even the 'legal families' described by comparative lawyers, are less and less independent of one another. Ideas about 'criminal justice', especially those represented by currently influential Anglo-American models, are being borrowed without too much attention being paid to their cultural origins or social preconditions, and (sometimes) this is bringing about change in the social contexts in which they are introduced. A given system of criminal justice will increasingly have its roots in more than one 'Legal culture'.[15] The current working of Italian criminal

---

[10] See for example, N Dorn, J Jepsen, and N Savona, (eds), *European Drug Policies and Enforcement*, Basingstoke (London, Macmillan, 1996); F Heidensohn and M Farrell, *Crime in Europe* (London, Routledge, 1991); P Robert and L van Outrive, (eds), *Crime et Justice en Europe* (Paris, L'Harmattan, 1993); V Ruggiero, H Ryan and J Sim, (eds), *Western European Penal Systems* (London, Sage, 1995); V Ruggiero, N South and I Taylor, (eds), *The New European Criminology: Crime and Social Order in Europe* (London, Routledge, 1998).

[11] G F Cole, *et al*, (eds), *Major Criminal Justice Systems: A Comparative Survey* (Beverly Hills, CA, Sage, 1987); CB Fields and RH Moore, (eds), *Comparative Criminal Justice* (Prospect Heights, IL, Waveland Press, 1996); and HG Heiland, LI Shelley and H Katoh, (eds), *Crime and Control in Comparative Perspectives* (Berlin, De Gruyter, 1992).

[12] K Zweigert, and H Kotz, *An Introduction to Comparative Law* (Oxford, OUP, 1987).

[13] See for example, J Feest and M Murayama, 'Protecting the Innocent through Criminal Justice: A Case Study from Spain, Virtually compared to Germany and Japan' in D Nelken, (ed), *Contrasting Criminal Justice* (Aldershot, Dartmouth, 2000).

[14] PL Reichel, *Comparative Criminal Justice Systems: A Topical Approach*, 2nd edn, (Upper Saddle River, NJ, Prentice Hall, 1999).

[15] D Nelken, (ed), *Comparing Legal Cultures* (Aldershot, Dartmouth, 1997); D Nelken, 'Comparative Sociology of Law' in R Banakar and M Travers, (eds), An Introduction to Law and Social Theory (Oxford, Hart Publishing, 2002) 329–44; and D Nelken and J Feest, (eds), *Adapting Legal Cultures* (Oxford, Hart Publishing, 2001).

justice for example is presently moulded both by the long standing hegemony of German penal law (which is still unchallenged amongst the law professors who deal in substantive criminal law), and the more recent influence of Anglo-American ideas which have come in as a result of the introduction of a large number of accusatorial elements in the penal process. Beyond this, the Italian system, like many others, is also more and more affected by wider general trends such as the rise of risk society, the growth of private police, the new emphasis on crime prevention and so on.

If we want to go beyond 'comparison by juxtaposition' we will need to establish some sort of working relationship with those who know more about other systems than we do. Some of those who write about comparative criminal justice may even be dependent on mediators to overcome their lack of proficiency in the local languages.[16] But, for almost any researcher, local experts and practitioners will inevitably be the direct or indirect source of most of their claims about other systems of criminal justice. Yet too little attention has been given to the implications of this reliance. There seems to be scant recognition, for example, of the extent to which the descriptions of the aims or results of legal institutions and procedures which local experts provide are themselves, in various ways, *part* of the context they are describing. Those whose opinions we rely on may often be partial to one side or other of contemporary political battles over criminal justice. In Italy for example, some academics and practitioners are notoriously pro-judges, others are anti-judges.[17] In France some commentators are strongly against importing ideas from the common law world, others are less antagonistic.[18] In Japan leading academics are involved in fierce controversy over the need for greater rights-consciousness. Others are against such developments.

Moreover, cultural variability means that the problem faced in different societies is not always the same. In some cultures, such as Italy, Spain or much of Latin America, it is considered appropriate for an academic to identify and be identified as a member of a group. In playing the role of what Gramsci called an 'organic intellectual' your prime duty is understood both by your allies and by your opponents to be the furtherance of a specific group ideal. In consequence, the question of social and political affiliation is one of the first questions raised (even if not always openly) in considering the point and validity of academic criticisms of current practices and of corresponding proposals for reform. In other societies, such as Anglo-Saxon cultures, however, the approved practice for many scholars and practitioners is to avoid such open identification. Relatively speaking, the extent of political consensus, or of admiration for allegedly neutral criteria based on

---

[16] See for example, D Downes, *Contrasts in Tolerance* (Oxford, OUP, 1988).

[17] D Nelken, 'Judicial Politics and Corruption in Italy' in M Levi and D Nelken, (eds), *The Corruption of Politics and the Politics of Corruption* (Oxford, Blackwell, 1996) 95–113.

[18] A Garapon, 'The Shock of Globalisation and French Legal Culture' (1995) 4 *Social and Legal Studies* 492–506.

'results' or 'efficiency', may be such that there is less pressure to take sides. And intellectuals may also simply count for less politically so their affiliations are less important! But if we think carefully about the allegiances of the experts we know personally in English-speaking cultures we will often be able to associate them with 'standing' for given political or policy positions. And those from more politicised cultures may have doubts about professed scientific neutrality. How then can we imagine that it is enough to cite foreign academics or practitioners without some knowledge about their affiliations, and an understanding of the role responsibilities of affiliation in the culture under investigation? Surely it would (or should?) make a difference when reading an article in the *British Journal of Criminology* by an Italian scholar that describes the work of Italian judicial prosecutors if we were to discover that the author has made an academic and even political career out of continually criticising the judiciary.

Even if we try to make proper allowance for the fact that our sources are 'partial' there still remains the problem that experts and practitioners are undoubtedly part of their own culture. This is, after all, why we consult them. But this means that they do not necessarily ask or answer questions based on where the outside researcher is 'coming from' (and may not even have the basis for understanding such questions). In a multitude of ways their descriptions and also their criticisms will also belong to their culture and may take for granted exactly what we most want to understand. In many cases those insiders we rely on will not necessarily even be aware of the ways their practices are special in a comparative perspective. Insofar as we are dependent only on them we will not therefore necessarily get to appreciate what makes their way of doing things 'special' in relation to our expectations. If, on the other hand, we insist nonetheless on asking questions from our own 'starting point'[19] we will at best learn about how different another society may be from what we are used to. But this is of strictly limited use for understanding how another society works as it does. Somehow we must try to transcend such partial perspectives.

A. THREE METHODOLOGICAL APPROACHES

There is unfortunately no methodological recipe which could give us a ready-made answer to how best to compare societies. But we can at least try to be clearer about how different approaches to gathering empirical data are likely to affect the way we do such research. In a recent edited collection I examined this question with reference to three of the most common

---

[19] D Nelken, 'Telling Difference: Of Crime and Criminal Justice in Italy' in D Nelken, (ed), *Contrasting Criminal Justice* (Aldershot, Dartmouth 2000) 233–64.

methods of doing comparative research in contemporary societies.[20] The three approaches I distinguished were those I called 'virtually there', 'researching there' and 'being there'. These distinctions are heuristic; in practice there may be considerable differences in the way research is carried out even within each of these categories. More important, these approaches are rarely found in a pure form, even if in different research projects one or other will usually be found to predominate.

The approach that I have called 'virtually there' aims to further the goal of accurate descriptions of relevant differences between systems of criminal justice by means of inter-cultural co-operation. Instead of going to learn about a foreign culture at first hand the researcher is content to be 'virtually there', by relying on an inside expert from the society or societies. Hence this approach is particularly conditioned by such reliance and this has to be borne in mind at all stages. A sophisticated example of what can nonetheless be achieved if care is taken in using this approach is provided by Brants and Field's study of legal cultures, procedural cultures and procedural traditions as they affect covert policing in England and in Holland.[21]

Brants and Field treated themselves as experts in the distinctive traditions of the societies in which each of them lived and worked and each took on the responsibility to mediate this expertise for the sake of the collaborator. Each therefore tried to familiarise the other with salient aspects of his own system in terms that the other could relate to aspects of his or her own society. This turned out to be more difficult than they had imagined. Such collaboration, they found, required a high degree of mutual trust and involved 'negotiating' mutually acceptable descriptions of legal practice in each of their home countries. They constantly came up against the dangers of not comparing like with like and the difficulties of reaching genuinely shared meanings between those socialised into different legal cultures. They discovered, for example that in England and Wales the idea of 'diversion' referred to a choice to take cases *out* of the system, as part of a pragmatic effort to avoid the negative, self fulfilling side-effects caused when people are drawn into the criminal justice process. In the Netherlands, on the other hand, diversion was part of a continuum of responses, which were considered *intrinsic to* the criminal justice system; and seen mainly as matter of re-routing offenders from the punishment option to more positive methods of conflict resolution. Again, in England and Wales, diversion was seen as a somewhat 'guilty secret', which compromises the ideals of

---

[20] See Nelken, *ibid*; and P Roberts, 'On Method: The Ascent of Comparative Criminal Justice' (2002) 22 *Oxford Journal of Legal Studies* 529–61.

[21] C Brants, and S Field, 'Legal Culture, Political Cultures and Procedural Traditions: Towards a Comparative Interpretation of Covert and Proactive Policing in England and Wales and the Netherlands' in Nelken, above, n 19, p 77–116.

adversary justice in the interests of making the criminal process more expeditious. Diversion in the Netherlands, by contrast, was understood as an aspect of the wider 'politics of accommodation', which encouraged an ample use of prosecution and other official use of discretion.

Through this sort of collaboration the authors learned that the correct interpretation of even the smallest detail of criminal justice organisation required sensitivity to what they call 'broader institutional and ideological contexts'. With this awareness the authors were able to show how contrasting ways of approaching the boundaries of criminal justice can have both good and bad consequences. The broad Dutch approach, for example, too easily allowed the gathering of police intelligence without it having to be justified as necessarily or directly connected to imminent prosecutions. In much the same way, the concern over proactive and covert forms of police activity in each country also related to the way in which cultural conceptions of the proper boundaries of criminal justice were being fought over within each of the legal and political cultures concerned. In the Netherlands it was seen as part of the growing challenge to the political culture of trusting the elites; in England in terms of the difficulties of holding to account the police as the key gatekeepers of the system.

Brants and Field also reconstructed the socio-historical relationship between forms of proactive and covert policing and the environing legal and political contexts in each of their two societies. They discovered that proactive police methods in England and Wales were first used to deal with 'problems' such as drugs and football hooliganism but were then legitimised by the slogan 'target the criminal not the crime', in the 1990's, so as to be applied to burglary, car crime, and eventually to the struggle against organised crime. These high profile techniques proved useful to the police because they gave the impression that they were 'doing something' and providing 'value for money'. They both helped defuse public expectations regarding the difficulties of apprehending other sorts of opportunistic crime, and also helped eased police anxieties over the limits to their investigative capacities introduced by the PACE rules on police interrogation. In the Netherlands, on the other hand, the 'management of crime' had always been seen as an essential role of the police. Organised crime was a long-standing 'Dutch demon' and intelligence gathering and the spread of disinformation were routine. Those who were suspected of being key criminals were targeted and harassed with all sorts of other administrative regulations as part of the process of defining and managing 'risk populations'. However, at a certain stage, this gave rise to a major scandal, as it became clear that the police had got 'out of control' in their exercise of their powers, and were not even being kept under their own hierarchical control. This then helped produce (but was also the result of) a breakdown of the political culture of 'pillarisation', which depended on a high level of trust in elites who corporatively arranged the pacification of the lower classes.

Many of Brants and Field's methodological strategies can be applied beyond their case study. Of particular value is their examination of the relationship between legal culture and political culture and the way in which changes in one affect the other. They set out a fruitful model for examining procedural traditions in criminal law as the site of intersections amongst four aspects of culture: traditions, institutions, intellectual formations and 'lived structures of feeling'. On the other hand, much as they stressed the need to capture contrasts in conceptions and contexts between cultures, the authors were also aware of the dangers of reifying differences between national systems of criminal justice as if they were totally independent. Thus they drew attention to the interaction between the local and the global and the way influences from the USA and the European Union were affecting both the Netherlands and England and Wales. The adoption of new policing techniques and the controversies which surrounded this therefore provided yet another illustration of the way developments in criminal justice were not restricted to any particular jurisdiction even if they were certainly affected by the contexts in which they operated.

The second type of approach I have called 'researching there'. This is well illustrated by a paper written by David Johnson in which he sets out to understand differences in 'role expectations' amongst prosecutors in the USA as compared to Japan.[22] Johnson went to Japan so as to carry out in the first person a systematic large-scale project of interviewing Japanese prosecutors. Though he also did some observation of trainees and made good use of the biographies of famous prosecutors that served as inspirational materials, he relied mainly on his many interviews in order to explain how Japanese prosecutors think and act. His methodology followed the positivist protocols. Rather than seeking to clarify cultural assumptions through collaboration with other experts, or by himself attempting to move backwards and forward between his own culture and that under observation, Johnson tried as far as possible to keep the researcher out of the picture. His interview schedule was carefully designed to produce the same stimulus for all respondents so as to be able to standardise their answers.

His survey of 235 Japanese prosecutors collected information about a range of background variables: age, gender, educational background (prosecutors have to have passed a very demanding examination), their reasons for choosing a career in the legal system and choosing the job of prosecutor in particular (the desire to do justice, the appeal of investigation, the fit between job and personality and the influence of significant others), and so

[22] D Johnson, 'Prosecutor Culture in Japan and USA' in Nelken, above, n 19, p 157–204; and D Johnson, *The Japanese Way of Justice*, (Oxford, OUP, 2002).

on. Johnson's main interest, however, was to understand why prosecutors in Japan so often go out of their way not to charge suspects. He used the evidence of their lack of interest in producing convictions so as to criticise those scholars who perpetuate the idea that all 'prosecutors' by the nature of their job must have the universal desire to maximise convictions. Even in the USA, he claims, such an assumption will often be misleading and it is seriously wide of the mark in Japan.

Of the possible objectives of prosecution that his respondents were asked to consider, thirteen in all were taken seriously. The most important goals to which they subscribed turned out to be that of 'discovering the truth' and 'making the correct decision whether to charge with an offence'. Prosecution aims which were standard in Anglo-American legal cultures, such as the goal of 'disposing efficiently of as many cases as possible', came low down the list, and 'prosecuting and convicting as many cases as possible' was espoused by a mere 8%. On the other hand, the answers which the prosecutors provided to his questions provided little support for the competing view that Japanese prosecutors avoid conviction because their aim is to rehabilitate or re-integrate offenders in the community. Low priority was given to the objective of 'invoking public condemnation of the crime', which was considered important by less than a third of his sample. More to the point, many of those interviewed did not even understand the question! 'Why would we want that?' they replied. Japanese prosecutors also said that they had little interest in repairing relationships between offenders and victims. But they did place enormous significance on searching for signs of remorse in the offender. And this was taken far more seriously than the token remorse which triggers guilty pleas and the consequent reduction in sentence after plea bargains in the USA and Britain. Genuine regret for one's actions was the necessary condition for receiving lenient treatment.

Johnson concluded that, as compared with the United States, the objectives of Japanese prosecutors have much less to do with the punitive ends of retribution and general deterrence. This relative leniency is made possible by the less adversarial nature of the criminal process in Japan, by the light caseloads which prosecutors carry, the absence of juries, and perhaps most of all by the way criminal convictions are not used as part of political battles. In Japan crime is far less of a 'public problem' than in the United States. Hence Japanese prosecutors' prudence in charging is ultimately explicable in terms of a combination of cultural differences and a lack of structural pressure on them to produce a high level of convictions.

The lack of external pressures clearly privileges 'internal legal culture', the ideas, values, expectations and attitudes that prosecutors have about criminal law, behaviour and justice. But these ideas also relate to wider aspects of Japanese culture. Johnson attributes particular significance to the Japanese belief that human nature is perfectible, in contrast to the Christian doctrine of original sin. As a vivid example he offers an account of a recidivist rapist who, court personnel insisted, could nonetheless be reformed if he only would take to the writing of poetic Haiku. Johnson's method also allows him to provide intriguing insights into the relationship between culture and crime control more generally. He notes how defendants in the USA contribute to their own stigmatisation by rejecting the authority of the courts and thus excluding the possibility of benefiting from the demonstration of remorse in place of punishment. But, he also suggests that the internal legal culture of the American courts, as compared with the Japanese criminal process, leaves accused persons with precious little opportunity for offering to show remorse.

Johnson's approach has its limits, however, which need to be set against its strengths. His arguments about which objectives count as most important for Japanese prosecutors certainly carry more weight because they are based on such a large sample. On other hand, large-scale survey and interview methods are subject to well-known criticisms, which are even more to the point when carrying out research in an unfamiliar context. How far can we take what prosecutors say they do as a reliable guide to what they actually do? Are answers given in the interview setting a reliable guide to everyday behaviour? Is it even plausible to believe that prosecutors actually act with all of 13 goals in mind? And what about the possibility of cultural variation as between the USA and Japan even in the degree to which subjects believe that their interview replies should mirror their actual behaviour. It is interesting that the questions Johnson planned to ask about whether prosecutors *actually achieved* their objectives were ruled off-limits by his official hosts. The reason that he was given was fear that the defence might use the findings as evidence of lenience, and by demanding such treatment, make this self-fulfilling. Johnson rightly argues that, whatever other information we may want to rely on so as to describe what prosecutors are doing, we can hardly dispense with asking them what they are trying to achieve. But this is not the same thing as showing what they do achieve.

The third approach I want to consider is that based on what may be called, for lack of a better term, 'living there'. This method is the mainstay of classical anthropological fieldwork in small-scale societies. But it is also the approach typically followed by expatriate scholars who live in, and may even intend to stay in, the country under investigation. Moving to work and live in another society is not quite the same as setting out to do ethnography as such. It has to do with wider participation in the general life of the country, which may often include an active consulting/critical role in relation to the criminal justice system itself. Thus the scholars who use this approach can be described as 'observing participants' (rather than participant observers) and come to enjoy the status of 'insider/outsiders'.[23]

---

[23] See D Nelken, 'Being There' in L Chao and J Winterdyk, (eds), *Lessons from Comparative Criminology* (Ontario, De Sitter Publications, 2004) 83–92.

Maureen Cain represents a good example of this new breed of expatriate academics, who move between countries by choice rather than as a result of forced emigration, and are hence less inclined to erase the past even as they engage with their new cultures. Cain spent a total of eight years in the West Indies before returning to Britain. Unlike those who only visit other countries on limited research assignments, she became an 'observing participant' in the society. (Those only involved in research projects are unlikely to be called 'family' and 'sister' by strangers in the road, as happened to her). As is typical of someone in this insider-outsider role, when writing about the West Indies she is therefore able to draw directly on her own experience of teaching and action rather than limiting herself to retailing what professionals or experts have to tell us about criminal justice in the country under observation.[24]

In her University work, Cain tells us, she increasingly felt uneasy about the ostensible universal truths of Western Criminology. The students wanted what they considered to be accredited knowledge but she felt ill at ease:

> Teaching about youth cultures in society which is not rigidly age stratified; of teaching community policing and democratic accountability while lacking a language to describe a post-colonial service lacking a sense of direction, having lost its *raison d'être*, of talking ethnic minorities where historically—and arguably today as well—it is the culture and identity of the black former *majority* which is under threat.[25]

Apart from teaching, however, Cain's activities in the West Indies also involved her in a consultancy role. In particular she was asked to help rethink the role of post-colonial police forces. The colonial force was established to serve the needs of the metropolis and the planter class, to ensure a steady supply of disciplined labour and to face down challenges to their culture and trade. Now, after independence, the islands increasingly struggled with the effects of tourism and drug trafficking, both of which increase street crime and stranger violence, but 'bring in money, at a lifestyle price'. The new police forces were starved of resources. In consequence, they tended to combine a normal passivity with sporadic raids against drugs and other crimes. For each newly identified problem a specialised police unit was created, and each island had a somewhat different way of organising policing in accordance with sometimes considerable historical and political differences. Cain was asked for her opinion over the future of 'community policing' and what such policing required. Some local scholars argued that,

---

[24] M Cain, 'Through Other Eyes: On the Limitations and Value of Western Criminology for Teaching and Practice in Trinidad and Tobago' in D Nelken, (ed), *Contrasting Criminal Justice* (Aldershot, Dartmouth, 2000a) 265–94; and M Cain, 'Orientalism, Occidentalism and the Sociology of Crime' (2000a) 40 *British Journal Criminal* 239–60.

[25] M Cain, above, n. 24 at 265.

at least in some of the islands, ensuring better responsiveness to the community should come before increasing professionalism. But Cain's view was that there was a need for more central co-ordination, more professionalism, and better resources as a pre-condition before encouraging debate over what the community wanted from the police. What is interesting methodologically here is the way in which Cain consciously reversed the priorities that she might have set down in Britain. Whatever she might think about the UK, in the West Indies, professionalism must come before community.

But this was not in any way part of a generalised attempt to bring in models from abroad. Cain was highly committed to tapping into ideas and practices being produced at local level as opposed to falling under the sway of the hegemonic Anglo-American ideas of what can be called 'globalising criminology'.[26] For her, it was always better to look for 'best practice' on the ground' rather than resort to foreign models. She was optimistic about the potential for self-policing in residential neighbourhoods, and the range of self-help strategies adopted by small businesses'. People facing risk of crime had invented ingenious strategies for sharing the costs of protecting their businesses. Hotel owners showed imagination in working out fruitful collaboration between themselves and beach vendors. Neighbourhood watch schemes in Trinidad did a lot to improve community spirit and even to control crime even though crime reduction was not their major goal.

B. CHOOSING A METHODOLOGY

The three methods described so far lie on a continuum running from least to greatest engagement with another society. But in deciding which method to choose we need to avoid some common misconceptions. In the first place we should not assume that there is any necessary relationship between the time spent in a culture and a tendency either to appreciate or to criticise its institutions. Some American comparative lawyers in the 1970's needed only a short time in Europe to satisfy themselves that the vaunted judicial oversight of the police was a 'myth'.[27] On the other hand, Marshall Clinard's short visit to Switzerland led him to a positive assessment of the country's way with crime,[28] but Balvig's even shorter visit there led him to quite different conclusions.[29] Downes needed only a short period to be impressed

---

[26] D Nelken, 'Criminology: Crime's Changing Boundaries' in P Cane and M Tushnet, (eds), *Oxford Handbook of Legal Studies* (Oxford, OUP, 2003) 250–70.

[27] A Goldstein and M Marcus, 'The Myth of Judicial Supervision in Three Inquisitorial Systems: France, Italy and Germany' (1977) 87 *Yale Law Journal* 240.

[28] MB Clinard, *Cities with Little Crime* (Cambridge, CUP, 1978).

[29] F Balvig, *The Snow White* Image: *The Hidden Reality of Crime in Switzerland* (Oslo, Norwegian University Press, 1987).

with prison policy in the Netherlands.[30] His Dutch critics, actually living there, were much more cynical.[31] On the basis of relatively short research visits, Adam Crawford criticises King, who lived for some years in France, for failing to see the downside of the French approach to crime prevention.[32] What seems to be most relevant to all these disagreements is the way the study of foreign cultures is so often 'really' more about debates in the home country. All we can reasonably assert is that the more time spent in a country the more chance the researcher has to become interested in understanding it in its own terms rather than be concerned only to discover or debate the lessons it supposedly has to teach those back home.

From this it might seem to follow that living in a society is the only really sound way to understanding it. Whilst there is something in this, it needs to be underlined that no methodology is ideal for all purposes. The choice to follow any particular approach to data gathering in comparative research will be linked to the many considerations which influence the feasibility of a given research project; the time available, whether one is able to visit the country concerned, and with what sort of commitment. Different research strategies have different merits and there are the usual tradeoffs, such as being able to cover more cases with questionnaires or interviews as opposed to in depth observation, and so on. Often there will be reasons to try for a mix of methodologies. Given the heavy investment required by going abroad for long periods, however, it is worthwhile to conclude by discussing what specific insights it can offer as well as what may be the disadvantages of this type of research.

There are certainly undeniable advantages to 'living there' for the purposes of comparative research. Spending a longish period in a society gives you a better chance to get relevant ideas about law and justice straight (or at least straighter) than more brief exposure, which can easily get things out of proportion. At the same time, you can also witness social change at first hand. Once one grants the point that crime and criminal justice are not artificially cut off from the rest of social life, being involved in everyday living offers a rich source of opportunities for interaction in the worlds of family, school, work and so on. Living in a country allows you to see whether you have a grasp of the way the culture works through the experience of trying to work with (or round) the rules and through making (or losing) group affiliations. Moving country as an adult moreover usually requires one to go through a process of re-socialisation, which tends to reveals some basic and sometimes painful truths about local methods of social control! And, as pre-

---

[30] D Downes, *Contrasts in Tolerance* (Oxford, OUP, 1988).

[31] H Franke, 'Dutch Tolerance: Facts and Fallacies' (1990) 30 *British Journal of Criminology* 81–93.

[32] M King, 'Social Crime Prevention à la Thatcher' (1989) 28 *Howard Journal of Criminal Justice* 291–312.

viously explained, long-term involvement in a culture can be invaluable in allowing you to grasp the intellectual and political affiliations of your and other people's informants. A further advantage of actually living in a country comes from being better placed to convey in a convincing way the experience of what Geertz calls 'being there'.[33] Whether this be seen as some sort of solution to the otherwise paralysing post-modern 'crisis of representation', or, more straightforwardly, as a way of dealing with the suspicion that one has not really got to grips with the culture being re-presented, there is no doubt that the descriptions that most influence an audience often take the form of vignettes drawn from life. The more opportunities to do this the more convincing the story that can be told. The story *of* the research comes to join the stories *in* the research.

But there are also some disadvantages. When you live in a place you can no longer pretend a useful naiveté. And once you have a recognised internal identity those with other loyalties will be less willing to trust you, and everyone will be in competition with you for scarce resources. This means that the insider-outsider is not someone above it all, without a role. Rather, he or she occupies exactly that role, which means that his or her experience corresponds neither to that of the native nor to that of the real outsider. There is also the danger of generalising too much and taking the part for the whole. The places where you live and work will not necessarily be representative of all other places, and you lack the long historical memory of the real insider. Because you can experience directly only a small slice of life you are still largely reliant on other people, like those who use the other methodological approaches, for ideas and information which lie beyond your direct experience. There is, finally, also the well-known problem of 'going native'. For those who move country as adults the problem can certainly be exaggerated, especially given the ease nowadays of keeping in touch with the country of origin. But it is true that as time passes your questions tend to lose their mooring in your original starting point and come to be linked more to the society in which you find yourself. In this partly positive sense you do indeed begin to go native. You are also led to examine how and why your own point of view has changed over time and so may even begin to question whether you ever really understood your own culture of origin. As you look back 'with others' eyes' you may come to realise that you saw your society before only as an insider and ethnocentric native. As an insider-outsider, striving to understand one society in the light of another, you may be able to manage the difficult trick of losing one type of ethnocentrism without taking on another. But, even if this can be achieved, the price which may then have to be paid is to find that the questions you now want to ask are not considered salient and important ones either by the audience in your original society or in that where you now live!

---

[33] C Geertz, *Works and Lives* (Cambridge, Polity Press, 1988).

13

Researching Legal Culture in Russia: From Asking the Question to Gathering the Evidence[1]

MARINA KURKCHIYAN

THIS PAPER GIVES an account of the steps that were taken to carry out a research project on the legal culture of post-soviet Russia. I intend to discuss what decisions were made and why; what was lost and what was achieved in the process of moving from the abstract initial research question to the practical business of collecting data; and the eventual outcome of the enterprise, which consisted—as is often the way with scholarly research—of realising the need to formulate a whole new set of questions. Hopefully, those new questions will be better-informed, and there will be some benefit to socio-legal studies in recording the internal logic that guided the project. Because the focus here is on the method rather than the substance, the findings themselves will not be discussed in detail.[2]

It follows that this paper deals with only some of the tasks required for a description of a completed project. The full sequence goes from stating an initial puzzle [the research question] to formulating practical questions about it [the research design], then to collecting answers to those questions [fieldwork], onward to analysis of the answers [findings], and finally to assessing the findings in the context of the initial puzzle [conclusions]. In the present discussion, the emphasis is on the first two stages. I shall look back at the questions that I had to ask myself and answer, from posing a research question through to collecting data about it.

[1] I would like to thank the staff at the Moscow School of Economic and Social Sciences, and in particular its rector Professor Teodor Shanin, for their generous provision of institutional support during my fieldwork in September and October 2002. I am also indebted to the many helpful people in various walks of life in Russia who helped me to establish the necessary contacts and arrange interviews.

[2] The findings of the research project were presented at the Law and Society Annual Conference, Pittsburgh, June 2003, and a publication is forthcoming.

Through its concentration on empiricism and on the formal requirements of disciplined method, the paper supports the validity of the research. Validity is generally defined as a consistency between what we measure and what we believe we measure. It is often a painful issue for researchers involved in empirical study, because they are vulnerable to the charge of employing what may appear to be a messy and iterative process of conceptualisation and data collection.[3]

Although in this study of Russian legal culture the appropriate methodological procedures were scrupulously executed and the volume of data collected was substantial, the project did have at least one characteristic of a pilot study. It started with a very broad research question, which caused it to lead to a correspondingly broad set of findings and conclusions. For this reason, the conclusions are probably best regarded as a set of hypotheses accompanied by suggestions about how to test them, even if the hypotheses are firmly grounded and the procedural recommendations are suitably well informed. Nevertheless a project aimed at a dependent variable as abstract as 'culture' did make it possible to acquire some insights into the overall shape of large-scale social change, and it also opened avenues for further inquiries into the specific processes set in motion by societal transition.

A. THE RESEARCH QUESTION

As is often the case, my basic question about Russian legal culture was formed at a crossroad where intuition, direct observation and research experience all came together. Being a researcher interested in all aspects of the post-soviet transition, I wondered whether people's dealings with the law might be changing. My interest was in the causal relationships at work in contemporary Russian society. The idea that socio-economic change tends to transform a society's legal culture is not new; mention of it can be found in the work of leading authorities on the sociology of law.[4] But is the amount of change in the legal culture significant enough to be treated as a dimension of the transition, and if so how could it be measured?

As a regular visitor to Moscow, I have noticed that since the mid–1990s law has steadily gained in prominence as the society has acquired a post-communist pattern. The country has been equipped with a relatively coherent body of legislation, and the process of lawmaking has become more transparent. There is more attention to law, so that ordinary people are becoming more knowledgeable about legislation and more willing to consult professionals if they get into trouble. In media analysis of public affairs,

---

[3] On issues on validity in qualitative research see J Kirk and ML Miller, *Reliability and Validity in Qualitative Research* (Beverley Hills, CA, Sage, 1986).

[4] R Cotterrell, 'Is there a Logic of Legal Transplants?' in D Nelken and J Feest, (eds), *Adapting Legal Culture* (Oxford, Hart Publishing, 2001) 71–92.

legal arguments have become common although they were once a rarity. Business is being conducted in a more orderly way, even at the level of street trading. It is clear that the law has changed, in procedure, content and institutions, and the changes seem to be continuing.

What is not clear, however, is whether thirteen years of transplanting, adapting and introducing the letter of the law have brought about a popular acceptance of a spirit of law. Have the expanded volume of laws and the increased number of lawyers created more genuine legality and respect for law into Russian society? What path is Russia following towards the development of its legal environment? Taking all these together, how has the post-soviet transition affected Russian legal culture? That is the question that inspired my research in the autumn of 2002.

B. EXPLORING CONCEPTS

To break the general research question down into a set of researchable ones, three concepts were adopted: legal culture itself, tradition, and transition. As the principal concern of the inquiry, 'legal culture' demanded a workable definition. What could the term mean? Which indicators would capture it? How could it be made 'visible' in concrete research? The second concept, tradition, emerged from the realisation that if the study dealt with change, there had to be something to compare the findings with. I settled upon the concept of 'traditional Russian legal culture', to be used as a starting point against which both transitional change and the current status of legal culture in Russian society could be examined. The final concept to be held up for examination was the post-communist 'transition'. In what ways, and why, was the transitional process thought likely to affect legal culture, and where should the changes be looked for?

1. Legal Culture

A browse through the literature on legal culture suggests that the concept is vague and open-ended. When scholars attempt to define it, they find themselves dividing into different camps on a variety of aspects. Clearly it is at its most useful for empirical research if it is defined narrowly, but most writers see benefit in defining it widely. Which social entity should be identified as a carrier of legal culture—the law professionals alone, or specific social groups who are not themselves associated with the law, or society as a whole? Or would it be reasonable to go even beyond that to the international level?[5] Should the definition lead to a quantifiable measure of legal

---

[5] On the definition of legal culture, see the exchange between R Cotterrell and L M Friedman in D Nelken, (ed), *Comparing Legal Cultures* (Aldershot, Dartmouth, 1997); for the

culture, such as the number of litigated cases? Or can legal culture be understood better by observing people's behaviour and recording the attitudes that they adopt and the language that they use whenever they speak about topics related to the law?[6]

Among these competing opinions on the interpretation of legal culture, two of the more prominent approaches deserve to be singled out. One is strict and narrow, focussing on the legal institution. It deals with issues related to law itself such as the activities of courts and other legal organisations, the models used for legal education in different countries, the values and behaviour of law professionals and the history of legal tradition.[7] The other is more contextual, analysing law in the setting of the wider context of the numerous social relationships that feel its impact. In this perspective law is embedded in the texture of a particular society and cannot easily be separated from it.[8] The approach lays particular emphasis on the law's main function, its contribution to the maintenance of order.

Having a research interest in how the post-Soviet transformation of social environment has affected the way in which people deal with the law, left me with no choice but to adopt the broader approach. It would have been inappropriate (though it was tempting) to simplify the inquiry by examining a single example of legal culture such as the newly introduced jury system, or an important social group such as the politicians. From a methodological point of view it would have been even safer to opt for a statistics-based procedure and examine the trends in litigation, or the patterns displayed by human rights cases, or the characteristics of economic disputes brought before the arbitration courts. If I had chosen to take that path I would have gained the benefit of unquestionably valid research findings and perhaps also some insight into the dynamics of a particular, albeit narrow, aspect of legal culture. But I would have lost the larger perspective and the overview of the way in which social institutions relate to one another. A wide-focus approach also supplies the data needed to address the largest questions, about the role of law and the meaning that Russian society allocates to law after having had its basic principles reshuffled by the transition. In other words, there was a tradeoff; what I would gain in the certainty

---

globalisation context see J Friedman, *Cultural Identity and Global Process* (London, Sage, 1994). Also on the 'internal' versus 'external' dichotomy in the sociology of law see R Banakar, *Merging Law and Sociology* (Berlin, Galda & Wilch Verlag, 2003).

[6] See E Blankenburg and F Bruinsma, *Dutch Legal Culture* (London, Kluwer Law International, 1994); and the commentary by D Nelken, 'Puzzling out Legal Culture: A Comment on Blankenburg' in D Nelken, (ed), *Comparing Legal Cultures* (Aldershot, Dartmouth, 1997).

[7] See the collection of papers in C Varga, (ed), *Comparative Legal Culture* (Aldershot, Dartmouth, 1992).

[8] See V Gessner, 'The Transformation of European Legal Cultures' in V Gessner, *et al*, *European Legal Cultures* (Aldershot, Dartmouth, 1996).

of my findings, I would lose in perspective on Russian society during the Putin era.

I therefore decided to work with the concept of legal culture as a reflection of the role that law plays in the society. If the role of law depends on the social environment in which it operates, then it will not be the same from one country to another. It is determined by such variables as people's attitudes to law, their expectations of how everyone else will behave towards the law, and the interplay of political institutions with the agents of the law such as police officers, lawyers and judges. Most importantly, it is determined by the professionalism—or lack of it—of those who work in the legal institution itself. In the widest possible terms, then, the role of law depends on the principles upon which social order is founded in that particular society; on what its dominant values happen to be; and on which form of problem-solving people are in the habit of choosing.[9]

With the definitional choice made, the next methodological question was how to measure legal culture when it is used in such a wide sense. I answered that by choosing to interpret the way in which people use language as an index of cultural meanings. I then set about recording what people said when they told me what they thought of the law, and also what they said indirectly about it while describing their own or other people's dealing with it. I also observed directly how people handled matters relating to law, both in their business dealings and in their instinctive reactions to challenging situations in everyday life.

2. Traditional Legal Culture in Russia

Any discussion of social change must begin with a judgment about where it starts from. So in this study, before I could test to establish whether there had been a shift to a new legal culture, I needed to have a clear understanding of what the old one was like. But how could the traditional legal culture in Russia be described? What were the distinct characteristics that needed to be monitored? The literature showed that everyone who was familiar either with soviet society or with pre-communist Russia would agree that law had never been among the dominant forces there, either in organising everyday life or in maintaining political stability. Commentators also agreed that the Russian people had long been cynical about law, and

---

[9] For discussion of the role of law in post-soviet Russia see M Kurkchiyan, 'The Illegitimacy of Law in Post-Soviet Societies' in D Galligan and M Kurkchiyan, (eds), *Law and Informal Practices: the Post-Communist Experience* (Oxford, OUP, 2003); P Murrell, (ed), *Assessing the Value of Law in Transitional Economies* (Ann Arbor, MI, University of Michigan, 2001); JD Sachs and K Pristol, (eds), *The Rule of Law and Economic Reform in Russia* (Oxford, Westview Press, 1997).

would not normally take it for granted either that legally correct behaviour would be rewarded or that illegal behaviour would be justly punished.[10]

In the literature on transition one can identify at least three explanations of the disrespectful way in which the public deals with law in post-Soviet Russia. Some authors attempt to explain it by current economic difficulties, or by the shortage of resources, or by the obviously bad leadership.[11] They argue that the questionable practices that they observe cannot be ascribed to culture. Their underlying argument is that although corruption is pervasive and illegalities of every kind are widespread, ordinary people in Russia should not carry the blame. In my view this argument is weak. It is significant that appropriate responses, such as making increased resources available for the public services or disproportionately increasing the salaries of civil servants, do not usually reduce corruption; often the opposite is true. Also, the emergence of an honest leadership within a corrupt environment is known to be unlikely, and in any case it is never clear whether leaders corrupt their followers or vice-versa.

Others tend to explain the Russian approach to law by attributing it to the soviet legacy.[12] The habits of being negative, cynical and disposed to cheat, they suggest, can be put down to the communist past. When ideological politics dominated all spheres of public life, the consequential hypocrisy encouraged sinecures, nepotism and bribery. There is little doubt that those 70 years did indeed leave a strong imprint on popular psychology and behaviour. But the Bolshevik Revolution did not happen in a historical vacuum. Lenin and his colleagues were attracted to the omnipotent secret police, the total centralisation, the instantly enforceable decrees and other features of the way things were done by the Tsars before 1917. They might not have admitted to such anti-progressive decisions, but they certainly adopted some features of the pre-existing political, social and legal culture.

My inclination, however, leans toward a third group of scholars, who suggest that in order to understand Russian society we need to probe farther back in history.[13] In doing so it is important not to fall into the trap of determinism, because societal modifications clearly do follow from explo-

---

[10] J Kampfner, *Inside Yeltsin's Russia* (London, Cassell, 1994) p x.

[11] C Humphrey and D Sneath, 'Shanghaied by the Bureaucracy: Bribery and Post-Soviet Officialdom in Russia and Mongolia' in I Pardo, (ed), *Corruption Between Morality and Law* (Dartmouth, Ashgate, 2004) pp 85–100; JL Gibson, 'Russian Attitudes Toward the Rule of Law' in Galligan and Kurkchiyan, above n 9, p 77–92.

[12] EP Hoffmann, 'Democratic Theory and Authority Patterns in Contemporary Russian Politics' in H Eckstein, *et al*, (eds), *Can Democracy Take Root in Post-Soviet Russia?* (Lanham, MD, Rowman and Littlefield, 1998) 105; K Jowitt, *New World Disorder: The Leninist Extinction* (Berkeley, CA, University of California Press, 1992); PH Solomon 'Legality in Soviet Political Culture' in N Lampert and GT Rittersporn, (eds), *Stalinism: Its Nature and Aftermath* (New York, NY, ME Sharpe, 1992) 260.

[13] See for instance M Newcity, 'Russian Legal Tradition and the Rule of Law' in JD Sachs and K Pristol, (eds), *The Rule of Law and Economic Reform in Russia* (Oxford, Westview Press, 1997).

sions like 1920s communism and 1990s capitalism. But even a glance at Russian legal culture through history reveals points that are relevant to research on today's legal culture.

To understand the Russian way of thinking and doing things, it is help-ful to bear in mind that the Russian tradition was rooted in the Byzantine culture and then cultivated throughout the Middle Ages by the Russian Orthodox Church. Being part of the 'Byzantine Commonwealth,'[14] Russia adopted the Roman legal code at an early stage. Thereafter it never experi-enced a formal separation of civil law from canon law, and until the 1990s it never had to adjust to the emergence of independent institutions.[15]

The scarcity of surviving data on Byzantine society leaves considerable room for speculation about how to interpret it, but it is widely accepted that it was a highly efficient social order held in place by a rigid political framework. Its organising principles were the primacy of political relation-ships, the dominance of a single undivided power, and a complete hierarchy of statuses from the top to the bottom of the whole society. It was radical-ly different from the slowly evolving legal norms, the continuous interplay between different branches of power, and the shifting coalitions of loyalties found elsewhere.[16]

In such a system, it is the power hierarchy, not the body of law, that keeps society together and enables it to function. Like all forms of social organisation, the model both shapes and is shaped by the way of thinking that rationalises it. It is underpinned by appropriate values such as loyalty, stability, patronage, and authority. The values are continually reaffirmed by habits and accepted practices in legal and bureaucratic activity that corre-spond directly to them. For example, one of its expressions is the Byzantine tradition of legal argumentation, which puts the recitation of dogma and the citation of authoritative quotations firmly ahead of logical reasoning, empirical analysis of evidence and resort to independent judgment.[17] Furthermore, the Byzantine tradition esteems an ability to take this style of discourse to the greatest possible lengths.

A society organised along such lines does not favour the growth of for-mal institutions managed by impersonal bureaucracies in the Weberian sense, and Russian institutions evolved quite differently.[18] At every level,

---

[14] The term 'Byzantine Commonwealth' was suggested and developed by D Obolensky. See D Obolensky, *The Byzantine Commonwealth: Eastern Europe, 500–1453* (London, Weidenfield and Nicholson, 1971).

[15] HJ Berman, *Justice in Russia* (Cambridge, MA, Harvard University Press, 1950) 127.

[16] On Byzantine society see AP Kazhdan and G Constable, *People and Power in Byzantium: An Introduction to Modern Byzantine Studies* (Washington DC, Dumbarton Oaks, Center for Byzantine Studies, Trustees for Harvard University, 1982).

[17] HJ Berman, *Justice in Russia* (Cambridge, MA, Harvard University Press, 1950) 116.

[18] On law in Byzantine see RJ Macrides, *Kinship and Justice in Byzantium, 11th–15th Centuries* (Aldershot, Ashgate, 1999) 187–96, ch XII; and HJ Berman, *Justice in Russia*

those in superior positions would grant special favours in exchange for the promise of loyal support by their inferiors, so that the working relationship was based on maintaining that relationship—not upon the law, nor upon the rationality of an order, nor upon getting the job done. What mattered was the political power of the person giving the instructions. If there was a universal understanding that loyalty was extended to a person, not to an office, and was always conditional upon reciprocal benefit, then rights and obligations were meaningless ideas.

The well-recorded attempt of Peter the Great to modernise the system in the 17th century was followed by that of Catherine II in the 18th century, by Alexander I and then by Nicholas I in the 19th century, and of course in the 20th century twice, by the early Bolsheviks and yet again by Gorbachev under late communism.[19] However, none of those reforms went far enough, which is why the Byzantine resonance remained so strong in the Russian society of 2002. Whenever reform was tried, the 'new' law was imposed by power—power being a commodity of which the state had a generous supply. While ordinary people changed their ways to fit the new law, the dominant elites stayed above it, unchanged. Although each reform did have a noticeable impact, none succeeded in modifying the fundamental interplay between law, politics and society. Even the revolution, despite being violent enough to tear most pillars of the social structure of the society away from their foundations, actually reinforced the political pillar—thereby extending the traditional Russian dominance of the political forces in society over the legal and economic ones.

In short, injections of law in Russia were never intended to make it competitive to the political will, and certainly never succeeded in doing so. Consequently law was never sufficiently empowered to enable it to become the main ordering principle in society. The entire legal institution in Russia has always been politically weak and underfunded, with little social prestige, and vulnerable to the manipulation that perpetuates its low status. Russian bureaucracy, in addition to being powerful and corrupt, has always worked on the basis of exchange of favours. Being secondary to political forces, law in Russia long ago acquired an instrumental character. It was used as a tool of the political leadership, for social engineering, for education, for moral instruction, for legitimisation of policies, for whatever task the rulers might choose—but never for creating a rule of law and not of men.[20]

(Cambridge, MA, Harvard University Press, 1950) 119; S Kucherov, *Courts, Lawyers and Trials under the Last Three Tsars* (New York, NY, FA Praeger, 1953).

[19] For a brief account of Russian reforms see R David and JEC Brierley, *Major Legal Systems in the World Today* (London, Stevens, 1985) 159–215.

[20] On the instrumental character of law, see D Galligan, 'Legal Failure: Law and Social Norms in Post-Communist Europe' in D Galligan and M Kurkchiyan, (eds), *Law and Informal Practices: The Post-Communist Experience* (Oxford, OUP, 2003) 1–24.

Not surprisingly, other potentially important components of society in Russia, especially the economic institutions, have always been more sensitive to the political climate than to law. If a private citizen needed anything, from a building permit to a defence against a criminal charge, it was more useful to know the right people than to know the right law. So he or she would seek personal access to a senior official, knowing that success was more likely to come his way in response to an *ad hoc* directive than through the routine application of abstract law to a particular case.

3. Transition

Since the collapse of the Soviet Union at the end of the 1980s, Russia has been making a serious attempt to modernise its society by restructuring all its institutions simultaneously—a project known as the 'post-soviet transition'.[21] The leadership, driven along by the impersonal forces of globalisation and warmly encouraged by foreign governments and international agencies, has energetically promoted the entire revolutionary process. The former USSR has been showered with consultants, advisers, observers, scrutineers and evaluators in every professional field.

The transition had ambitious goals. Initially it was intended to produce change in the governmental, economic and foreign policy systems, and subsequently in the entire social fabric of the country, everywhere and at every level. In politics, the reforms were supposed to transform Russia from an authoritarian regime into a transparently liberal democracy. In production, trade and distribution, there was to be a shift from centralised allocation to a competitive free market. And in international relations, the secretive, defensive regime of soviet times was to give way to an internationally-minded society, cooperative with the dominant western 'club' and fully integrated into global networks of communication and exchange.

(a) Transition to Democracy

To achieve the transition to democracy a new constitution was adopted in 1993. It laid the foundation for building up independent institutions such as a parliament, a judiciary, political parties, and an array of privately owned media. Subsequently, legislation was introduced to shield these new bodies from improper external influences.[22] But how well do these demo-

---

[21] On different aspects of the post-soviet transition see L Holmes, *Post-Communism* (Cambridge, Polity Press, 1997); and A Brown, (ed), *Contemporary Russian Politics* (Oxford, OUP, 2001).

[22] On post-soviet Russian legislation see WE Butler, *Russian Law* (Oxford, OUP, 2003); on democratisation in Russia see J Kahn, *Federalism, Democratisation, and the Rule of Law in Russia* (Oxford, OUP, 2002).

cratic initiatives work in practice? Has legality started to prevail? Has the introduction of a legal framework modelled upon western democracy led to a significant change in the way that the Russian people relate to law, as revealed by their attitude or their conduct?

Ideally, the way to arrive at a valid answer to this question would have been to scrutinise the legal culture within each of the main institutions subjected to democratic reforms. Doing that, however, would have been a major research project in itself, requiring greater resources than were available. I therefore chose instead to concentrate my scrutiny on the groups collectively described in socio-legal studies as 'the legal institution' itself. These are the judges, the barristers, the lawyers in private practice—that is, the legal professionals working exclusively on legal matters. The decision to concentrate on practices within the Russian legal institution was also predetermined by the initial research question. Self-evidently, the behaviour of lawyers themselves represents part of legal culture, and the legal institution is also a significant indicator of progress in democratising the wider society. As a slight widening of this focus, I decided to allocate any remaining time and effort to the interplay between the legal institution and the rest of society. In the event, that widening enabled me to examine the imprint of market forces on legal culture and to probe into the effects of opening up Russian society to foreign cultural influences.

All aspects of the public record—secondary literature, official documents, policy statements, successive acts of parliament—show that the legal institution attracted close attention from Russia's reformers in the transition decade, starting with the judiciary.[23] The 1992 Law on the Status of Judges established the principle of life appointment for judges and stipulated that their removal could come about only by the decision of a judicial qualification committee. There was also an attempt to ensure that sufficient resources for the judiciary would be allocated from the state budget, so as to allow them to operate independently.

Equally serious intentions are evident in relation to the legislative process, in which noticeable improvements have been made. The entire task of lawmaking has become more transparent, and the resultant body of law as a whole has become more consistent and stable. Nowadays, draft laws are published and openly debated. The media are given full opportunities to observe both the legislative process and the implementation of law in the courtrooms.

In consequence of this enhancement of legal institutions at the official level, an impressive increase in the number of professionals offering legal services has taken place. By 2002 one could see the dignified nameplates of newly established law firms and legal consultancies in every corner of the

---

[23] On judicial reforms in Russia see PH Solomon and TS Foglesong, *Courts and Transition in Russia: The Challenge of Judicial Reform* (Oxford, Westview, 2000).

city. There is good business for them, generated by a steady increase in the number of cases in which citizens choose to pursue their disputes by taking them to court.[24] There have also been substantial attempts to set up effective regulation, both for the legal profession as a whole and for the activities of its various agencies and organisations. My research coincided with the passage of a well-publicised new law intended to bring about the regulation of the advocacy services and of the Russian Advocacy Bar.

Overall, there is no doubt that we are witnessing the building up of a new legal institution in Russia. Its growth has already had a substantial effect on both the demand and supply sides of law.[25] Convincing evidence to demonstrate the scale and importance of that expansion has been assembled and reported by a number of researchers.[26] It is safe to conclude that the perceived value of law has increased in Russian society, meaning that it is much more actively in play today than it was even at the dawn of the Millennium in 2000. It is apparent that people generally, or at least those in Moscow, no longer have any problem in making the judgment of just when and how to bring law into the game.

However, it still remains to be seen whether we are indeed observing a qualitative change and not merely a quantitative one. It is one thing to note an increase in the number of events in which law plays a part, another to observe a shift in the relative importance of the legal factor in the situation compared to other factors, or an even deeper shift in the fundamental rules of life in society. In order to determine how significant the change really was, I included a number of specific questions in the research design. Given that the legal institution in Russia now enjoys legal and economic protection from outside influences for the first time in its history, how freely does it operate? What signals are the prominent legal bodies transmitting to the rest of the society? Have they started to convey a message that law is a valuable force for co-ordinating life in the society and a reliable means of problem-solving? Is the legal institution cultivating and defending a strong identity as a guardian of law in the society, or is professional identity only a secondary value in the self-image of the senior figures in the profession? How does the new situation affect the behaviour of lawyers, legislators and judges? If, after all the reforms, the institution still fails to display clear indications of its independence and integrity, then why? What are the sources and the mechanisms of the outside pressures?

---

[24] K Hendley, 'Suing the State in Russia' (2002) 18(2) *Post-Soviet Affairs* 122–47.
[25] On the demand and supply of law in Russia see K Pistor, 'Supply and Demand for Law in Russia' (1999) 8(4) *East European Constitutional Review.*
[26] GP Hendrix, 'The Experience of Foreign Litigants in Russian's Commercial Court' in P Murrell, (ed), *Assessing the Value of Law in Transitional Economies* (Ann Arbor, MI, University of Michigan Press) 94; K Hendley, 'Enforcing Judgements in Russian Economic Courts: Is Going to Court a Waste of Time?' Paper presented in *Annual Meeting of the Law and Society Association,* 5–8 June 2003, Pittsburgh, PA.

(b) Transition to a Free Market

Another dimension of the post-soviet transition is the transformation of the planned economy into a free market of the western type. According to classical economic theory, a market requires legality.[27] Effective law increases market efficiency by reducing the risks of business transactions and by protecting deals, both from delays and from arbitrary interference at the hands of bureaucrats.[28] Should we therefore assume that in parallel with the strengthening of the Russian market during the 1990s and even more during the boom years of the early 2000s, the law is also becoming a framework within which to manage dealings between business firms and to regulate relations between them and the state?[29]

Many sectors of commerce and industry are now fully marketised. Reforms began with the communist 'restructuring' programme of the 1980s, and since then Russia has experienced large-scale privatisation of nearly all the many forms of property formerly owned by the state: land, facilities for transport and communication, most of the public utilities, entire industries and services. Property ownership is secured by law, together with the necessary supporting apparatus of registries and associated procedures. A legal framework for enforcing contracts and otherwise maintaining orderly market relationships is largely in place. A formal mechanism for the resolution of economic disputes has been introduced. Although the new Russian market is obviously underdeveloped and remains relatively small by OECD standards, it has nevertheless taken shape. In the harsh judgment of fund managers on the London and New York stock markets, it has recently come to be regarded as one of the promising investments in the 'emerging economy' category.

Perhaps more importantly, there have been indications in the Putin era that transitional Russia is beginning to grow out of the initial phase in which it was labelled 'The Wild East' for its disorderly character, corrupt practices and violent criminality. In little more than a decade, the economy has already generated a capitalist class composed of business leaders, landowners, lenders and investors. All are keen to protect their rights and interests, and many are now sufficiently confident and strong enough to undertake legal

---

[27] On the relationship between the complexity of economic relations and law see P Stein, *Legal Evolution: The Story of an Idea* (New York, NY, CUP, 1980).

[28] Of course, greed does encourage some western firms to play sophisticated games with law. But many will argue that in the long run the market has a self-regulating capacity to protect itself from any illegalities that could distort it.

[29] In well-established markets, law does of course perform multiple functions including the regulation of relations between employers and workers. However, if professional (and therefore costly) legal services were to be made fully available in today's Russia, there is no obvious force that would drive demand for them: there is high unemployment, trade unions are extremely weak, and informal practices that solve problems at low cost are readily understood, expected and accepted.

action against individuals and organisations in the political system. Statistics suggest that suing the state has become common practice in Russia in the past few years, and that the number of litigations initiated by private companies is increasing.

The scale of the capital stock accumulated in the hands of the successful 'new Russians' is already huge, and the small group of entrepreneurs with holdings in the energy sector are among the world's richest. Merely to own so much automatically transforms them from free-wheeling innovators into risk-averse conservatives; they have acquired an objective interest in securing a safe, stable and predictable business environment in which to put their capital into play. Given that a disproportionately large chunk of the capital and business activities in all Russia are concentrated in Moscow, it is reasonable to expect that if indeed the development of an advanced market is sufficient in itself to bring legality to the whole system (that is, regardless of what the politicians do), then the process should be detectable in that city.

Having this in mind, and with an interest in how the coming of the market has affected the way that people think about law and deal with it in business transactions, I devised a set of questions to use in my inquiries. What meaning does the business community in Russia nowadays attach to the main legal instrument of exchange, the contract? What status do lawyers occupy in Russian companies, and what role do they play? How is communication evolving between business firms and the central government, in particular with the Tax Revenue Office? What is the preferred means of handling conflicts between business firms, and what happens when they come into conflict with the state? When, how, and on the basis of what assumptions do businesses choose to use the court system? Obviously, a complete answer to some of these questions would require massive research. But to gather all the details on matters such as tax was not my aim. What I wanted to discover was whether evidence existed to suggest that people in business firms are changing their attitudes towards law, and whether or not the law is gaining ground as an organising and regulating force in Russian commerce and industry.

(c) Transition to an Open Society

The end of the Cold War signalled a new relationship between Russia and the West, and it enhanced communication at every level. Government officials held consultations with western experts on designing and implementing reforms, business leaders formed collegial relations with their foreign counterparts, professionals and technicians were sent abroad for training, students sought admission to overseas universities rather than domestic ones, international collaboration on specific projects became more significant in every field, and the substantial numbers of Russians who travelled to the West as casual visitors began to cultivate their own understanding of how other societies work.

Today there are numerous and extremely varied channels of contact, communication and exchange between Russia and the West. In many thousands of occupations and activities, their existence undoubtedly facilitates a two-way flow of ideas and is capable of stimulating critical reflection on the traditional ways of doing things in Russia. Their actual impact, however, inevitably varies in both nature and extent. Globalising influences such as brand-name consumer goods or television soap operas reach virtually all members of the society, whereas an ethical code for stock market regulation reaches only a few people because it is of necessity localised and relatively esoteric in character. In this project I needed to find a means to assess the effect of external contact on the legal culture, so it was necessary to narrow the research focus down a single activity in which the building up of an image of the western concept of law is empirically detectable and potentially at its most intense. I chose to examine the interaction between western and Russian businesses, and among them especially the law firms, while fully appreciating that this was only facet of the much wider opening up of the entire society and its legal culture.

There is no need to employ sophisticated methodology to discover the scale and importance of the active western presence in Russia, especially in Moscow. Although some western or jointly owned companies abandoned their Russian operations during the financial crisis of the late 1990s, a substantial number remained—many of them staffed by local people—and others returned as the economy improved from 2000 onwards.

Western lawyers have followed western businesses. A collection of prominent western law firms have now established branch offices in Moscow, and most of them make it a policy to stick almost entirely to the western way of dealing with clients. If they employ Russian lawyers, they provide special training for them. The opening of the borders enabled many would-be lawyers of the 1990s to acquire their education outside Russia, and even those who did not do that mostly found ways to travel. As a result, many of the practising lawyers to whom I spoke to had western experience. Some had earned their full qualifications abroad while others had taken shorter courses or had occupied work placements with firms in Boston or London. Many were working with foreign partners in Moscow.

In this situation, I deduced that western cultural influence should be visible both directly, in the form of transplanted law reinforced by the local operations of multinational law firms, and indirectly through the many business deals that Russian companies make with foreign companies. Education is also a powerful channel of cultural transfer. Western courses and degrees in law, management, accounting and related fields are widely available and enthusiastically taken up by Russian and especially Moscow-based citizens. In addition, the internalisation of western culture is likely to be facilitated by the increasing access of Russian citizens to international courts, both for their economic disputes and for the protection of their human rights.

But this is all in theory. My research was directed at what is happening in practice. What do Russians think of the western way of dealing with the law, and how do they respond to it? How do local firms perceive the western law firms operating in Russia, and vice-versa? How do they interpret and assess each other's working culture? What is the outcome of the interaction between the two cultures? Are we now witnessing convergence or divergence in the legal environment? These were among the questions that I sought to answer in my research.

C. HYPOTHESES

To summarize, then: in the early stage my research project I identified three major trends within the post-soviet transition and described the various social forces associated with each of them. I concluded that in theory it was reasonable to expect that together these trends would push Russian society towards greater law-abidingness. Once this preliminary analysis had been set out, it was a straightforward matter to reformulate it as a set of three working hypotheses. The hypotheses were necessary in order to determine who should be interviewed and what kind of data should be collected while discussing contemporary Russian life with them. The hypotheses were:

(i) If Russia has introduced the necessary and sufficient conditions for a professional legal institution, then the degree of legality in the country will increase.
(ii) If Russia has moved from a planned economy to a free market economy, then self-interest will strengthen the role of law in that economy.
(iii) If the transition is taking place in the era of globalisation, then traditional practices in relation to law will be displaced by internationally accepted practices.

D. DESIGNING THE DATA COLLECTION

To enter the field, I next had to decide where to go, whom to talk to and what to ask them.

1. Where to Go?

The first decision was where to conduct the research—in many towns, in a few selected towns, or in just one? I was conscious that Russia is both vast and diverse. It would not be reasonable to base generalisations about the whole nation upon data gathered in a single city, even one with the pre-eminence of Moscow. However, my aim was not to describe contemporary

Russian legal culture as such, but rather to detect the changes that have resulted from the transition. I therefore chose to concentrate my resources on Moscow. As the centre of virtually every kind of activity in Russia, the capital city is where innovation would take place first and it is self-evidently the best place to monitor its progress.

2. Whom to Interview?

Whom to interview is another controversial question that needed to be addressed and it is one that has strong methodological implications. In the wider sense the carriers of the legal culture are ordinary people who belong to the society and who continually reproduce its distinctive pattern of behaviour and way of thinking about law. Yet, the population has to be sampled in a way that is viable for in-depth interviews with a limited number of respondents. The sample has to be so constructed that it makes sense for the validity of the eventual conclusions and allows us to generalise the findings as a socially significant phenomenon. But how should those 'ordinary' people be singled out, and how 'ordinary' should they be?

In each case the answer is very much determined by the research question. For instance, in an attempt to discover how ordinary people frame their everyday problems in legal terms and interact with the legal system, John M Conley and William M O'Barr interviewed those who took their cases to informal courts in six American cities.[30] In a different project intended to map out the various degrees of legal consciousness across a population, Patricia Ewick and Susan S Silbey conducted 430 semi-structured interviews with residents of New Jersey asking each of them general questions about their lives and problems.[31]

I approached the task of selecting respondents with a research interest in how legal culture can change, together with the set of hypotheses that stemmed from my initial research question. That interest directed me to the group of people most likely to be the first to practice, observe and identify new approaches to law—if indeed they were happening. I constructed my sample from the widest available range of active players in the transition who were also carriers of the experience that I was trying to understand.

The selection was based on the assumptions that any member of the society could inform us about how their culture is practised and that there is no strict division between 'ordinary people' and those actively involved in dealing with law. However, it should be acknowledged that this research cannot

---

[30] JM Conley and WM O'Barr, *Rules versus Relationships: The Ethnography of Legal Discourse* (Chicago, IL, University of Chicago Press, 1990).

[31] P Ewick and S Silbey, *The Common Place of Law: Stories from Everyday Life* (Chicago, IL, University of Chicago Press, 1998).

provide findings that inform us about deep-down settled changes in the society. It will only provide findings about newly emerged tendencies that can be attributed directly to the transition.

One set[32] of 34 interviews consisted of legal specialists, representing different groups of the profession: 9 advocates, 5 judges, 6 partners in Russian and 5 partners in western-based commercial law firms, and 9 company lawyers. The second set, comprising 16 interviews, was drawn from businessmen in charge of operations in Moscow, together with representatives of western companies working with Russians. The third set, made up of 6 interviews, was with Moscow-based westerners. Of these, four were human rights advocates and two were teachers of law. Each was able to compare Russian practices with western ones after years of first hand experience of how things were done on both sides.

I conducted 56 lengthy interviews in total, and supplemented them by observation of two cases in the Moscow Arbitration Court and a frustrating visit to the Ministry of Justice. The Ministry visit was made in an attempt to obtain appropriate statistical data. Although it turned out to be unsuccessful, it was nevertheless exceptionally revealing.

3. What to Ask?

As is normally the case in qualitative research, the set of questions that I asked in my interviews varied by the category of respondent. In addition, regardless of whether the person I was talking to was a barrister, a company manager or a judge, the questionnaire evolved from interview to interview as new avenues of inquiry opened. For instance, the first two interviews made it clear that the Russian economic crisis in 1998 had made a strong impact on the legal environment inside the country. I therefore had become interested in how firms had changed their legal behaviour in response to the crisis, how entrepreneurs reinterpreted their relationship with the state, how the crisis affected the image of the West (which Russians generally blame for it), and whether people perceived the law as a means of mitigating the damage.

Interviews usually began with the personal experience of the interviewees before using selected answers to move to deeper questions about how things work. For instance, I asked respondents to describe their professional activities, the kind of problems that they commonly face, their work before and after 1998 crisis, and their experience of dealing with other players such as

---

[32] The sample listed here describes only the lengthy, prearranged interviews that were carried out. It does not include the many other interviews that were shorter and conducted spontaneously during the research trip, although taking notes and reflecting on them was a general practice throughout the project.

business partners and managers, the courts, their clients, other lawyers, the tax collectors, the bureaucrats, etc. There were also questions about if, when, and in what circumstances they were exposed to western practices. I was particularly keen to ask people to support their accounts with examples and stories.

In every interview, I asked a series of general questions about the informant's understanding of other people's behaviour in relation to law and their view on established practices. Those questions revealed the informal dealings in business that the respondent knew of, and produced data critical to the analysis of legal culture, dealing with the unwritten ethical code among legal professionals, the operation of the courts, the mechanisms whereby external influence could be imposed on judges' decisions, the interviewees' view of the western firms operating in Russia, and the prevailing interpretation of western legal culture.

The interviews commonly lasted between one and a half and two hours. There were five cases in which the respondents were particularly informative and helpful, and those meetings were continued on a second day.

E. RESEARCH OUTCOMES

It is beyond the scope of this methodological paper to go into the details of the analysis. As is often the case in conducting qualitative research (which I find very rewarding) preliminary scrutiny had to be done after each interview in order to adjust the next one, leaving the more systematic work to be carried out once the fieldwork was completed. In this paper I will present in outline those conclusions that gave some answers to the research question.

In relation to my first hypothesis I would suggest that the message is mixed. On the one hand the legal institution is taking a more sophisticated shape in that democratic reform has freed the judiciary from direct political pressure, professional knowledge is becoming more highly valued, and the law is not as easily dismissed as it used to be. On the other hand there is no evidence that the judiciary is acting independently in practice. Judges are involved in the networking and exchange relationship with bureaucracy and business as well as being committed to the law and to their families, which means that they can easily be influenced by several categories of people—local governors, wealthy businessmen, people higher up the judicial hierarchy, family members, close friends. It seems that the law has not been internalised even by the legal professionals, and that the undoubted enhancement in the sophistication of how people talk about law has not resulted in a significant change in the more important role that it actually plays in relationships within the society.

In relation to market forces, one can discern two tendencies in the way in which the operation of the free market affects the role of law in society.

First, the market demands that losses be reduced. Companies respond to that imperative. They attempt both to cut down on payments to the corrupt bureaucracy and also to reduce their transaction risks. The effect is that they significantly improve the legality of their internal documentation and management procedures.

Second, the evidence shows that the free market uses, benefits from, and therefore strengthens, informal practices—that is, the old and well-established customary ways of taking short cuts and solving problems informally by non-legal means. The market does not resist the traditional network pattern in which mutually beneficial relationships grow up between businessmen and bureaucrats. It is instead adapting to it and making the system work for itself. At this stage of my research I can see firm evidence that the market is bringing new rules to the private sector of the economy. But at the same time its impact is not sufficient to bring radical change in the way in which things have been done in the past. Informal dealings benefit not only the bureaucrats and politicians, but also the corporate owners and managers.

Clearly, the interaction between the western and Russian cultures of law and business has not led to their convergence. Russian lawyers and managers generally reject the idea that the west can offer them something new and valuable in terms of how to deal with law and how to run their businesses. Although it is true that the interactions and contacts each have a substantial value in themselves and that what has been learned cannot easily be unlearned, there are also clear indications that the legal norms transmitted through these cultural interactions have not been internalised—which makes the very concept of learning somewhat suspect in this case.

To sum up, after inquiring into the effects of the several different social forces generated by the transition on the way in which Russian society is organised and how it functions, I suggest that despite all the intentionally far-reaching reforms there is no strong evidence that law is being transformed from its instrumental role in society into its organising principle. That is not to say that the legal culture is not changing; it certainly is changing. People can undoubtedly talk law, and some extent they do it too. The use of law has become more intensive, more professional, more self-conscious, more prestigious and more aggressive. More businessmen are resorting to law and more firms are practising it. But even so, I would argue that Russia is not on the way to a rule of law culture. Something new and quite different is being formed there, something that combines the glossy outward trappings of western law with the more cynical inward conniving of the Russian tradition.

Section Six

Socio-Legal Research in the UK

REZA BANAKAR AND MAX TRAVERS

I N THIS SECTION, we turn our attention to socio-legal research and debate in Britain. The first chapter, by Michael Adler, provides an example of how empirical research can address questions of interest to government departments. The last two chapters, written by Andrew Boon and Max Travers, discuss two developments that have changed the nature of socio-legal research, and are generating debate in Britain and internationally. The focus on the UK allows us to draw attention, very briefly, to some of the differences and similarities between various research orientations in continental Europe, the US and the UK.[1]

We have so far used 'socio-legal research' as a general term for three types of research. Firstly, there is empirical research that addresses the questions asked about law by black-letter lawyers and practitioners. This often views social science instrumentally as something that can be used to address legal concerns (the idea, famously expressed in the first issue of the *Journal of Law and Society*, that sociology should be 'on tap' rather than 'on top').[2] There is also the idea that one must acknowledge a wider context to law and legal institutions, but without engaging with the many theoretical and political debates in sociology about how to understand society. Secondly, there is the research conducted for government departments and agencies, such as the courts and police. Finally, there is research that engages with central issues in social theory.

This indiscriminate approach was justified because socio-legal research encompasses all three orientations. At the same time it is unjustified, because socio-legal research, as it has developed in the UK, does not accommodate these to the same degree and has certain specific institutional characteristics which distinguishes it from, for example, legal sociology in the

---

[1] Mary Seneviratne's study of ombudsmen, which was presented in Section Three, could have also been used here as an example of socio-legal research in the UK. At the same time, Michael Adler's chapters could have been presented in Section Four as examples of structural analysis.

[2] I Willock, 'Getting On with Sociologists' (1974) 1 *British Journal of Law and Society* 12.

Nordic countries, Germany or France. While the sociology of law in, say Sweden, has developed within the faculty of social sciences, socio-legal studies in the UK has grown out of law schools.[3] In the US, the law and society movement is also genuinely inter-disciplinary, in that law and society researchers belong to many academic departments. Perhaps because of their institutional base in law schools in Britain, socio-legal researchers remain more interested in applied empirical research about law, than in studying law from a sociological or anthropological perspective.[4] There is also a greater separation between researchers interested in using sociology to advance a critical view of law, and those doing empirical research for government departments.

The first chapter presented in this section is an example of the tradition of socio-legal research in the UK which strives to produce rigorous empirical research on law and legal institutions. We present it as an example of the type of quantitative, 'evidence-based' empirical research which the Nuffield Inquiry wishes to promote.[5] At the same time, we would argue that it is undesirable, and potentially dangerous, for any group of academics to secure a monopoly on doing publicly-funded research. The No Child Left Behind legislation enacted by the first George W Bush government requires any researcher doing funded research on education in the USA to conduct randomised experiments using quantitative methods. This reflects the growing influence of lobby groups such as The Campbell Collaboration,[6] and it would also appear that they might have influenced the Nuffield Inquiry.

Michael Adler reports on the initial stages of a quantitative study designed to investigate how people pursue complaints about government. This involved using focus groups to identify meaningful categories that were used to improve the design of a questionnaire. Adler's research was funded by the Nuffield Foundation, and in this case, one can see how a rig-

---

[3] On this point see the Introduction and Ch 1.

[4] Debates between socio-legal studies, which is often presented as being primarily concerned with applied research, and the sociology of law, which tries to address the theoretical issues raised within mainstream sociology and argues that empirical research need to be theoretically informed, is hardly new and in the UK goes back to 1970s. See for example, CM Campbell and P Wiles, 'The Study of Law and Society in Britain' (1976) 10 *Law and Society Review* 547–78. Since then more socio-legal researchers have become interested in theory, but there is still a debate as to the extent to which this should go, and whether theoretically-driven research is useful for policymakers. For an overview of socio-legal studies see P Thomas, (ed), *Socio-Legal Studies* (Aldershot, Dartmouth, 1997).

[5] See the concluding section in Chapter One on Research Training in the Law Schools for a brief summary of the Nuffield Inquiry.

[6] This is a consortium of mainly American quantitative researchers that seeks to establish internationally-agreed standards for scientific research, and promote these to governments. They represent a resurgence of confidence among positivists, following what they view as the defeat of interpretivist, realist and most recently postmodernist critics, but continue the tradition of policy-relevant, quantitative research developed by Lazarsfeld in the 1940s. See their website: <http://ww.campbellcollaboration.org>

orous scientific project that addresses general questions about how people experience administrative grievances can also be useful to government. Again, however, it is noticeable that, in contrast to continental researchers, Adler shows little interest (at least in this chapter) in social theory. It is easy to see why civil servants and managers in the public sector find this kind of empirical legal research useful; and how ethnographies of the kind conducted by interpretive researchers, or a systems theory analysis, might be less useful or even potentially unhelpful to developing government policies. One might still want to ask, however, from a continental perspective, whether one can address social problems effectively in the long-term without using some theoretical framework to make sense of the data. One can also argue that the range of methods employed in applied research is quite limited by the standards of academic social science (a point made by the Nuffield Inquiry).

Perhaps the most difficult issues of all are raised by the last two chapters, which consider changes in the way universities are funded and regulated in the UK, and how these may affect socio-legal research, although they should also interest a wider audience. Andy Boon looks at recent developments in law, such as the Human Rights Act, and the development of ethics committees in universities which are intended to regulate how researchers in Britain and elsewhere collect and use research data. Ethics committees were established in America in the 1970s, and in Canada and Australia during the 1990s. At present they do not exist in the UK outside hospitals, although there have been proposals from the Economic and Social Research Council, the main funding body for social science research, to make ethical review a requirement for doing funded projects, and this will probably affect all university-based research. Boon describes some aspects of ethical review from a legal perspective, and explains the political pressures that have contributed to form this new regulatory field.

One should be left in no doubt about the significance of these changes for socio-legal researchers. One example he gives, which is particularly relevant to researchers doing critical research, is that covert observation, of the kind pursued by many researchers during the 1960s and 1970s, will no longer be possible. He also notes that 'replacing professional responsibility with bureaucratic control will, in less enlightened environments, carry a risk of inflexible bureaucracy, rigidifying procedures and increasing paperwork'. There is growing dissatisfaction about ethical review in North America and Australia, given that committees are given the statutory power to determine what is valuable or scientifically worthwhile research (so it is not enough for a project to have been approved by a university department).

Qualitative researchers particularly resent the fact that the template for ethical review is the clinical trial in medicine, so the standard way of reducing risk is to require them to obtain signed forms to demonstrate 'informed consent' in every project.[7] The critics are not contesting the importance of ethical issues in social science, but whether it is appropriate that they should be regulated in this way. Boon's overview of what is happening should be taken seriously by all socio-legal researchers in Britain and Europe who will find that freedoms they took for granted may be eroded or removed in the name of protecting the research 'subject'.

In the last chapter, Max Travers also expresses worries about restrictions on academic freedom that are increasingly apparent in Britain and internationally. Responding to pressures to reduce costs, and use public resources more effectively, governments are tending to concentrate research funding in elite universities, and exercising greater control over what can be studied, and how academics use their time. In Britain, the Economic and Social Research Council, which replaced the Social Science Research Council at the start of the 1980s, has a narrowly utilitarian remit: research is only funded that benefits the economy or improves the effectiveness of public services. The withdrawal of research funding through the Research Assessment Exercise from many universities in 2003, has effectively compelled researchers to choose between taking on higher teaching loads or conducting evaluation research for government agencies.

Travers offers a sociological analysis of these developments which draws on the Foucauldian governmentality tradition and ethnomethodology. However, he also argues that evaluation research, especially of the kind commissioned by local agencies, has lower methodological standards than research published in peer-reviewed academic journals. Another side to the critique, already made forcefully by some criminologists and socio-legal researchers in Britain, is that consultancy necessarily has a managerial bias, so any findings that are uncomfortable to the agency funding the research are never published.[8] The idea that one should ask intellectual questions for their own sake motivates all the contributors to this collection, whatever their theoretical or political differences, as one might expect since they conduct research and teach in universities. Although one can exaggerate the extent to which universities are changing, these two chapters suggest that one can no longer take academic freedom for granted. We hope that socio-legal researchers will continue to raise and debate these difficult social and political issues.

---

[7] See, for example, Y Lincoln and W Tierney, 'Qualitative Research and Institutional Review Boards' in (2004) 10 *Qualitative Inquiry* 219–34.

[8] See R Collier, 'Research Capacity, Critical Social Science and the Paradox of Socio-Legal Studies' (2004) 43 *Socio-Legal Newsletter* 1.

14

Constructing a Typology of Administrative Grievances: Reconciling the Irreconcilable?

MICHAEL ADLER

I N THE UNITED Kingdom, there have been many empirical studies of people's experiences in dealing with a variety of government departments
and public bodies, eg with agencies responsible for social security, taxation, housing, immigration control etc.[1] There have likewise been many
studies of people's experiences in dealing with a wide range of redress mechanisms, eg internal review, complaints procedures, ombudsmen, courts, tribunals etc, which can be invoked when these experiences are experienced as
problematic and people wish to challenge them.[2] However, there have, as
far as I am aware, been no empirical studies which have taken an overview
of the entire spectrum of people's administrative experiences.

One consequence of this is that there is an absence of any comparative
data on administrative problems that people experience in dealing with

[1] The author would like to record his gratitude to the Nuffield Foundation, which funded
the research on which this chapter is based. He also wishes to acknowledge his indebtedness
to the other members of the research team—Jane Lewis, Steven Finch and Chris Farrell
(National Centre for Social Research) and Sue Morris (formerly of Robert Gordon University,
Aberdeen)–who were collectively responsible for the design of the research, and Chris Farrell,
who conducted the fieldwork. However, he would like to make it clear that he is solely responsible for the contents of this chapter. The chapter has benefited from some very helpful comments and criticisms made by those who attended seminars at the Centre for Socio-Legal
Studies at Oxford University and at the School of Social and Political Studies at Edinburgh
University.
[2] There have been a number of useful literature reviews on complaints and procedures for
dealing with them in the public sector. See, for example, T Williams and T Goriely, *An
Annotated Bibliography of Complaints Handling Literature* (London, TPR Social and Legal
Research for The Citizens Charter Complaints Task Force, 1995); D Leadbeater and L
Mulcahy, *Putting it Right for Consumers—A Review of Complaints Procedures and Redress
Services in Public Services* (London, National Consumer Council, 1996); L Mulcahy, *et al,
Small Voices, Big Issues—An Annotated Bibliography of the Literature on Public Sector
Complaints* (London, University of North London Press, 1996).

'government' in its many manifestations, or on administrative grievances, ie, on those experiences that are felt to be unjust or unfair. We do not, for example, know which government departments are experienced as most problematic and by whom. Likewise, we lack any systematic understanding of the nature of the problems that people experience and whether, and if so how, these problems vary from one administrative agency to another. Similarly, we do not know whether the mechanisms for challenging experiences and correcting decisions that are felt to be unjust or unfair are accessible or effective.

This chapter focuses on the first stage of a programme of research that is attempting to fill this gap in our understanding. The long-term aims of this research are, by means of a survey of the adult population, to

— estimate the incidence of administrative problems and administrative grievances;
— determine which government departments are experienced as most problematic and by whom;
— demonstrate how these problems vary from one government administrative agency to another; and
— assess how accessible and how effective the mechanisms for pursuing administrative grievances are for those who need to use them.

A. TERMINOLOGY

The vocabulary used above, in particular the references to 'problems' and 'grievances', is consistent with the usage developed by Felstiner, Abel and Sarat in their 'naming, blaming, claiming' model of disputes.[3] In their sequential or processual model of disputing behaviour, 'injurious experiences'—which we refer to as 'problems'—precede 'grievances', 'grievances' precede 'complaints', and 'complaints' precede 'legal remedies'. The logical steps along the path involve the recognition of particular kinds of experience as injurious ('naming'), the identification of the problem as a grievance for which some individual or institution is held to be responsible ('blaming'); the confrontation of the responsible individual or institution with the grievance ('complaining'); and finally, if the response is deemed to be unsatisfactory, the pursuit of a legal remedy. People may seek information or advice at several points, eg when they recognise that they have a problem, when they blame someone else for it and it has become a 'grievance', when they take up the matter with body in question and it becomes a 'complaint',

---

[3] W Felstiner, R Abel and A Sarat, 'Transforming of Disputes: Naming, Blaming and Claiming' (1980–81) 15 *Law and Society Review* 631–49.

and/or when they seek redress.[4] At the outset, seeking information or advice may be instrumental in persuading people that they have a grievance; later on, it may help them to decide whether to pursue it and, if so, whether to complain to the body in question and/or to pursue a legal remedy. If the outcome of the complaint or appeal is successful, or if it is unsuccessful but the person concerned is prepared to accept it, the grievance will have been resolved. However, if the outcome is unsuccessful and the person concerned does not accept it, he or she may continue to have a grievance.

It is clear that the incidence of administrative problems, ie of 'injurious experiences' with public bodies and public services, is far greater than the incidence of administrative grievances and that the incidence of administrative grievances is far greater than the incidence of complaints and appeals.

B. BACKGROUND

The programme of research outlined above was prompted by the publication of Hazel Genn's two 'Paths to Justice' studies—one in England[5] and the other in Scotland[6]—which set out to investigate how people use the legal system to deal with their problems. In both these studies, 'justiciable problems' were defined as problems that raise legal issues, whether or not they are recognised as such and whether or not any action is taken to deal with them. The range of justiciable problems was confined to civil (as distinct from criminal law) and was drawn up on the basis of focus group discussions with solicitors, advice agencies and members of the public. They comprised 16 broad categories, which included employment, divorce, money issues, health, injury, immigration, property, discrimination issues etc, and over 60 sub-categories which, taking employment problems as an example, referred to losing a job, problems associated with getting paid or receiving an occupational pension, other rights at work, changes to terms and conditions of employment, harassment at work and other disciplinary procedures.

Both studies were based on large-scale survey research. In a screening interview, respondents were asked to report all the justiciable problems that

---

[4] Although Felstiner, Abel and Sarat's model of disputing behaviour has undoubtedly been very influential and makes some important conceptual distinctions, it has been criticised for oversimplifying how people decide whether, and if so how, to respond to 'injurious experiences'. For example, Lloyd-Bostock's study of plaintiffs in personal injury actions demonstrates that the attribution of blame does not necessarily precede the decision to pursue a legal remedy and that knowledge of, or information about the availability of, a legal remedy is very important in determining whether people blame others for accidents they have had. See S Lloyd Bostock, 'Fault and Liability for Accidents' in D Harris, *et al*, *Compensation and Support* (Oxford, OUP, 1984) ch 4.

[5] H Genn, *Paths to Justice* (Oxford, Hart Publishing, 1999).

[6] H Genn and A Paterson, *Paths to Justice Scotland* (Oxford, Hart Publishing, 2001).

they had experienced, irrespective of their seriousness, over the last five years. Respondents were deemed eligible for the main interview if they had experienced one or more of these problems and had either taken some action to deal with it or had not taken any action for one of a number of 'good' reasons. Those who had not regarded the problem as important enough to justify taking action and those who were not in dispute with another party were excluded. However, respondents were automatically included if they had been involved in divorce proceedings, had had legal action taken against them, had been threatened with legal action over a disagreement about something, or had started or considered starting legal proceedings.

In total, about 40% of the 4125 individuals who answered the screening survey in England and 26% of the 2684 adults who did so in Scotland, reported having experienced one or more 'justiciable problems' during the past five years. Follow-up interviews with 1134 individuals who had experienced one or more 'non-trivial justiciable problems' during the past five years in England and with 472 individuals in Scotland who had done so in Scotland were then carried out and, for each type of problem, the action that was taken or the reasons for taking no action were recorded. The problems people encountered are set out in Table 1 below. It is clear from the table that the pattern of problem types about which respondents were interviewed in the main survey broadly reflects the pattern reported in the screening survey, and that the pattern of problem types encountered in Scotland is very similar to that found in England.

The two surveys indicate that the most common initial course of action reported by respondents was to try to resolve the dispute directly by making contact with the other side. 68% of respondents in England and 77% of respondents in Scotland contacted the other side, either in person or in writing. Some respondents did not take the matter further, either because they were able to resolve the problem or because they gave up. About six respondents in ten (60% in England and 64% in Scotland) sought advice, but most of them did so after first trying to resolve the problem themselves. Many sources of advice were used, but by far the most common were solicitors in private practice (used by 24% of those who sought advice in England and 29% Scotland) and citizens advice bureaux (used by 21% of those who sought advice in England and 17% in Scotland). The propensity to obtain advice and the advice obtained varied with the type of problem people faced and with income. However, this only led to legal proceedings in a small minority of cases (20% in England and 14% in Scotland).

Although these two studies have undoubtedly enhanced our understanding of the ways in which people deal with legal problems when they encounter them, it is striking how few of the problems involved public law disputes, ie disputes between the citizen and the state. They dealt primarily with private law disputes, ie disputes between two private parties, such as

Table 1: Distribution of 'Justiciable Problems' in England and Scotland

Type of Problem	England		Scotland	
	% of problems reported in screening survey	% of problems reported in main survey	% of problems reported in screening survey	% of problems reported in main survey
Employment	7	9	7	8
Owning residential property	12	11	11	12
Renting out property	2	2	1	2
Living in rented accommodation	12	11	18	14
Faulty goods and services	15	17	13	20
Money	13	15	13	17
Divorce proceedings	4	4	4	3
Family matters	8	5	7	5
Children under 18	4	3	2	3
Accidental injury/work-related ill health	9	11	6	6
Discrimination/police ill treatment/immigration/clinical negligence	4	3	6	3
Subject to legal action	5	3	3	2
Threatened with legal action	2	2	3	1
Started or considered legal proceedings	3	3	3	2
Weighted base	4125	1134	1845	472

Sources: Genn, n 3, Table 2.6 for England; Genn and Paterson, n 4, Table 2.9 for Scotland.

disputes between husband and wife, employer and employee, landlord and tenant, and contractor and consumer. This preponderance of private law disputes is clearly at odds with the experiences of many advice agencies whose caseloads are heavily weighted towards public law disputes in the fields of taxation, social security, housing, immigration control etc. It is not clear why this should be the case but it may well have resulted from the fact that people are more likely to think of the problems that they experience in dealing with government departments and other public bodies as 'adminis-trative problems' rather than 'legal problems'. This is not all that surprising since lawyers have little expertise in dealing with such problems, and few people would think of consulting a lawyer about them.

The research described in this chapter was designed to remedy the fact that more is known about disputes between private parties than about dis-putes between the citizen and the state. Adopting the model used in the *Paths to Justice* studies,[7] our original idea was to conduct a large-scale national survey of people who had experienced one or more 'non-trivial administrative problems' in their dealings with 'government' over the last five years, and then to question them about how they had dealt with them. However, survey research on this scale is extremely expensive. The Nuffield Foundation, to which an application for funding had been made, took the view that, before committing itself to a major outlay of expenditure, some development work needed to be undertaken. In particular, it took the view that a typology of grievances, which could be used to classify the problems that people experience in their dealings with government and to distinguish those problems that are justiciable from those problems that are not, with a view to excluding the latter from a survey of administrative grievances, needed to be developed. Because we were unable to locate any well-estab-lished typologies of grievances that we could take off the shelf and adapt for use in our own study, we had to develop a typology from scratch.

C. CONSTRUCTING A TYPOLOGY OF GRIEVANCES

A typology of grievances can not only be used to distinguish problems that are amenable to individual redress from problems that are not, but can also be used to classify grievances and compare the profiles of grievances asso-ciated with particular government departments and public bodies.

There would appear to be two contrasting approaches to devising such a typology: a 'top-down' approach and a 'bottom-up' approach. Each has its advantages and disadvantages. A 'top-down' approach, which might have involved reviewing the literature in administrative law and public administration and, possibly, consulting experts in these fields, could have been expected to result in a typology that made some valid analytic distinc-tions, eg between fact and law, rule and discretion, process and outcome, and law and policy. However, it would probably not have meshed well with the ways in which people define and describe the problems that they expe-rience and the grievances that they harbour. A 'bottom-up' approach, on the other hand, which might have involved asking people to describe the problems that they have experienced in their own words and using these

---

[7] See Genn, n 5, above, for England; and Genn and Paterson, n 6, above, for Scotland.

accounts to construct a typology, could have been expected to result in a typology that meshed well with the ways in which people define and describe the problems that they experience but would probably not have reflected some very important analytic distinctions.

Instead of choosing between a 'top-down' and a 'bottom-up' approach, an attempt was made to combine them and, by so doing, to produce a robust typology that maximises the strengths and minimises the weaknesses of the two approaches. Whether the 'top-down' typologies with which administrative lawyers and experts in public administration are familiar can be combined with the 'bottom up' typologies that members of the public use or whether this constitutes an attempt to 'reconcile the irreconcilable' is really the nub of the issue.[8] We thought that the attempt was worth making but whether it has been successful is quite another matter. An advisory committee of experts in the field[9] helped to develop and refine a 'top down' typology constructed from a review of the literature in administrative law and public administration, and the National Centre for Social Research conducted a programme of fieldwork with the dual aim of testing the 'top-down' typology and developing a 'bottom-up' typology.

The final version of the top-down typology, which contains 16 non-mutually exclusive typologies, is set out in Table 2 below. The original plan was to conduct two rounds of fieldwork, using focus groups in the first round and, depending on how successful they were, in-depth interviews or additional focus groups in the second round. However, the first round of fieldwork was so successful, and generated such rich material, that we decided to retain the focus groups in the second round and only to conduct a small number of one-to-one interviews where people whose socioeconomic characteristics were under-represented in the focus groups. We were worried that some people might not wish to talk about their personal experiences in a group setting but there was little evidence of this among those who took part. On the contrary, hearing others talk about their experiences seems to have helped participants to recall similar experiences of their own which they were keen to talk about. The 43 participants referred

---

[8] A belief that the 'top-down' and 'bottom up' approaches embody incompatible epistemological and ontological assumptions and represent alternative, and mutually exclusive, research strategies (a 'retroductive' research strategy in the case of the former, an 'ablative' research strategy in the case of the latter) would suggest that the two approaches are irreconcilable and that one has to choose between them. This is because they represent fundamentally different forms of knowledge and reflect fundamentally different theories of existence. For an account of these two research strategies, and the epistemological and ontological assumptions on which they are based, see N Blaikie, *Designing Social Research* (Cambridge, Polity Press, 2000) ch 4.

[9] Chaired by Mrs Elizabeth Filkin, formerly Parliamentary Commissioner for Standards, Adjudicator to the Inland Revenue and Customs and Excise, and Chief Executive of the National Association of Citizens Advice Bureaux (NACAB) and comprising a number of academics and 'practitioners'.

Table 2: The 'Top Down' Typology of Grievances

T1	the decision was based on facts that were incorrect (*error of fact*)
T2	the official did not apply the legal rules properly (*error of law*)
T3	the official did not exercise discretion properly, e.g. the official had not taken all the relevant circumstances or had taken some irrelevant circumstances into account, and/or had treated the person differently from other people in similar circumstances (*abuse or misuse of discretion/discrimination*)
T4	the official appeared not to have the requisite knowledge or experience (*incompetence*)
T5	the official did not do what they said they would do (*unreliability*)
T6	the person was not listened to and was not able to put their side of the case—the official did not seem to be interested in what they had to say (*lack of participation*)
T7	the person was treated badly by the staff—the staff were rude or unhelpful (*lack of respect*)
T8	the person was kept waiting for too long and/or the application took too long to process (*unacceptable delay*)
T9	the person had to disclose sensitive information in an inappropriate setting (*lack of privacy*)
T10	no one was prepared to deal with the problem—either because staff did not know who was responsible or because no one had responsibility (*lack of responsibility*)
T11	no explanation for an adverse decision was given (*no explanation*)
T12	the official did not acknowledge that a mistake had been made or apologise for it (*no apology*)
T13	the person was not offered a choice when they should have been (*lack of choice*)
T14	although the decision was technically correct, the policy which was being applied was a bad one, e.g. because they were not offered any choice (*policy*)
T15	although the decision was technically correct, the standards were too low because the policy wasn't properly resourced and because insufficient money was being spent on it (*resources*)
T16	what the person received represented poor value for money (*value for money*)

to a total of 71 grievances and it is clear that more grievances were discussed in the groups than would have been the case if the research design had been based on one-to-one interviews.

Because our long-term plan was to carry out a UK-wide study of administrative grievances, fieldwork was carried out in England and in Scotland

and participants were recruited in the London Boroughs of Islington and Camden and in Partick and the West End of Glasgow. The aim was to have roughly equal numbers of men and women and to structure the focus groups by age and social class, on the grounds that these two variables probably account for most variation in the experiences of members of the public. Consideration was given to recruiting focus groups made up of people from minority ethnic backgrounds and people living in rural areas but this was rejected on the grounds that, at this stage, we were not aiming to study a representative sample of the population. The aim was to put together relatively homogeneous groups in which people felt comfortable enough to talk about their experiences in front of others. We set out to conduct eight focus groups containing 6–8 participants. In Glasgow, the younger groups were intended to be more middle class and the older groups more working class; in London, the younger groups were intended to be more working class and the older group more middle class.

Unfortunately, the recruiters found it very difficult to recruit younger working class participants and, for this reason, the younger groups were more middle class and the older group more working class in both locations. They were also unable to recruit any Social Grade A respondents and Social Grade B respondents were under-represented among those who took part in the focus groups.[10] Four one-to-one interviews were therefore conducted with Social Grade A and B respondents. For reasons of convenience, these four interviews took place in London. The intended and achieved sample characteristics are set out in Table 3.

Table 3: Intended and Achieved Sample Characteristics

Age	Glasgow (Partick and the West End)	London (Islington and Camden)
Intended		
18–50	2 focus groups comprising Social Grades A, B, C1 and C2	2 focus groups comprising Social Grades C1, C2, D and E
30–70	2 focus groups comprising Social Grades C1, C2, D and E	2 focus groups comprising Social Grades A, B, C1 and C2
Achieved		
18–50	2 focus groups comprising Social Grades B, C1 and C2	2 focus groups comprising Social Grades B, C1 and C2
30–70	2 focus groups comprising Social Grades C1, C2, D and E	2 focus groups comprising Social Grades C1, C2, D and E 4 one-to-one interviews comprising Social Grades A and B

[10] The National Centre for Social Research uses 'Social Grade' as a measure of social class. Activities are graded on an A to E scale. Those in employment are generally graded A to D,

We aimed to recruit participants who had had problems with a wide range of government departments and public bodies. Some problems, eg those concerned with housing, council tax, education and health were well represented in the first round of fieldwork while others were not. An attempt was therefore made in the second round to recruit participants whose problems were in other areas, eg income tax, social security (including child support), employment services, local planning and environmental issues, policing and immigration issues. In addition to the problems that participants mentioned to the recruiters, participants raised other problems during the focus groups and, as a result, a wide range of problems and experiences was discussed. However, among the problems and grievances discussed in the focus groups and interviews, many referred to the provision of services, in particular health care and education, and relatively few concerned the provision of benefits, the imposition of taxes or the granting of licences. No references were made to problems with the Child Support Agency, the Driver and Vehicle Licence Agency or the Television Licensing Authority.

As far as the 'bottom up' typology was concerned, participants were encouraged by the focus group leader to explain their grievances and to describe them in their own way with as little prompting as possible. The transcripts of the focus group discussions, which lasted for about one and a half hours, and the one-to-one interviews were subsequently analysed using *Framework*, a sophisticated computer package developed by the National Centre for Social Research. Towards the end of the session, participants in the first round of fieldwork were also asked to consider the individual elements of the 'top-down' typology and to say whether or not they described some aspect of their grievance. To make the categories easier to grasp, they were expressed in terms that were intended to be easy to understand and written on a series of flashcards. The phrases used on the flashcards are set out in Table 4 below.

D. THE BOTTOM-UP APPROACH

As noted above, the focus groups and interviews generated some very rich, qualitative accounts of the administrative problems and administrative grievances that those who participated in the study had experienced in their dealings with various government departments and public bodies, the effects of these problems and grievances on their lives, and whether, and if so how, they had attempted to do something about them. In this chapter, we deal only with the first of these topics.

depending on the nature of their work, skills, education and seniority. Those on a retirement or disability pension are graded according to their former employment. Those who have not worked for more than six months and are entirely dependent on social security benefits or pensions are graded E. Lists of occupations are used to assign activities to the most appropriate typology. See Market Research Society, *Occupational Groupings: a Job Dictionary*, 5th edn, (London, Kogan Page, 2003).

Table 4: Focus Group Descriptors for Elements of the Top-Down Typology

'Top-Down' Typology		*Focus Group Descriptor*
T1	Error of fact	*The decision was based on facts that were incorrect*
T2	Error of law	*The law was not applied properly*
T3	Abuse or misuse of discretion/discrimination	*You were in a similar position to someone else but your treatment or the decision was different*
T4	Incompetence	*They did not know what they were doing*
T5	Unreliability	*They did not do what they said they would do*
T6	Lack of participation	*You were not listened to or they weren't interested.*
T7	Lack of respect	*They were rude or unhelpful.*
T8	Unacceptable delay	*You were kept waiting for too long or the matter took too long.*
T9	Lack of privacy	*You were not given any privacy in your dealings with them.*
T10	Lack of responsibility	*No-one accepted responsibility.*
T11	No explanation	*They did not explain the reasons for their decision.*
T12	No apology	*They did not acknowledge that a mistake had been made or apologise for it.*
T13	Lack of choice	*You were not offered a choice in the matter when you should have been*
T14	Policy	*The policy seemed wrong*
T15	Resources	*The policy couldn't be implemented properly due to a lack of resources*
T16	Value for money	*You didn't get value for money*

Framework, the computer package used to analyse the focus group discussions and interviews, is a sophisticated form of content analysis, which classifies and interprets qualitative data within a thematic matrix. Columns represent key themes and sub-themes while rows represent individual respondents. Data from each focus group discussion and each interview were recorded in the relevant column and a record of the context, along with references to where the original data could be found in the transcript, was kept. This facilitated an easy retrieval of the respondent's own words as required. The method allows for a detailed exploration of themes and sub-themes across all participants. Nevertheless, the construction of a typology from the data calls for the exercise of considerable judgement.

Judgement is required because administrative problems and grievances can be grouped together in different ways to produce different typologies. This does not mean that one typology is as good as another. The aim should be to produce a typology in which grievances are grouped together to form a coherent and differentiated set of categories. Coherence refers to the fact that grievances that raise similar issues should be grouped together. Differentiation, on the other hand, refers to the fact that grievances that raise different issues should be subsumed into separate categories. There is no hard and fast rule that determines how many categories there should be—emphasising what grievances have in common points in one direction while recognising how they differ points in the other and a degree of judgement is called for. Since grievances are often complex and can raise many issues, a given grievance may have several characteristics. Thus, the typologies are clearly not mutually exclusive.

With these concerns in mind, Table 5 shows how the grievances discussed in the focus groups and the one-to-one interviews were grouped together. It represents our 'bottom-up' typology.

The merits of this classification of grievances are that the sub-categories are grouped together to form a coherent categories, the categories refer to different areas of concern (although several of these areas of concern may characterise a given problem or grievance), and the number of categories (eight) is quite manageable. Since the classification of grievances is based on the ways in which participants in our study described the problems they experienced, it is reasonable to assume that, if the classification were to be used in a survey, people would be able to relate the categories and sub-categories to their own experiences. On the other hand, it is clear that the classification does not reflect many of the important analytic distinctions made by experts in administrative law and public administration.

E. THE TOP-DOWN APPROACH

In the first round of fieldwork, participants were asked—at the end of each focus group session and after talking, at some length, about their own problems and grievances—to consider the various elements of the 'top-down' typology and to say whether or not they described some aspect of their experiences. To make the typologies easier to grasp, they were expressed in terms that were intended to be easy to understand and written out on a series of flashcards (see Table 4 above). The focus group leader held up each of the flashcards in turn and asked participants to indicate whether or not the descriptor on the card described some aspect of their grievances.

Participants were able to recognise the relevance of almost all of the typologies in this typology. Although it is not clear whether they were referring to

Table 5: 'Bottom-Up' Typology of Grievances

'Bottom-Up' Typology		Sub-Typology
B1	Unjust decisions and actions	refusal to accept liability; decisions perceived to be wrong and/or unfair; decisions involving discrimination; unreasonable conditions imposed.
B2	Administrative errors	records lost or misplaced; no record of information received.
B3	Unacceptable treatment by staff	staff rude and unhelpful; presumption of 'guilt' by staff; threatening or intimidating behaviour by staff.
B4	Delay	delays in making appointments; delays in making decisions; delays in providing services.
B5	Information and communication shortfalls	lack of information; conflicting or confusing information; objections ignored by staff.
B6	Service unavailable	service withdrawn (either for everyone or for some people); service not available (either for everyone or for some people).
B7	Service deficient in quality or quantity	service not up to standard.
B8	General objections to policy	policy unacceptable.

their own grievance or to the grievances that had been talked about in the group, 14 of the 16 typologies were recognised as relevant. This is an interesting finding because it suggests that people experience a broad spectrum of grievances.

The two exceptions were 'error of law' and 'lack of privacy'. In the first case, many participants pointed out that they lacked the specialised knowledge to be able to say whether or not there had been an error of law. However, the failure of participants to recognise possible errors of law does not necessarily mean that none were present. If, instead of using as the descriptor the phrase 'the law was not applied properly' we had used a different descriptor, it is possible that participants would have been able to identify 'errors of law'. In the second case, comprehension did not appear to be a problem and the failure of participants to associate their grievances with a lack of privacy may indicate only that this problem is not very widespread.

The merits of the 'top-down' classification of grievances are that it reflects many of the important analytic distinctions made by experts in administrative law and public administration and that, even if the categories did not reflect the ways in which participants spoke about their administrative problems and grievances, they were—with the two exceptions referred to above—recognisable by those who took part in the study. Thus, it is reasonable to assume that, if a (slightly) modified version of the typology were used in a survey, people would be able to comprehend and respond to the categories from which this typology is constructed.

F. DEVISING A COMPOSITE TYPOLOGY

Although at least one of the participants in each of the focus groups in the first round of fieldwork was able to see the relevance of all but two of the categories in the 'top down' typology when they were shown a set of flash-cards containing a set of descriptors, it does not follow that, with the exception of these two categories, all the other categories in the 'top down' typology should necessarily be retained. To do so would have involved ignoring what we had learned about the ways in which people conceptualised and talked about the administrative problems and grievances they had experienced in the focus groups and interviews we conducted. Instead, we attempted to modify the 'top down' typology in light of our fieldwork and, in particular, in light of the 'bottom up typology' outlined above. To make clear what this involved, each of the categories in the 'top down' typology is considered in turn. It is important to recall that most of the grievances discussed by participants in our study related to the provision of services and relatively few referred to the provision of benefits, the imposition of taxes or the granting of licences.

— 'Top-down' Categories T1 ('Error of Fact'), T2 ('Error of Law') and T3 ('Abuse or misuse of discretion/discrimination') were combined and replaced by 'Composite' Category C1 ('Decision Wrong or Unreasonable'). This covers the issues grouped together in 'Bottom-up' Category B1 ('Unjust Decisions and Actions').

— Categories T4 ('Incompetence'), T5 ('Unreliability'), T7 ('Lack of Respect'), T9 ('Lack of Privacy'), T10 ('Lack of responsibility') and T12 ('No apology') were replaced by Categories C2 ('Administrative Errors') and C3 ('Unacceptable Treatment by Staff'), which cover the grievances included in Categories B2 ('Administrative Errors') and B3 ('Unacceptable Treatment by Staff').

— Category T8 ('Unacceptable Delay') was retained as Category C4 and comprises the grievances included in Category B4 ('Delay').

— Categories T6 ('Lack of Participation') and T11 ('No Information') were grouped together and replaced by Category C5 ('Information or Communication Problems'). This covers the grievances in Category B5 ('Information and Communication Shortfalls').
— Categories T13 ('Lack of Choice'), T15 ('Resources') and T16 ('Value for Money') were grouped together and replaced by Category C6 ('Benefit/Service Unavailable, Deficient in Quality or Quantity or too Expensive'). This includes the grievances in Categories B6 ('Service Unavailable') and B7 (Service Deficient in Quality or Quantity').
— Category T14 ('Policy') was retained as Category C7 ('General objections to policy'), which includes the grievances in Category B8 'General Objections to Policy'). Grievances about the application of policies to particular individuals were not included in Category C7.
— A residual category C8 'Other Grievances', for grievances not included in categories C1–C7, was also included.

Since our fieldwork indicated that participants felt that they lacked the specialised knowledge to say whether or not their grievance was caused by an error of law or to distinguish between a failure to apply a policy correctly from a correct application of a policy that they disagreed with, it follows that, in any future research, we should avoid questions that assume that people have this knowledge.

The process of constructing a 'composite' typology from the 'top-down' and 'bottom-up' typologies is represented in Table 6 below. This includes, in the right-hand column, some examples of grievances in each composite typology.

This typology seems to us to maximize the strengths and minimize the weakness of the 'top-down' and 'bottom up' typologies described above. It would appear to represent a successful combination of the 'top-down' typologies, with which administrative lawyers and experts in public administration are familiar, and the 'bottom up' typologies, which members of the public use to describe their grievances. Moreover, because the composite categories reflect the public's conceptualisation of their grievances and the language that they use to describe them, the typology should constitute a robust instrument for data collection.

What may have seemed like an attempt to 'reconcile the irreconcilable' turns out to have been a reasonably straightforward exercise.[11] It provides

---

[11] This is because the 'top-down' and 'bottom up' approaches do not actually represent fundamentally different forms of knowledge or reflect fundamentally different theories of existence. Both approaches utilise the accounts that individuals gave to researchers of their own

Table 6: Combining 'Top-Down' and 'Bottom-Up' Typologies

'Top-Down' Typologies	'Bottom-Up' Typologies	'Composite' Typologies	Examples
T1 'Error of Fact' T2 'Error of Law' T3 'Abuse or misuse of discretion/discrimination	B1 'Unjust Decisions and Actions'	C1 'Decision wrong or unreasonable'	decisions perceived to be wrong or unfair; decisions involving discrimination; decisions that involve imposition of unreasonable conditions; refusal to accept liability.
T4 'Incompetence' T5 'Unreliability' T7 'Lack of Respect' T9 'Lack of Privacy' T10 'Lack of responsibility' T12 'No apology'	B2 'Administrative Errors' B3 'Unacceptable Treatment by Staff'	C2 'Administrative errors' C3 'Unacceptable treatment by staff'	records lost or misplaced;no record of information received. staff rude and unhelpful; staff incompetent or unreliable; presumption of 'guilt' by staff; threatening or intimidating behaviour by staff; staff did not acknowledge mistake or offer apology.
T8 'Unacceptable Delay'	B4 'Delay'	C4 'Unacceptable delays'	delays in making appointments; delays in making decisions; delays in providing services.
T6 'Lack of Participation' T11 'No Information'	B5 'Information or Communication Problems'	C5 'Information and communication problems'	lack of information; conflicting or confusing information; poor communication; objections ignored by staff; lack of privacy.
T13 'Lack of Choice' T15 'Resources' T16 'Value for Money'	B6 'Service Unavailable' B7 'Service Deficient in Quality of Quantity'	C6 'Benefit/service unavailable or deficient n quality or quantity or too expensive'	benefit/service withdrawn (either for everyone or for some people); benefit/service not available (either for everyone or for some people); benefit/service deficient in quantity or quality.
T14 'Policy'	B8 'General Objections to Policy'	C7 'General objections to policy' C8 'Other Grievances'	policy unacceptable. other types of grievance not covered by typologies C1–C7.

actions in their own language and the concepts that individuals used to structure and make sense of their own experiences. The key differences between the two approaches reflect the contrasting social roles and positions of the individuals concerned. In the case of the 'top-down' approach, they are decision makers and people in positions of authority, whose views are reflected in the writings of administrative lawyers and public administration experts; in the case of the 'bottom up' approach, they are members of the public who are on the receiving end of decisions taken by others, whose views were elicited in focus groups and interviews. The fact that the two approaches do not actually embody incompatible epistemological and ontological assumptions or represent alternative, and mutually exclusive, research strategies makes it possible to reconcile what may, at first sight, have seemed to be irreconcilable forms of knowledge.

a good illustration of why it is sometimes important to carry out a development project (or scoping exercise) prior to embarking on large-scale research. The composite typology will, of course, need to be piloted but, on the face of it, it would seem to have the potential to generate profiles of the administrative problems that people experience in their dealings with different government departments and public bodies and the administrative grievances that result from them. Thus it would enable us better to understand how these problems and grievances vary from one administrative agency to another. Whether or not it would be sensible to use the typology to distinguish those problems that are justiciable from those problems that are not—in order to exclude the latter from any future survey of administrative grievances—is another matter.

15

The Formalisation of Research Ethics

ANDREW BOON*

RESEARCH ETHICS ARE concerned, by definition, with research as it *ought to be* conducted. In recent years the focus has changed from dilemmas confronted in the field, seen as individual responsibilities for the researcher, to embrace a range of institutional, disciplinary and structural issues. The main focus of this paper is the change in practice brought about and presaged by these processes, particularly in the socio-legal sphere. The paper attempts this task in two parts. The first describes the pressures behind the trend of formalisation. The second explores the way in which formalisation reshapes ethical issues for socio-legal research. This task is approached through a chronological examination of the research process in its constituent phases, from intention to evaluation. The context discussed here is broadly that relating to the United Kingdom, although research and publication from other legal and research jurisdictions is cited where relevant.

A. ORIENTATION

The formalisation of research ethics in British universities is a development fuelled by globalisation and commercialisation. One of many localised drivers is the transformation of the European higher education sector under the Bologna process, itself a reflection of worldwide competition for the brightest students, most innovative researchers and the social capital that they

* I would like to thank my colleagues John Flood, Penny Green, Julian Webb and the anonymous referees for their careful reading of, and comments on, drafts of this, Linda Mulcahy for drawing the case of Russell Ogden to my attention and Avis Whyte for research assistance.

bring. Since the European Union has no formal jurisdiction in the field this can be seen as an example of Foucault's concept of 'governmentality',[1] which emphasises the role of knowledge systems in the institutional construction of 'truth' and 'legitimate' power, and which therefore enters the normative realm of ethics. Through this transformation, higher education's traditional values and ideals, 'students who "learn for life", researchers who enjoy "the freedom of teaching and research" and a state that considers education as a public good, or even a human right, are replaced by a view of education as a private career investment.'[2] This is assigning a new role for research, both an audited commodity and a tool of economic growth.[3] While the place of research in the universities is reconceived, the movement of research ethics up the agenda of higher education institutions can be seen to reflect a different aspect of governmentality, the demand of the neo-liberal state for informal governance, which seeks to extend ethical concerns to social and business activity. Allied to direct political appeals, higher education institutions experience localised pressures, as concerns over privacy issues, the security of new technologies and the directions and implications of scientific discovery and quality management. The ramifications are widespread, from specific demands for ethical governance[4] to debates within academic disciplines regarding purpose and values.

The field of research ethics has enjoyed a surprising degree of consensus around fundamental values. Respect for autonomy, non-maleficence (not doing harm), beneficence (doing good) and justice transcend disciplinary boundaries, but do so because of their high level of abstraction. Proponents of these universal values recognise that, as research regulation develops, factors such as efficiency, institutional rules, law and client acceptance splinter values and create tensions between them.[5] Philosophical perspective also plays a part in ethical problem-solving and decision-making in the field, particularly when either provisions in codes, or broad ethical principles, conflict. Beauchamp and Childress argue that abhorrence of paternalism leads us to place autonomy over beneficence, that is, to place individual

---

[1] T Lemke, 'The Birth of Bio-Politics', Michel Foucault's lecture at the College de France on Neo-liberal Governmentality (2001) 30 *Economy and Society* 190.

[2] A Oels, 'The informalisation of the state in a globalising world: a neoliberal restructuring?' at www.angelaoels.de/person/research.html.

[3] The government white paper *The Future of Higher education* (London, Department of Education and Skills, 2003) Cm 5735, contains 26 references to higher education's growing role in 'knowledge transfer', the latter defined by AURIL as '... the organised exchange and application of public sector funded research, intellectual property, expertise and training to meet business and community needs', and the potential for it replacing research in parts of the Higher education sector.

[4] A Fazackerley and S Farrar, 'Agree Ethics Code or Face State Control', *The Times Higher Education Supplement*, 14 November 2003, p 1.

[5] T L Beauchamp and J F Childress, *Principles of Biomedical Ethics*, 4th edn, (New York, NY, OUP, 1994) 28.

relationships over broader social good. While these issues are likely to remain in flux, it is anticipated that formalisation will clarify the relative importance of values. Indeed, it is anticipated that this process will elevate further the autonomy of participants as the key value for research. This will have profound implications for field methodology.

B. THE FORMALISATION TRAJECTORY

The three linked pressures towards formalisation of ethical obligations in research are legalisation, regulation and institutionalisation. The research ethics field is constituted by three normative areas; legal, regulatory and moral. Law provides the outer boundary of the system of research ethics, touching on areas as diverse as intellectual property rights and rights to reputation. Law also, increasingly, intrudes in the other areas. There has been a recent increase in legislation in areas once regarded as matters of individual conscience or professional duty,[6] notably the Human Rights Act 1998, which brings research activity within the scope of several of the articles of the European Convention on Human Rights. The right to publish is protected by the right to freedom of expression[7] and a right to respect for private and family life[8] supports potential research participants' wish not to participate in research, or to do so only on terms. The most likely point of conflict between these rights, the issue of confidentiality, is perhaps less problematic than might be imagined because of data protection legislation. Additionally, data protection requirements are the main vehicle for formalisation of the ethical relationship between researchers and those they research. The legislation, the Data Protection Act 1998, as amended by the Freedom of Information Act 2000, establishes a regime affecting the obtaining, holding, using or disclosing of personal data.

The regime prevents unauthorised access to personal and confidential data identifiable, or potentially identifiable, as that of an individual. Data that cannot be linked to an individual is not covered by the Act, but may be protected under the common law relating to confidence.[9] Data are classified as sensitive personal data and other data, and the ability to collect

---

[6] Regarding inroads into the principle of professional confidentiality, for example in relation to money laundering—see A Boon and J Levin, *The Ethics and Conduct of Lawyers in England and Wales* (Oxford, Hart Publishing, 1999).

[7] The 'freedom to hold opinions and to receive and impart information without interference by public authority' (HRA Sch 1 Article 10, para 1).

[8] Article 8.

[9] *R v Dept of Health, Ex parte Source Informatics Ltd*, EWCA Civ (21 December 1999), (there is no breach of confidence where general practitioners and pharmacists disclose to a third party, without a patient's consent, information in the patient's prescription form but not the patient's identity).

data in either category is subject to conditions.[10] Information about individuals held on computer, or on paper, and sorted by reference to individuals is subject to the Act, affecting both quantitative and qualitative research.[11] Although the definition of personal data gives the Act a potentially narrow application,[12] obtaining consent to any data collection and processing will increasingly become the norm. The Act also constrains the handling of data, so that researchers conducting research covered by the Act are under an individual obligation to register with an Information Commissioner specifying the nature, purpose and intended recipients of the intended data. The Commissioner can investigate complaints, prevent processing of data and order its destruction.

The Act provides limited exemptions for research, provided that the data are not used to support measures or decisions with respect to particular individuals and are not processed in such a way as to cause substantial damage or distress.[13] In such circumstances, the right of data subjects to access data is exempted provided that they are processed so as to comply with the relevant conditions, and provided also that the results are not in a form that permits the identification of data subjects.[14] Another significant exemption is that data processed in compliance with the relevant conditions and only for research purposes may be kept indefinitely.[15] The prohibition against further processing in principle 2 is also abrogated if such further processing is for research purposes.[16] Subject to these limited exceptions, the obligations in the data protection regime relating to collecting, handling and storing data still obtain and particularly requirements for the provision of information, and the conditions of storage and processing.[17] The complexity of the Act exacerbates pressure on institutions to ensure that the legal requirements are observed, increasing the likelihood of regulation and pushing it into the area formerly defined as an area of individual moral concern for researchers.

---

[10] Sensitive personal data, concerning an individual's race, gender, sexuality or political or religious beliefs, should not be processed unless one of the conditions set out in Sch 3 is satisfied. Other data may only be processed where one of the conditions set out in Sch 2 are met.

[11] 'Data' includes information processed by automatic equipment or with the intention that it should become part of a relevant filing system or form part of an accessible record. (S 1(a) to (d)).

[12] Mere mention of a data subject does not amount to 'personal data'. The information must affect his privacy, whether his personal or family life, business or professional capacity' (*Durant ibid*, Auld LJ at para 28) or be an opinion about him personally (*ibid*, Buxton LJ at para 80).

[13] DPA s 33(1)(a) and (b).

[14] DPA s 33(4)(a) and (b).

[15] DPA s 33(3).

[16] See DPA s 33(2) and note that the research exemption is not lost by certain kinds of disclosure (33(5)(a) to (d)).

[17] Sch 1 Part II, s 7 and 9.

Regulation of data collection and handling has increased pressure by home universities, grant-giving institutions[18] and external regulators for greater institutional control of research[19] and for professional and disciplinary-based organisations to create codes of conduct and develop educational programmes. Tighter regulation of research may be achieved most effectively by collaboration between disciplinary-based associations and employing institutions. The Associations can provide ethical guidance, with university ethics committees best placed to provide control and enforcement. Whether the work of the Associations will be simplified by creating one ethics regime for the social sciences is moot, however, with current plans limited to providing guidelines for scrutiny and practice, and with more detailed guidelines for different areas of research.[20] The institutional incentive to formalise research ethics stems from increased consciousness of the ethical obligations of universities and anxiety over the risks of injury to reputation, and of liability inherent in uncontrolled research activity.[21] A well-established model of ethical oversight operates in the medical field with peer review of research proposals[22] operating at local and regional levels. The spread of the medical model to the social sciences will end the low visibility that ethics has had in socio-legal research.[23]

The narrow aim of ethics committees, scrutiny of the research proposals, inevitably produces new issues for consideration. It is predictable that these university committees will acquire jurisdiction over tangential issues

[18] See, for example, the current application form for grants over £5000 to the Arts and Humanities Research Board requiring a description of '... the nature of your institution's arrangements for scrutinising the ethical implications of specific funded projects and describe, where appropriate, how these arrangements have been brought to bear in relation to your particular programme of work' (s 11).

[19] Codes may include provisions for formal accreditation of research facilities, A Fazackerley, '"Pointless" new code worries scholars' *The Times Higher Education Supplement*, 16 May 2003, p 4.

[20] The UK Economic and Social Research Council project to develop a framework for social science research ethics (http://york.ac.uk/rcs/rcf/).

[21] Researchers in the USA found confidential information on 42 out of 158 second-hand drives purchased second-hand and conclude that it is difficult to successfully clean hard discs in such a way that they can be sold on with confidence. SL Garfinkel and A Shelat, 'Remembrance of Data Passed: A Study of Disk Sanitization Practices' (2003) *IEEE Security and Privacy* 17, http://computer.org/security./.

[22] See P Williamson, *et al*, 'Statistical Review by Research Ethics Committees' (2000) 163 *Journal of the Royal Statistical Society* 5.

[23] A survey conducted for the Nuffield Foundation found that ethical scrutiny was widespread in British universities but that there were wide variations in types of committee, frequency of meetings and jurisdiction, A Tinker and V Coomber, *University Research Ethics Committees: Their Role, Remit and Conduct* (London, King's College, 2004); C Johnston 'Ethics Scrutiny Found Wanting', *The Times Higher Education Supplement*, 5 November 2004, p 5.

such as the treatment of junior researchers and research assistants, the handling of publication credits and intellectual or other property rights. This may result in removal of some long neglected blemishes,[24] providing an infrastructure of support for research training, mentoring, and counselling[25] that places the relationship of universities with research staff on a sounder ethical footing and reinforces the cultural and structural support for ethical practice.[26] But ethics committees will be a mixed blessing. Replacing professional responsibility with bureaucratic control will, in less enlightened environments, carry a risk of inflexible bureaucracy, rigidifying procedures and increasing paperwork.[27] A tendency to withdraw within the safety of routines and procedures[28] will constrain risk-taking. For example, some features of qualitative work, inductive methods, emergent design, deliberative sampling and small samples risk misunderstanding and leave much to be worked out in the field, tempting ethics committees to overspecification. Ethics committees need protocols and procedures that recognise differences in methodology and qualitative researchers must specify the procedures that underpin and reinforce the ethicality of qualitative work; formal observance of the principle of consent, 'member checking'[29] and keeping trail notes, a history of the research process that sheds light on the data.[30] In whatever ways these matters are handled, the interface between legal and regulatory requirements and ethical decision making in the field will be renegotiated. The remainder of this chapter explores areas of potential conflict and interaction between the elements of the research ethics field.

---

[24] Research academics in universities find the higher education culture unsupportive and their prospects blighted by low status work, job insecurity, lack of career structure, lack of training and development and lack of resources. J Campbell, *et al*, *Supporting Research Staff: Making a Difference* (Sheffield, University of Sheffield, 2003).

[25] Particularly where qualitative researchers are uncovering particularly disturbing information, MQ Patton, *Qualitative Research and Evaluation Methods*, 3rd edn, (Thousand Oaks, CA, Sage, 2002) 406.

[26] Improving the prospects of researchers and research active academics might diminish competitive pressures and incentives to 'spice up' results, R Dingwall, 'Ethics and Ethnography' (1980) 28 *Sociological Review* 871.

[27] For example, letters delineating the research and its aims, signed consent forms, updating participants and sending them materials.

[28] Different groups, medical researchers, healthcare politicians, district nurses and members of Ethics Research Committees (RECs), evaluate the ethical issues in hypothetical scenarios differently but REC members converge on a meticulous regard for the autonomy of their subjects, which are consistently placed before the interests of research or of society, N Lynoe, M Sandland and L Jacobson, 'Research Ethics Committees: A Comparative Study of Assessment of Ethical Dilemmas' (1999) 2 *Scandinavian Journal of Psychiatry* 152.

[29] YS Lincoln and EG Guba, *Naturalistic Inquiry* (Newbury Park, CA, Sage, 1985).).

[30] M Punch, *The Politics and Ethics of Fieldwork* (London, Sage, 1986) 15; P Ramcharan and JR Cutliffe, 'Judging the Ethics of Qualitative Research: Considering the "Ethics as Process" Model' (2001) 9 *Health and Social Care in the Community* 358.

C. IMPLEMENTATION

Ethics pervade every stage of research, from conception to evaluation. Ethics therefore affects all socio-legal scholars, not just the empirical researcher in the field. What is seen as an ethical issue is socially constructed as, for example, the academic role is shaped by debates about the role and value of universities and research.

1. Intention

A controversial question is whether academics have an ethical obligation to research, arising from the universities' historic and contemporary mission to generate and disseminate knowledge, from terms of employment or from the synergy between high level teaching and research activity.[31] The issue became highly political when the higher education sector mobilised to resist government proposals to focus research resources on elite universities through the Research Assessment Exercise, in the process creating 'teaching only' institutions.[32] The ethical dimension of such debates are wide, ranging from arguments about the disadvantage faced by students not taught in a research rich environment[33] to the collegiality engendered by individual and collective responsibility for the standing of researchers.[34] The linkage of the existence and amount of research funding to research performance weakens the argument that an obligation arises merely from working in a university. The academic contract of employment is also a tenuous basis because academics specialise on both sides of the teaching and research divide. The question of whether socio-legal scholars have special obligations arises from concerns about the level of empirical fieldwork being conducted and the replacement of the scholars leaving the socio-legal field.[35] This may create obligations on the research community to be more active or to provide a new generation with training and support. Another issue arises from attempts to make more explicit the relationship between research and teaching,[36] despite evidence that there is no correlation

---

[31] See further the discussion in A Bradney, *Conversations, Choices and Chances: The Liberal Law School in the Twenty-First Century* (Oxford, Hart Publishing, 2003) ch 5.

[32] The assessment occurs at intervals of approximately five years, generating substantial recurrent core funding for research orientated Law Schools.

[33] A Fazackerley, 'Research Linked to Teaching-Official', *The Times Higher Education Supplement*, 19 November 2004, p 4 and Leader at 12.

[34] F Cownie, *Legal Academics: Culture and Identities* (Oxford, Hart Publishing, 2004) 133–42.

[35] The Nuffield Foundation will fund an inquiry into the issue of socio-legal research capacity to report in 2005: 'Empirical Socio-legal Research Capacity: Announcement of an Inquiry' (2003) 41 *Socio-Legal Newsletter* 3.

[36] See the Dearing Report NCIHE (1997) *Higher Education in the Learning Society*, Report of the National Committee.

between research productivity and teaching effectiveness.[37] It is an implausible argument that academics teach in their research areas, irrespective of its relevance to their audiences. This is fortunate since many socio-legal researchers teach doctrinal subjects and their research is often outside a standard law curriculum.

2. Conception

The purpose of socio-legal scholarship is not obvious and to some extent changes over time. Selznick argued that there is little point to studying normative behaviour for its own sake.[38] For him, empirical work in the field is theoretically grounded in a quest to explain why some norms are given the sanction of law. The collaboration between law and sociology is an intermediate stage in the evolution of the core principles of a version of natural law. This view ignores the impact that socio-legal work has on policy and on the development of law,[39] of the taken for granted assumptions and norms associated with legality[40] and on the boundaries and horizons of legal study. Socio-legal work is now inextricably linked to the proposition that legal institutions cannot be understood without seeing the entire social environment.[41] While it is now broadly accepted that socio-legal work need not exist in support of jurisprudential theory, Selznick's injunction that socio-legal studies should only be linked to wider theory remains arguable to the extent that the academic concern should be disciplinary development, and subversion of accepted power relations, rather than service of policy or speaking to power.[42]

The tradition in university research is that 'choice of method and subject is a purely personal one',[43] although three areas of potential threat constitute loose boundaries of enquiry; subjects that are considered private, stressful or sacred, subjects that may incriminate or stigmatise and subjects that impinge on political alignments and vested interests.[44] Socio-legal topics

---

[37] J Hattie and HW Marsh, 'The Relationship between Research and Teaching: A Meta-analysis' (1996) 66 *Review of Educational Research* 507.

[38] P Selznick, 'The Sociology of Law' in RK Merton, L Broom and LS Cottrell, (eds), *Sociology Today: Problems and Prospects* (New York, NY, Basic Books, 1959).

[39] See further S Silbey and A Sarat, 'Reconstituting the Sociology of Law' in JF Gubrium and D Silverman, (eds), *The Politics of Field Research: Sociology Beyond Enlightenment* (Beverley Hills, CA, Sage, 1989) 150.

[40] S Silbey, 'On the Relationship of State Theory to Sociolegal Research: The Example of Minor Dispute Processing' (1990) 10 *Studies in Law, Politics and Society* 67.

[41] S Silbey and A Sarat, 'Critical Traditions in Law and Society Research' (1987) 21 *Law and Society Review* 165.

[42] A Sarat and S Silbey, 'The Pull of the Policy Audience' (1988) 10 *Law and Policy* 97.

[43] See Bradney, above, n 31, p 125.

[44] RM Lee, *Doing Research on Sensitive Topics* (London, Sage, 1993).

may be found in each of these areas, raising questions about appropriateness of research and, conversely, whether important topics are ignored for fear of exciting controversy, with negative consequences for understanding important areas of social activity.[45] The law and society movement in the United States and the socio-legal movement in the United Kingdom traditionally embraced a range of methodologies, disciplines and perspectives. They existed as a counterpoint to traditional doctrinal emphasis and are defined by what they are not, as much as by what they are. While there is no single methodology employed in socio-legal work, its distinctiveness hinges on the use of sociological research methods in fieldwork, and the use of sociological modes of analysis rather than purely legal analysis.[46] The issue of subject matter that arises in relation to much of the work done under the socio-legal banner is, however, often one of theoretical perspective rather than methodology.

It is generally accepted that the perception of any subject depends on the position taken in relation to it, one's perspective or standpoint. The term standpoint has been defined as a site occupied in order to produce knowledge and practice of which researchers are aware in a special way,[47] and the 'special way' is often a position of interest, conceived of as engagement, that seeks to reveal real relations between humans that are, on the surface, invisible.[48] Examples of the conscious development of standpoint include feminist and socialist theorists, sharing common roots,[49] a desire to understand social power relations and make such relations more satisfactory.[50] While feminism embraces a range of perspectives and approaches, those at the radical end of the feminist spectrum posit that it is necessary to see the world from the position of women in order to reveal the nature of, and reasons for, women's oppression otherwise hidden in male-generated paradigms and generally accepted in the 'malestream'. Standpoint theory provides a position from which to re-conceptualise the world in a way that

---

[45] Researchers on human sexuality are apparently stigmatised by colleagues (*ibid*, p 9).

[46] See further R Cotterell, *Law's Community* (Oxford, Clarendon Press, 1995); R Banakar, *Merging Law and Sociology: Beyond the Dichotomies in Socio-Legal Research* (Berlin, Galda & Wilch Verlag, 2003).

[47] M Cain, 'Realist Philosophy and Standpoint Epistemologies or Feminist Criminology as a Successor Science' in L Gelsthorpe and A Morris, (eds), *Feminist Perspectives in Criminology* (Milton Keynes, Open University Press, 1990) 124, 132.

[48] NCM Hartsock, 'The Feminist Standpoint: Developing the Ground for a Specifically Feminist Historical Materialism' in S Harding and MB Hintikka, (eds), *Discovering Reality: Feminist Perspectives on Epistemology, Metaphysics, Methodology, and Philosophy of Science* (Dordrecht, Reidel, 1983) 283.

[49] B Ellis and R Fopp, 'The Origins of Standpoint Epistemologies: Feminism, Marx and Lukacs' paper for the TASA 2001 Conference, The University of Sydney, 2001.

[50] NCM Hartsock, 'Comment on Hekman's "Truth and Method: Feminist Standpoint Theory Revisited": Truth or Justice?' (1997) 22 *Signs: Journal of Women in Culture and Society* 367.

reflects women's interests and values in order to suggest new ways of being. By reshaping the way in which the world is perceived feminists, like Marxist researchers,[51] reason that it may be possible to change the way it is.

While, practically, certain theoretical perspectives are distinctive because they are taken with a view to espousing a cause,[52] choice of methodology also represents a perspective on the subject of study. The plethora of contemporary socio-legal traditions approach research from different perspectives, contradicting the rationale of the positivist tradition's claim to merely discover and understand 'reality' through a standardised examination of evidence. Postmodernists, arguing that knowledge is rooted in the values and interests of social groups, wish to understand the construction of discourses, the frameworks of ideas within which other ideas can be understood. A constructionist viewpoint is that no knowledge is neutral; it is necessary to view the world from a chosen perspective in order to understand just one strand of the multiple realities that are 'truth'. While theoretical positions can be construed as bias, explicit recognition of standpoint is consistent with modern conceptions of knowledge emphasising the elusiveness of 'reality'. Conceptually, therefore, perspective affects every stage of research, from the theoretical position that underpins the research idea, through selection and implementation of method to interpretation and presentation of data.

Despite the wide range of theoretical positions informing research agendas, the range of methods available to socio-legal scholars is limited to three main kinds of investigation; textual, quantitative and qualitative. There are wide variations in these broad categories, with text-based research potentially covering everything from historic archives to law reports, quantitative research including various types of survey method, and qualitative research everything from interviews to ethnography. Some methodologies are dictated by, or associated with, particular theoretical backgrounds. The historical sweep favoured by grand theorists requires that a large amount of text, and quantitative data, be distilled. In contrast, postmodernists, favouring small, incremental understandings of 'reality', and the debunking of grand theory, prefer small but intensive qualitative studies and detailed textual deconstruction.

Ethical developments also stem from the interaction between perspective and methodology. In terms of methodology, for example, Lincoln and Guba assert that qualitative research is a superior paradigm, methodologically and ethically, to quantitative methodology.[53] Part of its justification is that

---

[51] See, for example, P Green, 'Taking Sides: Partisan Research in the 1984–1985 Miners' Strike' in D Hobbs and T May, (eds), *Interpreting the Field: Accounts of Ethnography* (Oxford, Clarendon Press, 1993).

[52] Cain, above, n 47, p 135.

[53] YS Lincoln and EG Guba, 'Ethics: The Failure of Positivist Science' (1989) *The Review of Higher Education* 221.

the role of the researcher in producing new knowledge is explicitly recognised, rather than hidden behind the conventional 'scientific' pretensions and value neutrality of quantitative methodology. Therefore, it is arguable that clear adoption of a standpoint improves the process and outcomes of fieldwork,[54] a proposition clearly reflected in feminist researchers' preference for qualitative methods, and the extensions they have proposed. Standpoint theory, for example, provides a basis for feminist empirical researchers to explicitly use the tacit knowledge and understanding that derives from their own experience[55] so that other women might benefit from their research.[56] This is an extension of Lincoln and Guba's assertion that research participants should be consulted about the interpretation of data, a process that they call 'member checking',[57] and the standpoint theorist's position that (women) participants in research should be treated as partners, determining the object and methods employed. The corollary of this, and a view sometimes advocated, is that feminist researchers should run counter to conventional norms for scientific research and forsake pretensions of neutrality. Such ideas may have receded as feminist standpoint theory, stressing the unity of women, has blended with feminist postmodernism, stressing their differences, and a feminist empiricist tradition, yet feminists continue to debate the issue of partial perspective, objectivity and the relationship between methodological theory and practice.[58]

The interposition of university ethics committees between researchers and funding bodies promises interesting debates on the ethics of 'partisanship' in research. The significant role that feminist researchers have played in articulating the ethical argument for shifting the balance of power in the research relationship towards 'the subjects' of research, and the general acceptance of this shift by the research community, underlines the importance of ethics committees heeding divergent views. The issue of partisan theoretical approaches raises interesting issues about perspective and

---

[54] Green, above, n 51, her influence on the nature and type of response to her interviews with miners was 'minimal' (p 111) and her political sympathies facilitated access (p 110).

[55] D Smith, 'Women's Perspective as a Radical Critique of Sociology' in S Harding, (ed), *Feminism and Methodology: Social Science Issues* (Bloomington, IN, Indiana University Press, 1987) 84.

[56] PH Collins, *Black Feminist Thought: Knowledge, Consciousness and the Politics of Empowerment* (New York, NY, Routledge, 1990).

[57] Lincoln and Guba, above, n 15.

[58] S Harding, *Whose Science? Whose Knowledge? Thinking from Women's Lives* (Milton Keynes, Open University Press, 1991) (arguing for 'strong objectivity' and against 'going native') and the discussion in C Ramazanoglu and J Holland *Feminist Methodology: Challenges and Choices* (London, Sage, 2002) particularly ch 3; and DJ Haraway, 'Situated Knowledges: The Science Question in Feminism and the Privilege of Partisan Perspective' in *Simians, Cyborgs, and Women: the Reinvention of Nature* (New York, NY, Routledge, 1991) ch 9.

particularly standpoint theory. While the proposition that no research is value-free is unanswerable, the theoretical foundation for the position that 'some perceptions of reality are partial and others true and liberatory', continues to be debated.[59] Nevertheless, the recognition sharpened by standpoint theory, that knowledge is situated and perspectival, underlines the importance of specifying the implications of a theoretical stance in researching an issue, in much the same way as empirical researchers acknowledge the limitations of a chosen methodology in tackling a particular research question. When issues of perspective and methodology have been identified, the ethical debate lies in balancing the values of veracity and justice. With fields changing almost constantly, and with the importance of perspective to understanding the truth claims of research, it is important that researchers identify their perspective on their field of study, for the benefit of readers who do not know their work. Explicit recognition of perspective remains the best way of maintaining the integrity of research and supporting an area of academic life still tolerant of relativistic values.

3. Design

Of necessity, research design is the area in which University research committees will wield the most influence. In the medical field, Local Research Ethics Committees have well-established procedures that tend to address three sets of questions in considering research proposals: whether the proposed project asks a reasonable or important question; whether the procedures that subjects will undergo are acceptable and whether they will be protected in terms of consent, confidentiality and compensation.[60] While slightly different considerations may arise in non-medical research, this formulation raises some interesting issues about research design in the socio-legal sphere and so is adopted here.

4. Justification

In medical research it is considered unethical to conduct pointless research, that is when research addresses a research question that has already been satisfactorily answered, uses an inappropriate methodology or is based on an

---

[59] S Hekman, 'Truth and Method: Feminist Standpoint Theory Revisited' (1997) 22 *Signs: Journal of Women in Culture and Society* 341, 343.

[60] C Foster and S Holley, 'Ethical Review of Multi-Centre Research: A Survey of Multi-Centre Researchers in the South Thames Region' (1998) 32 *Journal of the Royal College of Physicians* 242.

inadequate understanding of the methodology of choice.[61] Each of these is a matter of judgement likely to be even more complicated outside the medical sphere where, at least, there is likely to be some measure of agreement about standpoint and methods. The contested issue in medical science, what constitutes a 'satisfactory answer', imposes the burden on researchers of citing all previous work and defining the scope of proposed research so as to clearly indicate the novel area of investigation. Selecting an appropriate methodology requires researchers to understand what available alternatives involve and what they have to offer. This leaves a question mark over the ethicality of conducting research where there are insufficient resources available to determine fully the issue addressed. This applies particularly to quantitative work, where sample size is often crucial to reliable and valid conclusions.[62] 'Underpowered' studies, however, arguably make some contribution to the development of understanding of an issue and are routinely accepted by ethics committees.[63] A particular area of difficulty, however, is research conducted by students. This may be conceived of as research training but, if it involves human participants, whether there is sufficient time, expertise and resource available to conduct the research bears significantly on the issue of whether the research can be justified as training rather than for the knowledge produced.

5. Acceptability and Implementation

With increased levels of sensitivity to the human rights of participants, or those affected by the research, researchers intending to delve into areas of sensitivity for some participants should be required to justify their plans. In such cases, it might be argued that the importance of the research and the nature of the subjects are both matters that are crucial in deciding whether the intrusion is justified.[64] By analogy with the medical field, it could be argued that research should be conducted with some groups, for example the very young, only where it is for their personal benefit, a very focused application of the principles of beneficence and justice. On a practical note, studies that are conducted badly may affect willingness to participate in other studies. They might also contribute to 'survey fatigue' among the populations researched, making it more difficult for other researchers to build an adequate response rate for their studies.

---

[61] N Lynoe, M Sandland and L Jacobson, 'Research Ethics Committees: A Comparative Study of Assessment of Ethical Dilemmas' in 2 *Scandinavian Journal of Psychiatry* 152.

[62] J Cohen, 'A Power Primer' (1992) 112 *Psychological Bulletin* 155.

[63] Williamson, *et al*, above, n 22, p 10.

[64] In qualitative research the interview process may affect a person's state of mind, or the choices they make. Interviewers must consider their questions and avoid offering advice.

6. Protection

While protection for participants has a number of dimensions in medical research, in social science research it often revolves around issues of anonymity and confidentiality. Technically, anonymity exists where researchers do not know who has provided data[65] and confidentiality exists were the researcher does know, but will not reveal the participant's identity, even by implication. It is not safe to assume that all quantitative research automatically guarantees anonymity or that all qualitative research must be subject to confidentiality rules. Institutional research committees tend to favour participants not being identified in studies, but there is a serious issue about whether or not this is an ethical necessity, an excess of caution or patronising of participants who want to be named. Should the researcher insist that participants remain anonymous when they have reasons, commercial or personal, for wishing to be named? Does it increase the risk of dishonest responses? Does naming some subjects increase the risk that unnamed subjects are identifiable? These matters need to be dealt with in planning research if the assumption that participants will receive anonymity or confidentiality is not to apply.

An increase in institutional regulation may complicate ethical issues arising in research and occasionally bring researchers into conflict with their universities. An example arises in relation to confidentiality in research revealing possible crimes. There are relatively few cases where a researcher's right to protect confidences have been tested, outside the analogous sphere of journalism, but the dangers are illustrated by a Canadian case involving a graduate criminology student at Simon Fraser University, Vancouver, Canada. In the early 1990s the student, Russell Ogden, was researching assisted suicide and euthanasia among AIDS victims. A coroner subpoenaed him to give evidence before his court in the hope that he could throw some light on a suspected assisted suicide.[66] Ogden refused to divulge any information on the grounds that it would compromise the promise of confidentiality given to participants in his study. He was charged with contempt of court, but successfully argued that his communications with his research participants were privileged. The incident ignited a debate in the University about the role of the ethics committee.

Simon Fraser University's Ethics Committee distanced itself from the contempt of court proceedings brought against Russell Ogden,[67] amending its approval mechanism for research proposals so that researchers were

---

[65] Anonymity may also mean that participants will not be identifiable in published material.
[66] This account is based on an article J Lowman and T Palys, 'When Research Ethics and the Law Conflict' (1998)(June Issue) *Canadian Association of University Teachers Bulletin*. (http://www.sfu.ca/~palys/cautbull.htm)
[67] Ogden was forced to sue the institution for the cost of his legal defence.

required to give to research participants promises of 'limited confidentiality' only where crimes, or even breaches of civil law, might be revealed and to state that 'a researcher may be required to divulge information obtained in the course of this research to a court or other legal body'.[68] This potentially compromised the value of information provided to researchers, and therefore undermined the claim of their work to veracity. It also reduced the cogency of an argument for privilege based on Wigmore's test for recognising the public interest in confidences, at that time applied by the Canadian Supreme Court.[69] The test required, first, that communication must originate in confidence that it will not be disclosed and, second, that it must be essential to the full and satisfactory maintenance of the relation between the parties. It would be difficult to argue that a communication originated in a confidence when only limited confidentiality had been promised. The use of such undertakings also undermined the case of other researchers that confidentiality is an essential feature of research relations. The case illustrates the permeability of the ethical, legal and regulatory spheres while serving as a warning of the dangers for higher education institutions in sailing these waters.[70]

The availability of the Contempt of Court Act 1981 means that researchers threatened with contempt of court proceedings in the UK need not rely on the Wigmore test, although it might be seen to produce similar outcomes. Section 10 of the Act provides that:

> No court may require a person to disclose, nor is any person guilty of contempt of court for refusing to disclose, the source of information contained in a publication for which he is responsible, unless it is established to the satisfaction of the court that disclosure is necessary in the interests of justice or national security or for the prevention of disorder or crime.

The section appears to offer a good deal of protection to researchers threatened by contempt proceedings. Publication is broadly defined and includes material received for the purposes of publication. The court is not bound to order disclosure, even when satisfied that disclosure is necessary in the interests of justice, national security or in order to prevent disorder or crime, where such disclosure would be against the public interest. The case law developed around the section, however, most of which concerns journalists, is ambiguous. The situation of journalists is similar to that of researchers and one would expect the courts to treat researchers in a similar way. The approach of the courts is to recognise a high public interest in

---

[68] Lowman and Palys, above, n 66, p 2.
[69] *Slavutych v Baker* (1975) 55 DLR (3d) 224 (SCC).
[70] Ogden subsequently registered for a PhD in England and obtained damages of £62,000 from Exeter University for negligence after it withdrew a promise to give him legal backing (*The Times Online*, 31 March 2004).

freedom of the press and, therefore, in the protection of journalistic sources, particularly when their disclosures further the public interest. The benefits of disclosure must outweigh the public interest in the protection of sources.[71] For example, putting informants at physical risk requires there to be a substantial benefit from ordering disclosure. Similarly, where justice or national security is not substantially advanced, nor significant disorder or crime avoided by ordering disclosure, the courts would probably not find it 'necessary', in the words of the section, to make an order.

Several of the cases in which disclosure of information by journalists has been ordered have involved breach of the duty of confidence implicit in the employment relationship[72] and, usually, a risk that, unless the source is identified, there will be a repetition of such breaches. In one such case, how-ever, the European Court of Human Rights overturned a conviction and fine under the Contempt of Court Act on the grounds that the journalist's right to free expression under Article 10 of the European Convention on Human Rights had been infringed by the order to reveal an employee source. The risk of further harm to the employer had been curtailed by an injunction against the journalist and the order was not 'proportionate' given the 'chilling effect' on press freedom.[73] Since then, the European Convention on Human Rights has been incorporated into English law through the Human Rights Act (1998),[74] thereby increasing the likely prominence of its principles in such decisions.[75]

Cases involving journalists merely point the way to how researchers like Ogden may fare before the courts. Independent academic research would appear to have at least as high a social value as press freedom, and it is like-ly that there will be seen to be a strong public interest in protecting sources. Evidence that one of the four reasons mentioned in section 10 was more powerful than this legitimate interest would need to be strong. In Ogden's case, for example, the uncertain nature of any evidence he might give, its dubious evidential value as hearsay and a lack of any concrete indication that his research participants might be involved in a campaign of 'assisted deaths', would make the 'interests of justice' and 'prevention of crime' cri-teria of section 10 of the Contempt of Court Act weak, and, therefore, arguably insufficient to rebut the presumption in favour of research. This

---

[71] Per Lord Bridge in *X Ltd*, pp 7–8.
[72] Ashworth Hospital Authority v MGN Ltd [2002] 1 WLR 2033; Interbrew SA v Financial Times Ltd [2002] EWCA Civ 274.
[73] *Goodwin v UK* (17488/90) (1996) 22 EHHR 123 (ECHR).
[74] Sch 1.
[75] Both *Ashworth* and *Interbrew* (above n 72) went against journalists, but the employment breaches were serious, involving leaking of medical notes in *Ashworth* and confidential finan-cial information in *Interbrew*.

would indicate that there should be no finding of contempt of court, were an academic researcher to face a charge of contempt of court on similar facts before the courts in the UK. The assumption thus far is that researchers do not wish to break confidences. Deeper issues of conscience arise where they wish to do so, despite a promise of confidentiality. Researchers might face such a situation where, for example, corporate antisocial activity or individual abusive behaviour towards others is discovered and where, in the absence of legal obligations to report, that researcher must decide whether to break a promise of confidentiality. Ethics committees need to be alert to the risks of both kinds of case and to ensure that their policies do not undermine the position of researchers in protecting confidences, nor inhibit research into powerful interests.

7. Implementation

Implementation of research projects should produce relatively few unanticipated issues. Interaction with individuals in the field is, however, reflexive and underpinned by the notion of informed consent, and it has been subtly changed by the Data Protection Act. The traditional view is that informed consent is given when there has been no pressure exerted and no manipulation in obtaining consent. It, therefore, implies that consent is given by adults able to make an informed decision. By requiring, for example, explanation of the purpose of the research, and by creating the possibility that data subjects might withdraw consent to handling of their data, the legislation encourages a more expansive conception of the rights of those researched. In some types of research, in qualitative studies certainly but also in some kinds of quantitative work, this will lead to a reappraisal of the relationship between researchers and researched, and may move 'data subjects' closer to the concept of participants. This would call for an adjustment to the conceptions of researchers who, while observing the formal requirements of informed consent, may yet still conceive of their partners in the research venture as the 'objects' of *their* research. Conceiving of those contributing data as 'participants' in research suggests that their involvement should be both willing and witting.

The willingness and wittingness that turns data subjects into research participants arises from their awareness of what the research is about, how it will be conducted, and how it will be used, and their understanding of what risks it poses to them or to others. The introduction of formal requirements for collecting, handling and processing some kinds of data could easily lead to the informal extension of participant protections. This raises an issue about how much and which information is necessary before it can be said that consent is truly informed. Even if the information provided is full and clear, an audience may have widely divergent perceptions based on the same presentation, placing a premium on the quality and variety[76] of information available about the project, but also on the follow-up. Provision of information sheets should be followed by a briefing given by a person willing to encourage questions and able to give answers and briefing must be more considered and comprehensive where intended participants are unable to read. From an ethical point of view, the extent to which either information or briefing must be full and frank is a moot point. It might be argued that, if participants are too well informed about the purposes of the study, they may give inaccurate information either in an attempt to be helpful or to ensure that the research will produce a result they personally favour. But information and briefing should be honest. If there are concerns about the impact of providing information on the responses of research participants, an ethical approach must include exploration of ways of providing sufficient explanation of the research and the reason for incompletely explaining it.

Raising expectations of what constitutes informed consent, because it increases demands placed on research participants, increases concerns about achieving adequate levels of research participation. It is necessary to consider the point at which pressure to participate compromises willing and witting participation. An interviewee who is initially reluctant to provide information should be under no pressure to do so. This is particularly the case where participation poses a 'substantial threat' to those involved. Where participants are vulnerable, even mild persuasion is not justified. Another dimension of this problem is providing inducements to participate. One argument for payment of participants is that, particularly when working with disadvantaged groups, it is exploitative to take their time but not pay for it. On the other hand, does paying increase the risk that participants will affect a status, or pretend to views in order to qualify for interview, or exaggerate their experiences to 'give value'? The answer to the problem of achieving a balance between willing and honest participation may lie with offering benefits in kind rather than direct financial incentives.[77] Securing willing and witting participation in research is only the start of a relationship between researchers and research based on principles of autonomy and individuality. What was previously seen as good practice, asking whether participants wish to read interview transcripts, know the outcome of research or receive details of publications arising from it, may become integral to the research relationship. Researchers increasingly seek to justify

---

[76] Anticipating different levels of understanding and, where written explanations are provided in advance, checking that they have been received, read and understood.

[77] Providing tape recordings or transcripts of interviews or copies of reports, may be as much of an incentive and less of a threat to integrity, MQ Patton, *Qualitative Research and Evaluation Methods*, 3rd edn, (Thousand Oaks, CA, Sage, 2002) 414.

research by asserting that participation can be therapeutic, draw attention to a situation or influence debate and policy.

These developments mark a discernible shift away from beneficence as the main determinant of the ethicality of access towards the notion of participant autonomy. The move towards engagement in feminist methodologies is echoed in the resentment of disempowered groups of the intrusion represented by research.[78] This rejection is based on the grounds that outsiders cannot accurately represent the experience, for example, of a disabled person, and may further disempower those studied, including by insensitivity and unintended exploitation. While ethical counter arguments against research by outsiders are possible,[79] they constantly run up against the barrier that truly informed consent might involve a discussion of such issues and views with intended participants if the principle of autonomy is to be truly respected. An ancillary consideration is whether the research is justified on principles of beneficence and justice; is it capable of benefiting the participant or only the researcher, perhaps at the expense of the participant? In all situations researchers are under an obligation to consider their relationship with participants, particularly where those participants are from disadvantaged groups. The possibility that the relationship will prove therapeutic for the participant is a strong consideration, but the risk that research relationships may become abusive also requires that attention be given to issues of differential power, to the duration of the relationship and the clarity of its termination.[80]

Issues of autonomy and beneficence are highly problematic in dealing with those unable, because they lack legal or mental capacity, to give informed consent for the purposes of research. Where researchers wish to conduct research with participants whose ability to give informed consent is in doubt, the convention is to seek consent from a proxy, authorised to act on behalf of that individual, who can assess whether it is in the individual's interests to participate, on what terms and under what conditions. If the intended participant is also able to express a preference and wishes to participate, the participant's agreement, or assent, should be sought as well. The problem however, despite having two 'consents', lies in determining whether the participation can be said to be witting. The difficulties are acute in the case of children, who may legally consent to participate in

---

[78] JI Charlton, *Nothing About Us Without Us: Disability Power and Oppression* (Berkeley, CA, University of California Press, 1998).

[79] D Bridges, 'The Ethics of Outsider Research' at http://www.dur.ac.uk/r.d.smith. Bridges.html.

[80] B Bordeau, 'Dual Relationships in Qualitative Research' (2000) 4 *The Qualitative Report*, http://www.nova.edu/sss/QR/QR4-3bourdeau.html.

research at the age of 16,[81] but where the consent of a proxy is required before that age. In order to give effect to the principle of autonomy, researchers should seek consent of the child as well as the consent of a proxy. What ethical principles govern the decision to seek such consent? In the medical field proxy consent is not normally acceptable for non-therapeutic research on children, although there is a view that children have the ability and right to assent on their own behalf around the age of eight.[82] Between the ages of eight and sixteen, it is advocated that children be recognised as 'social actors', and their assent, as opposed to consent, to research be obtained. In order to meet potential objections to the ethicality of involving them in research, it may be necessary that they and their guardians are involved in a continuous dialogue aimed at mutual understanding of the research process and its aims.[83] These principles appear equally relevant to social science research and are increasingly reflected in ethics codes for those working with children.[84]

Covert research also presents vexed questions for an expanded notion of participation. Research subjects in such studies are completely unaware of their participation in research, in breach of the principle of autonomy protected by the informed consent of participants. The most extreme example of ethical concern arises where the researcher misrepresents who they are or the purpose of the research in order to gain access to the group studied.[85] Assuming that the study is one for which consent would normally be required, it must be asked whether the need for such consent could ever be abrogated. Is the importance of the purpose pursued by the research significant to this question? Could research that pursues an important purpose, the exposure of racism in the police force for example, justify the use of covert methods? Methods that were both intrusive and which compromised the autonomy of the individuals researched were used in some of the most groundbreaking and well-known social science research projects of the past fifty years.[86] These studies would have been impossible had the informed

---

[81] Children do not have capacity to enter contracts, under the Family Law Reform Act s 8 (1969) but consent of 16 year olds is adequate consent for research purposes, including clinical trials.

[82] S Grover, 'On the Limits of Parental Proxy Consent: Children's Rights to Non-Participation in Non-Therapeutic Research' (2004) 1 *Journal of Academic Ethics* 349; JB Kotch, 'Ethical Issues in Longitudinal Child Maltreatment Research' (2000) 15 *Journal of Interpersonal Violence* 696.

[83] M Cuttini, 'Proxy Informed Consent in Paediatric Research: A Review' (2000) 60 *Early Human Development* 89; L Fasoli, 'Research with Children: Ethical Mind-Fields' (2001) 26 *Australian Journal of Early Childhood* 7.

[84] See, for example, Australian Early Childhood Association Code of Ethics (1990).

[85] KT Erikson, 'A Comment on Disguised Observation in Sociology' (1967) *Social Problems* 366.

[86] See further Punch, above, n 30, pp 38–48; and N Fielding, 'Observational Research on the National Front' in M Bulmer, (ed), *Social Research Ethics* (London, Macmillan, 1982).

consent of participants been required. Research Ethics Committees must be expected to approach such studies with extreme caution.

Covert studies in which the identity of researchers or their intentions are misrepresented are unusual. Most covert studies are very low risk, as when researchers observe traffic flows or patterns of playground interaction. In these cases, it would be unreasonable to require that consent be sought from participants, although the consent of a reliable gatekeeper or suitable proxy should be obtained. Yet, where the line lies between these cases and those where consent is required from individual participants is not easily drawn. The points at which, it is suggested, consent requirements are triggered is research where, for purposes integral to the research, the participant ceases to be a number and becomes a person. Examples of this include where the research design requires that the individual interacts with the researcher or where reaction to an event is material. In some circumstances, the issues may be made more obscure by familiarity or proximity to the research context. Action research based on experience of one's own students, for example, might fall into the category of covert research, raising questions, first, about the need for consent and, second, whether, given the power inherent in the teaching relationship, any consent obtained is truly willing.[87]

Concerns about the absence of informed consent in covert studies extend to classic ethnography. The participant observer may maintain anonymity to prevent a Hawthorn effect, or changed behaviour in the observed. Since the researcher may be investigating the operation of an institution he or she may be unable to state precisely what information is sought or even what might be regarded as relevant to the study. Moreover, where researchers are conducting studies in large institutions there are issues about the extent to which members or users of those institutions, employees, patients, clients, are, or need to be, willing and witting participants in the study.[88] Typically, 'fear of scrutiny' and concern about how information gleaned may be used is palpable in such situations. The conventional way of addressing this problem is to seek the consent of those controlling the organisation as proxy for other groups. But proxy consent of this kind, on behalf of people who are capable of making their own decision, negates the principle of informed consent. How far is it safe to assume that a few people can consent to research on behalf of many others, whose individual concerns and interests they may not even have considered? Does leaving the decision in the hands of one group give elites too much power over fieldwork at the

---

[87] KB Lucas and JG Lidstone, 'Ethical Issues in Teaching About Research Ethics' (2000) 14 *Evaluation and Research in Education* 53.

[88] M O'Neill, 'Participation or Observation? Some Practical and Ethical Dilemmas' in DN Gellner and E Hirsch, (eds), *Inside Organizations: Anthropologists at Work* (Oxford, Berg, 2001) 223, 227.

expense of other interest groups?[89] It is unlikely that researchers will be able to avoid dealing with these issues in future.[90]

It is no longer safe to assume that ethics codes are purely public relations or that all ethical decisions must be left to the judgment of researchers in the field.[91] Ethics Committees will want to know how the more troublesome ethical questions that inevitably arise in fieldwork will be dealt with, in principle if not in detail. In probing these issues, ethics committees may not seek definitive answers. Rather, they may seek reassurance that researchers are aware of the issues that they are likely to face in the field, and assess their competence to recognise and deal with ethical dilemmas. It is unlikely that work with groups that lack capacity to consent or ethnography will be prohibited although they may become more constrained and controlled. It is likely that researchers will need to provide more detail of how the problematic and unforeseen aspects of fieldwork will be dealt with. They may even confront situations that force them to rethink these plans and perhaps be required to seek revised approval. But it should not be concluded that ethics committees will necessarily impede empirical research. One of the benefits that may arise from the presence of ethics committees is that such committees will develop rules or guidelines for proxy consent or ethnography, providing suitable foundations, and even support,[92] for research that may otherwise come to be seen as ethically dubious.

D. PRESENTATION

There are ethical considerations affecting the presentation of all research, from doctrinal to purely theoretical work including plagiarism, referencing and attributing ideas. In work sponsored by bodies outside the university, it may be necessary to protect the integrity of research from undue interference, including pressure to omit matters or adjust findings. One of the more tangled arising from the obligation to treat colleagues fairly is giving credit for work. The conventions regarding credit vary from discipline to discipline and the socio-legal field broadly follows the social sciences in this

---

[89] For a general description of the difficulties associated with 'front door access' see T Gronning, 'Accessing Large Corporations: Research Ethics and Gatekeeper Relations in the case of Researching a Japanese-invested Factory' (1997) 2 *Sociological Research Online* http://www.socresonline.org.uk/socresonline/2/4/9.html.

[90] The Market Research Association has promised guidance on 'observation research' but currently advises that any staff in an organisation must be informed when the organisation is subject to observation or 'mystery shopping' research, where, for example, services are tested by researchers posing as clients (The Market Research Society Code and Guidelines (2002 revision paras 6.2. and 6.7).

[91] See above, n 26, p 884.

[92] O'Neill had two meetings with a medical ethics committee to explore the implications of his possible involvement in future emergencies. See above, n 88, at 238.

respect. The expectation is that contributors to publication, and only contributors, will be credited as authors and contributors to fieldwork, or other background research activity, acknowledged as such. Similarly, reading, comments or ideas from colleagues should also be acknowledged. These conventions, while well established, may sometimes operate unfairly and are, therefore, *prima facie*, unjust and unethical. The main problem is article authorship, which, while the most prestigious part of research activity, is only the tip of the research iceberg. Unequal power relations between academic staff and research assistants mean that the latter's contribution may be inadequately represented by an acknowledgement, particularly when they have not had the opportunity to translate a large contribution to a project into an authorial contribution.

Researchers may also accrue obligations to research participants over how work is presented. The core values concerned include respect for the autonomy of individuals, justice, specifically, in the way people are represented, and veracity, in presentation of data and findings. Researchers must be ever-conscious of the responsibility to the communities which they research because of the implications of published work for policy that may affect these communities. They must note the limitations and constraints on their fieldwork, consider whether their data support their conclusions and the scope of those conclusions. But they may also owe duties to individuals in the way that they are presented. For example, a recent debate concerns how research participants are represented through quotations appearing in research. A specific example of such an issue is whether researchers should use edited or unedited transcripts in qualitative work.[93] One view is that reproducing vernacular speech adds to the accuracy, and hence the veracity of research, another that it is potentially patronising and demeaning to do so.[94] While dilemmas of this kind can be resolved by consulting participants as to their preferences, the emergence of this kind of issue is symptomatic of a decisive shift in the concept of individual autonomy. Where participants disagree with substantive research findings or conclusions the balance must, ultimately, remain with presenting the truth. In certain circumstances however, there may well be difficult decisions to be made about dissemination of the research.

---

[93] It has been argued that repeating interviews with 'working class and less educated people', with local accents, poor grammar or repeated stumbling do not further the interests of truth and are patronising and discriminatory. S Nelson 'It's I Mean Like uh Disrespectful', *The Times Higher Education Supplement*, 28 March 2003, p 16.

[94] The response to Nelson's article (*ibid*) in the letters page of *The Times Higher Education Supplement* the following week, suggested that it is 'disrespectful' for one person to define what is proper speech for another: S MacKlan, *The Times Higher Education Supplement*, 4 April 2003, p 15.

E. DISSEMINATION

The dissemination of research findings is protected under the Human Rights Act by the right to freedom of expression. The existence of an ethical duty to disseminate is almost as clear. The rationale for a duty to disseminate is undermined by the existence of two, superficially competing, ethical issues in relation to dissemination of research; one the consequence of too much and the other of too little dissemination. The first arises from multiple publication of what is essentially the same material, made possible by the proliferation of journals and the growth of international publication. It is dubious ethically because academics might secure career advancement by deceptively appearing to have published more original material than they have actually produced. This is increasingly seen as a serious ethical infraction within some research communities.[95] The other pressure is on universities and individual researchers to disseminate the products of research more widely. A general duty to disseminate research findings derives from the responsibility of universities to produce and transfer new knowledge. They are the institutions that house the great bulk of the nation's independent research capital and they receive public money for research and teaching. The dominant concern may be public accountability, but it may also be argued that an ethical duty to publish research data exists independently.[96]

As will be observed, trends against multiple-publication, and towards wider dissemination, are not necessarily contradictory. Dissemination implies a requirement to publish beyond a relatively small circle through peer-reviewed journals, amongst different relevant communities and through a range of media. These might include seminars, conferences and popular journals as well as the more heavyweight academic outputs. Researchers can therefore publish widely, from the same data but for different audiences, while being open about the fact. Publishing similar but differently titled articles in journals of the same type, concealing their similarity, is clearly distinguishable. It is not surprising therefore, that a duty to disseminate research findings is the dominant trend for research active academics. The prevalence of requirements to disseminate as a condition of research grants ensures that empirical researchers are familiar with the distinction between dissemination and multiple-publication. Such an obligation might also be urged on academics using other research methods, since

---

[95] Some editors advocate 'whistle-blowing' by peers and investigation by journal editors, with the publication of apologies in appropriate cases, and reference back to employing institutions. A Saxon, 'Research, Ethics and Publishing' (2001) 98 *Clinical Immunology* 155.

[96] The source of the argument is that monopolising, or not publishing, research data gathered at the public expense is 'robbing the poor', because the policy framed in the absence of satisfactory data may further disadvantage such groups. D Hulme, 'Hand Over Your Data!', *The Times Higher Education Supplement*, 28 March 2003, p 16.

they operate in a similar institutional context and circumstances and might have just as much impact on groups and individuals through their work.

Some research is conducted in universities under condition that there is to be no dissemination of findings. The general move towards wide dissemination raises ethical questions for academics about conducting research for the sole use of commercial sponsors. It is inconsistent with the public role of universities in knowledge production and dissemination that academic researchers should not disseminate findings. Wider issues arise where, for example, something is discovered that the public interest demands should be made public. Whether research ethics demands that a duty to break silence transcends the duty to honour obligations could depend on the public interest served by disclosure. Publishing research that further disadvantages a disempowered group presents more difficult ethical questions. Presumably, if access to members of such a group was granted because of the assumed benefits to the group, the principle of non-maleficence provides a foundation for rebutting the presumption in favour of dissemination. If ethical approval was granted to such a project on the grounds of beneficence, the approving ethics committee might also be consulted on the ethics of publication.

F. EVALUATION

Issues of reflection and accountability are wrapped up in the evaluation stage of research projects. The social importance of research creates multiple obligations for researchers of trust, honesty, integrity, that are usually only dimly perceived. Ethical dilemmas that arise in the field must be resolved in an instant, often under pressure. The period following the completion of research is an opportunity to take seriously the professional obligation to reflect critically on what has been undertaken, to learn from the experience and, perhaps most importantly, to ensure that the research team also absorbs lessons. In future, these lessons from the field may be so important that there will be an expectation of sharing with a wider audience, the research community and, perhaps formally, the local ethics committee.

G. CONCLUSION

The formalisation of ethics under the shadow of law and its institutionalisation through university ethics committees threatens a period of difficulty as weak professionalism gives way to bureaucratic and administrative control. This is inevitable, however, under the pressure of demands to monitor and regulate standards of research, to limit risk and liability, particularly in relation to more demanding regimes for data protection and human rights, and to anticipate moves to a regulatory regime based on institutional research competence. It is predicted that the formalisation of ethics will change the nature of the relationship between researchers and those they research, irrespective of minimum legal requirements, and that the autonomy of subjects of research will become a dominant concern for such committees. This will force re-examination of the relative values of research and make explicit the roles of beneficence, non-maleficence and justice in research ethics discourse. Ethics committees may well treat covert studies, proxy consent, and even some ethnography, as problematic and either refuse consent for, or impose onerous conditions on, such studies. This issue needs to be more widely understood and managed appropriately.

The challenges that researchers will face are, however, commensurate with the importance of a field producing new knowledge often intended to have practical or policy consequences. Institutional developments will increase the attention paid to the ethics of field research but the widening conception of the ethical field will raise awareness of a range of issues on which the research community has found it difficult to gain purchase, such as the place of research in the universities and the conditions and prospects of junior staff. This may, in turn, lead to stronger collegial bonds in the research community. One product will be a much needed increase in research training informed by ethics, to 'continuing professional development' through production of codes, publication of tried and tested solutions to practical problems, including hypothetical problems, and more informed debates concerning ethical issues. It may also stimulate interest in the ethical dimensions of the socio-legal discipline, its content, its personnel and its audiences. These will be significant developments in, and for, a marginalized field.

16

Evaluation Research and Legal Services

MAX TRAVERS

S OCIAL SCIENTISTS WORKING in British universities face increasing pressures not only to publish in peer-reviewed academic journals, but also obtain external income from consultancy. This often means writing a report evaluating the work of some public agency, using a mixture of quantitative and qualitative methods.[1] My objective in this paper is to provide a critical review of evaluation research, contrasting this with sociological approaches to evaluation and quality assurance. I will particularly focus on legal services, and the implications for socio-legal researchers based in departments of law or social science in British universities.

The paper starts with an overview of what evaluation research involves, and how it is relevant to the delivery of legal services. It then reviews two criticisms that have been made of evaluation as a research paradigm, and explain why many university-based researchers would prefer not to conduct this kind of research. One criticism is that methodological standards are often lower than in other areas of social science, partly because most 'small-scale' evaluations are poorly resourced, but also because the managers and civil servants who commission these studies have little interest in how academics understand and debate methodological questions. Another is that evaluation research has a managerial bias, and researchers are required to become 'hired hands' and give up their intellectual independence.

The next part of the paper reviews how sociologists in different traditions have studied this new form of regulation. It starts by considering the writings of Michael Power, the 2002 Reith Lecturer Onora O'Neill, and the Foucauldian governmentality tradition.[2] It suggests that these all make a

---

[1] See, for example, A Clarke, *Evaluation Research: An Introduction to Principles* (London, Sage, 1999); I Shaw, *Qualitative Evaluation* (London, Sage, 1999); and C Robson, *Small-Scale Evaluation: Principles and Practice* (London, Sage, 2000).

[2] M Power, The Audit Society: Rituals of Verification (Oxford, OUP 1997); O O'Neill, A Question of Trust: The 2002 Reith Lectures (London, BBC, 2002).

powerful moral and political case against quality assurance, and also implicitly against evaluation research, but that qualitative or ethnographic research on how quality reports are produced and used, and the alleged burdens created by excessive regulation, is needed to test their general arguments. I will argue that ethnomethodology goes considerably further than these critical approaches in addressing the day-to-day work involved in quality assurance, and makes it possible to understand the deteriorating relationship between managers and professionals across the public sector.

The paper concludes by considering how socio-legal researchers should respond to the opportunities offered by evaluation research. Following Payne, Dingwall and Carter, it suggests that we should pursue the difficult course of constructive engagement, rather than withdrawing into textually-based critical scholarship.[3] We face the twin challenges of not only raising our own methodological standards, which are low in relation to mainstream sociology and social policy, but also persuading the organisations commissioning research that they will benefit from more thoughtful and rigorous evaluations.

A. WHAT IS EVALUATION RESEARCH?

According to Carol Weiss, one of the most respected figures in this field, 'evaluation is the systematic assessment of the operation and/or the outcomes of a program or policy, compared to a set of explicit or implicit standards, as a means of contributing to the improvement of the program or policy'.[4] In contrast to academic research which is concerned with the production of knowledge, or perhaps delivering a general political message, the aim of an evaluation is to make a practical difference to the delivery of government programmes and policies.

This kind of applied research has a long history in America. Private foundations funded studies of the social welfare programmes that they supported in the 1940s. From the mid–1960s, the federal government evaluated the various programmes established during the War on Poverty, and 'by the end of the 1970s evaluation had become common-place across federal agencies'.[5] Although there were fewer new social programmes to evaluate during the Reagan administration, there was a revival in the 1990s. A large number of consultancy firms, in-house government agencies, and university-based researchers conduct evaluation studies for federal, state and local government. They have established several journals, such as *Evaluation*

---

[3] G Payne, R Dingwall and M Carter, *Sociology and Social Research* (London, Routledge, 1981).

[4] C Weiss, Evaluation: Methods for Studying Policies and Programs (New York, NY, Prentice-Hall, 1998) 4.

[5] Weiss, *ibid*, p 13.

Review and the *American Journal of Evaluation*, that publish evaluation research and debate methodological issues. They also have a professional association, the American Evaluation Association, and hold regular conferences.

Evaluation took longer to develop in Britain, although the present New Labour government is committed to what is termed 'evidence-based' policy.[6] This has involved commissioning pilot studies of new initiatives such as the New Deal, and making evaluation a statutory requirement for local government programmes under the 1998 Crime and Disorder Act. Evaluators have also benefited from a shift in philosophy across the public sector, the New Public Management, in which government services previously provided by Departments of State are devolved to *quasi*-independent agencies that must demonstrate they provide a good service to the customer, and value for money to the tax-payer. Britain now has its own Evaluation Society and academic journals such as *Evaluation* which was established in 1994.

1. Methods of Investigation

The majority of studies have employed quantitative methods, and focus on whether government programmes make a difference. A typical research question might be whether an educational initiative to reduce juvenile delinquency had a demonstrable effect on the youths who participated. The researcher, in this case, would measure attitudes using a questionnaire before and after the programme. A major concern would be to establish a randomised experimental design, modelled on natural science, so that one could also measure a change of attitudes in youths with the same characteristics who did not attend the programme.[7] It has also become increasingly

---

[6] This was introduced by D Blunkett 'Influence or Irrelevance: Can Social Science Improve Government' lecture to the *Economic and Social Research Council as Secretary of State for Education and Employment* (London, ESRC, 2 February 2000). He argued that government needed social scientific research, but then went on to attack educational researchers for producing irrelevant and ideologically-motivated findings. For discussion on the relationship between New Labour and social science, see R Walker, 'Great Expectations: Can Social Science Evaluate New Labour's Policies' (2001) 38 *Evaluation* 305–30; and H Davies, S Nutley and P Smith, (eds), *What Works? Evidence-Based Policy and Practice in Public Services* (Bristol, Policy Press, 2000).

[7] For examples of a 'random assignment' and 'program implementation' study, see J Grossman and J Tierney, 'Does Mentoring Work? An Impact Study of the Big Brothers Big Sisters Program' (1988) 22 *Evaluation Review* 403–26; and C Sellers, T Taylor and F Esbensen, 'Reality Check: Evaluating a School-Based Gang Prevention Model' (1998) 22 *Evaluation Review* 590–608. Many studies that employ similar quantitative techniques are published each year by the American evaluation journals. For a review of methodological debates in this field, see H Davies, S Nutley and N Tilley, 'Debates on the Role of Experimentation' in H Davies, S Nutley and P Smith, above, n 6.

common to employ qualitative methods, such as structured interviews, focus groups, and short periods of fieldwork to obtain more detailed information on whether a programme is working. In some cases, large numbers of interviews are carried out, and the data analysed into themes using software programmes such as NUDIST. In small-scale evaluations, a researcher might interview a few practitioners, attend a planning meeting or observe the delivery of some service, and draw on this data.[8] To the best of my knowledge, no researchers have obtained funding in recent years to conduct ethnographic projects based on a long period of observation in one organisation.[9]

Whatever combination of quantitative and qualitative methods is used, it is important to recognise that the logic of explanation, and the assumptions informing evaluation research, are usually positivist in character. It is assumed that one can identify causal relationships between variables, and measure phenomena such as attitudes, provided that one employs the right techniques. Qualitative studies are often used to establish whether programmes are being administered correctly, so that it is then possible to conduct comparisons or 'meta-analysis' on a series of evaluations.

The only sustained interpretive challenge within the evaluation community has come from Egon Guba and Yvonne Lincoln.[10] They argue that reality is socially constructed, so the version of the setting produced by the evaluator should have no special status. Conventional evaluations also uncritically support the official definition of reality in the sponsoring organisation, whereas the views and actions of professionals and clients are equally important in shaping outcomes.[11] The objective of 'fourth generation' evaluation should be to promote dialogue between these different groups, and reflexive learning, rather than produce some spuriously objective account that privileges the perspective of managers. One might add, however, that only a few American evaluators have experimented with these ideas, and most evaluations are based on the assumption that it is possible to determine what happens in organisations, and make authoritative recommendations, without being troubled by the existence of different versions.

---

[8] Robson, above, n 1.

[9] During the golden age of American sociology, researchers were funded to conduct long periods of fieldwork by the main Research Foundations. For examples of ethnographic classics produced by researchers who were given free reign to pursue their own intellectual interests while working on applied projects, see E Goffman, *Asylums* (Harmonsdworth, Penguin, 1961); and E Liebow, *Tally's Corner* (Boston, MA, Little Brown).

[10] E Guba and Y Lincoln, *Fourth Generation Evaluation* (Newbury Park, Sage, 1989).

[11] M Patton, 'A Vision of Evaluation that Strengthens Democracy' (2002) 8(1) *Evaluation* 125–39, advances a similar argument, although he has no interest in the epistemological debates that take place between positivists and interpretivists in sociology.

2. Some Definitional Problems

It will be apparent from this short review that the evaluation industry (Weiss calls it a 'community') draws on mainstream social science for its methods, but often tries to keep its distance from the theoretical and methodological debates that interest university-based researchers. This is because it is primarily concerned with providing useful knowledge in an accessible form to the organisations that provide government services. At the same time, evaluators see themselves as doing more than collecting facts, or offering recommendations based on intuition or opinion, and this is because they have a commitment to scientific method: 'Doing evaluation through a process of research takes more time and costs more money than offhand evaluations that rely on intuition, opinion, or trained sensibility, but it provides a rigor that is missing in these more informal activities.'[12]

This does not fully explain how evaluation differs from applied social scientific research in general. In the United Kingdom, for example, the Economic and Social Research Council will mainly allocate funding to projects that improve economic performance, or the efficiency and effectiveness of public services. This is also evaluation research, although it is usually funded at higher level than consultancy, and must also contribute to the development of theory or methodology in an academic discipline.

Another difficulty is whether one should include the research conducted by a large number of organisations that are concerned with evaluation, but have no interest in creating a new academic discipline. This is the growing field of quality assurance that is overseen by the General Accounting Office (GAO) in America and the Audit Commission.[13] There are also a large number of inspectorates in the United Kingdom which examine the activities of schools, the social services, universities and the criminal justice system. The majority of people writing these reports are civil servants or practitioners without any background in social science, but they also conduct evaluation research.

B. EVALUATION AND LEGAL SERVICES

Socio-legal researchers should be interested in evaluation for two reasons. In the first place, it is an important, but under-researched, area of regulation. Local authorities and other agencies have a statutory obligation to conduct evaluations, and provide statistical data to inspectorates and the Audit Commission. There is almost no part of society untouched by quality

---

[12] Weiss, above, n 2, p 5.
[13] These bodies were originally concerned with financial auditing, but they now produce numerous reports about the quality of service provided by public services.

assurance, and more routine evaluations are conducted than at any time in British history.[14]

One should also remember that, although many lawyers work in private practice, the legal system is part of public services, and subject to the same pressures to cut costs and demonstrate value for money. Legal aid firms are now regularly assessed and audited by the Legal Services Commission (Sherr, *et al*, 1994; *cf* Travers 1994, Somerlad 1999). There has also been a greater emphasis on performance targets in the courts following the Woolf Report, although the Lord Chancellor's Department has resisted pressures to make the judiciary more accountable. Finally, law schools along with other university departments are subject to review by the Quality Assurance Agency for Higher Education (QAA), and the Research Assessment Exercise which are intended to raise standards, allocate scarce resources, and encourage competition between institutions.

It is difficult to assess the extent to which British socio-legal researchers (who are primarily based in law departments) are engaged in doing evaluation research. This is because, unlike other areas of academic inquiry, the majority of evaluation studies are never published. One can get some idea of what research has been commissioned or conducted by government departments by looking at the publications produced by the Home Office Research Unit, the Lord Chancellor's Department and the Law Society, or at studies cited in The Macpherson Report on the murder of Stephen Lawrence or the Auld Review of the Criminal Courts. However, a much larger number of local evaluations, commissioned by local authorities, police forces, and the voluntary sector are never distributed beyond a local policy network.

C. OBJECTIONS TO EVALUATION RESEARCH

Although evaluation can be viewed as an opportunity to make social science interesting and relevant to a wider audience, relatively few university-based researchers have welcomed these developments.[15] There are two main objections. The first is that most evaluation research is less rigorous and offers less intellectual satisfaction than publishing in peer-reviewed academic journals. The second is that there is an inevitable political bias in evaluation studies towards the needs and perspective of managers, rather than practitioners or clients: the researcher becomes a hired-hand serving government, and loses the ability to represent subordinate or disadvantaged groups.

---

[14] Power, above n 1, uses the phrase 'audit explosion' although he acknowledges that it is difficult to quantify the amount of time and money spent on auditing.

[15] See C Payne, R Dingwall and M Carter, above, n 3; R Scott and A Shore, *Why Sociology Does Not Apply: A Study of the Use of Sociology in Public Life* (New York, NY, Elsevier-North Holland, 1979).

1. The Charge of Lower Standards

When discussing the issue of standards, it is important to make a distinction between the 'small-scale' evaluations commissioned by local agencies, and the 'flag-ship' projects that are more generously funded by government departments. There is, for example, no evidence to suggest evaluation research is inferior to peer-reviewed social science if one looks at the many highly rigorous quantitative studies that are published in the American evaluation journals. This has not, however, prevented some academics from complaining about the routine character of work in this field, and the need for a more thoughtful or critical approach to data collection and analysis.[16]

Methodological standards are considerably lower in the average small-scale study commissioned by a local agency to demonstrate its efficiency or effectiveness for the purposes of some external or internal review. Unsurprisingly, one finds that many studies measure the effect of programmes without using a randomised control group. Although a layperson might regard the findings as persuasive, from a scientific perspective they are virtually worthless.[17] Similarly, one finds far-reaching conclusions being drawn from tiny samples, and less care and attention to the problems involved in measuring variables, and using appropriate statistical tests.

In the case of qualitative research, there is arguably an even greater gulf between the methods used in evaluation research, and those taught in university departments. One major difference is that the assumptions informing evaluations are broadly positivist in character, in the sense that it is assumed one can make objective findings through measuring and relating variables, whereas there are also interpretive, realist and post-modern traditions in ethnography that could be employed in studying any social setting. None of the main texts on evaluation mentions standard qualitative traditions like symbolic interactionism, ethnomethodology or conversation analysis. Even grounded theory hardly gets a mention, which is strange since this is informed to some extent by positivist assumptions, and widely used in applied social science.[18]

There are all kinds of methodological debates about representation in qualitative research, but these are largely irrelevant to evaluation studies. Instead extracts from interviews are used to support some argument about the processes that produce outcomes in an organisation, without considering

---

[16] See, for example, R Pawson and N Tilley, *Realistic Evaluation* (London, Sage, 1997).

[17] It would be interesting to look more systematically at how standards of proof and argument differ in academic life from those employed in practical fields like management or politics.

[18] Grounded theorists employ an elaborate method based on analytic induction that seeks to produce formal theory grounded in evidence that can help practitioners and policy-makers. See A Strauss and J Corbin, *Basics of Qualitative Research: Techniques and Procedures for Producing Grounded Theory* (London, Sage, 1998).

any of the philosophical issues about representation that trouble sociologists or anthropologists. These include the possibility there might be different perspectives, or the extent to which interviews can adequately address the practical issues involved in delivering a service, each of which should be highly relevant in an evaluation.

This is one reason why academics often look down on evaluation, and it is still a small field, relative to other areas of social science, despite the pressures on universities to secure external income from consultancy. Irrespective of political considerations, which I will consider next, one can see that one cannot usually pursue cutting edge intellectual questions, or state-of-the-art methods in evaluation: rather, as Weis notes, the skill lies in making 'research simultaneously rigorous and useful' while dealing with 'the complexities of real people in real programs run by real organizations'.[19]

2. The Charge of Political Bias

Social scientists have also kept their distance from policy research because it has an inevitable managerial bias. The classic statement of this position is Alvin Gouldner's critique of symbolic interactionists who conducted liberal studies about deviance during the 1960s.[20] Gouldner saw them as making a mutually profitable compact with middle-managers in the welfare state that provided ideological support for liberal capitalism. Although, on the face of things, it appeared that they were siding with disadvantaged groups against state institutions, in fact this diverted attention away from massive structural inequalities in American society.

Most academics have liberal or left-wing political views (they are more likely to read *The Guardian* than *The Daily Mail*), so it is hardly surprising that sociologists and socio-legal researchers have maintained a critical distance towards agencies like the police, courts and social services. The best empirical studies about law and criminal justice from the late 1960s and 1970s have a strong ideological bias. This is evident in how they collect and present data selectively to support a left-wing political case.[21]

By contrast, evaluators generally have no qualms about serving the needs of managers, and do not question the objectives of government policy.

---

[19] Weiss, above, n 4, p 18.

[20] A Gouldner, *The Coming Crisis of Western Sociology* (London, Heinemann, 1970).

[21] There is an interesting parallel here in that both evaluation reports and studies by left-wing sociologists usually present a one-sided view of the institution that they are studying. For a discussion of how this is done in criminal justice, see M Travers, 'Preaching to the Converted? Improving the Persuasiveness of Criminal Justice' (1997) 37 *British Journal of Criminology* 359–77.

Weiss, for example, appears to have complete faith that policies and programmes improve over time, and that people in authority can be trusted to make good decisions based on the latest scientific knowledge: 'Evaluation is a practical craft, designed to make programmes work better and to allocate resources to better programs. Evaluators expect people in authority to use evaluation results to take wise action. They take satisfaction from the chance to contribute to social betterment.[22]

Most evaluators recognise that there are groups with different perspectives and political interests in real organisations, and there is likely to be conflict between front-line workers and management, especially if cuts are being introduced. However, most evaluation reports are written for senior managers, and inevitably address the questions that they feel are important, rather than allowing other groups to express their concerns. Most of the evaluation reports published by the Home Office give the bland and reassuring impression that government policies and programmes are working, and that managers are overcoming various problems.

To give an example, a key objective of current government policy is to reduce crime through encouraging professionals in different agencies to work together in multi-agency partnerships. Various studies are being commissioned to evaluate their success. One can predict that these will not reveal the true extent of distrust and hostility between, for example, social workers and the police, and the cynical attitudes of some practitioners towards partnerships. This is because political considerations ultimately determine what is published in any evaluative study. Inevitably, the agency and the government program being evaluated are portrayed in a good light.[23]

One might add that, despite their radical intentions, 'fourth generation' evaluators inevitably have to produce findings that are acceptable to the organisations that commission their research.[24] One also suspects that the full range of views one might hear as an insider (which include complaints about individual managers, dissatisfaction about policy and resources, and deep cynicism about excessive bureaucracy) are not usually revealed to consultants.

---

[22] Weiss, above, n 4, p 5.

[23] For a recent complaint about censorship in the United Kingdom, see D Tombs and D Whyte, 'Shining a Light on Power? Reflections on British Criminology and the Future of Critical Social Science' (2003) 41(Winter) *Socio-Legal Newsletter* 1–2.

[24] This parallels the way ethnographers, who are committed to the idea there can only be multiple verisons of reality, often find it difficult to avoid privileging their own authorial viewpoint. For a discussion of postmodern ethnography, see J Clifford, 'On Ethnographic Authority' in J Clifford, *The Predicament of Culture: Twentieth Century Ethnography, Literature and Art* (Cambridge, MA, Harvard University Press, 1988) 21–54.

D. STUDYING EVALUATION FROM A SOCIOLOGICAL PERSPECTIVE

Having described the nature of evaluation research, and discussed two criticisms, I now want to consider how one might study evaluation, and quality assurance more generally, from a sociological perspective. The next part of the paper is, therefore, a contribution to sociology of law, and reviews the actual or potential contribution of a few traditions.[25] It starts by considering the sociological critique advanced by Michael Power and the 2002 Reith Lecturer Onora O'Neill about the negative effects of inspection and auditing.[26]

1. A Sociological Critique of Quality Assurance

The continuing relevance of sociology as an academic discipline, and the reason why it has become a central part of the undergraduate curriculum in democratic societies, lies in the fact that it forces the student to question and reflect critically on areas of social life that one might otherwise take for granted. Law is a good example, in that the ordinary citizen does not usually question or even think about the legitimacy of legislators, judges and lawyers, and the entire technical apparatus of government. The objective of sociology is to problematise these activities: to ask not simply how things could be different, but how institutions like the legal system and politics actually work behind the official front presented to the public.

From the very beginning of socio-legal studies as an academic discipline, there has been a debate over whether it should provide technical services to the legal profession and government, or develop a critical stance towards law drawing on different sociological perspectives.[27] One can see that exactly the same choice faces contemporary socio-legal scholars in relation to evaluation research. We are well-placed to contribute to the evaluation of different government programmes, particularly in the area of legal services. However, it is also possible to adopt a sociological approach towards evaluation, and quality assurance more generally. This involves asking moral and political questions about how contemporary societies are developing which are not open to applied researchers

---

[25] There are, of course, many different sociological perspectives, and a neo-functionalist or Marxist analyst, to give two examples, could offer alternative ways of understanding the rise of quality assurance. For an introduction to a number of traditions in sociology of law, see R Banakar and M Travers, (eds), *An Introduction to Law and Social Theory* (Oxford, Hart Publishing, 2002).

[26] See above, n 1.

[27] See CM Campbell and P Wiles, 'The Study of Law and Society in Britain' (1976) 10 *Law and Society Review* 547–78; M Travers, 'Sociology of Law in Britain' (2001) 32 *The American Sociologist* 26–40; and S Silbey and A Sarat, 'The Pull of the Policy Audience' (1988) 10 *Law and Policy* 98–116.

The most compelling moral and political critiques of quality assurance have been made by Michael Power in his (1997) book *The Audit Society* and in the 2002 Reith Lectures delivered by Onora O'Neill. Neither are strictly speaking sociologists, although they draw on ideas from different sociological traditions, so one can see Power has been influenced by Weber and Foucault, and O'Neill by Durkheim. Although they draw on different intellectual sources, each argues that quality assurance is largely ritualistic, and damages the delivery of public services through reducing levels of trust, and creating excessive regulation and red-tape.

O'Neill blames the media for creating the anxieties that fuel quality assurance through irresponsible reporting. She believes, along with many conservative philosophers and social theorists over the last two hundred years, that trust is necessary for a cohesive society, but that this is threatened by the relentless changes associated with industrialisation and modernity.[28] Whereas Emile Durkheim believed that the professions, and scientific experts, could create new forms of social solidarity, O'Neill argues that trust in experts has broken down, with damaging consequences for our sense of well-being. The rise of quality assurance is, therefore, seen as a social pathology that damages the quality of service provided by professionals, and encourages individualistic and anti-social attitudes among the public.[29]

Power's central argument is that quality assurance is 'a growing industry of comfort production' that makes us feel better rather than offering any benefit to public sector organisations or the economy.[30] Clients are rarely consulted, so there is no real bite to auditing, and institutions are rarely allowed to fail. Power asks 'whether audit provides deluded visions of control and transparency which satisfy the self-image of managers, regulators and politicians but which are neither as effective nor as neutral as commonly imagined'.[31]

A second claim is that quality assurance, instead of improving performance, might actually damage it by creating the requirement to produce mountains of paperwork. He shows, for example, how once measures to assess quality are introduced, organisations quickly learn how to produce information that satisfies the auditors. This can, however, have unintended negative effects: '... audits may turn organizations on their heads and generate excessive preoccupations with, often costly, auditable process. At the

---

[28] For two recent examples, see R Putnam, *Bowling Alone: The Collapse and Revival of an American Community* (New York, NY, Simon & Schuster, 2001); and F Furedi, *Culture of Fear: Risk Taking and the Morality of Low Expectation* (Leicester, Continuum, 2002).

[29] Functionalists are fond of using biological or organic metaphors, and from this perspective quality assurance could be viewed as a cancer that feeds on our fears and anxieties about public services, but damages the host organism.

[30] Power, above, n 1, p 147.

[31] *Ibid*, p 143.

extreme, performance and quality are in danger of being defined largely in terms of conformity to such process.[32]

Without going into the detail of their argument, Power and O'Neill provide an intellectual version of the objections many professionals working in the public sector have towards quality assurance.[33] One can note that this is strongly opposed to the view of managers and professional evaluators who believe that professionals cannot be trusted to provide a good service without regular auditing, and that this measurably improves the quality of service provided to customers.[34]

2. Foucault, Governmentality and Quality Assurance

Another group of scholars who have made critical observations about quality assurance is the Foucauldian governmentality tradition. Foucault's writings on governmentality, like the rest of his work, are difficult and complex, and open to multiple interpretations.[35] A central theme is the rise of the administrative and legal apparatus of the modern state, based on liberal ideas about governance. One can read Foucault as saying something similar to Weber about the loss of human freedom in an over-rationalised world. On the other hand, he also sees power as productive, as well as oppressive, so there is something in the theory to please everyone, and it can be used for a variety of purposes.

These ideas broadly inform an area of inter-disciplinary scholarship, embracing sociology, law and political theory, that has examined different aspects of government, and how this has changed in the modern world.[36] In recent years, they have increasingly focused on the changes that have taken place in our own times, which are theorised as a shift from the welfare state to neo-liberalism. This includes 'the privatization of public utilities and welfare functions' and 'the introduction of new forms of management into the civil service modelled upon an image of methods in the private sector'.[37]

---

[32] *Ibid.*

[33] See also H Somerlad, 'The Implementation of Quality Initiatives and the New Public Management in the Legal Aid Sector in England and Wales: Bureaucratisation, Stratification and Surveillance' (1999) 6 *International Journal of the Legal Profession* 311–43.

[34] H Davies, S Hutley and P Smith, above n 6, introduce a collection on 'evidence-based' policy by stating that professionals, such as doctors and police officers have lost the trust of the public, due to higher levels of education. The solution is a new profession of evaluation. It remains unclear, however, whether they believe that 'evidence-based practice' is mainly concerned with 'reassurance', or whether it is meant to address real problems in how professionals deliver services.

[35] See G Wickham, 'Foucault and Law' in Banakar and Travers, above, n 25.

[36] See M Dean, *Governmentality: Power and Rule in Modern Society* (London, Sage, 1999); and G Burchell, C Gordon and P Miller, (eds), *The Foucault Effect: Studies in Governmentality* (London, Harvester Wheatsheaf, 1991).

[37] N Rose, 'The Death of the Social? Re-figuring the Territory of Government' in (1996)25/3 *Economy and Society*, 327, 327–28.

More generally 'government at a distance' encourages individuals to take responsibility for their own welfare instead of relying on state provision.

The rise of auditing is also seen as a significant new development in the way public services are delivered. Under the welfare state, there was a cosy relationship between unaccountable professionals and government. This has changed under neo-liberalism since everyone is subject to audit or inspection:

> Audits of various sorts come to replace the trust that social government invested in professional wisdom and the decisions and actions of specialists. In a whole variety of practices—educational, medical, economic, organizational—audits hold out the promise—however specious—of new distantiated forms of control between political centres of decision and the autonomized loci—schools, hospitals, firms—who now have the responsibility for the government of health, wealth and happiness.[38]

Like other macro-sociological approaches, the governmentality tradition encourages you to understand the rise of quality assurance as part of much wider changes in how human populations are governed. Although Foucauldians often claim to be value-neutral in the Weberian sense, they usually seem happiest in siding with marginal or disadvantaged groups, although this still allows for a wide variety of responses.[39] It is possible, from this perspective, to complain about the 'bullying, waste and suffering' associated with the 'increasingly influential and well-paid new class of managers' who are 'the principal conduit of neo-liberal technologies of management and audit'[40]; but at least one theorist has argued that 'such mechanisms may perhaps contain some innovative possibilities for contesting and reshaping the relations of power between experts and their subjects'.[41]

3. An Ethnomethodological Approach to Quality Assurance

One weakness of this critical literature is that there is very little emphasis on empirical research beyond the analysis of official documents. This is

---

[38] *Ibid*, p 351.

[39] Dean explains the value-free nature of Foucauldian analysis in the following terms:
There is no single standard for deciding whether a form of power or state of domination is contingent or necessary. Such evaluations are made by various actors in the course of contestation and resistance to regimes of government as acts of the exercise of capacities for self-determination. All an analytics of government can do is to analyse the rationalities of resistance and the programmes to which they give rise and to make clear what is at stake and what are the consequences of thinking and acting in such a way. *Ibid*, p 37.
In fact, there is usually a concealed or explicit value position in Foucauldian writings (see, for example, what is implied by the term 'resistance'), which explains their appeal to left-wing intellectuals, following the difficulties experienced by Marxism.

[40] K Stenson, 'Beyond Histories of the Present' (1998) 27 *Economy and Society* 333, 347.

[41] Rose, above, n 37, p 346.

important if you believe that one should address the 'messiness of human practices' in addition to the history of ideas,[42] and how individual human beings respond to these changes. My own view is that any properly scientific sociological account needs to address what happens at the local level in some detail, and with more sensitivity to the perspectives and practices of social actors.

Although it is not well-understood, or widely used in socio-legal studies, I would argue that the sociological tradition that is best placed to address this local level is ethnomethodology, and particularly the ethnographic tradition associated with Harold Garfinkel, and also Egon Bittner, David Sudnow and Aaron Cicourel during the 1960s. These studies examined the interpretive procedures employed to make decisions by the police, defence lawyers, educational counsellors and coroners, and the political and organisational constraints that determined adequate work in those settings.[43] They focus on the practical considerations involved in day-to-day work that produces official statistics such as crime rates, guilty pleas and suicides.

Statistical measures are routinely collected and analysed as part of the management process in large organisations, and also used to present performance to the public in league tables required by government. In what some have described as an evaluation society, every organisation has to present itself, and become accountable to outside audiences through annual reports, evaluations, annual monitoring, and the new occupation of quality assurance that has grown as a sub-field of management with the task of producing and managing this information.[44]

One way to read a study like Cicourel's *The Social Organization of Juvenile Justice* is as a critique of official statistics like crime rates at a time when these were used to justify political action. The statistics suggested rising levels of black juvenile crime, whereas Cicourel's study drew attention to the prejudicial judgments made by the police about the motivation and likely criminal careers of youths from different ethnic and socio-economic backgrounds. The fact that there is no similar political interest in criticising evaluation studies, or the reports produced by inspectorates is itself

---

[42] Stenson, above, n 40, p 350.

[43] See A Cicourel, *The Social Organisation of Juvenile Justice* (New York, NY, Wiley, 1968); E Bittner, 'The Police on Skid Row: A Study in Peace-Keeping' (1967) 32 *American Sociological Review* 699–715; D Sudnow, 'Normal Crimes: Sociological Features of the Penal Code in a Public Defender's Office' (1965) 12 *Social Problems* 255–76; A Cicourel and J Kitsuse, *The Educational Decision-Makers* (New York, NY, Bobbs-Merrill, 1968); and H Garfinkel, 'Practical Sociological Reasoning: Some Features in the Work of the Los Angeles Coroner's Office' in Banakar and Travers, above, n 25, 25–42.

[44] Pawson and Tilley, above, n 16 p xi–xii, note that the rise of evaluation research can be explained by the fact that more people are doing managerial and administrative jobs: 'We live in a knowledge-centred, value-adding, information-processing, management-fixated world which has an obsession with decision-making. As we write, managers and administrators have become the largest group of employees in Britain. There are 3,921,000 of them, 15.8% of the labour force, all charged with judgements to better their organisations'.

interesting, since it suggests that whether an agency like a police force or law court performs well or badly is not something that particularly concerns the public, and is not even usually reported in the newspapers. This does not mean, however, that managers and practitioners may not have sleepless nights worrying about the possibility of obtaining a low grade from an inspection, or obtain tremendous pride from, for example, obtaining a Chartermark.[45] What exactly is at stake, and for whom, are questions one would need to address in an empirical study.[46]

To study quality assurance from an ethnomethodological perspective, would also require obtaining access to examine the practical work of conducting and preparing for inspections. We know that a tremendous amount of effort is expended in preparing the rules and regulations that govern inspections, in recruiting and training inspectors, in scrutinising paper documents, and in conducting inspection visits. This happens regularly in law courts, prisons, police forces, and legal offices. On the other side, there are people preparing for inspections, having coaching sessions, and holding innumerable meetings concerned with quality. Outside the inspection process itself, annual monitoring and evaluation forms part of everyone's work, and discussions about quality are held and recorded in countless meetings.

It is tempting to consider this whole procedure in dramaturgical terms, or as an absurd ritual. An ethnomethodological analysis, however, would resist the temptation to ironicise, and instead focus on the serious concerns of the different groups and organisations involved in these procedures. One has to begin by recognising that managers are always worried and anxious about quality, and that getting a good score matters. But one also has to remember that professionals are also usually concerned about quality, and resent the organisational and financial constraints that prevent them from giving a good service to clients.

Another topic one could investigate from this perspective is the effectiveness of measurement. The problem faced by quality assurers and by managers more generally is how to translate the intangible service provided by professionals into objective measures of quality that can be used in league tables or, in some cases, to allocate resources. Inspectors in criminal justice have to decide, for example, whether a court is processing cases quickly or slowly, whether prison officers are behaving correctly, and whether a programme designed to reduce offending works. It seems clear that statistics

---

[45] A Chartermark is a quality standard established by the Cabinet Office and awarded to organisations that demonstrate excellence in setting and achieving goals.

[46] See also C Wiener, *The Elusive Quest: Accountability in Hospitals* (New York, NY, Aldine de Gruyter, 2000) for a symbolic interactionist study about evaluation in American health care. This does not describe practical, day-to-day work in much detail, although there are interesting chapters on the history of different initiatives, and how professionals are coached so they can demonstrate an understanding of quality assurance procedures during inspections.

and other indicators on their own are potentially ambiguous. The task of a research project would, therefore, be to explicate the procedures and methods used to make quality judgments, and how these are sometimes challenged.[47]

Without pre-judging the findings of such a study, one can imagine that many lawyers working in public sector organisations are deeply cynical about quality assurance, and what they perceive as growing levels of bureaucracy. On the other hand, managers and evaluators sincerely believe that inspections, and auditing, improve quality of service. These competing moral claims are arguably central to understanding the deteriorating relationship between managers and professionals in the public sector, although it has not so far resulted in widespread industrial action.[48]

One should also add that, if taken seriously as a form of analysis, ethnomethodology is not especially helpful to either politically-motivated forms of analysis, or management consultancy, since it requires you to acknowledge inconvenient facts, and the difficulty of changing existing social relationships.[49] There is already, for example, considerable evidence that quality assurance is viewed with considerable suspicion by professionals like doctors, teachers and lawyers: everyone in these groups believes that the measures do not measure anything important,[50] and that they are used to control and brow-beat professionals. Similarly any ethnographic study in a public sector organisation is likely to find that complaints about low-levels of resources, excessive levels of bureaucracy and poor management are regularly made. This would be particularly apparent from attending union meetings, which are outside the remit of the average evaluation study.

On the other hand, many critical analysts do not acknowledge the concerns that politicians and managers have about delivering quality. We know, for example, in the case of legal services that many clients get a poor deal from incompetent lawyers, and that the professional mechanisms to redress

[47] See R Harper, 'The Social Organisation of the IMF's Mission Work: An Examination of International Auditing' in M Strathern, (ed), *Audit Cultures: Anthropological Studies in Accountability, Ethics and the Academy* (London, Routledge, 2000) 21–54. He used this approach to study how judgments were made by officials working for the International Monetary Fund on an inspection visit.

[48] This is a matter for political debate since one can argue that there has been a great deal of industrial action by public sector workers during the New Labour government, including the 2002–03 fire service dispute. Other symptoms of unrest would be higher levels of sickness and greater use of disciplinary procedures. It can, of course, be argued that other grievances, particularly relating to pay and workload, are more important than the burdens of auditing, or concerns about maintaining professional standards.

[49] See also Max Weber's comments on 'inconvenient facts' in his 'Science as a Vocation' in H Gerth and CW Mills, (eds), *From Max Weber: Essays in Sociology* (London, Routledge, 1991) 147.

[50] See M Travers, 'Measurement and Reality: Quality Assurance and the Work of a Firm of Criminal Defence Lawyers in Northern England' (1994) 1 *International Journal of the Legal Profession* 173–89.

these complaints are slow and inadequate. We also know that public services are expected to provide a better service, to more people, with fewer
resources, in a society that is reluctant to pay higher levels of income tax.
Quality assurance from this perspective becomes a form of rationing, a
struggle between professionals who refuse to compromise on their professional standards and managers forced to use budgets more effectively.

To complain that quality assurance is ritualistic, or destroys trust may be
true, but this tells us little about what is happening inside legal institutions
like law courts, the police or law firms. It also, arguably, diverts attention
from what is the most interesting topic for sociology of law: the nature of
professional competence. Studies based on interviewing legal professionals
have found that many have highly negative or cynical views about quality
assurance.[51] However, because there have been so few ethnographic studies,
we still know very little about how lawyers, judges or the police understand
and display quality and competence in their day-to-day work. One reason
why professionals are so dismissive towards quality assurance is because
the 'objective' measures used by auditors and inspectors seem alien and
irrelevant to their practical concerns.

E. SOCIOLOGICAL RESEARCH AND EVALUATION: A PRAGMATIC RESPONSE

The term socio-legal rather unhelpfully conflates at least three distinct,
although often over-lapping and complementary, research agendas. Critical
legal researchers employ mainly textual means in advancing a progressive
political viewpoint. Sociologists of law draw on numerous theoretical traditions in sociology in conducting empirical research on law and legal phenomena from a scientific perspective.[52] Finally, policy-driven socio-legal
research is concerned with improving the effectiveness and fairness of legal
services. The field of evaluation research, which I have considered in this
paper, is a sub-field of policy-driven research, although it is likely to become
increasingly significant as Britain becomes an audit or evaluation society.[53]

The financial and political pressure brought to bear on universities to do
'useful' research is unlikely to persuade academics with left-wing political
views who are deeply worried about these developments. This has certainly been the case in mainstream British sociology for a thirty-year period,
where many researchers have viewed policy research almost as an immoral
enterprise, and certainly as not offering the intellectual satisfaction that
one can obtain from pure, scientifically-driven research. It will also not

---

[51] See, for example, Somerlad, above, n 33.
[52] Banakar and Travers, above, n 25.
[53] Power, above, n 1; E Chelimsky, 'Thoughts for a New Evaluation Society' (1997) 3(1)
Evaluation 97–118.

persuade those doing textually-based critical scholarship in law schools who can continue quite happily with only limited funding from central government.

Notwithstanding the objections to evaluation research reviewed in this paper, I would agree with Payne, Dingwall and Carter that we should pursue the difficult course of constructive engagement rather than withdrawing into textually-based critical scholarship.[54] Although one can complain about the pressures on university-based researchers to do applied research that is not especially interesting or valuable in academic terms, there are many examples of studies funded by government agencies in the past, including evaluations, that have also made a contribution to knowledge, and allowed academic disciplines to develop. What seems disappointing is that evaluations in Britain tend to employ a narrow range of methodologies, and seldom raise difficult questions about how government policies and programmes are working. One does not need to have radical or left-wing political views to be disturbed by these developments.

To achieve the climate for more theoretically-informed policy research in Britain, and persuade cash-starved public sector organisations to fund studies more generously, and experiment with more imaginative data-collection strategies, may be an uphill task, but it is clearly important that we should try to do this. We could start by becoming more pro-active in teaching and promoting a wider range of methodologies through the UK Socio-Legal Studies Association, that can be used in applied research.

The growing importance of evaluation may also eventually lead to changes in the law school curriculum, since it is clearly relevant for law students to know about these changes, and acquire some basic research methods training in law schools. Arguably both sociology of law and policy-oriented socio-legal studies will remain weak, both theoretically and methodologically, until students get experience of doing empirical research, as happens in degrees in nursing and management. There has so far been a lack of enthusiasm for introducing social science, as opposed to history or philosophy into law degrees, but an optional methods course would be extremely useful for law students entering a profession that is increasingly subject to evaluation.

Finally, it is worth noting that a rather darker future for applied social science was predicted by Robert Scott and Arnold Shore who reviewed the difficulties faced by American sociologists in making theoretical concepts and arguments relevant to policy-makers over a thirty year period. Scott and Shore concluded that, once those in power realised that sociology could not solve social problems, they might decide to withdraw funding from universities:

---

[54] Payne, Dingwall and Carter, above, n 3.

In an environment where public bodies, which have traditionally supported research and the development of the discipline, are calling for immediate and concrete answers to questions that they insist on formulating, we should expect that what little public money may exist for the social sciences will go to policy-related research done in independent research firms.[55]

One can argue that this has subsequently happened, although with an unexpected twist. Universities have become the main providers of policy-relevant research through self-funding centres of criminal justice and social policy that employ researchers on temporary contracts to process data and conduct evaluations for different agencies and government departments. One can even argue that there is a link between the relative scarcity of interesting theoretically-informed, empirical studies in the last 15 years that one can use in undergraduate teaching and might interest a general audience, and the rise of evaluation research.

---

[55] Scott and Shore, above, n 15, p 238.

Bibliography

ABEL RL, *The Legal Profession in England and Wales* (Oxford, Blackwell, 1988).

——, *English Lawyers between Market and State: The Politics of Professionalism* (Oxford, OUP, 2003).

ABEL RL and LEWIS PSC, (eds), *Lawyers in Society: The Civil Law World* (Berkley, CA, University of California Press, 1988).

——, (eds), *Lawyers in Society: The Common Law World* (Berkley, CA, University of California Press, 1988).

ALEXIADOU N, 'Researching Policy Implementation: Interview Data Analysis in Institutional Contexts' (2001) 4 *International Journal of Social Research Methodology* 51.

ALI S, *Gender and Human Rights in Islam and International Law: Equal before Allah? Equal before Man?* (London, Kluwer Law International, 2000).

ALLAN G, 'Qualitative Research' in ALLAN G and SKINNER C, (eds), *Handbook for Research Students in the Social Sciences* (London, Falmer Press, 1993) 12.

ANDERSEN H and SPENCER H, ANDERSEN H and KASPERSEN B, (eds), *Classical and Modern Social Theory* (Oxford, Blackwells, 2000).

ANDERSEN ML, 'Studying Across Difference: Race, Class and Gender in Qualitative Research' in STANFIELD JH and DENNIS RM, (eds), *Race and Ethnicity in Research Methods* (Newbury Park, CA, Sage, 1993) 127.

ANTHIAS F, 'Beyond Feminism and Multiculturalism: Locating Difference and the Politics of Location' (2002) 25 *Women's Studies International Forum* 275.

ANTHIAS F and YUVAL-DAVIS N, *Racialized Boundaries: Race, Nation, Gender, Colour and Class and the Anti-Racist Struggle* (London, Routledge, 1992).

APPELBAUM RP, FELSTINER WLF and GESSNER V, (eds), *Rules and Networks: The Legal Culture of Global Business Transactions* (Oxford, Hart Publishing, 2001).

ARBIB MA and HESSE MB, *The Construction of Reality* (Cambridge, CUP, 1986).

ARNAUD AJ, 'Structuralist Theories of Law' in AMSELEK P and MACCORMICK N, (eds), *Controversies about Law's Ontology* (Edinburgh, EUP, 1991).

ASHMORE M, *The Reflexive Thesis: Righting the Sociology of Scientific Knowledge* (Chicago, IL, University of Chicago Press, 1989).

ATKINSON P and SILVERMAN D, 'Kundera's Immortality: The Interview Society and the Invention of the Self' (1997) 3 *Qualitative Inquiry* 304.

AUBERT V, 'The Changing Role of Law and Lawyers in Nineteenth and Twentieth Century Norwegian Society' in MACCORMICK DN, (ed), *Lawyers in Their Social Setting* (Edinburgh, Green & Son, 1976) 1.

——, *Rettens Sosiale Funksjon* (Oslo, Universitetsforlaget, 1976).

AXELROD R, (ed), *Structure of Decision: The Cognitive Maps of Political Elites* (Princeton, NJ, Princeton University Press, 1976).

——, 'The Analysis of Cognitive Maps' in R Axelrod, (ed), *Structure of Decision: The Cognitive Maps of Political Elites* (Princeton, NJ, Princeton University Press, 1976) 55.

——, 'The Cognitive Mapping Approach to Decision Making' in AXELROD R, (ed), *Structure of Decision: The Cognitive Maps of Political Elites* (Princeton, NJ, Princeton University Press, 1976) 3.

AYLETT S, *Sydney Under the Wigs: The Memoirs of a Legal King-Maker* (London, Eyre Methuen, 1978).

BABBIE E, *The Basics of Social Research* (Kentucky, Wadsworth, 2002).

BALVIG F, *The Snow White Image: The Hidden Reality of Crime in Switzerland* (Oslo, Norwegian University Press, 1987).

BANAKAR R, *Merging Law and Sociology: Beyond the Dichotomies of the Socio-Legal Research* (Berlin, Glada and Wilch Verlag, 2003).

——, 'Det offentliga samtalet om ethnokulturella frågor' (Public Discourse on Ethno-Cultural Issues) (1993) 1(2) *Häften för kritiska studier* (The Swedish Critical Studies Review) 8.

——, *The Dilemma of Law: Conflict Management in a Multicultural Society* (Swedish title: *Rättens Dilemma: Om konflikthantering i ett mångtkulturellt samhälle*) (Lund, Bokbox, 1994).

——, 'Integrating Reciprocal Perspectives: On Georges Gurvitch's Theory of Immediate Jural Experience' (2001) 16 *Canadian Journal of Law and Society*.

——, 'Reflections on the Methodological Issues of the Sociology of Law' (2002) 27 *Journal of Law and Society* 273.

——, 'Sociological Jurisprudence' in R Banakar and M Travers, (eds), *An Introduction to Law and Social Theory* (Oxford, Hart Publishing, 2002) 33.

——, *The Doorkeepers of the Law: A Socio-Legal Study of Ethnic Discrimination in Sweden* (Aldershot, Dartmouth, 1998).

BANAKAR R and TRAVERS M, (eds), *An Introduction to Law and Social Theory* (Oxford, Hart Publishing, 2002).

BAUMAN Z, *Intimations of Postmodernity* (London, Routledge, 1992).

BEAUCHAMP TL and CHILDRESS JF, *Principles of Biomedical Ethics*, 4th edn, (Oxford, OUP, 1994).

BECKER HS, 'Becoming a Marijuana User' (1953) 59 *American Journal of Sociology* 235.

——, 'Theory: The Necessary Evil' in FLINDERS DJ and MILLS GE, (eds), *Theory and Concepts in Qualitative Research: Perspectives from the Field* (New York, NY, Teachers College Press, 1993).

——, 'The Politics of Presentation: Goffman and Total Institutions' (2003) 26 *Symbolic Interaction* 659.

BERMAN HJ, *Justice in Russia* (Cambridge, MA, Harvard University Press, 1950).

M Bertilsson, (ed), *Rätten i Förvandling: Jurister mellan stat och marknad* (Stockholm, Nerenius & Santerus Förlag, 1995).

BHABBA HK, 'Cultures in Between' in BENNETT D, (ed), *Multicultural States: Rethinking Difference and Identity* (London, Routledge, 1998).

BIKAAKO W and SSENKUMBA J, 'Gender, Land and Rights: Contemporary Contestations in Law, Policy and Practice in Uganda' in MUTHONI WANYEKI L, (ed), *Women and Land in Africa: Culture, Religion and Realizing Women's Rights* (London, Zed Books, 2003) 31.

BITTNER E, 'The Police on Skid Row: A Study in Peace-Keeping' (1967) 32 *American Sociological Review* 699.

BIX B, *Law, Language, and Legal Determinacy* (Oxford, OUP, 1996).

BLACK D, *The Behavior of Law* (New York, NY, Academic Press, 1980).
——, *Sociological Justice* (Oxford, OUP, 1989).
BLACK J, 'Regulatory Conversations' (2002) 29 *Journal of Law and Society* 163.
——, *Talking about Regulation* (1998) *Public Law* 77.
BLANKENBURG E and BRUINSMA F, *Dutch Legal Culture* (London, Kluwer Law International, 1994).
BLOOR D, *Knowledge and Social Imagery* (London, Routledge and Kegan, 1976).
BLUMER H, *Symbolic Interactionism: Perspective and Method* (Englewood Cliffs, NJ, Prentice-Hall, 1969).
BOGDAN M, *Comparative Law* (Stockholm, Norstedts juridik, 1994).
BOHANNAN P, *Justice and Judgment Among the Tiv* (London, OUP for the International African Institute, 1957).
BOON A and LEVIN J, *The Ethics and Conduct of Lawyers in England and Wales* (Oxford, Hart Publishing, 1999).
BORDEAU B, 'Dual Relationships in Qualitative Research' (2000) 4 *The Qualitative Report*, http://www.nova.edu/sss/QR/QR4-3bourdeau.html.
BOURDIEU P, 'L'illusion biograpique' in (1986) XII *Actes de la recherche en sciences sociales* 69.
——, 'The Force of Law: Toward a Sociology of the Juridical Field' (1986) 38 *Hastings Law Journal* 814.
——, *Homo Academicus* (Cambridge, Policy Press, 1988).
——, *et al*, *The Craft of Sociology: Epistemological Preliminaries* (Berlin, Walter de Gruyter, 1991).
——, *The State Nobility* (Cambridge, Policy Press, 1996).
BOURDIEU P and WACQUANT LJD, *An Invitation to Reflexive Sociology* (Chicago, IL, University of Chicago Press, 1992).
BRADNEY A, 'Law as a Parasitic Discipline' (1998) 25 *Journal of Law and Society* 71.
——, *Conversations, Choices and Chances: The Liberal Law School in the Twenty-First Century* (Oxford, Hart Publishing, 2003).
BRADNEY A and COWNIE F, *Living Without Law: An Ethnography of Quaker Decision-Making, Dispute Avoidance and Dispute Resolution* (Aldershot, Ashgate, 2000).
BRANNEN J, *New Mothers at Work: Employment and Childcare* (London, Unwin Hyman, 1988).
BRANTS C and FIELD S, 'Legal Culture, Political Cultures and Procedural Traditions: Towards a Comparative Interpretation of Covert and Proactive Policing in England and Wales and the Netherlands' in NELKEN D, (ed), *Contrasting Criminal Justice* (Aldershot, Dartmouth, 2000) 77.
BREWER JD, 'Sensitivity as a Problem in Field Research: A Study of Routine Policing in Northern Ireland' (1990) 33 *American Behavioural Scientist* 578.
BROOKMAN F, NOAKES L and WINCUP E, *Qualitative Research in Criminology* (Aldershot, Ashgate, 1999).
BROWN A, (ed), *Contemporary Russian Politics* (Oxford, OUP, 2001).
BROWN B, 'The Impact of Male Labour Migration on Women in Botswana' (1983) 82 *African Affairs* 367.
BROWN B and COUSINS M, 'The Linguistic Fault: The Case of Foucault's Archaeology' in GANE M, *Towards a Critique of Foucault* (London, Routledge and Kegan, 1986) 36.

BRYMAN A, *Quantity and Quality in Social Research* (London, Routledge, 2000).
——, *Social Research Methods* (Oxford, OUP, 2001).
BUDAK AC and GESSNER V, (eds), *Emerging Legal Certainty: Empirical Studies of the Globalisation of Law* (Aldershot, Ashgate, 1998).
BUGLER J, 'NCOs of the Law', *New Statesman*, 5 March 1976, p 287.
BUNT G, 'Decision Making Concerns in British Islamic Environments' (1998) 19 *Islam and Christian-Muslim Relations* 103.
BURAWOY M, 'Revisits: An Outline of a Theory of Reflexive Ethnography' (2003) 68 *American Sociological Review* 645.
BURCHELL G, GORDON C and MILLER P, (eds), *The Foucault Effect: Studies in Governmentality* (London, Harvester Wheatsheaf, 1991).
BURLEY AM and WALTER M, 'Europe before the Court: A Political Theory of Legal Integration' (1993) 47 *International Organization* 41.
BUTLER WE, *Russian Law* (Oxford, OUP, 2003).
CAIN M, 'Realist Philosophy and Standpoint Epistemologies or Feminist Criminology as a Successor Science' in GELSTHORPE L and MORRIS A, (eds), *Feminist Perspectives in Criminology* (Milton Keynes, Open University Press, 1990) 124.
——, 'Orientalism, Occidentalism and the Sociology of Crime' (2000b) 40 *British Journal Criminal* 239.
——, 'Through Other Eyes: On the Limitations and Value of Western Criminology for Teaching and Practice in Trinidad and Tobago' in NELKEN D, (ed), *Contrasting Criminal Justice* (Aldershot, Dartmouth, 2000) 265.
CAMBROSIO A, LIMOGES C and PRONOVEST D, 'Representing Biotechnology: An Ethnography of Quebec Science Policy' (1990) 20 *Social Studies of Science* 195.
CAMPBELL M and MANICOM A, (eds), *Knowledge, Experience and Ruling Relations* (Toronto, University of Toronto Press, 1995).
CAMPBELL CM and WILES P, 'The Study of Law and Society in Britain' (1976) 10 *Law and Society Review* 547.
CAMPBELL J, *et al*, *Supporting Research Staff: Making a Difference* (Sheffield, University of Sheffield, 2003).
CARABINE J, 'Unmarried Motherhood 1830–1999: A Genealogical Analysis' in WETHERELL M, *et al*, (eds), *Discourse as Data* (London, Sage, 2001) 276.
CARSON WG, (1974) 'Symbolic and Instrumental Dimensions of Early Factory Legislation: A Case Study in the Social Origins of English Law' in R Hood, (ed), *Crime, Criminology and Public Policy* (London, Heinemann, 1980) 107.
——, *The Other Price of Britain's Oil: Safety and Control in the North Sea* (Oxford, Martin Robertson, 1981).
DE CERTEAU M, *The Practice of Everyday Life* (Berkeley, CA, University of California Press, 1984).
CHELIMSKY E, 'Thoughts for a New Evaluation Society' (1997) 3 *Evaluation* 97.
CHENITZ WC and SWANSON JM, 'Qualitative Research using Grounded Theory' in CHENITZ WC and SWANSON JM, (eds), *From Practice to Grounded Theory: Qualitative Research in Nursing* (New York, NY, Addison-Wesley, 1986) 471.
CHIBA M, *Asian Indigenous Law in Interaction with Received Law* (London, Kegan Paul International, 1986).
CICOUREL A, *The Social Organisation of Juvenile Justice* (New York, NY, Wiley, 1968).

CICOUREL A and KITSUSE J, *The Educational Decision-Makers* (New York, NY, Bobbs-Merrill, 1968).

CLARKE A, *Evaluation Research: An Introduction to Principles* (London, Sage, 1999).

CLAUSEN S, *Applied Correspondence Analysis: An Introduction* (London, Sage, 1998).

CLIFFORD J, 'On Ethnographic Authority' in CLIFFORD J, *The Predicament of Culture: Twentieth Century Ethnography, Literature and Art* (Cambridge, MA, Harvard University Press, 1988) 21.

CLINARD MB, *Cities with Little Crime* (Cambridge, CUP, 1978).

COFFEY A, *The Ethnographic Self: Fieldwork and the Representation of Identity* (London, Sage, 1999).

COHEN J, 'A Power Primer' (1992) 112 *Psychological Bulletin* 155.

COLE GF, *et al*, (eds), *Major Criminal Justice Systems: A Comparative Survey* (Beverly Hills, CA, Sage, 1987).

COLLIER R, 'Research Capacity, Critical Social Science and the Paradox of Socio-Legal Studies' (2004) 43 *Socio-Legal Newsletter* 1.

COLLINS H, *Changing Order: Replication and Induction in Scientific Practice* (Beverly Hills, CA, Sage, 1985).

COLLINS PH, *Black Feminist Thought: Knowledge, Consciousness and the Politics of Empowerment* (New York, NY, Routledge, 1990).

——, 'Learning from the Outsider Within: The Sociological Significance of Black Feminist Thought' (1996) 33 *Social Problems* 14.

COLLINS R, 'The Romanticism of Agency/Structure versus the Analysis of Micro/Macro' (1992) 40 *Current Sociology* 77.

COMAROFF JL and ROBERTS SA, *Rules and Processes: The Cultural Logic of Dispute in an African Context* (Chicago, IL, University of Chicago Press, 1981).

COMTE A, *System of Positive Polity* vol 1–4 (New York, NY, Burt Franklin, 1968).

CONLEY JM and O'BARR WM, *Rules versus Relationships: The Ethnography of Legal Discourse* (Chicago, IL, University of Chicago Press, 1990).

——, *Just Words: Law, Language and Power* (Chicago, IL, University of Chicago Press, 1998).

COOPER DM, *An Overview of the Botswana Class Structure and its Articulation with the Rural mode of Production: Insights from Selebi-Phikwe* (Cape Town, University of Cape Town, 1982).

COTTERRELL R, *Sociology of Law: An Introduction* (London, Butterworths, 1992).

——, *Law's Community* (Oxford, Clarendon Press, 1995).

——, 'Why Must Legal Ideas be Interpreted Sociologically?' (1998) 25 *Journal of Law and Society* 171.

——, 'Is there a Logic of Legal Transplants?' in NELKEN D and FEEST J, (eds), *Adapting Legal Culture* (Oxford, Hart Publishing, 2001) 71.

COTTERRELL R and BERCUSSON B, 'Introduction: Law, Democracy and Social Justice' (1988) 15 *Journal of Law and Society* 1.

COULON R, 'Discourse Analysis versus Text Analysis: The Reading of Ideology in Foreign Language Texts' (1988) 1 *International Journal for the Semiotics of Law* 195.

COULSON NJ, *A History of Islamic Law* (Edinburgh, EUP, 1964).

COWNIE F, *Legal Academics: Culture and Identities* (Oxford, Hart Publishing, 2004).

CRAWFORD A, 'Contrasts in Victim/Offender Mediation and Appeals to Community in Comparative Cultural Contexts: France and England and Wales' in NELKEN D, (ed), *Contrasting Criminal Justice* (Aldershot, Dartmouth, 2000) 205.

CRENSHAW K, 'Demarginalising the Intersection of Race and Sex: A Black Feminist Critique of Antidiscrimination Doctrine' in CRENSHAW K, *Feminist Theory and Antiracist Politics* (Chicago, IL, University of Chicago Forum) 139.

CUTTINI M, 'Proxy Informed Consent in Paediatric Research: A Review' (2000) 60 *Early Human Development* 89.

SACHS JD and PRISTOL K, (eds), *The Rule of Law and Economic Reform in Russia* (Oxford, Westview Press, 1997).

DANET B, 'Toward a Method to Evaluate the Ombudsman Role' (1978) 10 *Administration and Society* 335.

DAVID R and BRIERLEY JEC, *Major Legal Systems in the World Today* (London, Stevens, 1985).

DAVIES H, NUTLEY S and SMITH P, (eds), *What Works? Evidence-Based Policy and Practice in Public Services* (Bristol, Policy Press, 2000).

DE SAUSSURE F, *Course in General Linguistics* (London, Fontana, 1974).

DE SOUSA SANTOS B, 'Science and Politics: Doing Research in Rio's Squatter Settlements' in LUCKHAM R, (ed), *Law and Social Enquiry: Case Studies of Research* (Uppsala, Scandinavian Institute of African Studies, and New York, International Center for Law in Development, 1981).

——, *Toward a New Common Sense: Law, Science and Politics in the Paradigmatic Transition* (London, Routledge, 1995).

DEAN M, *Governmentality: Power and Rule in Modern Society* (London, Sage, 1999).

DEEGAN J, 'The Chicago School of Ethnography' in P Atkinson, *et al*, (eds), *Handbook of Ethnography* (London, Sage, 2001).

DELEUZE G and GUATARRI F, *A Thousand Plateaus: Capitalism and Schizophrenia* (London, Athlone, 1988).

DEZALAY Y and GARTH BG, *Dealing in Virtue: International Commercial Arbitration and the Construction of a Transnational Legal Order* (Chicago, IL, University of Chicago, 1996).

——, *The Internationalization of Palaces War: Lawyers, Economists, and the Contest to Transform Latin American States* (Chicago, IL, University of Chicago Press, 2002).

DINGWALL R, 'Ethics and Ethnography' (1980) 28 *Sociological Review* 871.

——, 'Ethnomethodology and Law' in R Banakar and M Travers, (eds), *An Introduction to Law and Social Theory* (Oxford, Hart Publishing, 2002) 227.

DOERING H and HIRSCHAUER S, 'Die Biographie der Dinge: Eine Ethnographie musealer Repräsentation' in AMANN K and HIRSCHAUER S, (ed), *Die Befremdung der eigenen Kultur: Zur Ethnographischen Herausforderung Soziologischer Empirie* (Frankfurt aM, Suhrkamp, 1997).

DORN N, JEPSEN J, and SAVONA N, (eds), *European Drug Policies and Enforcement*, (London, Macmillan, 1996).

DOUGLAS M, *Purity and Danger: An Analysis of the Concepts of Pollution and Taboo* (Harmondsworth, Penguin, 1970).

DOWNES D, *Contrasts in Tolerance* (Oxford, OUP, 1988).

DREW P, 'Contested Evidence in Courtroom Cross-Examination: The Case of a Trial for Rape' in DREW P and HERITAGE J, (eds), *Talk at Work: Interaction in Institutional Settings* (Cambridge, CUP, 1992) 470.

DREYFUS HL and RABINOW P, *Michel Foucault: Beyond Structuralism and Hermeneutics* (Brighton, Harvester Press, 1982).

DURKHEIM E, *The Rules of Sociological Method* (New York, NY, Free Press, 1966).

DWORKIN M, 'Is Law a System of Rules?' in RW Dworkin, (ed), *Legal Philosophy* (Oxford, OUP, 1977) 43.

EDWARDS D, *Discourse and Cognition* (London, Sage, 1990).

EHRLICH E, *Principles of the Sociology of Law* (Cambridge, MA, Harvard University Press, 1936).

EKBERG J, *Inkomsteffekter av Invandring* (Högskolan i Växjö, Centrum för ArbetsMarknadspolitisk Forskning, 1983).

——, *Yrkeskarriärer under 1970–Talet* (Stockholms läns Landsting, Regionplanekontoret, Rapport, 1985).

EKELÖF PO, 'Teleological Construction of Statutes' *Scandinavian Studies in Law* 2 (Stockholm, Almquist and Wiksell, 1958).

EKSTRÖM M, 'Sociologiska förklaringar och Variabelanalysens Gränser: En Kritisk Analys med Exempel Från Medicinsk Sociologi' (Swedish Sociological Explanations and the Limits of Variable Analysis: A Critical Analysis with Examples from Medical Sociology) (1993) 30(2) *Sociologisk Forskning* 26.

ELKINS J, 'Frederick Schauer on the Force of Rules' in MEYER L, (ed), *Rules and Reasoning* (Oxford, Hart Publishing, 1999).

ELLIS B and FOPP R, 'The Origins of Standpoint Epistemologies: Feminism, Marx and Lukacs' paper for the TASA 2001 Conference, The University of Sydney, 2001.

EMERSON R, *Judging Delinquents: Context and Process in Juvenile Court* (Chicago, IL, Aldine, 1969).

ENDICOTT TAO, 'Law and Language' in *Oxford Handbook of Jurisprudence and Philosophy of Law* (Oxford, OUP, 2003).

ERIKSON KT, 'A Comment on Disguised Observation in Sociology' (1967) *Social Problems* 366.

EVAN WM, (ed), *The Sociology of Law: A Social-Structural Perspective* (New York, NY, Free Press, 1980).

EWALD F, 'The Law of Law' in G Teubner, (ed), *Autopoietic Law: A New Approach to Law and Society* (Berlin, de Gruyter, 1987) 36.

EWICK P and SILBEY S, *The Common Place of Law: Stories from Everyday Life* (Chicago, IL, University of Chicago Press, 1998).

FASOLI L, 'Research with Children: Ethical Mind-Fields' (2001) 26 *Australian Journal of Early Childhood* 7.

FAZACKERLEY A, 'Research Linked to Teaching Official', *The Times Higher Education Supplement*, 19 November 2004, p 4.

FAZACKERLEY A and FARRAR S, 'Agree Ethics Code or Face State Control', *The Times Higher Education Supplement*, 14 November 2003, p 1.

FEELEY M, 'Comparing Criminal Law for Criminologists' in NELKEN D, (ed), *Comparing Legal Cultures* (Aldershot, Dartmouth, 1997) 93.

FEEST J and MURAYAMA M, 'Protecting the Innocent through Criminal Justice: A Case Study from Spain, Virtually compared to Germany and Japan' in NELKEN D, (ed), *Contrasting Criminal Justice* (Aldershot, Dartmouth, 2000).

FELSTINER W, ABEL R and SARAT A, 'Transforming of Disputes: Naming, Blaming and Claiming' (1980–81) 15 *Law and Society Review* 631.

FIELDING N, 'Observational Research on the National Front' in M Bulmer, (ed), *Social Research Ethics* (London, Macmillan, 1982).

——, (ed), *Researching Social Life* (London, Sage, 1993).

FIELDS CB and MOORE RH, (eds) *Comparative Criminal Justice* (Prospect Heights, IL, Waveland Press, 1996).

FLOOD J, 'The Middlemen of the Law: An Ethnographic Inquiry into the English Legal Profession' (1981) *American Bar Foundation Research Journal* 377.

——, *Barristers' Clerks: The Law's Middlemen* (Manchester, MUP, 1983).

——, *Anatomy of Law: An Ethnography of a Corporate Law Firm* (PhD dissertation, Department of Sociology, Northwestern University, 1987).

FORM K, *Approaches to Social Enquiry* (Cambridge, Polity Press, 1983).

FOSTER C and HOLLEY S, 'Ethical Review of Multi-Centre Research: A Survey of Multi-Centre Researchers in the South Thames Region' (1998) 32 *Journal of the Royal College of Physicians* 242.

FOUCAULT M, SHERIDAN AM, (tr), *The Archaeology of Knowledge and the Discourse of Language* (London, Tavistock, 1972).

FRANKE H, 'Dutch Tolerance: Facts and Fallacies' (1990) 30 *British Journal of Criminology* 81.

FRANKEL PH, *Essentials of Petroleum: A Key to Oil Economics* and *Essentials* (London, Frank Cass, 1968).

FRIEDMAN K, 'Realisation of Ombudsman Recommendations' (1988) *Fourth International Ombudsman Conference Papers*.

FRIEDMAN J, *Cultural Identity and Global Process* (London, Sage, 1994).

FUREDI F, *Culture of Fear: Risk Taking and the Morality of Low Expectation* (Leicester, Continuum, 2002).

GALANTER M, 'Justice in Many Rooms: Courts, Private Ordering and Indigenous Law' (1981) 19 *Journal of Legal Pluralism and Unofficial Law* 1.

GALLIGAN D, 'Legal Failure: Law and Social Norms in Post-Communist Europe' in GALLIGAN D and KURKCHIYAN M, (eds), *Law and Informal Practices: The Post-Communist Experience* (Oxford, OUP, 2003).

GANE N, *Max Weber and Postmodern Theory: Rationalisation versus Re-enchantment* (London, Routledge, 2002).

GARAPON A, 'The Shock of Globalisation and French Legal Culture' (1995) 4 *Social and Legal Studies* 492.

GARFINKEL SL and SHELAT A, 'Remembrance of Data Passed: A Study of Disk Sanitization Practices' (2003) *IEEE Security and Privacy* 17, http://computer.org/security.

GARFINKEL H, '"Good" Organisational Reasons for "Bad" Clinic Records' in GARFINKEL H, (ed), *Studies in Ethnomethodology* (Englewood-Cliffs, NJ, Prentice-Hall, 1967) 186.

——, 'Practical Sociological Reasoning: Some Features in the Work of the Los Angeles Coroner's Office' in TRAVERS M and MANZO J, (eds) Law in Action: Ethnomethodological and Conversation Analytic approaches to Law (Aldershot, Adngate, 1997) 25.

GARLAND D, *Punishment and Modern Society* (Oxford, OUP, 1990).

——, 'The Limits of the Sovereign State: Strategies of Crime Control in Contemporary Society' (1996) 36 *British Journal of Crimina*l 445.

——, *The Culture of Control* (Oxford, OUP, 2000).

GARRETT G, 'The Politics of Legal Integration in the EU' (1995) 49 *International Organisation* 171.

GEERTZ C, 'Thick Description: Toward an Interpretive Theory of Culture' in GEERTZ C, (ed), *The Interpretation of Culture* (New York, NY, Basic Books, 1973) 3.

——, *Works and Lives* (Cambridge, Polity Press, 1988).

GEIGER T, *Vorstudien zu Einer Soziologie des Rechts* (Preliminary studies for a sociology of law), (Acta Jutlandica XIX, Aarhus, 1947).

——, *Den Danske Intelligens fra Reformationen til Nutiden* (Copenhagen, Ejnar Munksgaard, 1949).

GENN H, *Paths to Justice: What People Do and Think about Going to Law* (Oxford, Hart Publishing, 1999).

GERTH H and MILLS CW, (eds), *From Max Weber: Essays in Sociology* (London, Routledge, 1991).

GESSNER V, (ed), *Foreign Courts* (Aldershot, Dartmouth, 1996).

——, 'The Transformation of European Legal Cultures' in V Gessner, *et al*, *European Legal Cultures* (Aldershot, Dartmouth, 1996).

GIDDENS A, 'Structuralism, Post-Structuralism and the Production of Culture' in GIDDENS A, *Social Theory and Modern Sociology* (Cambridge, Polity Press, 1987).

GLASER BG and STRAUSS A, *The Discovery of Grounded Theory, Strategies for Qualitative Research* (New York, NY, Aldine de Gruyter, 1967).

GLUCKMAN M, *The Judicial Process Among the Barotse of Northern Rhodesia (Zambia)* (Manchester, MUP, 1955).

GOFFMAN E, 'On Cooling the Mark Out: Some Aspects of Adaptation To Failure' (1952) 15 *Psychiatry: Journal for the Study of Interpersonal Processes* 451.

——, 'The Interaction Order' (1983) 48 *American Sociological Review* 1.

——, 'Footing' in WETHERELL M, *et al*, (eds), *Discourse Theory and Practice: A Reader* (London, Sage, 2002) 97.

GOLDSTEIN A and MARCUS M, 'The Myth of Judicial Supervision in Three Inquisitorial Systems: France, Italy and Germany' (1977) 87 *Yale Law Journal* 240.

GOODRICH P, *Legal Discourse: Studies in Linguistics, Rhetoric and Legal Analysis* (London, Macmillan, 1986).

GORER G, *Himalayan Village: An Account of the Lepchas of Sikkim* (London, Michael Joseph, 1938).

GOULDNER A, *The Coming Crisis of Western Sociology* (London, Heinemann, 1970).

GRAHAM C, SENEVIRATNE M and JAMES R, 'Publicising the Bank and Building Societies Ombudsman Schemes' (1993) 3(2) *Consumer Policy Review* 85.

GREEN P, 'Taking Sides: Partisan Research in the 1984–1985 Miners' Strike' in HOBBS D and MAY T, (eds), *Interpreting the Field: Accounts of Ethnography* (Oxford, Clarendon Press, 1993).

GREENACRE MJ, *Correspondence Analysis in Practice* (London, Academic Press, 1993).

GREGORY R and GIDDINGS P, 'The Ombudsman Institution: Growth and Development' in GREGORY R and GIDDINGS P, (eds), *Righting Wrongs: The Ombudsman in Six Continents* (Amsterdam, IOS Press, 2000).

——, *The Ombudsman, the Citizen and Parliament* (London, Politico's Publishing, 2002).

GREGORY R and HUTCHESSON P, *The Parliamentary Ombudsman: A Study in the Control of Administrative Action* (London, Allen & Unwin, 1975).

GRIFFITHS A, *In the Shadow of Marriage: Gender and Justice in an African Community* (Chicago, IL, University of Chicago Press, 1997).

——, 'Mediation, Gender and Justice in Botswana' (1998) 154 *Mediation Quarterly* 335.

——, 'Reconfiguring Law: An Ethnographic Perspective from Botswana' (1998) 23 *Law & Social Inquiry* 587.

——, 'Gendering Culture: Towards a Plural Perspective on Kwena Women's Rights' in COWAN JK, DEMBOUR MB and WILSON RA, (eds), *Culture and Rights: Anthropological Perspectives* (Cambridge, CUP, 2001) 102.

——, 'Siblings in Dispute over Inheritance: A View from Botswana' (2002) 49(1) *Africa Today* 61.

GRIFFITHS J, 'What is Legal Pluralism?' (1986) 24 *Journal of Legal Pluralism* 1.

——, 'Legal Pluralism and the Theory of Legislation: With Special Reference to the Regulation of Euthanasia' in PETERSEN H and ZAHLE H, (eds), *Legal Polycentricity: Consequences of Pluralism in Law* (Aldershot, Dartmouth, 1995).

GROSSMAN J and TIERNEY J, 'Does Mentoring Work? An Impact Study of the Big Brothers Big Sisters Program' (1988) 22 *Evaluation Review* 403.

GROVER S, 'On the Limits of Parental Proxy Consent: Children's Rights to Non-Participation in Non-Therapeutic Research' (2004) 1 *Journal of Academic Ethics* 349.

GRUNDMANN R, *Marxism and Ecology* (Oxford, Clarendon Press, 1991).

GUARNIERI C and PEDERZOLI P, *The Power of the Judges: A Comparative Study of Courts and Democracy* (Oxford, OUP, 2002).

GUBA E and LINCOLN Y, *Fourth Generation Evaluation* (Newbury Park, Sage, 1989).

GUBRIUM J and HOLSTEIN J, (eds), *Handbook of Interview Research: Context and Method* (Thousand Oaks, CA, Sage, 2002).

GUIBENTIF P, *Pierre Guibentif in Bielefeld 1991*, Interview first published (in French) in ARNAUD AJ and GUIBENTIF P, (eds), *Niklas Luhman: Observateur du Droit*, (1993) 5 Droit et société 187.

——, 'Niklas Luhmann und die Rechtssoziologie: Gespräch mit Niklas Luhmann in Bielefeld on 7 January 1991'(Interview with N Luhmann) in (2000) 21(1) *Zeitschrift für Rechtssoziologie* 217.

GÜNTHER G, 'Cybernetic Ontology and Transjunctional Operations' in GÜNTHER G, (ed), *Beiträge zur Grundlegung einer operationsfähigen Dialektik I* (Hamburg, Meiner, 1976).

——, 'Life as Poly-Contexturality' in GÜNTHER G, (ed), *Beiträge zur Grundlegung einer operationsfähigen Dialektik I* (Hamburg, Meiner, 1976).

HABERMAS J, *The Theory of Communicative Action*, vols 1 and 2 (Boston, MA, Beacon Press, 1987).

HAGAN FE, *Research Methods in Criminal Justice and Criminology* (New York, NY, Allyn & Bacon, 2001).

HALL S, 'The Multi-Cultural Question' in HESSE B, (ed), *Un/settled Multi-culturalisms* (London, Zed Books, 2000).

HALLIDAY TC and JANOWITZ M, *Sociology and its Public: The Forms and Fates of Disciplinary Organisation* (Chicago, IL, University of Chicago Press, 1992).

HAMMERSLEV O, *Danish Judges in the 20th* Century: *A Socio-Legal Study* (Copenhagen, DJØF-Publishing, 2003).

HAMMERSLEY M and ATKINSON P, *Ethnography: Principles in Practice* (London, Tavistock, 1983).

HARAWAY DJ, 'Situated Knowledges: The Science Question in Feminism and the Privilege of Partisan Perspective' in *Simians, Cyborgs, and Women: the Reinvention of Nature* (New York, NY, Routledge, 1991).

HARDING S, (ed), *Feminism and Methodology* (Bloomington, IN, Indiana University Press, 1987).

——, *Whose Science? Whose Knowledge? Thinking from Women's Lives* (Milton Keynes, Open University Press, 1991).

HARPER R, 'The Social Organisation of the IMF's Mission Work: An Examination of International Auditing' in M Strathern, (ed), *Audit Cultures: Anthropological Studies in Accountability, Ethics and the Academy* (London, Routledge, 2000) 21.

HARRIS O, (ed), *Inside and Outside Law: Anthropological Studies of Authority and Ambiguity* (London, Routledge, 1996).

HARRIS S, 'Fragmented Narratives and Multiple Tellers: Witness and Defendant Accounts in Trials' (2001) 3 *Discourse Studies*.

HART HLA, *The Concept of Law* (Oxford, OUP, 1988).

HARTSOCK NCM, 'The Feminist Standpoint: Developing the Ground for a Specifically Feminist Historical Materialism' in HARDING S and HINTIKKA MB, (eds), *Discovering Reality: Feminist Perspectives on Epistemology, Metaphysics, Methodology, and Philosophy of Science* (Dordrecht, D Reidel, 1983) 283.

——, 'Comment on Hekman's "Truth and Method: Feminist Standpoint Theory Revisited": Truth or Justice?' (1997) 22 *Signs*: 367

HATTIE J and MARSH HW, 'The Relationship between Research and Teaching: A Meta-analysis' (1996) 66 *Review of Educational Research* 507.

HAWKINS K, *Environment and Enforcement: Regulation and the Social Definition of Pollution* (Oxford, Clarendon Press, 1984).

——, *Law as Last Resort* (Oxford, OUP, 2002).

HEEDE K, *European Ombudsman: Redress and Control at Union Level* (The Hague, Kluwer Law International, 2000).

HEIDENSOHN F and FARRELL M, *Crime in Europe* (London, Routledge, 1991).

HEILAND HG, SHELLEY LI and KATOH H, (eds), *Crime and Control in Comparative Perspectives* (Berlin, De Gruyter, 1992).

HEKMAN S, 'Truth and Method: Feminist Standpoint Theory Revisited' (1997) 22 *Signs*: 341.

HELD D and THOMPSON JB, *Social Theory of Modern Societies: Anthony Giddens and his Critics* (Cambridge, CUP, 1989).

HENDLEY K, 'Rewriting the Rules of the Game in Russia: The Neglected Issue of the Demand for Law' (1999) 8(4) *East European Constitutional Review*.

——, 'Suing the State in Russia' (2002) 18 (2) *Post-Soviet Affairs* 122.

——, 'Enforcing Judgements in Russian Economic Courts: Is Going to Court a Waste of Time?' Paper presented in *Annual Meeting of the Law and Society Association*, 5–8 June 2003, Pittsburgh, PA.

HENDRIX GP, 'The Experience of Foreign Litigants in Russian's Commercial Court' in MURRELL P, (ed), *Assessing the Value of Law in Transitional Economies* (Ann Arbor, MI, University of Michigan Press) 94.

HERITAGE J, *Garfinkel and Ethnomethodology* (Cambridge, Polity Press, 1984).

HILL LB, *The Model Ombudsman: Institutionalizing New Zealand's Democratic Experience* (Princeton, NJ, Princeton University Press, 1976).

HOBSBAWM E and RANGER T, (eds), *The Invention of Tradition* (Cambridge, CUP, 1992).

HOFFMANN EP, 'Democratic Theory and Authority Patterns in Contemporary Russian Politics' in H Eckstein, *et al*, (eds), *Can Democracy Take Root in Post-Soviet Russia?* (Lanham, MD, Rowman & Littlefield, 1998) 105.

HOFSTADTER DR, *Gödel, Escher, Bach: An Eternal Golden Braid* (New York, NY, Basic Books, 1979).

——, 'Nomic: A Self-Modifying Game Based on Reflexivity in Law' in HOFSTADTER DR, (ed), *Metamagical Themas: Questing for the Essence of Mind and Pattern* (New York, NY, Bantam, 1985) 70.

HOLMES L, *Post-Communism* (Cambridge, Polity Press, 1997).

HOOKS B, *Feminist Theory: From Margin to Center* (Boston, MA, South End Press, 1984).

HOWE RJ, 'Evolution of Offshore Drilling and Production Technology' (1986) 4 *Offshore Technology Conference* 593.

HUGHES EC, *The Sociological Eye: Selected Papers on Work, Self, and the Study of Society* (Chicago, IL, Aldine Atherton, 1971).

HUGHES J and SHARROCK W, *The Philosophy of Social Research* (London, Longman, 1997).

HULME D, 'Hand Over your Data!', *The Times Higher Education Supplement*, 28 March 2003, p16.

HUMPHREY C and SNEATH D, 'Shanghaied by the Bureaucracy: Bribery and Post-Soviet Officialdom in Russia and Mongolia' in PARDO I, (ed), *Corruption Between Morality and Law* (Dartmouth, Ashgate, forthcoming).

HUNT A, *The Sociological Movement in Law* (London, Macmillan, 1978).

HUNT A and WICKHAM G, *Foucault and Law: Toward a Sociology of Law and Governance* (London, Pluto Press, 1994).

HUTTER B, *The Reasonable Arm of the Law? The Law Enforcement Procedures of Environmental Health Officers* (Oxford, Clarendon Press, 1988).

——, *Regulation and Risk: Occupational Health and Safety on the Railways* (Oxford, OUP, 2001).

HYLAND R, 'Comparative Law' in PATTERSON D, (ed), *A Companion to Philosophy of Law and Legal theory* (Oxford, Blackwell, 2000).

IZZARD W, 'The Impact of Migration on the Roles of Women' in *Migration in Botswana: Patterns, Causes, and Consequences* (*Final Report National Migration Study* vol 3) (Gaborone, Government Printer, 1982) 654.

JAMES R, *Private Ombudsmen and Public Law* (Aldershot, Dartmouth, 1997).

JAMES S R, (ed), *The Sociology of Law* (San Francisco, CA, Chandler, 1968).

JAMES R and MORRIS P, 'The New Financial Ombudsman Service in the UK' in RICKETT CEF and TELFER TGW, (eds), *International Perspectives on Consumers Access to Justice* (Cambridge, CUP, 2002).

JAMES R, GRAHAM C and SENEVIRATNE M, 'Building Societies, Customer Complaints and the Ombudsman' (1994) *Anglo-American Law Review* 214.

JAMES R and SENEVIRATNE M, 'The Building Societies Ombudsman Scheme' (1992) *Civil Justice Quarterly* 157.

JAMES R and SENEVIRATNE M, 'The Legal Services Ombudsman—Form versus Function' (1995) 58 *Modern Law Review* 187.

JOHNSON D, 'Prosecutor Culture in Japan and USA' in NELKEN D, (ed), *Contrasting Criminal Justice* (Aldershot, Dartmouth 2000) 157.

——, *The Japanese Way of Justice*, (Oxford, OUP, 2002).

JOHNSTON C 'Ethics Scrutiny Found Wanting', *The Times Higher Education Supplement*, 5 November 2004, p 5.

JONES M and BROOKS L, 'Addressing Organisational Context in Requirements Analysis Using Cognitive Mapping' (1993–94) 17 *University of Cambridge Research Papers in Management Studies* 6.

JOWITT K, *New World Disorder: The Leninist Extinction* (Berkeley, CA, University of California Press, 1992).

JUPP V, *Methods of Criminological Research* (London, Routledge, 1999).

KAHN J, *Federalism, Democratisation, and the Rule of Law in Russia* (Oxford, OUP, 2002).

KALMAN L, *The Strange Career of Legal Liberalism* (New Haven, CT, Yale University Press, 1996).

KAMPFNER J, *Inside Yeltsin's Russia* (London, Cassell, 1994).

KASTNER F, *et al*, (eds), ZIEGERT KA (tr), *Law as a Social System* (Oxford, OUP, 2004).

KAUPEN W, 'Das Verhältnis der Bevölkerung zur Rechtspflege' (Attitudes towards the administration of justice) (1972) 3 *Jahrbuch für Rechtssoziologie und Rechtstheorie* 555.

KAZHDAN AP and CONSTABLE G, *People and Power in Byzantium: An Introduction to Modern Byzantine Studies* (Washington DC, Dumbarton Oaks, Center for Byzantine Studies, Trustees for Harvard University, 1982).

KELLE U, (ed), *Computer-Aided Qualitative Data Analysis: Theory, Methods and Practice* (London, Sage, 1995).

KELSEN H, *Introduction to the Problems of Legal Theory* (Oxford, Clarendon Press, 2001).

KENDALL G and WICKHAM G, *Using Foucault's Methods* (London, Sage, 1999).

KERVEN C, *Urban and Rural Female-Headed Households' Agricultural Productivity in Botswana* (Gaborone, Ministry of Finance and Development Planning, Central Statistics Office, 1979).

——, 'The Effects of Migration on Agricultural Production' in *Migration in Botswana: Patterns, Causes, and Consequences (Final Report National Migration Study* vol 3) (Gaborone, Government Printer, 1982) 544.

——, 'Academics, Practitioners and all Kinds of Women in Development: A Reply to Peters' (1984) 10 *Journal of Southern African Studies* 259.

KIDDER RL, *Connecting Law and Society: An Introduction to Research and Theory* (New Jersey, Prentice Hall, 1983).

KING M, 'Social Crime Prevention à la Thatcher' (1989) 28 *Howard Journal of Criminal Justice* 291.

——, 'The "Truth" About Autopoiesis' (1993) 20 *Journal of Law and Society* 218.

KIRK J and MILLER ML, *Reliability and Validity in Qualitative Research* (Beverley Hills, CA, Sage, 1986).

KNOCKE W, *Invandrare Möter Facket—Betydelsen av Hemlandsbakgrund och Hemvist i Arbetslivet* (Stockholm, Arbetslivscentrum, 1982).

KOCKEN EM and UHLENBECK GC, *Tlokweng: A Village Near Town* (Leiden, Leiden University Institute of Cultural and Social Studies, ICA Publication No 39, 1980).

KONRADI A, 'Too Little Too Late: Prosecutors' Pre-Court Preparation of Rape Survivors' (1997) 22 *Law and Social Inquiry* 1.

KOPTYTOFF I, 'The Cultural Biography of Things: Commodification as Process' in APPADURAI A, (ed), *The Social Life of Things: Commodities in Cultural Perspective* (Cambridge, CUP, 1986) 1.

KOTCH JB, 'Ethical Issues in Longitudinal Child Maltreatment Research' (2000) 15 *Journal of Interpersonal Violence* 696.

KROHN W and KÜPPERS G, 'Selbstreferenz und Planung' (1990) 1 *Selbstorganisation* 101.

KRONMAN AT, *Max Weber* (Stanford, CA, Stanford University Press, 1983).

KUCHEROV S, *Courts, Lawyers and Trials under the Last Three Tsars* (New York, NY, FA Praeger, 1953).

KURKCHIYAN M, 'The Illegitimacy of Law in Post-Soviet Societies' in GALLIGAN D and KURKCHIYAN M, (eds), *Law and Informal Practices: the Post-Communist Experience* (Oxford, OUP, 2003) 25.

KUTCHINSKY B, 'Knowledge and Attitudes Regarding Legal Phenomena in Denmark' in CHRISTIE N, (ed), *Scandinavian Studies in Criminology II* (Universitetsforlag, Oslo, 1967).

——, 'Law and Education: Some Aspects of Scandinavian Studies into the "General Sense of Justice"' (1967) 10 *Acta Sociologica* 21.

LANGE B, 'From Boundary Drawing to Transitions: The Creation of Normativity under the EU Directive on Integrated Pollution Prevention and Control' (2002) 8 *European Law Journal* 246.

LATOUR B, *Science in action: How to follow Scientists and Engineers through Society* (Cambridge, MA, Harvard University Press, 1987).

——, *Pandora's Hope: Essay on the Reality of Science Studies* (Cambridge, MA, Harvard University Press, 1999).

——, *La Fabrique du Droit: Une Ethnographie du Conseil d'Etat* (Paris, la Decourverte, 2002).

——, 'Scientific Objects and Legal Objectivity—Portrait of the Conseil d'Etat as Laboratory' in A Pottage, (ed), *Making Persons and Things* (Cambridge, CUP, 2004) 73.

LATOUR B and WOOLGAR S, *Laboratory Life: Social Construction of Scientific Facts* (New York, NY, Sage, 1979).

LEADBEATER D and MULCAHY L, *Putting it Right for Consumers—A Review of Complaints Procedures and Redress Services in Public Services* (London, National Consumer Council, 1996).

LEE RM, *Doing Research on Sensitive Topics* (London, Sage, 1993).

LEMKE T, 'The Birth of Bio-Politics', Michel Foucault's lecture at the College de France on Neo-liberal Governmentality (2001) 30 *Economy and Society* 190.

LEWELLYN KN and HOEBEL EA, *The Cheyenne Way: Conflict and Case Law in Primitive Jurisprudence* (Norman, OK, University of Oklahoma Press, 1941).

LINCOLN YS and GUBA EG, *Naturalistic Inquiry* (Newbury Park, CA, Sage, 1985).

——, 'Ethics: The Failure of Positivist Science' (1989) *The Review of Higher Education* 221.

LINCOLN Y and TIERNEY W, 'Qualitative Research and Institutional Review Boards' in (2004) 10 *Qualitative Inquiry* 219.

LLEWELLYN KN and HOEBEL EA, *The Cheyenne Way* (Norman, OK, University of Oklahoma Press, 1940).

LLOYD BOSTOCK S, 'Fault and Liability for Accidents' in HARRIS D, *et al, Compensation and Support* (Oxford, OUP, 1984).

LOFLAND J and LOFLAND L, *Analyzing Social Settings* (Belmont, CA, Wadsworth, 1994).

LOGIE JG and WATCHMAN PQ, *The Local Ombudsman* (Edinburgh, T & T Clark, 1990).

LOWMAN J and PALYS T, 'When Research Ethics and the Law Conflict' (1998)(June Issue) *Canadian Association of University Teachers Bulletin.* (http://www.sfu. ca/~palys/cautbull.htm).

LUCAS KB and LIDSTONE JG, 'Ethical Issues in Teaching About Research Ethics' (2000) 14 *Evaluation and Research in Education* 53.

LUCKE D and SCHWENK OG, 'Rechtsbewusstsein als empirisches Faktum und symbolische Fiktion' (Legal consciousness as an empirical fact and symbolic fiction) (1992) 13(2) *Zeitschrift für Rechtssoziologie* 185.

LUHMANN N, *Soziologische Aufklärung* (Opladen, Westdeutscher Verlag, 1970).

——, *Ausdifferenzierung des Rechts: Beiträge zur Rechtssoziologie und Rechtstheorie* (Frankfurt, Suhrkamp Verlag, 1981).

——, *Soziale Systeme: Grundriss einer allgemeinen Theorie* (Frankfurt, Suhrkamp, 1984).

——, 'The Self-Reproduction of Law and its Limits' in TEUBNER G, (ed), *The Dilemma of Law in the Welfare States* (Berlin, Walter de Gruyter, 1986) 111.

——, 'The Third Question: The Creative use of Paradoxes in Law and Legal History' (1988) 15 *Journal of Law and Society* 153.

——, *Die Wirtschaft der Gesellschaft* (Society's economy) (Frankfurt, Suhrkamp, 1988).

——, *Legitimation durch Verfahren* (Frankfurt aM, Suhrkamp, 1989).

——, *Die Wissenschaft der Gesellschaft* (Society's science) (Frankfurt, Suhrkamp, 1990).

——, 'Meaning as Sociology's Basic Concept' in LUHMANN N, *Essays on Self-Reference* (New York, NY, Columbia University Press, 1990).

——, 'The Coding of the Legal System' in G Teubner and A Febbrajo, (eds), *State, Law and Economy as Autopoietic Systems: Regulation and Autonomy in a New Perspective* (Milan, Giuffrè, 1992) 145.

——, 'Operational Closure and Structural Coupling: The Differentiation of the Legal System' (1992) 13 *Cardozo Law Review* 1419.

——, *Das Recht der Gesellschaft* (Frankfurt, Suhrkamp, 1993).

——, *Risk: A Sociological Theory* (Berlin, Walter de Gruyter, 1993).

——, *Social Systems* (Stanford, CA, Stanford University Press, 1995).

——, 'The Paradoxy of Observing Systems' (1995) 31 *Cultural Critique* 37.

——, *Die Kunst der Gesellschaft* (Society's fine art) (Frankfurt, Suhrkamp, 1995).

——, *Die Gesellschaft der Gesellschaft* (Frankfurt, Suhrkamp, 1997).

——, 'Limits of Steering' (1997) 14 *Theory, Culture and Society* 41.

——, *Die Religion der Gesellschaft* (posthumously, Society's religion) (Frankfurt, Suhrkamp, 2000).

——, *Die Politik der Gesellschaft* (posthumously, Society's politics) (Frankfurt, Suhrkamp, 2000)

——, ZIEGERT KA, (tr), *Society's Law*, (Sydney, Faculty of Law Notes, 2000).

——, KASTNER F, *et al*, (eds), ZIEGERT KA, (tr), *Law as a Social System* (Oxford, OUP, 2004).

LYNCH M and BOGEN D, *The Spectacle of History—Speech, Text, and Memory at the Iran-Contra Hearings* (Durham, NC, Duke University Press, 1996).

LYNOE N, SANDLAND M and JACOBSON L, 'Research Ethics Committees: A Comparative Study of Assessment of Ethical Dilemmas' (1999) 2 *Scandinavian Journal of Psychiatry* 152.

VAN MAANEN J, 'Afterword: Natives 'R' Us: Some Notes on the Ethnography of Organisations' in GELLNER DN and HIRSCH E, (eds), *Inside Organisations: Anthropologists at Work* (Oxford, Berg, 2001).

MACRIDES RJ, *Kinship and Justice in Byzantium, 11th–15th Centuries* (Aldershot, Ashgate, 1999).

MARCUS G, *Ethnography through Thick and Thin* (Princeton, NJ, Princeton University Press, 1998).

MASON J, *Qualitative Researching* (London, Sage, 1996).

MATHIESEN T, *Ideologi og Motstand* (Oslo, Pax Forlag, 1979).

MATURANA HR and VARELA FJ, *Autopoiesis and Cognition* (Boston, MA, Reidel, 1980).

MAYNARD D, *Bad News, Good News: Conventional Order in Everyday Talk and Clinical Settings* (Chicago, IL, Chicago University Press, 2003).

MAYNTZ R, 'The Conditions of Effective Public Policy: A New Challenge for Policy Analysis' (1983) 2 *Policy and Politics* 1.

MCBARNET DJ, *Conviction: Law, the State and the Construction of Justice* (London, Macmillan, 1981).

MCCARTHY JR, HOLLAND J and GILLIES V, 'Multiple Perspectives on the "Family" Lives of Young People: Methodological and Theoretical issues in Case Study Research' (2003) 6 *International Journal of Social Research Methodology* 1.

MERRY S, *Getting Justice and Getting Even: Legal Consciousness Among Working Class Americans* (Chicago, IL, University of Chicago Press, 1990).

MILLER G, 'Introduction' in MILLER G and DINGWALL R, (eds), *Context and Method in Qualitative Research* (London, Sage, 1997) 6.

MILLS S, *Michel Foucault* (London, Routledge, 2003).

MJÖSET L, 'Stein Rokkan's Thick Description' (2000) 43 *Acta Sociologica* 381.

MOERMAN M, *Talking Culture: Ethnography and Conversation Analysis* (Philadelphia, PA, University of Pennsylvania Press, 1988).

MOORE HL, *Feminism and Anthropology* (Minneapolis, MN, University of Minnesota Press, 1988).

MOORE SF, 'Law and Social Change: The Semi-Autonomous Social Field as an Appropriate Subject of Study' (1973) 7 *Law & Society Review* 719.

——, *Law as Process: An Anthropological Approach*, (London, Routledge and Kegan Paul, 1978).

MORAN J, *Interdisciplinarity* (London, Routledge, 2002).

MORIN E, *La Méthode Tome 3: La Connaissance de la Connaissance* (Paris, Seuil, 1986).

MORISON J and LEITH P, *The Barrister's World and the Nature of Law* (Buckingham, Open University Press, 1992).

MORRILL C, 'Towards an Organizational Perspective on Identifying and Managing Formal Gatekeepers' (1999) 22 *Qualitative Sociology* 51.

MULCAHY L, et al, *Small Voices, Big Issues - An Annotated Bibliography of the Literature on Public Sector Complaints* (London, University of North London Press, 1996).

MULKAY M, 'Conversations and Texts' (1986) 9 *Human Studies*.

MURRELL P, (ed), *Assessing the Value of Law in Transitional Economies* (Ann Arbor, MI, University of Michigan, 2001).

NADER L and YNGVESSON B, 'On Studying Ethnography of Law and its Consequences' in HONIGMAN J, (ed), *Handbook of Social and Cultural Anthropology* (Rand Chicago, IL, McNally, 1973).

NAHAMOWITZ P, 'Difficulties with Economic Law: Definitional and Material Problems of an Emerging Legal Discipline' in TEUBNER G and FEBBRAJO A, (eds), *State, Law and Economy as Autopoietic Systems: Regulation and Autonomy in a New Perspective* (Milan, Giuffrè, 1992) 515.

NELKEN D, 'Law in Action or Living Law? Back to the Beginning in Sociology of Law' (1984) 4 *Legal Studies* 163.

——, 'The Future of Comparative Criminology' in NELKEN D, (ed), *The Futures of Criminology* (London, Sage, 1994) 220.

——, 'Judicial Politics and Corruption in Italy' in LEVI M and NELKEN D, (eds), *The Corruption of Politics and the Politics of Corruption* (Oxford, Blackwell, 1996) 95.

——, 'Puzzling out Legal Culture: A Comment on Blankenburg' in NELKEN D, (ed), *Comparing Legal Cultures* (Aldershot, Dartmouth, 1997) 69.

——, (ed), *Comparing Legal Cultures* (Aldershot, Dartmouth, 1997).

——, 'The Globalization of Crime and Criminal Justice: Prospects and Problems' in FREEMAN M, (ed), *Law at the Turn of the Century* (Oxford, OUP, 1997) 251.

——, 'Blinding Insights? The Limits of a Reflexive Sociology of Law' (1998) 25 *Journal of Law and Society* 407.

——, (ed), *Contrasting Criminal Justice* (Aldershot, Dartmouth, 2000).

——, 'Telling Difference: Of Crime and Criminal Justice in Italy' in NELKEN D, (ed), *Contrasting Criminal Justice* (Aldershot, Dartmouth 2000) 233.

——, 'Comparative Sociology of Law' in BANAKAR R and TRAVERS M, (eds), *An Introduction to Law and Social Theory* (Oxford, Hart Publishing, 2002) 329.

——, 'Criminology: Crime's Changing Boundaries' in CANE P and TUSHNET M, (eds), *Oxford Handbook of Legal Studies* (Oxford, OUP, 2003) 250.

——, 'Being There' in CHAO L and WINTERDYK J, (eds), *Lessons from Comparative Criminology* (Ontario, De Sitter Publications, 2004) 83.

NELKEN D and FEEST J, (eds), *Adapting Legal Cultures* (Oxford, Hart Publishing, 2001).

NELSON S 'It's I Mean Like uh Disrespectful', *The Times Higher Education Supplement*, 28 March 2003, p 16.

NEWCITY M, 'Russian Legal Tradition and the Rule of Law' in SACHS JD and Pistor K, (eds), *The Rule of Law and Economic Reform in Russia* (Oxford, Westview, 1997) 41.

NIELSEN JS, 'Emerging Claims of Muslim Populations in Matters of Family Law in Europe' (1992) 13 *Research Papers: Muslims in Europe*.

NONET P and SELZNICK P, *Law and Society in Transition: Toward Responsive Law* (New York, NY, Harper & Row, 1978).

NYAMU-MUSEMBI C, 'Are Local Norms and Practices Fences or Pathways? The Example of Women's Property Rights' in AN-NA'IM A, (ed), *Cultural Transformation and Human Rights in Africa* (London, Zed Books, 2002) 126.

O'BRIEN N, 'Ombudsmen and the Courts: Time for Dialogue' (2002) 19 *The Ombudsman* 15.

O'NEILL M, 'Participation or Observation? Some Practical and Ethical Dilemmas' in GELLNER DN and HIRSCH E, (eds), *Inside Organizations: Anthropologists at Work* (Oxford, Berg, 2001) 223.

O'NEILL O, *A Question of Trust: The 2002 Reith Lectures* (London, BBC, 2002).

OAKLEY A, 'Gender, Methodology and People's Ways of Knowing: Some Problems with Feminism and the Paradigm Debate in Social Science' (1998) 32 *Sociology* 707.

——, *Experiments in Knowing: Gender and Method in the Social Sciences* (Cambridge, Polity Press, 2000).

OBOLENSKY D, *The Byzantine Commonwealth: Eastern Europe, 500-1453* (London, Weidenfield & Nicholson, 1971).

OBOLER RS, 'For Better or Worse: Anthropologists and Husbands in the Field' in WHITEHEAD TL and CONWAY ME, (eds), *Self, Sex and Gender in Cross-Cultural Fieldwork* (Urbana, IL, University of Illinois Press, 1986) 28.

OELS A, 'The Informalisation of the State in a Globalising World: A Neoliberal Restructuring?' www.angelaoels.de/person/research.html.

OKIN SM, *Is Multiculturalism Bad for Women?* (Princeton, NJ, Princeton University Press, 1999).

PARSON J, 'Cattle, Class and State in Rural Botswana' (1981) 7 *Journal of Southern African Studies* 236.

PARSONS T, *The Social System* (Glencoe, IL, Free Press, 1937).

——, *Essays in Sociological Theory* (New York, NY, Free Press, 1954).

——, 'Some Problems Confronting Sociology as a Discipline' (1959) 24 *American Sociological Review* 527.

PATERSON A, *The Law Lords* (London, Macmillan, 1982).

PATERSON J, *Behind the Mask: Regulating Health and Safety in Britain's Offshore Oil and Gas Industry* (Aldershot, Ashgate, 2000).

PATTON M, 'A Vision of Evaluation that Strengthens Democracy' (2002) 8 (1) *Evaluation* 125.

PATTON MQ, *Qualitative Research and Evaluation Methods*, 3rd edn, (Thousand Oaks, CA, Sage, 2002).

PAWSON R and TILLEY N, *Realistic Evaluation* (London, Sage, 1997).

PAYNE G, DINGWALL R and CARTER M, *Sociology and Social Research* (London, Routledge, 1981).

PEARL D and MENSKI W, *Muslim Family Law* (London, Sweet & Maxwell, 1998).

PECZENIK A, 'Can Philosophy Help Legal Doctrine?' (2004) 17 *Ratio Juris* 107.

——, *On Law and Reason* (Dordrecht, Kluwer, 1989).

PETERS P, 'Gender, Developmental Cycles and Historical Process: A Critique of Recent Research on Women in Botswana' (1983) 10(1) *Journal of Southern African Studies* 100.

PHILLIPS A, *Lawyers' Language: The Distinctiveness of Legal Language* (London, Taylor & Francis, 2002).

PHOENIX A, 'Practising Feminist Research: The Intersection of Gender and "Race" in the Research Process' in MAYNARD M and PURVIS J, (eds), *Researching Women's Lives from a Feminist Perspective* (London, Taylor & Francis, 1994) 49.

PIERCE J, *Gender Trials: Emotional Lives in Contemporary Law Firms* (Berkeley, CA, University of California Press, 1995).

PISTOR K, 'Supply and Demand for Law in Russia' (1999) 8(4) *East European Constitutional Review*.

PODGÓRECKI A, 'The Prestige of Law (Preliminary Results)' (1967) 10 *Acta Sociologica* 81.

PODGÓRECKI A and WHELAN CJ, (eds), *Sociological Approaches to Law* (London, Groom Helm, 1981).

POSPISIL L, *Kapauka Papuans and Their Law* (New Haven, CT, Yale University Publication in Anthropology, No 54, 1958).

POTTER J and WETHERELL M, *Discourse and Social Psychology* (London, Sage, 1989).

——, 'Discourse Analysis' in SMITH JA, (ed), *Rethinking Methods in Psychology*, (London, Sage, 1995) 81.

POULTER SM, *Ethnicity, Law and Human Rights*, (Oxford, Clarendon Press, 1998).

POUND R, 'Law in Books and Law in Action' (1910) 44 *American Law Review*.

POWER M, *The Audit Society: Rituals of Verification* (Oxford, OUP 1997).

PUNCH M, *The Politics and Ethics of Fieldwork* (London, Sage, 1986).

PUTNAM R, *Bowling Alone: The Collapse and Revival of an American Community* (New York, NY, Simon & Schuster, 2001).

RAGIN C, *The Comparative Method: Moving beyond Qualitative and Quantitative Strategies* (CA, University of California Press, 1987).

RAMAZANOGLU C and HOLLAND J *Feminist Methodology: Challenges and Choices* (London, Sage, 2002).

RAMCHARAN P and CUTLIFFE JR, 'Judging the Ethics of Qualitative Research: Considering the "Ethics as Process" Model' (2001) 9 *Health and Social Care in the Community* 358.

RAWLS A, 'Editor's Introduction' in GARFINKEL H, (ed), *Ethnomethodology's Program: Working Out Durkheim's Aphorism* (Lanham, Rowman & Littlefield, 2002) 6.

REICHEL PL, *Comparative Criminal Justice Systems: A Topical Approach*, 2nd edn, (Upper Saddle River, NJ, Prentice Hall, 1999).

REINHARZ S, *Feminist Methods in Social Research* (Oxford, OUP, 1992).

RIBBENS J, 'Interviewing—An "Unnatural Situiation?"' (1996) 12 *Women's Studies International Forum* 579.

ROBERT P and VAN OUTRIVE L, (eds), *Crime et Justice en Europe* (Paris, L'Harmattan, 1993).

ROBERTS P, 'On Method: The Ascent of Comparative Criminal Justice' (2002) 22 *Oxford Journal of Legal Studies* 529.

ROBERTS S, *Order and Dispute: An Introduction to Legal Anthropology* (Oxford, Martin Robertson, 1979).

ROBSON C, *Small-Scale Evaluation: Principles and Practice* (London, Sage, 2000).

ROSE N, 'The Death of the Social? Re-figuring the Territory of Government' (1996) 25(3) *Economy and Society* 327.

ROSS HL, 'Housing Code Enforcement as Law in Action' 17(2) *Law and Policy* 133.

ROTTLEUTHNER H, *Einfuehrung in die Rechtssoziologie* (Darmstadt, Wissenschaftliche Buchgesellschaft, 1987).

——, 'The Limits of Law: The Myth of a Regulatory Crisis' (1989) 17 *International Journal of the Sociology of Law* 273.

RUGGIERO V, RYAN H and SIM J, (eds), *Western European Penal Systems* (London, Sage, 1995).

RUGGIERO V, SOUTH N and TAYLOR I, (eds), *The New European Criminology: Crime and Social Order in Europe* (London, Routledge, 1998).

Runnymede Trust, *Islamaphobia: A Challenge For Us All* (London, Runnymede Trust, 1997).VARELA FJ, 'A Calculus for Self-Reference' (1975) 2 *International Journal of General Systems* 5.

SANDERS C, 'Law Courses set for Radical Shake-Up', *Times Higher Education Supplement*, 21 November 2003, 15.

SARAT A and FELSTINER WLF, *Divorce Lawyers and Their Clients: Power and Meaning in the Legal Process* (New York, NY, OUP, 1995).

SARAT A and SILBEY S, 'The Pull of the Policy Audience' (1988) 10 *Law and Policy* 97.

SAVELSBERG J, 'The Making of Criminal Law Norms in Welfare States: Economic Crime in West Germany' (1987) 21 *Law and Society Review* 529.

SAXON A, 'Research, Ethics and Publishing' (2001) 98 *Clinical Immunology* 155.

SCHEFFER T, *Asylgewährung. Eine Ethnographische Analyse des deutschen Asylverfahrens* (Stuttgart, Lucius & Lucius, 1999).

——, 'Jenseits der Konversation: Zur Konzeptualisierung von Asylanhörungen anhand der ethnographischen Analyse ihrer Eröffnung' (1998) 24 *Schweizerische Zeitschrift für Soziologie* 291.

——, 'The Duality of Mobilisation: Following the Rise and Fall of an Alibi-story on its Way to Court' (2003) 33 *Journal for the Theory of Social Behaviour.*

——, 'Materialities of Legal Proceedings' (2004) 17 *International Journal for Semiotics of Law* 365.

SCHIERUP C-U and PAULSON S, *Arbetets Etniska Delning* (Stockholm, Carlsson, 1994).

DE BERG H and SCHMIDT J, (eds), *Rezeption und Reflektion. Zur Resonanz der Systemtheorie Niklas Luhmanns außerhalb der Soziologie* (Frankfurt, Suhrkamp, 2000).

SCHUYT CJM and RUYS JCM, 'Die Einstellung Gegenüber Neuen Sozio-ökonomischen Gesetzen' (Attitudes towards new socio-economic legislation) (1972) 3 *Jahrbuch für Rechtssoziologie und Rechtstheorie* 565.

SCOTT J, 'Flexibility, "Proceduralization", and Environmental Governance in the EU' in DE BÚRCA G and SCOTT J, (eds), *Constitutional Change in the EU: From Uniformity to Flexibility* (Oxford, Hart Publishing, 2000) 260.

SCOTT R and SHORE A, *Why Sociology Does Not Apply: A Study of the Use of Sociology in Public Life* (New York, NY, Elsevier-North Holland, 1979).

SELLERS C, TAYLOR T and ESBENSEN F, 'Reality Check: Evaluating a School-Based Gang Prevention Model' (1998) 22 *Evaluation Review* 590.

SELZNICK P, 'The Sociology of Law' in RK MERTON, et al, (eds), *Sociology Today: Problems and Prospects* (New York, NY, Basic Books, 1959).

——, 'Sociology and Natural Law' in BLACK D and MILESKI M, (eds), *The Organisation of Law* (New York, NY, Seminar Press, 1973).

SENEVIRATNE M, 'Estate Agents, the Consumer and the Ombudsman for Corporate Estate Agents' (1997) *Consumer Law Journal* 123.

——, *The Legal Profession: Regulation and the Consumer* (London, Sweet & Maxwell, 1999).

——, 'Joint Regulation of Consumer Complaints in Legal Service: A Comparative Study' (2001) 29 *International Journal of the Sociology of Law* 311.

——, *Ombudsmen: Public Services and Administrative Justice* (London, Butterworths, 2002).

SENEVIRATNE M and CRACKNELL S, 'Consumer Complaints in Public Sector Services' (1988) 66(2) *Public Administration* 181.

SENEVIRATNE M, JAMES R and GRAHAM C, 'The Banks, the Ombudsman and Complaints Procedures' (1994) *Civil Justice Quarterly* 253.

SHAMIR R, 'Suspended in Space: Bedouin Under the Law of Israel' (1996) 30 *Law and Society* 231.

SHAW I, *Qualitative Evaluation* (London, Sage, 1999).

SILBEY S, 'On the Relationship of State Theory to Sociolegal Research: The Example of Minor Dispute Processing' (1990) 10 *Studies in Law, Politics and Society* 67.

SILBEY S and SARAT A, 'Critical Traditions in Law and Society Research' (1987) 21 *Law and Society Review* 165.

——, 'The Pull of the Policy Audience' (1988) 10 *Law and Policy* 98.

——, 'Reconstituting the Sociology of Law' in GUBRIUM JF and SILVERMAN D, (eds), *The Politics of Field Research: Sociology Beyond Enlightenment* (Beverley Hills, CA, Sage, 1989) 150.

SILVERMAN D, 'The Logics of Qualitative Research' in MILLER G and DINGWALL R, (eds), *Context and Method in Qualitative Research* (London, Sage, 1997) 24.

SMANDYCH R, (ed), *Governable Places: Readings on Governmentality and Crime Control* (Aldershot, Dartmouth, 1999).

SMART C, *Feminism and the Power of Law* (London, Routledge, 1995).

SMART B, *Michel Foucault*, (London, Routledge, 2002).

SMIGEL EO, 'Work of the Wall Street Lawyer' in JAMES S, (ed), *The Sociology of Law* (San Francisco, CA, Chandler, 1968).

SMITH D, 'Textually Mediated Social Organization' (1985) 99 *International Social Science Journal* 59.

——, 'Women's Perspective as a Radical Critique of Sociology' in HARDING S, (ed), *Feminism and Methodology: Social Science Issues* (Bloomington, IN, Indiana University Press, 1987) 84.

——, *The Everyday World as Problematic* (Milton Keynes, Open University Press, 1987).

SMITH P, (ed), *Feminist Jurisprudence* (Oxford, OUP, 1993).

SOLOMON PH 'Legality in Soviet Political Culture' in LAMPERT N and RITTERSPORN GT, (eds), *Stalinism: Its Nature and Aftermath* (New York, NY, ME Sharpe, 1992) 260.

SOLOMON PH and FOGLESONG TS, *Courts and Transition in Russia: The Challenge of Judicial Reform* (Oxford, Westview, 2000).

SOMERLAD H, 'The Implementation of Quality Initiatives and the New Public Management in the Legal Aid Sector in England and Wales: Bureaucratisation, Stratification and Surveillance' (1999) 6 *International Journal of the Legal Profession* 311.

SONG M and PARKER D, 'Commonality, Difference and the Dynamics of Disclosure in In-depth Interviewing' (1998) 6 *Qualitative Research* 112.

SPENCER H, *On Social Evolution: Selected Writings* (Chicago, IL, Chicago University Press, 1972).

SPENCER-BROWN G, *Laws of Form* (New York, NY, Julian, 1972).

STACEY F, *The British Ombudsman* (Oxford, Clarendon Press, 1971).

STACEY J, 'Can there be a Feminist Ethnography? (1998) 11 *Women's Studies International Forum* 21.

STANLEY L, (ed), *Feminist Praxis: Research, Theory and Epistemology in Feminist Sociology* (London, Routledge, 1990).

STANLEY L and WISE S, *Breaking Out Again* (London, Routledge, 1988).

STAR S and STRAUSS A, 'Layers of Silence, Arenas of Voice: The Ecology of Visible and Invisible Work' (1999) 8 *Computer Supported Cooperative Work* 9.

STEIN P, *Legal Evolution: The Story of an Idea* (New York, NY, CUP, 1980).

STENSON K, 'Beyond Histories of the Present' (1998) 27 *Economy and Society* 333.

STJERNQUIST P, *Organised Cooperation Facing Law: An Anthropological Study* (Stockholm, Almqvist & Wiksell International, 2000).

STRAUSS A and CORBIN J, *Basics of Qualitative Research: Techniques and Procedures for Producing Grounded Theory* (London, Sage, 1998).

STREET WR, 'United Kingdom Regulations for Permanent Offshore Structures' (1975) 3 *Offshore Technology Conference* 731.

SUBER P, *The Paradox of Self-Amendment: A Study of Logic, Law, Omnipotence and Change* (New York, NY, Peter Lang, 1990).

SUCHMAN L, *Plans and Situated Actions: The Problem Of Human-Machine Communication* (Cambridge, CUP, 1987).

——, 'Making a Case: "Knowledge" and "Routine" work in document production' in LUFF P, HINDMARSH J and HEATH C, (eds), *Workplace Studies: Recover-ing Work Practice and Informing System Design* (Cambridg, CUP, 2000).

SUDNOW D, 'Normal Crimes: Sociological Features of the Penal Code in a Public Defender's Office' (1965) 12 *Social Problems* 255.

Swedish Official Investigation (SOU 1989: 111) *Invandrare i storstad* (Underlagsrapport från Storstadsutredningen, 1989).

TAMANAHA BZ, *Realistic Socio-Legal Theory: Pragmatism and a Social Theory of Law* (Oxford, Clarendon Press, 1997).

——, *A General Jurisprudence of Law and Society* (Oxford, OUP, 2001).

TAYLOR SJ, 'Leaving the Field: Research, Relationships and Responsibilities' in SLIVERMAN D, (ed), *Qualitative Research, Theory, Method and Practice* (London, Sage, 1998) 274.

——, 'Locating and Conducting Discourse Analytic Research' in M Wetherell, *et al*, (eds), *Discourse as Data* (London, Sage, 2001) 10.

TERKEL S, *Working: People Talk about What They Do All Day and How They Feel About What They Do* (New York, NY, Pantheon Books, 1984).

TEUBNER G, 'Substantive and Reflexive Elements in Modern Law' (1983) 17 *Law and Society Review* 1443.

——, 'Juridification: Concepts, Aspects, Limits, Solutions' in TEUBNER G, (ed), *Juridification of Social Spheres: A Comparative Analysis in the Areas of Labour, Corporate, Antitrust and Social Welfare Law* (Berlin, Walter de Gruyter, 1987) 3.

——, *Law as an Autopoietic System* (Oxford, Blackwell, 1993).

THOMAS PA, 'Introduction' in THOMAS PA, (ed), *Legal Frontiers* (Aldershot, Dartmouth, 1996).

——, 'Socio-Legal Studies: The Case of Disappearing Fleas and Bustards' in PA Thomas, (ed), *Socio-Legal Studies* (Aldershot, Dartmouth, 1997).

TINKER A and COOMBER V, *University Research Ethics Committees: Their Role, Remit and Conduct* (London, King's College, 2004).

TOMBS D and WHYTE D, 'Shining a Light on Power? Reflections on British Criminology and the Future of Critical Social Science' (2003) 41(Winter) *Socio-Legal Newsletter*, 1.

TRAVERS M, 'Putting Sociology Back into Sociology of Law' (1993) 20 *Journal of Law and Society* 443.

——, 'Measurement and Reality: Quality Assurance and the Work of a Firm of Criminal Defence Lawyers in Northern England' (1994) 1 *International Journal of the Legal Profession* 173.

——, *The Reality of Law: Work and Talk in a Firm of Criminal Lawyers* (Aldershot, Ashgate, 1997).

——, 'Preaching to the Converted? Improving the Persuasiveness of Criminal Justice' (1997) 37 *British Journal of Criminology* 359.

——, 'Sociology of Law in Britain' (2001) 32 *The American Sociologist* 26.

——, *Qualitative Research Through Case Studies* (London, Sage, 2001).

——, 'Symbolic Interactionism and Law' in BANAKAR R and TRAVERS M, (eds), *An Introduction to Law and Social Theory* (Oxford, Hart Publishing, 2002) 209.

——, 'Understanding Talk in Legal Setting: What Law and Society Studies Can Learn from a Conversation Analyst' (forthcoming). *Law and Social Inquiry.*

TRAVERS M and MANZO JF, (eds), *Law in Action: Ethnomethodological and Conversation Analytic Approaches to Law* (Aldershot, Ashgate, 1997).

TRINCH S, *Latina's Narratives of Domestic Abuse* (Philadelphia, PA, John Benjamins, 2003).

TUROW S, *One L: The Turbulent True Story of a First Year at Harvard Law School* (New York, NY, Farrar Straus, 1977).

TWINING W, *Globalisation and Legal Theory* (London, Butterworths, 2000).

TWINING W and MIERS D, *How to Do Things With Rules* (London, Butterworths, 1996).

UNICEF, *Children, Women and Development in Botswana: A Situational Analysis* (Gaborone, Government of Botswana/UNICEF, 1993).

VARGA C, (ed), *Comparative Legal Culture* (Aldershot, Dartmouth, 1992).

VICK DW, 'Interdisciplinarity and the Discipline of Law' (2004) 31 *Journal of Law and Society* 163.

VOLPP L, 'Talking "Culture": Gender, Race, Nation and the Politics of Multiculturalism' (1996) 96 *Columbia Law Review* 1573.

VON FÖRSTER H, *Observing Systems* (Seaside, CA, Intersystems, 1981).

WACQUANT L, 'Review Symposium: Scrutinizing the Street: Poverty, Morality, and the Pitfalls of Urban Ethnography' (2002) 107 *American Journal of Sociology* 1468.

WALKER R, 'Great Expectations: Can Social Science Evaluate New Labour's Policies' (2001) 38 *Evaluation* 305.

WEBER M, *Max Weber on Law in Economy and Society* (Cambridge, MA, Harvard University Press, 1954).

——, *Economy and Society: An Outline of Interpretive Sociology* (Berkeley, CA, University of California Press, 1968).

WEILER J, 'Community, Member States and European Integration: Is the Law Relevant?' (1982) *Journal of Common Market Studies* 39.

WEISS C, *Evaluation: Methods for Studying Policies and Programs* (New York, NY, Prentice-Hall, 1998).

WETHERELL M, 'Part Three: Minds, Selves and Sense-Making: Editor's Introduction' in WETHERELL M, *et al*, (eds), *Discourse Theory and Practice: A Reader* (London, Sage, 2000) 193.

WHEELER S and THOMAS PA, 'Socio-Legal Studies' in HAYTON DJ, (ed), *Law's Future(s)* (Oxford, Hart Publishing, 2002) 271.

WIEDER DL, *Language and Social Reality: The Case of Telling the Convict Code* (The Hague, Mouton, 1974).

WIENER C, *The Elusive Quest: Accountability in Hospitals* (New York, NY, Aldine de Gruyter, 2000).

WILLIAMS R, *Keywords: A Vocabulary of Culture and Society* (London, Fontana, 1976).

WILLIAMS T and GORIELY T, *An Annotated Bibliography of Complaints Handling Literature* (London, TPR Social and Legal Research for The Citizens Charter Complaints Task Force, 1995).

WILLIAMSON P, *et al*, 'Statistical Review by Research Ethics Committees' (2000) 163 *Journal of the Royal Statistical Society* 5.

WILLOCK I, 'Getting On with Sociologists' (1974) 1 *British Journal of Law and Society* 12.

WOOD D, *The Power of Maps* (London, Routledge, 1993).

WOOLGAR S and ASHMORE M, 'The Next Step: An Introduction to the Reflexive Project' in S Woolgar, (ed), *Knowledge and Reflexivity: New Frontiers in the Sociology of Knowledge* (London, Sage, 1988).

WOOLGAR S and PAWLUCH D, 'Ontological Gerrymandering' (1985) 32 *Social Problems* 214.

YILMAZ I, 'Law as Chameleon: The Question of Incorporation of Muslim Personal Law into English Law' (2001) 21 *Journal of Muslim Minority Affairs* 297.

——, 'Muslim Law in Britain: Reflections in the Socio-Legal Sphere and Differential Legal Treatment' (2001) 20 *Journal of Muslim Minority Affairs* 353.

YOUNG J, *The Exclusive Society* (London, Sage, 1999).

ZEDNER L, 'In pursuit of the Vernacular; Comparing Law and Order Discourse in Britain and Germany' (1995) 4 *Social and Legal Studies* 517.

ZIEGERT KA, *Zur Effektivität der Rechtssoziologie: die Rekonstruktion der Gesellschaft durch Recht* (Towards the Effectiveness of Sociology of Law: The Reconstruction of Society Through Law) (Stuttgart, Enke, 1975).

——, 'Legal Education at Work: The Impossible Task of Teaching Law' (1988) 5 *Tidskrift för rättssociologi* 184.

——, 'Courts and the Self-Concept of Law: The Mapping of the Environment by Courts of First Instance' (1992) 14(2) *Sydney Law Review* 196.

——, 'Aufgaben der Rechtssoziologie als Soziologie für Juristen in der Rechtsforschung und Juraausbildung' (Objectives of the Sociology of Law as a Sociology for Lawyers in Legal Research and Legal Education) (1994) 15(1) *Zeitschrift für Rechtssoziologie* 13.

——, 'The Complex Courtroom Communication Scheme: Towards a Transnational and Transcultural Inventory for Measuring Legal Impact: Observations from a Study of Australian, Danish, German and Swedish Courts', paper presented at the *Law & Society Association Annual Meeting*, Phoenix, AZ, 16–19 June 1994.

——, 'The Thick Description of Law: An Introduction to Niklas Luhmann's Theory of Operatively Closed Systems' in BANAKAR R and TRAVERS M, (eds), *An Introduction to Law and Social Theory* (Oxford, Hart Publishing, 2002).

ZIMAN J, *Reliable Knowledge: An Exploration of the Grounds for Belief in Science* (Cambridge, CUP, 1978).

ZIMMERMAN D, 'Record-Keeping and the Intake Process in a Public Welfare Agency' in WHEELER S, (ed), *On Record: Files and Dossiers in American Life* (New York, NY, Russell Sage, 1969) 319.

ZWEIGERT K and KOTZ H, *An Introduction to Comparative Law* (Oxford, OUP, 1987).

ZWEIGERT K and KÖTZ H, *An Introduction to Comparative Law*, 3rd edn, (Oxford, OUP, 1998).

Index